Asymmetric Marketing

Asymmetric Marketing

**Tossing the 'Chasm' in the Age of the Software
Superpowers**

Joseph E. Bentzel

ISBN : 1-4196-4980-9

To order additional copies, please contact us.
BookSurge, LLC
www.booksurge.com
1-866-308-6235
orders@booksurge.com

Asymmetric Marketing

Contents

Acknowledgments

During the course of finishing this book, I lost my younger brother Barry to cancer. Barry (the Bear) would have loved to see this project completed, as he always enjoyed jumping in to any worthwhile street fight I chose to initiate.

You are missed brother. And feel free to pass this book around wherever you are hanging out these days. Especially if it's in purgatory. My kind of people, those purgatorians. Poised between heaven and hell, order and chaos. Kind of like the marketing profession.

I'd like to thank those colleagues who took the time to give me valuable feedback and encouragement during the writing process, especially Tim Eades, Charley Walton, Zor Gorelov, Al Sisto, Bruce Klein, Stephanie Brown, Lisa Cradit, and Sophia Stewart. And a special thanks to Nancy Chou for letting me bounce these ideas off her Stanford night school class.

This book is dedicated to the great marketing unwashed.

Who never got their products across the chasm.

But kept stubbornly trying anyway.

Right up to the end.

Chapter One

ASYMMETRIC STRATEGY FOR THE AGE OF THE SOFTWARE SUPERPOWERS

'Sacred cows make the best hamburger.'
Mark Twain

I n the 21st century software industry, there's more than one right way to begin a book about marketing strategy.

Plan A. Do I gently put my hand on your shoulder, swab the competitive blood from your nose, and point out the painfully obvious? That we are well into an age of brass knuckles market combat...Combat honed to perfection by a veteran contingent of cross-category, natural monopoly cage fighters.

Plan B. Do I rat-tat-tat you into a state of heretical hyper-attention? Pepper you with a full-frontal, Dennis Miller machine-gun-rant against a venerable marketing religion. A marketing religion that disarms independent software vendors (ISVs) on today's winner-take-all battlefield.

I'm a gambler. I'll flip a coin to decide.

Uh oh. Don't ask me how...My shiny new quarter is neither heads nor tails. It hit the ground hard, bounced around a few seconds... and settled on its side. Probably another tech-fad marketing aftershock rumbling through Northern California.

Plan C. Let's outsource the opening to a really brilliant guy.

'Cargo Cult Science'

In 1974, Nobel-winning physicist Richard Feynman gave a commencement address at CalTech he called *'Cargo Cult Science'*. In the address, Feynman tells the following story about a group of ambitious islanders with big ideas.

"In the South Seas there is a cargo cult of people. During the war (WWII) they saw airplanes with lots of good materials, and they want the same thing to happen now. So they've arranged to make things like runways, to put fires along the sides of the runways, to make a wooden hut for a man to sit in, with two wooden pieces on his head to headphones and bars of bamboo sticking out like antennas--he's the controller--and they wait for the airplanes to land. **They're doing everything right.** *The form is perfect. It looks exactly the way it looked before.* **But it doesn't work. No airplanes land.** *So I call these things* **cargo cult science,** *because they follow all the apparent precepts and forms of scientific investigation, but they're* **missing something essential,** *because the planes don't land."*[1]

Within the U.S. software industry, would it be heresy to suggest that *"cargo cult science"* is the 'marketing thought leadership' guiding the strategy of far too many under-performing ISVs? ISVs perpetually waiting for cargo planes that never land. Despite the bright, roaring technology fires lighting their runways.

And is it conceivable that *"something essential"* actually is missing from the marketing strategy of those under-performing, cargo-challenged ISVs? Perhaps a practical grasp of the marketing science necessary to win...In this age where software natural monopolies move the bulk of the cargo.

Wait...I'm getting ahead of myself.

If I'm going to keep bench-pressing these heavy metaphors, I need a minute to super-charge my batteries. How? By plugging into that infinite power grid of American comedic genius known as the Seinfeld reruns. They always seem to provide me with at least one battery-charging belly laugh, and one *'aha moment'* to get me through my marketing day.

Cargo Cult Science...Meet the Bubbleboys!

Have you seen the Seinfeld episode[2] called 'the Bubble Boy'? If you missed it (or the show never made it to your corner of Bangalore, Beijing or Berlin), here's a quick synopsis.

The fictional character of the Seinfeld Bubble Boy (like the real boy on which the episode is loosely based) was born without a rugged, ready-for-the-real-world immune system. So his devoted parents provide him with an environmentally perfect plastic bubble---Inside which he is seemingly protected from life's threatening realities. But in the twisted Seinfeld version of the tale, the Bubble Boy (by now an angry young man forced to live life in a plastic prison) has the karmic misfortune to get into verbal fisticuffs with George Costanza, Jerry Seinfeld's short, bald, always-argumentative sidekick---Over a game of *Trivial Pursuit*!

When the shouting match between George and the Bubble Boy disintegrates into an all-out mini-brawl...Take a wild guess what happens? Exactly. The Bubble Boy's bubble bursts, liberating him from his Trivial Pursuit...But also earning him an ambulance trip to the hospital. All while a mob of local villagers sets out on a torch-bearing Frankenstein-hunt for the evil George, that "little bald guy from the city" who tried to kill our Bubble Boy. Belly laugh. Big, big belly laugh. Batteries all charged.

"But what was the 'aha' moment?" Thanks for reminding me.

Large parts of the 2006, post-bubble software marketing profession continue to function in insular worlds like that of the Seinfeld Bubble Boy... Worlds in which cargo cult marketing appears to be normal.

"No way! What kind of BS aha moment is that...How did you end up there?"

OK. Let's pause Seinfeld...And hit the play button on that depressing old Bubble History tape you haven't looked at in a few years. And no cheating. Let's begin at the beginning.

However well intentioned, don't many 2006-model-year marketing strategists persist in harboring the bubbleboy illusion that the latest and greatest software fad-du-jour... the latest and greatest prescription for "creative destruction" (*on-demand this, Web 2.0 that, open source everything*), will serve as their protective marketing shield?

Any of this sounding familiar to you? Or do you need a little more 'context'?

Wouldn't you agree that Feynman's description of a cargo cult resembles the marketing behavior of those dead and buried bubble companies? From the outside looking in, didn't those practitioners of creative destruction appear to be *"doing everything right"?*

Didn't their celebrity thought leaders behave as if they had all the strategic marketing answers to that seeming *'Trivial Pursuit'*... Of building world-class software and web companies at the dawn of the information age?

Did not Tier 1 VCs fund countless bubbleboy startups at a 'premium' valuation? At which point, didn't these well-funded bubbleboys proudly shout from the rooftops that their protective cash cocoon, not profitable customers, constituted 'market validation' of their creative destruction?

Flush with cash and their new found validation, did they not network all night at those lavish coming-out parties---And then confidently refer to these parties, as well as to their demo website or prototype application, as a 'new category launch'?

Chronic namedroppers all, weren't the bubbleboys obsessed with issuing those wildly optimistic press releases about their latest 'partner synergy'? Synergy with the bubbleboy startup next door that nobody else had actually heard of.

And didn't they spend small fortunes 'branding' their deals up the proverbial wazoo, sincerely believing they were creating more than a hip logo? More than a few even 'succeeded' in floating these 'brands' on the Nasdaq. In many cases making mega-millions for their VCs, investment bankers, and founders.

Yet despite *"doing everything right"*, as did Feynman's cargo cult islanders, researchers of bubble history have determined that as many as **5000 tech, software and internet companies went out of business**[3] *over the 4 year period between 2000 to 2003.* **Some** death-spiraling in a resounding thud... Some gobbled up by **another company.** Often at fire sale prices. 5000 companies. "OK ...Pause that **tape**".

By the way, all it took was one Barrons article[4] that rudely intruded (like Seinfeld's George Costanza) on the validated, synergistic, well-branded, cash-cocooned, bamboo sticks of the bubbleboys. And sent them on that one-way ambulance trip to Marketing Memorial Hospital. Don't you just love creative destruction?

What Went Wrong? The Bubbleboys Had All Those Sexy 'New Rules'

When you rewind, and watch the Bubble History tape all the way to the end, one thing you can state with confidence is this. Many bubbleboy entrepreneurs, stoned on cash, and tripping on the 'creative destruction' of that period, *chose to reject both the competitive history and marketing best practices of today's dominant software natural monopolies* (e.g. the much maligned Microsoft).

Instead of going to school on the cross-category conquests of these market gladiators, instead of embracing their brass knuckles best practices, the bubbleboys figured out an easier way to go. A more romantic way to go. They fell head-over-heels in love with those *"new rules for the new economy"*[5].

Don't get me wrong...I love new rules too. For some reason, they always seem to be much sexier than those old rules. No joke ...If you've got enough VC cash in the bank, enough 'validation', enough creative destruction Kool-Aid, enough bamboo sticks, enough cargo cult runway, who wouldn't love a 'rule' like *"abandoning the highly successful"*[6]?

So whenever I miss too many Seinfeld reruns...Whenever I get nostalgic for those 'new rules', I follow a simple program to feel better. I smack myself in the face.

Then I can't help but recall that the most avid practitioners of the 'new rules' were the same marketing rocket scientists that brought us the company formerly known as WebVan (*I'll sell you $2 worth of groceries for $1...And oh yeah, I'll drive it to your house in my well-branded truck. Psst..and don't worry, we raised a billion.'*). And Kozmo.com (*'I'll bring* *you anything you want on a bicycle in an hour... Seriously dude, that's what we do...yeah, we raised 280 million').*

And didn't the 'new rules' marketers of the bubble also believe that the original Napster would succeed with a business model based on... Wait a second...My brain isn't as caffeinated as it used to be...Now it's coming to me...*stealing copyrighted music and sending it to your friends.*

I know. You already told me once to pause the history tape. I promise. Right after these bonus scenes. They're just too good to miss.

Remember how the bubbleboys creatively concocted near-metaphysical constructs like B2B 'net markets'...Net *markets* they knew would never attract buyers and sellers[7]. Many of their Wall Street celebrity analysts also waxed eloquent about how these B2B cargo cult marketers were locking in pre-product 'land-grabs'... Land-grabs of non-existent market turf.

And while we're at it, what was the deal with all those biz-dev VPs with the metrosexual designer eye-ware and the corporate platinum cards? Correct me if I'm wrong, but didn't many of them hold the deep-seated cargo cult conviction that they could conjure their own *'ecosystems'* from scratch...Usually with enough sponsored lunches at the right conferences.

And let's not leave out those 'incubators' that failed to generate a stable business heartbeat for those fortunate enough to get incubated. Translation, kept artificially safe in an easy-cash bubble.

And I don't know about you, but there are times that I can just close my eyes, and I'm tele-ported back to one of those rousing keynote addresses at this or that bubbleboy conference. Pacing to and fro on the stage, this born-again 'new rules' rock-star is going on and on...and on, about how some well-pedigreed cargo cult startup would achieve automatic market traction...Safely 'nurtured' inside some VC-brokered 'keiretsu'. As opposed to bootstrapping his deal with all that messy garage sweat.

I hear you. Bubbleboy overdose.

Hey...If Seinfeld isn't your cup of comedic chai, let me recommend one last laugh about cargo cult marketing in action. It's the mockumentary film simply titled *dot*,[8] about not-so-fictional startup Zectek.

Zectek's bubbleboy marketing tagline was...Get this.... '*the Solution for e-Tomorrow*'. Unfortunately for the imaginary entrepreneurs in the film, and for those thousands of other "new rules" cargo cult marketers--Their e-tomorrow never came. The cargo planes never landed.

And that might have been the whole tragicomic tale. But as much as I'd like to think that cargo cult science and "new rules" marketing were confined to the Zecteks of that period, that would be a lie.

The bubbleboys did go extinct. But 'Bubbleboy-ism' is more rugged than that. A mutated virus. A more adaptive and intractable strain of 'creative destruction'. Even giant brick and mortar companies were infected by it, slipping into temporary marketing comas in pursuit of their very own e-tomorrow. Enron to name one.

Magazine cover sexy, hailed at the time by almost every analyst on the planet as a business innovator. Enron floated B2B web offerings[9], and funded these cash-draining 'Solutions for E-tomorrow' with their brick and mortar assets. As well as with a series of off-balance sheet, 3rd party-bankrolled ventures that turned out to be e-voodoo economics for their shareholders.

But hey... Enron *was* successful in creatively marketing its story to the world. They even had their auditors and 'new rules' business model consultants, Arthur Andersen, 'validate' that story for them.[10] Right up to the moment Arthur Andersen itself experienced 'creative destruction' from the negative relationship equity of their ties to Enron. OK. Now we can turn off the tape. Because what more can I add about those 'new rules', and those new, new, good old days except... this.

"Hey... you over there by the runway...Mr. e-Tomorrow...Can you pass me those well-branded bamboo sticks and a few blocks of website wood. I need to create the antennas ... I mean business models ... that will make the planes land with the new economy cargo. I read all about it in the Enron annual report".

I know. While you're marginally amused by all this retro-sarcasm, you think it's time to get back to being serious. Because being a diligent student of tech marketing history, you are convinced of one thing. That the bubbleboy brand of cargo cult marketing was, and remains, no laughing matter. It's for real. As real as it gets.

Because the software industry in the United States is a major stronghold of global innovation. And its entrepreneurial vitality remains an indispensable pre-condition for the health and competitive strength of the U.S. economy. Not to mention a fail-safe, tech-advantaged homeland security policy. It's not surprising that leaders of both major U.S political parties agree on this, if seemingly they agree on little else.

Having said that, wouldn't you suppose that after all these new rules, after all this creative destruction, there would be no conceivable way in hell that cargo cult thinking could remain alive in the post-bubble software industry? But it's been my experience that exactly the opposite is true.

Behind that poor, unfortunate CEO trapped in the latest class action lawsuit stands a committed bubbleboy (or bubblebabe). Energetically practicing cargo cult marketing. Enthusiastically getting his bamboo sticks in a row. Excitedly pitching the latest brand of e-tomorrow.

Perhaps you've even met him or her. Just close your eyes, and visualize them standing in the boardroom in front of that graphically correct, wall-sized PowerPoint slide. Now focus. See them tag-teaming their CEO for a marketing budget increase, while passionately pointing to that huge, hyper-growth market displayed on their colorful pie chart?

If only their penny-pinching CEO 'got it', he would fund and execute their marketing strategy... You know... The new, new strategy they *guarantee* will get those new, new, new, new cargo planes to land. Unfortunately, the only thing landing anytime soon is that poor, unfortunate CEO---Landing in Eliot Spitzer's courtroom, looking oh-so-radiant in his Martha Stewart tangerine jump suit.

But fear not, gentle reader. Tangerine is not your color. That CEO's humiliating fate shall not befall you. The solution for your triumphant e-tomorrow is at hand. But before I share that solution with you, I need you to do me one small favor. Come a little closer.

Help me slip on these blood-spattered, testosterone-drenched, monopoly-loving, marketing brass knuckles. Where we're going, it gets dangerous. We've been invited to a software cage fight.

Market Superpowers & the Asymmetric Landscape in the Software Industry

Everywhere you look in 2006, the dynamics of ***intensified winner-take-all competition*** are at work in the software industry. Every sober marketer should see this brass knuckles gladiator fight as the main trend in the industry. The trend shaping and driving smart ISV strategy in every dimension of the marketing challenge. Why is that, you ask?

In the period since the bursting of the bubble (I call it the *after-bubble*), a select contingent of natural monopolies (I'll define *natural* in a moment) has solidified their cross-category domination of the software landscape. And, as special ops practitioners of asymmetric warfare are known to say, they are committed to continuing that domination 'by any means necessary'.

Shoplifting a term from the language of geopolitics, I call this elite group of ***cross-category, natural monopoly cage fighters... the software superpowers.***

In addition to their war chests of cash, the software superpowers have built up large repositories of ***brass knuckles marketing practices*** from years (decades in many cases) of successful competitive engagements. Consequently, these veteran marketing gladiators have consistently grown their top line revenue in the economic uncertainty of the post-bubble, post-9.11 period.

Moreover, these natural monopolies have progressively gone on the competitive offensive in the after-bubble, continuing to capture asymmetric market advantage at the expense of those ISVs whose executive leadership, like Feynman's tropical islanders, keeps relying on the bamboo antennas and wooden sticks of cargo cult science, rather than embracing and applying the brass knuckles marketing of the superpowers.

So who are the software superpowers that have created this ***anything-but-flat asymmetric market landscape?*** The superpower Top

10 List would of course include the usual suspects like Microsoft and Oracle, SAP, Cisco and IBM.

And in the context of Software-as-a-Service (SaaS), the list would also include the native web natural monopolies like eBay and Yahoo, as well as search powerhouse Google.

But emerging superpowers like security leader Symantec (in the wake of its merger with Veritas), and other natural monopolies, e.g. Adobe with its Acrobat franchise, have also adopted *and adapted* the Microsoft, IBM and Oracle superpower marketing playbooks to drive their own style of winner-take-all economics.

The brass knuckles, cross-category, winner-take-all wisdom of the superpowers...Wisdom that enables them to grow and dominate...and keep growing and dominating... is what I call **asymmetric marketing.**

Ripped From the After-Bubble Headlines

It's important to understand that whatever the latest stock-picking guru, or cable TV talking head, tells you about software becoming just another kind of cyclical 'rust belt' industry during the post-bubble, post-9.11 period of overall tech market uncertainty...It's just not true. The software superpowers have done everything but stand still in the after-bubble. They didn't simply engage in 'consolidation'. Instead, they creatively turned to their asymmetric marketing playbooks to conquer and annex new categories for themselves while expanding their existing ones.

Just scan a few of the more memorable headlines from the 2001-2005 after-bubble period. I've taken creative license with the copy to make my point.

- Microsoft Plans Ad-sponsored Software as a Service, Takes on Google in Search
- Microsoft to Incorporate Security into Windows, Takes on Anti-virus Vendors
- Microsoft Acquires PlaceWare and Groove Software, Takes on Conferencing and Collaboration ISVs
- Oracle Initiates Hostile Takeover of PeopleSoft (After PeopleSoft Acquires JD Edwards)
- PeopleSoft CEO Removed by Board for Opposing Oracle Takeover

- Oracle Completes Takeover of PeopleSoft, Also Acquires CRM Category 'Gorilla' Siebel (And Then Buys Open Source Database Provider)
- IBM Acquires Rational Software, FileNet, Internet Security Systems—Expands Tools, Content Management, Security Lines of Business
- IBM Acquires PWC Consulting, Becomes World's Largest Professional Services Provider
- IBM Professional Services Muscle Powers It to Number One in Middleware Shipments Worldwide

I could throw a few hundred more headlines at you...Headlines from the other superpowers. I think you catch my drift. But M&A, and the cross-category annexation of turf formerly staked out by another ISV, is only one component of intensified superpower market asymmetry. Here's another one.

Superpower R&D/Marketing Spend Trumps Venture Capital Investment

The mantra of Silicon Valley, or any other regional hub of high tech innovation, has always been... *'Let's found and fund the next great disruptive innovation startup, and pound those slow-moving superpowers with creative destruction (and oh yeah... let's order lots of pizza)'.* To do that has historically taken large cargo planes full of venture capital.

In calendar 2005 (according to Price Waterhouse Coopers), total US venture capital investment in software and web deals combined was around $7.6 Billion[11]. While that figure reflects recovery from the lows of the immediate post-bubble period, it's important to point out that the lion's share of those dollars went to follow-on investment in later stage deals spread across lots and lots of emerging categories. Only around 25% went to Series A investments in pure startups[12].

In stark contrast to that $7.6 billion in software and web venture capital, the Microsoft R&D and sales/marketing budget combined[13] in fiscal 2005 was north of $14 Billion or almost twice the total U.S. VC software/web investment. In fiscal 2006 it grew to more $16 billion. And lest anyone forget, the Microsoft R&D/marketing investment was not spread across 1250 plus deals, like VC money. It's 100% focused on the Windows platform, so says Mr. Bill Gates, asymmetric marketer numero uno.

Uh oh...I think I just accidentally outed myself in the first chapter. Oh well, if you're going to stop reading, I figure I'd do you a favor, let you close the book early on, curse me out loud and hiss, "*I demand a refund. I just won't read a book by a closet Bill Gates fan...Even if he does like Seinfeld...And even if Gates is going to retire in 2008. Sure...Bill Gates may be a philanthropist giving away his money to worthy causes... but he's also the software anti-Christ. Why the hell would I want to learn anything from the marketing practices of the software anti-Christ?*"

For those of you who choose not to believe in the marketing boogeyman, or practice guilt by intellectual association, let's get back to my discussion of superpower asymmetry.

The Software Superpowers Are Driving Both Innovation & New Market Creation

When you fold in Oracle, SAP, IBM, Cisco and the R&D and sales/marketing budgets of the other superpowers, you can begin to see the dimensions of the ISV competitive challenge emerge. This is real asymmetric market power we are witnessing in the 21st century software industry. And my simple observation about the superpower's growing asymmetry of R&D and marketing spend, relative to new VC investment, should underscore for you that the agenda of the software superpowers is not some rust-belt exercise in zero-sum-game industry consolidation.

What is happening is that the ***superpowers are now effectively driving both innovation and new market creation*** with their investments in R&D and marketing around their platforms. So what is the practical implication of this for ISVs?

I know it's counter-intuitive, but try to wrap your brain around the notion that this increasing asymmetric market dominance by an elite contingent of cross-category superpowers may actually bring increasing market opportunity for the ISV "great unwashed"---If that great unwashed can shed certain marketing illusions holding them back in the age of the software superpowers. My experience tells me time and again that this is the case. So if you're looking for one consistently positive message you will find in this book, it is this---***Embrace the age of the software superpowers.***

I'll return to this theme over and over again, but for now I'll just cite the anecdotal evidence. Scores of thousands of Microsoft, Cisco, Oracle, eBay and other superpower partners can't all be wrong.

But hold on a minute Mr. Superpower Cheerleader. While the superpowers advanced, grew their revenue, made acquisitions, expanded their R&D and marketing efforts, and increased their overall industry dominance in the 2001-2005 post-bubble period, didn't more than a few of those thousands of extinct 'disruptive technology innovators' actually create that next 'visionary killer app'? At least according to some analyst firm or other 'compensated endorser'? Let's assume that in fact they did create that next visionary killer app. What does that have to do with *marketing* vision?

On a superpower-dominated, asymmetric market landscape, it's no longer advisable to doze off on your laptop after a late night of writing code, and blissfully dream about lovable old Ed McMahon playing the role of software industry angel investor. Unexpectedly knocking on your garage door with a three-foot long check for millions, because you managed to get penciled in to some analyst's 'visionary magic quadrant'[14] sweepstakes.

As you open the garage door to take jolly old Ed's three-foot long visionary sweepstakes check, the dream morphs into a nightmare. Must have been that day-old pizza you ate at midnight. You look down at the check, and see that it is dated 1999. It has expired. When you cry out in anguish that there must be some kind of mistake, Ed speaks this mysterious phrase, a phrase you suspect you might have heard before on some bad music video. *'Hate the game, not the player'!*

Neo-Jungian translation. Dreamy attachment to the visionary fad-du-jour does not equate with visionary marketing in the age of the software superpowers. But there is good news.

The nightmare of the software fad-du-jour cannot be blamed on the thousands of mid-level marketing and sales professionals (the *players*). These players always immerse themselves in day-to-day, campaign-to-campaign combat, passionately committing themselves to the good fight on behalf of their corporate tribe. Instead, it is a faulty perception of today's software industry *game* that has failed the dreamers. A faulty perception maintained by a high priesthood of armchair advisors and desk-jockey consultants.

One thing you can always bank on in the U.S. software industry. For those 1999 visionaries still committed to thinking like Richard Feynman's cargo cult islanders, there will always be one more cargo plane just over the software market horizon. Fortunately, we are focused on the superpower market horizon. Where the cargo planes fly as far as the eye can see.

The Locked-In Installed Base of the Superpowers---That's Serious Asymmetry

In the after-bubble, the software superpowers have also become adept at both contending and colluding with each other in an always-on, cold/hot cage fight for the connected enterprise, the high-growth SMB and the digital consumer. Why are the software superpowers well positioned to contend and collude for these markets? Answer---They own the cage. They possess *locked-in customer installed bases, the real foundation of their asymmetry and 'natural' monopoly*. I told you I'd eventually come back to the 'natural' part of that phrase.

When I was a freshman marketer, I worked for AT&T during the time the company was still a government-sanctioned monopoly. And as we saw after the divestiture of the RBOCs (Regional Bell Operating Companies), the old AT&T didn't keep its market monopoly for long.

But *software natural monopolies* (unlike government-blessed monopolies like the old AT&T) *are based on a customer-sanctioned lock-in* that is extremely difficult to break, if not impossible... Unless a superpower accidentally hands you the key to their cage.

Hey...Don't chuckle at that observation just yet. This *can* and does happen---Just ask an IBM marketing veteran whether they would like to go back in time and negotiate a do-over on the original Microsoft DOS OEM agreement. Or ask Yahoo marketing leadership whether they would like a similar do-over when they selected Google as their search provider back in 2000. These guys handed Microsoft and Google the keys.

But for those thousands of ISVs *not* implementing the best practices of the natural monopolies---It is spasmodic market development, sales uncertainty, and fuzzy market visibility that have become the new normal in this age of the software superpowers. And that's especially true if (in spite of everything we learned in the bubble) you are still committed to building your business around a marketing strategy transmitted to you over the bamboo antennas of the cargo cult scientists. Which leads me to my next point.

It's Time for Software Entrepreneurs to Toss the 'Chasm'

Since the early 1990's 'chasm theory', as articulated by Geoffrey Moore in his book *Crossing the Chasm*[15], and in follow-on books like *Inside the Tornado*[16], has been perceived by many startup entrepreneurs and their VC backers as the proven strategic marketing path to category leadership in the software industry. But in this age of market superpowers, the *software natural monopolies entrench themselves across both established and emerging categories*. These cross-category superpowers creatively implement brass knuckles strategy and tactics to defend their cage fighter customer lock-in and competitor lockout.

The result...The superpowers create the equivalent of *market 'no-fly-zones'*. Vast, extensible, locked-in market 'cages' that provide the strategic foundation of their ongoing dominance.

Recognizing this no-fly-zone marketing of the superpowers as both the main challenge to, and main opportunity for, ISV success, it has become clear to me that the *software industry is long overdue in tossing the legacy 'chasm' model as a theoretical framework*. A framework capable of being universally applied by ISVs to develop successful marketing strategy.

Like many, I have not always felt that tossing the 'chasm' was necessary. And in the wake of the bubble, I've even believed it was important to defend Moore's chasm theory[17] as a pragmatic alternative to the 'new rules' mantra of the bubbleboys, many of whom felt it was their God-given right to deconstruct and marginalize everything on the planet that was pre-internet or pre-'new economy'. So what changed my mind about chasm theory? Actually, none other than Geoffrey Moore himself convinced me that it's time for a change, time to toss the chasm as a strategic marketing framework for ISVs.

Here's his rear-view-mirror observation, excerpted from the transcript of a 2004 speech published on the Always-On Network weblog---An observation by Moore that crystallized my thinking about the necessity of tossing the chasm as a practical framework for software marketers.

"The issue is, can you get the technology across the chasm inside the company that invented it? The answer historically has been not very often[18]."

Wow. Where does one begin to tackle this kind of comment from an industry veteran about his own intellectual property? Do I seize on the obvious truth of Moore's statement---That not a lot of companies seem to have successfully applied his chasm model, leading him to state that *'the answer historically has been not very often'*, that a tech company creating something new and innovative had successfully marketed that particular something into mainstream markets, i.e. crossed his chasm. I could begin there. But in the end, that conclusion could just as easily be chalked up to poor execution by marketers, not any intrinsic flaw in Geoffrey Moore's chasm framework.

That Oh-So-Nuanced, Historically Revisionist Flip-Flop

It was that other part of Moore's comment that really got me to sit up and pay attention. You know, that *nuanced* part of the comment. *'Can you get the **technology** across the chasm'* is the way he framed the question. Ahhhh. Enlightenment at last.

Up until that white light moment of marketing satori, that moment of coming to terms with how historically revisionist this comment actually is, I naively thought that Geoffrey Moore, and his associates like Paul Wiefels (*The Chasm Companion*), were in the business of providing strategic marketing services to *specific marketers with specific commercial products* who either paid for Moore's help, or bought and read his books, in order to help themselves move their products across the 'chasm'.

Not 'technology' in the abstract moving across the chasm, but commercial products and services.

Think about it. Moore could have chosen to say something like, "*I believe that chasm theory had legitimacy and applicability in the pre-pubescent phase of the evolution of the software industry. But it may no longer be that practical in an age of the natural monopolies"*. But that's not what Moore says in the Silicon Valley 4.0 speech. What he says is that all along, it was about 'technology' in the abstract crossing the chasm to mainstream markets.

So late one night, after chug-a-lugging way too many bright blue bottles of Bawls energy drink, the question I asked myself was this: ***"If by it's creator's own admission, the outcome of chasm theory's application is that companies other than the technology originator usually win, then the only question worth answering is this. What's it all about Geoffrey?"***

So I decided to dig a little deeper. After digging a while, here's where I ended up as the thesis for this book, for better or worse, richer or poorer.

Twenty first century ISVs need to execute their marketing initiatives around a strategic marketing framework that detoxes them from the Kool-Aid of chasm theory. A theory I would now regrettably characterize as one of the foremost examples of cargo cult science in the software industry.

Furthermore, ISVs need to begin cultivating a new generation of creative thinkers from within their own ranks who will not fall into the trap of providing a revisionist history of their own ideas. Or flip-flop on the relevance of the application of those ideas.

My Turn to Flip-Flop Too

In the context of Moore's comments, why would any responsible marketer at a software or web company try to apply chasm theory to today's superpower-dominated landscape? Following Moore's example, I decided to flip-flop as well. I no longer see any intellectually honest way to articulate the ideas that I call asymmetric marketing, if I try to accommodate or incorporate chasm theory as a legacy foundation. Instead, I decided to begin thinking of chasm theory as a legacy industry artifact. Something ancient a marketing archeologist might dig up in the software desert. A software industry fossil.

Or perhaps the better metaphor is the one suggested by my reference to Mark Twain at the top of this chapter... a Sacred Cow 'chasm-burger'.

And rather than provide yet one more abstract model of market development (or perfect instantiation of cargo cult science that appears to the marketing tropical islander as *graphically correct* on a PowerPoint slide---You know graphical correctness...It's that iconic bell curve with that scary hole on the bottom left where you fall into the chasm), I decided that the promise of asymmetric marketing is to provide ISVs with ***pragmatic, actionable guidelines for how to succeed in the context of superpower-dominated landscapes***. How to win in the age of natural monopolies. How to leverage the 'cage' lock-in of the veteran cage fighters.

By understanding and practicing these asymmetric marketing guidelines, ISVs can stop investing their time, their market window, their marketing spend---In the fruitless task of ***trying to force-fit the chasm model to today's conditions***. Trying to make the chasm model perform in the face of the ongoing market reality of superpower asymmetry. Trying to get the cargo planes to land on the chasm runway.

That result alone should resonate with those VCs who have placed the lion's share of their dollars into later stage deals, replete with big 'chasm-crossing' marketing budgets. Having been convinced by that marketing exec with the bamboo sticks on his head, and the graphically correct PowerPoint slide, of that vast market that awaits in the 'tornado', if only....

Step One: Unlearning the 4 Core Ideas in Chasm Theory
So I return to the first sentence in this book. "In the 21st century software industry, there's more than one right way to begin a book about marketing strategy." That's true. I stand by it. But I'd be lying if I said there wasn't a right *right* way. Here is that right right way.

It's critical for software marketers in the age of the superpowers to start thinking like recovering addicts, and take the 'first step'. Detox from the marketing Kool-Aid of the 90's.

This requires ***unlearning the 4 core ideas in chasm theory***. So feel free to think of this book as one of those self-help pamphlets you pick up at your first meeting of *'Cargo Cult Marketers Anonymous'*...Only feel free to take a pass on the day-old coffee and nicotine-stained fingertips.

For the remainder of this chapter, and in the next 3 chapters of this book, I'm going to turn a critical eye toward each one of the 4 core 'big marketing ideas' in chasm theory as follows:

- Tornadoes of disruptive innovation-driven market growth,
- TALC or technology adoption lifecycles, the basis of the chasm metaphor,
- The notion of 'whole products', and the
- Go-to-market approach referred to as the 'bowling alley'.

I'll provide an alternative to each of these 4 core building blocks of chasm theory that many ISV marketers (and a sub-industry of chasm-clad marketing mullahs) see as industry religion.

As our first destination on this journey, I invite you to join me on the maiden voyage of an asymmetric marketing time-folding machine. Let's back-jump all the way to those pre-internet olden days of the now quarter-century young PC industry. Together, let's gaze down into the primordial ooze of software industry evolution to behold the embryonic emergence of that awesome life form known as the software superpower.

And on our time trip, let's draw a few conclusions that will determine if the early experience and market development of this unique species of 21st century, cross-category natural monopoly *ever really validated chasm theory at all.*

Or if in fact, this embryonic superpower was an *asymmetric marketer all along.*

The Microsoft Way of Asymmetric Marketing

We marketing dinosaurs (Let's define a dinosaur as a marketer past the age of 50 that still looks forward to having fun with the challenge and the work) remember all too well that Microsoft, the much-maligned 'predatory competitor' of today, did not start out in life as a natural monopoly, or even as the next sexy startup focused on disruptive technology innovation.

As a startup, Microsoft did not enjoy the commitment of cargo planes of VC dollars. VC dollars committed on a term sheet hastily scribbled down on the back of a Palo Alto bar napkin. As did many of the now extinct companies of the bubble. Instead, Microsoft did it the old fashioned way.

Founded by a poker playing college dropout, Microsoft didn't have the luxury of cargo cult science to follow, just entrepreneurial instinct and common sense. So Microsoft-the-startup decided that its primary path to opportunity lay in *leveraging the market power of IBM*, the dominant computing colossus of the early 80's.

Through aligning with IBM by successfully selling them a PC operating system that Microsoft had in fact purchased from someone else[19] (hint to future asymmetric marketers—even the little guy can acquire IP on the cheap), Microsoft helped to define the IBM standard PC platform as the alternative to Apple and other innovators of that time. It was this validation provided by the IBM imprimatur on Microsoft products, and the fact that Microsoft's early strategy was one of *détente with the IBM agenda, not disruptive technology innovation against that agenda,* that allowed Microsoft the opportunity to grow from a small developer of programmer tools to discover the single biggest secret of today's software superpowers, the asymmetric advantage of the customer lock-in. The way of the cage.

The lock-in of IBM, and the hundreds and hundreds of IBM clone wannabe's with bargain basement names like PCs Limited (by the way, it's now referred to by it's founder's name, Dell) gave Microsoft not just market share, but market power. And all of it on IBM's nickel.

It is this *creative cooptation of the market power of incumbent market leaders (even market power in embryonic form) that should be the goal of every asymmetric marketer at every stage of the evolution of your business strategy*. I hear you thinking *'How can a startup have anything approximating market power*? We'll get there, I promise. But these time-folding ships are expensive to rent, so let's get back to our ancient history lesson.

After a while, as other PC-compatible vendors entered the market that IBM was creating, and the PC clone industry began to take off, IBM execs understood how powerful Microsoft's strategy of creative cooptation of the IBM PC agenda really was. So they tried to break that rising Microsoft market power, first by changing the PC hardware architecture[20] (the now vanished PS/2 MicroChannel bus). And after that failed, by attempting to force Microsoft to develop its software roadmap around IBM's OS/2, their big blue alternative[21] to Windows. From our window in the time machine, we can lip-read IBM execs growling under their breath to themselves, *"Hey, we created this PC mass market and we brought these guys from Redmond to the game. Sure we thought the PC would only amount to a worldwide base of a few hundred thousand units. But hey...It's our damn market, not theirs. Get out the brass knuckles. Let's change the hardware and software standards."*

But by that point, the asymmetric Redmondistas had already done the math. They saw that there were going to be lots more unit shipments of PCs produced by IBM-compatible cloners than by IBM itself. So there was no turning back for the poker-playing Gates tribe. For Microsoft, the future now lay in leveraging its growing asymmetric market power in new directions. So they openly committed to Windows as their future client and server development roadmap, bidding sayonara to OS/2. To borrow a term from the latest, in-vogue IBM marketing terminology, this decision was 'transformative' for Microsoft.

Asymmetric Marketers Do Not American Idolize the Next 'Big Thing'

Let me pause here for a moment. Am I just shilling for Microsoft with my little time travel parable? Perhaps currying favor in order to get on the short list for a little bit of Bill Gates retirement philanthropy. Or am I just making the simple point that ISV marketers who want to break with cargo cult thinking should begin by abandoning graphically correct, abstract market development models (like chasm theory). And instead, begin examining the ***specific best practices and actual competitive history of the superpowers*** in their march to the top of the software mountain.

Once you dig into this history of the superpowers, you will understand that asymmetric marketers and future superpowers never focus on 'American Idolizing' abstract market models, get drunk on romantic concepts like disruptive innovation-driven tornadoes, or get hypnotized by the latest cool fad. Whether it's open source this, on-demand that, or Web 2.0 all of the above. Instead, asymmetric marketers focus on assembling those sets of initiatives that allow them to co-opt the power of incumbent market leaders, and iteratively begin migrating from relative weakness to absolute strength---As did the young Microsoft.

For you software CEOs who may have come up through the development ranks, try thinking of the young Microsoft's evolving practice of asymmetric marketing as the extreme programming[22] of marketing. Extreme programming (also called agile programming) is an ongoing movement within the software development community that is all about delivering *'good enough'* software products in short time frames. Under rapidly changing requirements that tend to have the effect of locking in the customer at every phase of the project. It's all about creating working software that addresses a customer's short and medium range needs. As opposed to creating exhaustively comprehensive and well documented code in some perfect future. Extreme programming often incorporates hands-on customer collaboration, thereby making the approach highly adaptive to change, as distinct from following a long-range roadmap on paper.

Asymmetric marketers imitate this approach taken by extreme programmers. They rely on 'good enough' marketing best practices, and break down marketing and sales organizational silos in a 'no huddle offense' operating approach focused on achieving iterative dominance. ***Infiltrating the IBM PC initiative of that time, and then co-opting the IBM standard as its own---These were the Microsoft expression of extreme or asymmetric marketing.*** So what else can we learn from the young Microsoft in its journey to marketing superpower status? How about this?

Category 'Regime Change', Not Market Share, is the Expression of Market Power
Microsoft, evolving from its humble beginning as an IBM supplier in a ***product that many inside IBM perceived to be 'non-strategic'***[23] (the IBM PC line of business had a worldwide 5 year unit forecast topping out at 250,000 boxes), began developing a system of asymmetric marketing that capitalized on its initial success in providing the critical software component of the IBM PC. It began leveraging what noted economist Brian Arthur called the *'law of increasing returns'*[24]. The tendency for that which is ahead to get further ahead, especially in the software industry.

Here a quick clarification is in order. More than a few cargo cult marketers cited Brian Arthur during the bubble period to justify spurious business models, usually around creative distortions of the concept of 'network effects', one component of Arthur's increasing returns analysis. But Arthur was explicit that the defining pre-requisite for increasing returns market leadership was what he referred to as *path dependence*.

For asymmetric marketers like Microsoft, the path on which increasing returns and iterative market dominance were dependent did not simply consist of network effects in the abstract. But on those *specific marketing practices* that enabled them to *capture asymmetric advantage via customer lock-in and competitor lockout*. Stated another way...*Increasing returns market leadership always proceeds through the 'path' of a particular vendor's product and marketing strategy.*[25]

That's why Geoffrey Moore's 'observation', cited above, about a given "technology" crossing the chasm vs. a specific company's product crossing the chasm is, sad to say, just so much neo-revisionist history of the tech industry in general. And the software superpowers in particular. *"Hmmm..........in retrospect, chasm theory didn't prove to be all that accurate. So therefore I should retro-spin it for the new conditions. After all, I have to make sure my new Darwin stuff is backwards compatible with my chasm stuff"*. Uh oh...I feel a new metaphor coming on.

My study of Microsoft's pioneering experience in asymmetric marketing has led me to see it not as a validation of chasm theory, but as *asymmetric warfare theory applied to software markets*. That is... the ability of a market gladiator to wage unconventional or unorthodox market warfare against both emerging players, *and* market share leaders. The ultimate outcome...To successfully carry out *category 'regime change'* against those market share leaders that prove to be deficient in path-dependent asymmetric marketing muscle.

Let me break this down. One key indicator of an asymmetric marketer and future superpower is the ability to go on the offensive against, and *out-compete, a market share leader in an adjacent category*, effectively restructuring that adjacent category or market segment around one's own rules, one's own path to increasing returns. This is what I mean when I use the expression *category regime change*. This is why there's no question that today's after-bubble startups and emerging market share leaders need to understand and study the relevant early history of Microsoft (and the other superpowers).

In addition to unseating IBM for market control of the PC standard, Microsoft has carried out full blown category regime change in at least 3 other major competitive engagements, and now has a set of best practices in place to replicate this strategy in both emerging and mature categories (all within the constraints of anti-trust law of course).

This is why pejoratively referring to Microsoft's category regime change practices as 'predatory' competition, which many do, simply doesn't help you and your team deal with, or learn from, those practices. So to continue with our time travel lesson, here are 3 classic market restructurings in which *Microsoft carried out category regime change against overwhelming market share leaders.*

Desktop Applications: Leveraging its Windows platform and OEM marketing clout with IBM-compatible cloners, Microsoft rolled over WordPerfect's word processor and Lotus' spreadsheet with its Office package. It's important to note that both WordPerfect[26] and Lotus[27] were the *market share leaders* in their respective categories of word processor and spreadsheet software when Microsoft went on the offensive against them.

This is an important point for future asymmetric marketers. When Microsoft and other superpowers undertake category regime change, it is usually always against an incumbent leader with majority market share. This underlines my point about the critical distinction between market share and market power. If you possess market power....even nascent market power.... you can eventually take market share.

I remember a conference call with a group of individuals in the senior marketing leadership at one of Redmond's desktop regime change targets at the time Microsoft's early offensive was just getting started. I inquired as to their strategy to defeat Microsoft's OEM marketing program for desktop apps. One VP, sounding like he had just stepped out of a seminar run by MBA cargo cult marketers, responded that *"We're the top-of-mind brand, we command strong retail pricing power, and we'd be undermining and cannibalizing our own growth if we switched gears and launched an OEM marketing program"*. Having witnessed Redmond's capture of the IBM standard, this was a suicidal position for him to take.

For Microsoft, it's offensive in desktop apps constituted regime change number two. After its displacement of IBM for control of the PC standard. As both Lotus 1-2-3 and WordPerfect were unseated by the asymmetric marketers from Redmond.

By the way, another lesson from this history is that cargo cult marketing mentality in the software industry clearly pre-dates the bubble. That's why I would have to disagree with any analyst or pundit who rationalizes the bubble as primarily a period of stock market excess, as distinct from an ongoing crisis of entrepreneurial vision in the software and larger technology industries. I'll come back to this point in Chapter 6, when I drill down on the operating culture of asymmetric marketing.

Local Area Networks: The next Microsoft market regime change target was Novell. Novell had captured overwhelming market share[28] in network server software, and had even purchased Digital Research to try to boldly expand into the PC DOS OS market. But Microsoft's Windows server systematically overtook Novell Netware. Creative product management that emphasized common developer APIs for both client and server turned the tide in Microsoft's favor, helping them build an army of 3rd party developers and solutions providers. One of the key catalysts of a path dependent, increasing returns market lock-in. Centuries ago, legendary Chinese general and asymmetric warfare poster child Sun Tzu described the effect of sound strategy against his enemies as the equivalent of *'stones thrown on eggs'.*[29] The army of third party developers that morphed into today's Microsoft partner network became the stones thrown onto the eggs of Novell's market share leadership.

Web Technology: The Netscape/Microsoft 'browser wars' are well documented[30]. Microsoft gave away Internet Explorer as part of the Windows platform, triggering the DOJ actions. Which should be seen by today's software marketing professionals for what they were---Marketing countermeasures against Microsoft by a company that was unable to defend its own franchise in the marketplace. Because it had *not been practicing a path dependent market lock-in* from day one. Because it had not been constructing its own 'cage' to fight in.

The reality of the browser wars was this. Netscape had not created any significant market power for itself despite their overwhelming 80% market share. Microsoft then went on to build web server capability into their Windows platform, eating away at Netscape's growing enterprise software business. And it was this enterprise software business that was Netscape's real revenue base in the year prior to their joint acquisition by AOL (they got the Netscape.com portal and the Netscape brand) and Sun (they got the enterprise software).

The browser wars demonstrated that Microsoft had perfected this powerful practice of category regime change. The browser wars also demonstrated that Microsoft's competitors, having neglected to study their marketing practices, would resort to government intervention to attempt to reverse the situation.

The inability to grasp the fundamental marketing implications of this concept of category regime change is an ongoing saga in the software industry. The fines levied in recent years by the European Union against Microsoft's bundling of Media Player (and other marketing practices labeled as 'predatory'), demonstrate once again that Redmond's competitors that fail to develop either a practical working relationship with them, or effective countermeasures against them, usually resort to government intervention as a temporary marketing strategy. But government intervention will not change the 'path' or reverse the course of increasing returns over the long term. Only asymmetric marketing can do that.

That's why every ISV should ask themselves one simple question: *"Do I have a strategy to resist regime change should Microsoft (or another superpower) eye my market?*

Do I have a strategy to either aggressively partner with them, or develop effective counter-measures against them (as Microsoft itself successfully did with IBM, when IBM attempted to rein in the Microsoft advance)? I'm going to pick up on this theme later in this chapter. But first let's time-jump back to the software here and now, and pick up on my discussion of that first 'big idea' of chasm theory, the notion of disruptive innovation-driven 'tornadoes'. Let's see whether or not this notion conforms in any way to this asymmetric marketing path followed by Microsoft...A path open to every ISV today.

Tossing the 'Tornado': the First Core Concept in Chasm Theory

The first big chasm commandment worthy of tossing is that deeply ingrained (almost cult-like) belief that the only really promising software companies are those focused on *disruptive technology innovation*. And that an exercise in disruptive technology innovation is somehow the path to a market 'tornado'[31]. But first let's briefly answer the question 'What is disruptive technology innovation'? It's pretty simple to conceptualize... and it's been the main mantra of Silicon Valley technology and financial elites for as long as most of us can remember.

The concept of disruptive innovation means that a new discontinuous or disruptive technology paradigm unseats the dominant paradigm. Metaphorically speaking, it means that small and weak David can ultimately defeat big and strong Goliath because of technology innovation contained in his slingshot. So David's superior slingshot technology provides the disruption necessary to knock out the dominant Goliath.

In the 80's and 90's, disruptive innovation came to mean things like the PC disrupting the minicomputer, or the PDF laser printer disrupting the printing press. There are many more examples that can serve to illustrate this concept. Pick your own. But for now, please note that I am *not* referring here to the application of the concept of disruptive innovation to business models, but to disruptive innovation as a technology paradigm that many suggest translates into a strategic path to unseat dominant vendors from their installed base of customers.

Disruptive technology innovation became the core tenet of the 'best of breed' ISV explosion of the 90's. Disruptive technology innovation meant the latest and greatest 'killer app' delivering new competitive advantage to corporate IT or to consumers. And the promise of disruptive technology innovation as a foundation for marketing strategy is simple. That emerging categories based on disruptive technology innovation can evolve into a market 'tornado' of explosive hyper-growth that will benefit a specific vendor, often bestowing on that vendor category dominance, i.e. category 'gorilla' status[32].

Historically however, there have been important prerequisites for disruptive technology innovation to succeed. Here's three.

For Startups: Disruptive technology innovation (even today's free open source variety) assumes ***significant VC investment*** to underwrite the marketing spend needed to 'cross the chasm'. Aha. So that must be why 75+% of U.S. software industry venture capital in 2005 went into later stage deals.

For Emerging Segment Leaders: Disruptive technology innovation (if it is to succeed) assumes an ***IPO path to a large war chest of dollars*** to fund later stage market promotion of the disruption, as it moves into the 'tornado' of mainstream adoption. Aha. Not so many IPOs in the after-bubble, not a lot of disruptive technology innovators who can afford very much 'disrupting'.

For Market Share Leaders: Disruptive technology innovation assumes that a high priesthood of anointed technology ***analysts validate and position the disruptive innovator*** in various 'leader magic quadrants' relative to older 'continuous innovations'. Hey...Who says they don't love religion here in California? Not me.

The Reality of Disruptive Innovation: The Superpowers Have Co-opted It!

So what is the reality of disruptive technology innovation in 2006? Here's my take on it. The software superpowers, through their R&D investments and acquisitions mentioned above, have become increasingly adept at out-maneuvering the upstarts and their VC backers, and are ***co-opting the notion of disruptive innovation.*** The superpowers are themselves getting into the business of introducing new technology disruption into their own installed bases (e.g. Oracle and IBM's embrace of Linux and Open Source, Microsoft's embrace of on-demand and sponsored applications), all while intensifying their market lock-ins. This creative form of asymmetric marketing on the part of the superpowers is serving to destabilize disruptive innovation ISVs. And ***'dry up' the market for pure play disruptive innovation***.

Why else do I believe this to be true? For me it's the simple fact I've had more than a few phone calls from more than a few marketing VPs telling me the same thing: *"Gartner (the creator of the 'magic quadrant' concept) says we have the best technology... technology that will disrupt the prevailing paradigm. But the customers don't seem to want our disruptive innovation even if we gave it away for free. And until we show some serious traction, the VCs don't seem to want to put any more money into our deal."*

That's why in 2006, I can't help but see the long held marketing belief---that disruptive technology innovation should remain the driving vision behind future ISV success---as a formula for continuing marketing masochism in the age of the software superpowers. It's like beating your head on the outside of the superpowers' cage, when all the action is going on inside the cage.

After-Bubble Changes in the Nasdaq 100 Support Tossing the 'Tornado'

You can see some very interesting evidence of how superpower cooptation of disruptive technology innovation plays out in the real world, simply by looking at the changes in the composition of the Nasdaq 100, the index of the strongest (by market cap) Nasdaq stocks.

In order to grow or maintain the price of the Nasdaq Index Tracking Stock, QQQQ, the Nasdaq 100 goes through additions and deletions of various companies on an annual basis. When a software company is added to the Nasdaq 100, it has usually meant that analysts grounded in chasm theory perceive that company to be a category leader that stands at the threshold of the 'tornado phase' of market growth. And that validation of the company's growing market share leadership, combined with big future market real estate, warrants inclusion in the Nasdaq 100. As a corollary to this, removal from the Nasdaq 100 usually means that something happened to kill the tornado, or snuff out that leadership, at least as far as that specific vendor is concerned. This was a common occurrence during the period of the tech bubble. In fact, most emerging 'tornado category players' entering the Nasdaq 100 index during the past few years have been deleted.

Let's illustrate this phenomenon by examining the fate of Broadvision, a representative example from bubble history of an ISV that delivered disruptive technology innovation, succeeded in 'crossing the chasm' into the tornado of mainstream market adoption, and was added to, and then rapidly deleted from, the Nasdaq 100.

Broadvision was the poster child and category leader of '1:1 e-commerce' software, and was added to the Nasdaq 100 in 1999 at the peak of the bubble. Who would argue that highly personalizable, one-to-one e-commerce infrastructure was not perceived by many as one of the next big software things? A major disruptive technology innovation that could sweep its creator into a market tornado of growth.

By 2000, Broadvision's annual revenue had ramped to a more-than-respectable $415 million (bigger than Webex, Salesforce, Akamai, Red Hat, and RSA Security at the end of 2005). In this same period of time, IDC, a leading research and analyst firm, declared Broadvision the category leader in e-commerce application software[33]. But in 2001, only one year later, Nasdaq deleted Broadvision from the Nasdaq 100 as it's revenue fell to $248 million. By 2002, revenue had declined again by more than 50% to $116 million, and to $88 million a year later in 2003[34]. By mid-2006, Broadvision's market capitalization, once in the billions, fell below $50 million dollars, as its annual revenue continued to decline, and management first decided, then un-decided, taking the company private[35].

I don't know about you, but this Broadvision history looks more like a reverse tornado to me. And here's the asymmetric rub. Broadvision's revenue collapsed, its market cap dwindled, and for a time management considered taking the company private---Despite the fact that e-commerce as a way of doing business has continued to be adopted by companies of all sizes. And personalized 1:1 marketing models are flourishing everywhere on the web.

In the interest of fairness, one could argue that it was the bursting of the bubble, and the subsequent collapse of many e-retailing startups, magnified by the post 9.11 economic downturn, that contributed to knocking Broadvision from it's perch as a member of the elite Nasdaq 100. But I see it differently. I see it as a picture-book example of the kind of superpower *category regime change* discussed above. While it was not generally apparent at the time Broadvision was being removed from the Nasdaq 100, we can now see that ***e-commerce had evolved into a 'feature' or module of end-to-end enterprise software platforms provided by Microsoft, SAP, Oracle, IBM and others***.

And this wholesale annexation of Broadvision's target market opportunity happened despite the fact that respected analysts validated Broadvision as the leading, best-of-breed vendor in the emerging 'e-commerce category'. I suspect that this Broadvision experience may be exactly the kind of thing Geoffrey Moore is referring to when he asks and answers his own question referenced above.

"...can you get the technology across the chasm inside the company that invented it? The answer historically has been not very often."

So why not come right out and say that this is what happens when cross-category, natural monopoly superpowers annex an emerging category? And the vendor with the disruptive technology innovation fails to develop countermeasures against superpower "no-fly-zone" marketing, category annexation and market leader regime change. Because for Moore to do so may open the door to closer scrutiny of chasm/tornado theory itself.

Because Broadvision is certainly not an isolated example. A similar superpower reverse tornado ravaged every single software company deleted from the Nasdaq 100 in the 2001-02 period, including companies like *i2* (the previous supply chain management category leader), *Ariba* (a B2B spend management ISV), and *Inktomi* (an early search infrastructure leader). Fortunately for Inktomi, a superpower by the name of Yahoo wisely decided to kick out competitor Google as their 'powered-by' search provider, and buy them. But the folks at Nasdaq appear to have temporarily learned their lesson about premature software tornado picking in the after-bubble. Because no software companies were added to the index in 2002 and 2003, while in 2004 only outsourcer Cognizant was added. In 2005, Google and Red Hat joined the elite Nasdaq 100 club, while Akamai gained admission in 2006. So what's the big point I'm trying to make with this Nasdaq 100 evidence?

The big point is this. Today's software superpowers, unlike the IBM of old that unwittingly allowed Microsoft to creatively leverage its market power in PC software, have *gone to school on how to cage, contain and co-opt disruptive technology innovation*. They are institutionalizing the process of category regime change in order to grow their cross-category installed base 'no fly zones', while protecting their existing customer lock-in. One day and one category at a time, the cross-category superpowers are hard at work to co-opt disruptive innovation, and make it one of *their* brass knuckles. Make it one of the strongest bars in the cage of their natural monopoly lock-in.

So if disruptive technology innovators appear to be unable to enter the Nirvana of the 'tornado' in the face of superpower co-optation of their mantra, then there is only one 'right right' question for future asymmetric marketers to ask.

What is the marketing path forward for ISVs in the 21st century software industry?

I call it *superpower symbiosis*. And it is the first practical guideline for asymmetric marketers.

Tornados and Disruption---Fuggeddabouddittt! Practice Superpower Symbiosis

I do have to give 2006-model-year cargo cult marketing folks some credit. In the face of after-bubble ISV uncertainty and superpower gains, they've become more predictable. While still intoxicated by the software fad-du-jour, they've given up a lot of the new economy rhetoric of the bubble years. In favor of more traditional, 'doing everything right' approaches to identifying market opportunity and developing sales and marketing strategy. Whenever they get into trouble, they like to call their favorite headhunter to recruit that next expensive new sales VP with the thick rolodex, or the right rolodex, or sometimes just a rolodex. And they seem to love to over-pay their favorite analyst firm to provide them with a bright, shiny, rear-view mirror market opportunity analysis to justify those later rounds of funding.

But asymmetric marketers (like the embryonic Microsoft described above), are too busy paying attention to pay money. They pay attention to the defining aspect of today's software landscape. Superpower market asymmetry. That's why *asymmetric marketers embrace this natural monopoly market landscape as the starting point of their strategy*. They do not run away from the simple (however counter-intuitive) conclusion that most of their future customers, whoever they may turn out to be, are probably *superpower customers today*. Are already locked up in the superpower cage. Are already in the no-fly-zone.

So asymmetric marketers creatively attach their businesses to the installed base of locked-in superpower customers in ways that are sustainable. All the while seeking to capitalize on the superpowers' own cooptation of disruptive technology innovation. I call this pro-active marketing process *superpower symbiosis*.

Symbiosis is a well-known concept in the biological sciences that literally means *'living together'* or species co-existence. However, what isn't on the radar of many software marketers is that scientists have identified *multiple forms of symbiosis*[36]. The 3 most significant for our purposes are:

- Mutualism: The association between 2 co-existing species *benefits both parties.*
- Parasitism: The association between 2 species *benefits only one species while harming the other.*
- Commensalism: One species benefits while the other is *unaffected.*

From the standpoint of asymmetric marketing, the systematic application of the concept of symbiosis to the software industry means this. Creating a strategic roadmap for successfully living together with the superpowers. And in the real world of the after-bubble, that means living together with them *on their terms...in their cross-category cage... with their brass knuckles 'no-fly-zone' lock-in... as well as with their ongoing predisposition for category regime change.*

Let's take a look at a few examples of how these 3 distinct forms of symbiosis are playing out in the 2006 software industry.

Mutualism

In 2006, Microsoft and SAP rolled out Duet[37], a jointly developed offering that makes it easier to integrate Redmond's vision of MS Office apps and web services-advantaged personal computing, with SAP's Netweaver enterprise SOA (services oriented architecture) foundation. This is an example of two superpowers practicing mutualism, or 'détente', for those readers who got temporarily freaked out when I switched gears from a political (superpower) to a biological (symbiosis) metaphor.

Another example. The relationship held by 'certified' ISVs with the MSDN (Microsoft Developer Network) is also mutualistic in nature.

But market adversaries can also practice a mutualistic form of symbiosis in the age of the software superpowers. In the aftermath of their court settlement in 2004, Microsoft announced a 10 year joint development effort[38] with Sun Microsystems, historically their unabashed market foe. If anything proves my earlier point about market share vs. market power, it is this deal. Sun may still have significant enterprise market share, and even unite with Google to promote their vision of a web-based MS Office-killer. But their deal with Microsoft is an acknowledgement by Sun of Redmond's market power. The upside of this form of superpower symbiosis. For Sun it holds the promise of taking back a little market power[39] from Java ISVs, e.g. BEA Systems, a company that has capitalized well on the historic gap and competing agendas between Microsoft and Sun software infrastructure. I'll come back to this in Chapter 2 in discussing ISV opportunities for symbiosis in the context of the 'No-Fly-Zone Imperative' of the superpowers.

Parasitism

The companies discussed above (WordPerfect, pre-IBM Lotus, Novell, Netscape), on which Microsoft perfected its practice of category regime change, are examples of ISVs that were symbiotic with Microsoft as an OS provider... but had adopted a marketing form of in-your-face parasitic symbiosis.

They leveraged Microsoft's OS market lock-in, but were a net negative to Microsoft's own growth plans. Take Netscape as an example. Netscape's leverage of, and association with the Windows platform was not just mildly parasitic, but openly parasitic. Their public marketing mantra was based on the point of view of committed disruptive technology innovators that the *'browser is the new desktop'*. When in fact their browser clearly *depended on the ubiquity of the Microsoft desktop* for it's early market share leadership.

It's a huge understatement to say that ISVs want to avoid being in a similar situation of open, in-your-face parasitism with a veteran superpower. From a software marketing perspective, ***openly telling an asymmetric marketer that you are going to ride on his platform to topple his empire is the industry equivalent of the Howard Dean scream***[40] during the 2004 Democratic primary campaign.

The Dean scream clearly generated lots of enthusiasm and good vibes from Dean's core following of Democratic Party 'disruptive innovators'. But everyone else had the nagging feeling that something was not quite right about the content of the scream (and the screamer). Especially after seeing it replayed and caricatured a hundred times a day on TV.

But wait a minute Mr. Dean Scream-basher. Wasn't parasitic symbiosis exactly what Microsoft practiced relative to IBM during the PC 'standards wars' in the 90s? Exactly! But the Redmondistas were asymmetric enough to employ a marketing strategy that 'cloaked' their long-term agenda of cooptation inside a wrapper of near-term mutualism. And they also didn't publicly flaunt parasitic symbiosis to the market detriment of their original 'biological host', IBM. They respected the fact that they were fighting inside the IBM cage. They acknowledged the boundaries of the cage.

So yes…It is possible to creatively engage in multiple forms of strategic symbiosis over the course of your marketing evolution, as has Microsoft. I'll come back to this point in Chapter 4 in discussing asymmetric sales strategy.

Commensalism

This is the default form of symbiosis for most pure-play vertical or specialty market providers that are intent on remaining vertical or specialized. What do I mean by 'intent on remaining vertical or specialized'? I'll also go into this in Chapter 4 while discussing the chasm theory notion of the 'bowling alley'[41], a concept that often translates into practicing *verticalization*, or industry segment specialization, on the way to Moore's tornado. But here's the big picture regarding commensalism.

Practitioners of commensalist symbiosis benefit from leveraging superpower platforms, but consciously do not choose to encroach on the superpowers actual or perceived turf, instinctively sensing that they would be targeted for regime change as parasitic competitors.

Horizontally focused companies can also practice commensalist symbiosis. These companies can often grow and develop market power by operating *in the gap* between multiple superpowers, or *on the overlap* between or among superpowers. Akamai, added to the Nasdaq 100 in 2006, and a pioneer in web application acceleration[42], is a good example of this form of symbiosis.

As I indicated above, it is my belief that today's ever-expanding dominance by natural monopoly market superpowers can only serve to increase, not decrease, entrepreneurial opportunity for ISVs. But only if they make it their marketing business to **understand and successfully practice one or more of these 3 forms of symbiosis.**

By adopting symbiosis as the starting point for marketing strategy in the age of the superpowers, ISVs place themselves in a position to capitalize on market opportunity in both the installed base of the superpowers (their locked in cage), as well as in the new market creation activities of the superpowers outside their existing installed base. In those emerging and disruptive technology-driven segments that the superpowers are co-opting.

It's important here in Chapter 1 to underline the point that ISVs committed to winning through asymmetric marketing see the practice of symbiosis not simply as some kind of business development or partnering issue for one silo of the company. It's not. ***Symbiosis is a CEO and end-to-end management team imperative*** that will separate the survivors from the market road kill.

Isn't Symbiosis Just That Whole 'Ecosystem Thing'?

Sorry...one more sacred cow on which to dine. No, I'm not talking about the 'ecosystem thing'. Because to execute around strategic symbiosis, it's critical to get a practical handle (non-cargo cult, non-bubbleboy) on the application of bioscience concepts to marketing. And unfortunately, the application of bioscience concepts to software marketing was something that the cargo cult marketers turned on its head during the bubble. By muddying up the concept of 'ecosystems'. Here's an example to illustrate the point I want to make before concluding this chapter.

There's a website focused on portal and e-business news you might have heard of called Line56.com. If you haven't heard of them, then I just gave them a free plug for their news and info. But Line56 also publishes a promotional poster it calls the 'Line56 e-Business Ecosystem'[43]. The poster illustrates the process flow of a generic e-business-enabled enterprise with colorful boxes identifying ERP, EAI, CRM and other functional building blocks that populate the 'ecosystem'. I'll give them this...it's a really nice promotional poster. Especially nice if you find yourself needing to put something colorful on your office wall to cover up that gaping hole you punched in it during a missed quarter. When a few of those 'in the bag', big deals slipped.

But for asymmetric marketers seeking to apply this concept of superpower symbiosis, the Line56 poster is a representative example of the wrong way to think about bioscience concepts like ecosystems.

Calling any abstraction-level overview of supply chain and demand chain relationships an ecosystem is exactly the kind of thinking that fueled much of the B2B bubble. Really, what's a guy to do with a process abstraction except pop it into a 1999 business plan and go public. Damn. I wish I would have thought of that.

Seriously...I'm not trying to beat up on Line56. But do yourself a favor and consider the practical implications of developing marketing strategy around this way of thinking about ecosystems, and my point becomes clear. Which part of your organization needs to own this whole 'ecosystem thing'? What's the way to infiltrate the ecosystem and capitalize on opportunities in it? How do you identify ecosystem opportunities if the ecosystem is a process abstraction, and not a living market environment populated by contending species?

This whole notion of ecosystems as process abstractions was one of the theoretical foundations of the whole failed 'net markets' movement of the late 90's. Many B2B suppliers decided not to join these net market 'ecosystems' of the 90's, choosing instead to embrace *private exchanges* that would allow them continue their critical work of locking in their existing customers, not introducing them to their competitors[44]. For this very reason, many startup participants in the B2B net markets movement mistakenly believed that B2B e-commerce itself was dead on arrival, because of this twisting of the concept of ecosystems. But what really happened was that one more graphically correct cargo cult marketing abstraction died---Not the application of biological science concepts to the software industry.

Real biological systems are not approached as process abstractions. They are *living environments supporting certain species (market participants) while eliminating others over time.* Here's a sobering statistic to back that up. 99% of all life forms that have ever existed on planet Earth are now extinct[45]. 99% ...all life forms...extinct! If that sounds kind of like what happened to those 5000 deceased bubble companies...Keep reading.

As I pointed out above, there are still lots of startups and emerging category players out there running around telling folks that they are going to *create their own ecosystems.* What can I say about that, except that just like superpower marketers, cargo cults die hard. So when the concept of ecosystems got more than a little muddied up for me by the bubbleboy penchant for graphically correct process abstraction, I decided to flesh out my approach to superpower symbiosis by utilizing two much more specific, harder to muddy-up, related terms from the biological sciences. These terms are *ecozones*[46] and *ecoregions*[47].

Ecozone: a Superpower Installed Base

In the biological sciences, an ecozone is defined by the natural terrestrial *boundaries* that distinguish it from other ecozones. For example, the Nearctic ecozone is distinct from the Palearctic ecozone. And I do know that to be true...Just don't ask me to find the Nearctic ecozone on a map.

Building on this notion, think of a software *ecozone as a boundaried opportunity landscape that is defined by the market footprint of the superpower that dominates it*. In other words, see the *installed base of locked-in superpower customers defining the boundaries of a given ecozone,* e.g. the Microsoft ecozone, or the Oracle ecozone or the eBay ecozone. The superpower cross-category mega-cage where the marketing war is being fought.

And yes...While the specific superpower setting the boundaries of the ecozone maintains an agenda of long-term lock-down of this market territory, they are not, and never will be, the only potential beneficiary of that lock-down. The existence of superpower ecozones also provides immediate and tangible value creation opportunities for other ISV participants who choose to practice symbiosis vs. disruptive technology innovation.

And these opportunities are not simply limited to participation in the formal partner networks of the particular superpower defining the market boundaries of the ecozone. You can practice non-permissioned symbiosis with a superpower in their ecozone, i.e. NOT be a business partner of the host of the ecozone, if you understand this practice of symbiosis from the standpoint of asymmetric marketing.

Need a high profile example of non-permissioned symbiosis? Of using your opponents cage to defeat your opponent? How about the Google 'Toolbar' that piggybacks on the Microsoft Internet Explorer browser, delivering search via Google.com, as well as other 'one-button' capabilities for Google-allied ISVs. This is an example of high profile, in-your-face parasitic symbiosis by Google with the Microsoft ecozone.

So is it any wonder that when Microsoft announced its intention to place MSN search into Internet Explorer (*as an asymmetric cage-fighting counter-measure against Google's free ride on their installed base*), the folks at Google starting yelling for the government lawyers to jump in.[48]

Through the course of the book, I'll continue going into how the various forms of symbiosis are expressed in product marketing, sales strategy, customer management, and brand messaging. But since definitions are important in real marketing science, as opposed to cargo cult marketing science, let me close out this chapter by introducing the related concept of 'ecoregions'.

Ecoregions

Ecozones in natural geography are subdivided into ecoregions. Likewise the ecozone of a given software superpower market geography is subdivided into various ecoregions. Ecoregions often appear as *product/partner/customer clusters* and serve as focal points for superpower marketing warfare, particularly the maintenance of a no-fly-zone policy against those ISVs perceived to be parasitic competitors. Ecoregions are like the category cage where specific battles within the overall war are being fought.

So what would be a few representative examples of the ecoregion concept in the software industry? Continuing on with Microsoft as my lab sample, here's three of their established, well-defined ecoregions that qualify as ISV opportunities for the creative practice of superpower symbiosis.

The PC OEM Ecoregion: Microsoft's first---It consists of branded PC suppliers who license the Windows platform. This ecoregion has grown and evolved around Microsoft's asymmetric marketing success in PC markets. But even before Microsoft fostered it's own ecoregions (let's not forget our time travel lesson), Microsoft had successfully practiced symbiosis within *the IBM PC ecoregion as a software partner*, and learned the importance of cultivating ecoregion relationships with dominant market players. Note to self. Keep underlining the fact that superpowers like Microsoft did not start out in life as disruptive technology innovators, but as practitioners of mutualistic (and later parasitic) symbiosis.

The Microsoft Developer & ISV Ecoregion: Microsoft is at the center of business opportunity for tens of thousands of small, midsize, and large developers who profit by selling applications on the Windows server platform. These partners have been instrumental in Microsoft's ability to evolve out of its original PC focus into enterprise, web and SMB software businesses.

The MSN Ecoregion: Microsoft has been steadily building up MSN by attracting a base of ecoregion partners in content, music, video and commerce. This ecoregion is critical to Microsoft's future as a portal, paid search and sponsored-application-services provider. And when you practice asymmetric marketing across multiple ecoregions, you can leverage one to deal with problems in another. In the wake of the European Union's 2004 ruling[49] forcing Microsoft to un-bundle Windows Media Player from the Windows desktop platform, the MSN content provider ecoregion served as an alternative engine of distribution for Media Player. This effectively enables Microsoft to continue to make Media Player ubiquitous through content and media partnerships, not PC platform bundling. Remember…These veteran cage fighters are not 'category gorillas'. They are cross-category superpowers.

Summing Up Chapter One: the TAO (of Asymmetric Marketing)

Let me close this chapter by leaving you with this. While the traditional starting point for ISV marketing strategy has been the identification and projected quantification of some future 'tornado' market opportunity represented by the 'target end customer', asymmetric marketers begin differently.

Asymmetric marketers seek to build their businesses on the basis of superpower symbiosis, and so they think in terms of the *TAO (targets of asymmetric opportunity)*.

This TAO of Asymmetric Marketing…these targets of asymmetric opportunity…are the installed base ecozones, and discrete product/partner ecoregions of the superpowers. These ecozones and ecoregions can be thought of as the biological 'host' to which you can attach your business, practice symbiosis, and leverage the market momentum of the superpowers.

By concentrating on creatively attaching to superpower ecozones and ecoregions, asymmetric marketers place themselves in position to harness the asymmetry of superpower success (and failure) for themselves, as the young Microsoft did with IBM. Within the framework of a symbiosis-advantaged strategic approach, asymmetric marketers at every stage of their evolution can turn their own relative weakness into absolute strength.

The message of asymmetric marketing is simple. If you are in the software industry, your future customers are already superpower customers, or will in the future become superpower customers. So meditate on the TAO, these targets of asymmetric opportunity, and make them the starting point for the development of your marketing strategy.

Let's briefly rewind, and review a few key points before moving on to the next chapter.

Software marketers in 2006, whether or not they are up to their eyeballs in on-demand this, Web 2.0 that, open source everything, or the next big fad-du-jour...Face the fundamental strategic challenge of surviving, competing and winning in this age of cross-category software superpowers. And if ISVs want the cargo planes to land, they must face this fundamental challenge. While simultaneously detoxing from the cargo cult marketing mentality of the bubble period of tech history.

As the superpowers out-invest VCs in software R&D and marketing, and systematically co-opt disruptive technology innovation (including open source, on-demand and Web 2.0) to reinforce their installed base lock-in, emerging ISV leaders risk falling victim to category regime change if they fail to accumulate sufficient asymmetric market power to build and defend their own customer and category no-fly- zones.

Rather than build software marketing strategy on the basis of 'crossing the chasm', asymmetric marketers get busy tossing the chasm in favor of the practice of superpower symbiosis, i.e. *leveraging incumbent, cross-category leader dynamics for their own benefit.* This is the path followed by the embryonic Microsoft when it co-opted IBM's PC leadership for itself. When it entered the IBM cage and leveraged the power of that cage.

When over the course of its evolution, Microsoft expanded its 'no-fly-zone' from PC operating systems to desktop applications to network servers to browsers to e-business infrastructure and beyond---that's asymmetric marketing (not 'predatory' competition) in action.

And for you Microsoft-player-haters, let's also stipulate that this very same path of symbiosis (in various forms) has also been the marketing approach taken by ascendant superpower Google in it's 'powered by' search services agreements with Yahoo, AOL and other portal providers. Agreements that have enabled Google to effectively harness and co-opt the market power of Yahoo and AOL to catapult its own market momentum. And Google's other forms of superpower symbiosis (the Google Toolbar parasitically attaching itself to Internet Explorer) are the asymmetric icing on their cake.

In the chapters that follow, I will focus on the application of symbiosis along the full spectrum of the software marketing challenge in the age of the superpowers. Here's a glimpse ahead:

- Asymmetric product strategy has evolved beyond Geoffrey Moore's chasm theory notion of 'whole products'. I'll get into this in Chapter 3.
- Asymmetric sales strategy is not based on the chasm theory notion of a vertically focused 'bowling alley'. I'll get into this in Chapter 4.
- Asymmetric marketers maintain a no-fly-zone approach to their customers that I call 'CBM' or *customer barrier management*. CBM is the market-craft of progressively creating one's own customer lock-in and competitor lockout. I'll cover this in Chapter 5, and surprise, surprise! The most successful ISVs in the open source Linux segment (e.g. Red Hat) have not only been known to follow this asymmetric marketing path, they have been successful at it. So much so that they were publicly attacked by companies 40 times their size.

In Chapter 6, I'll discuss the tribal operating culture of asymmetric marketing, and a Culture Management Systems (CMS) approach that will help your team execute a 'no huddle offense' in the age of the software superpowers.

And in Chapter 7, I'll take up the issue of asymmetric brand messaging strategy for an age of continuous superpower reputation conflict, and the 24/7 market conversations I call the 'messaging mashup'.

But for now, let's turn a critical eye toward that second big idea in chasm theory, the so-called TALC or 'technology adoption lifecycle'. And while we're at it, let's see if we can zoom in on a new 'post-chasm' metaphor to describe the persistent challenge of competing in the on-again/off-again ISV market uncertainty that has become a fact of life in the age of the software superpowers.

And before I forget. When you do eventually get around to taking that next bite out of your sacred cow chasm-burger...Like mom used to say, Don't forget to chew before you swallow.

Chapter 2

ASYMMETRIC MARKET DEVELOPMENT IN THE SUPERPOWER SANDSTORM

"There's something's happening here. What it is ain't exactly clear. There's a man with a gun over there...Telling me I've got to beware." 60's Rock Band, Buffalo Springfield

I f this chapter were an episode of my favorite counter-terror TV action program, *24*, a deep voice-over from Jack Bauer[1] would start us off something like this. *Previously on Asymmetric Marketing...* (quick jump-cut to the following action scenes tightly edited for effect):

In the after-bubble, we're witnessing the accelerated growth of cross-category market clout in the hands of a select group of superpowers. It is this *asymmetry of cross-category market power*, not market share leadership alone, which defines a true winner-take-all superpower marketer.

Check. Software superpowers. Got it.

One key manifestation of the market power wielded by the cage-fighting software superpowers is their *installed base of locked-in customers.* I call them *ecozones* and *ecoregions*, e.g. the ecozone of all Microsoft customers, and it's specific subsets, e.g. the Windows Client OEM ecoregion, the Windows server ecoregion, or the MSN ecoregion.

Check. A non-fuzzy bioscience metaphor to characterize asymmetric market power over clearly demarcated market landscapes. The biology that pays off the 'cage' metaphor.

Locked-in superpower ecoregions can be transformed into powerful marketing brass knuckles to carry out *category regime change* against market share leading ISVs in emerging and/or adjacent categories. Remember how Microsoft defeated WordPerfect, Lotus, Novell and Netscape, all market share leaders. And let's not forget what these companies did to themselves by not developing effective defenses of their own installed base customers against brass knuckles, regime change competition.

Category regime change against market share leading ISVs. Check.

As for the promised land of tornadoes of ISV disruptive technology innovation ... think again. Disruptive technology innovation (including open source, on-demand, and Web 2.0) is being creatively co-opted by the *asymmetry of R&D and marketing investment made by the superpowers*. Superpower R&D and marketing spend has significantly out-paced VC investment in innovative startups in the after-bubble period.

Summing Up....

As natural, i.e. customer-sanctioned monopolies, the software superpowers implement a set of strategic marketing practices designed to transform their customer ecoregions into defensible no-fly-zones against competitive ISVs who choose not to practice effective marketing symbiosis with them. The challenge of ISV leadership in the age of the superpowers is to break with all forms of cargo cult thinking, defined primarily by the legacy marketing religion of disruptive technology innovation. The goal: *To develop strategy, products, and go-to-market initiatives that capitalize on symbiosis with the superpowers in order to co-opt, not disrupt, their market power.*

OK, now that we've reviewed the voice-over notes for Chapter 1, I'm going to start off this chapter by turning a critical eye toward the second basic pillar and big idea in Moore's chasm theory. After those 'tornadoes' of disruptive innovation.

I'm going to suggest an alternative approach to thinking about adoption and market development in the age of the software superpowers. An approach more suited to ISVs seeking to advance their own marketing agendas by creatively leveraging the asymmetric advantage of the superpowers.

Tossing the TALC As the Market Development Framework for ISVs

The practical foundation of Geoffrey Moore's chasm theory is the notion of a *technology adoption lifecycle* or *TALC²*. Here's a quick summary of the highlights of that notion.

The TALC approaches markets through the prism of a lifecycle framework---a framework that seemingly explains how technology users adopt a specific innovation. This TALC framework segments markets based on how quickly, or *when* in the lifecycle, discrete sets of customers purchase a given technology, referring to them accordingly as technology enthusiasts, visionaries, pragmatists, conservatives, and skeptics.

According to Moore's TALC, at some point in the lifecycle, an adoption *chasm* between enthusiast and visionary 'early adopters', and the 'early majority' of pragmatists, must be crossed. In order for a given technology provider to gain mainstream market acceptance of its offering. And if the Gods of Software happen to be smiling on a particular chasm-crosser, that company may be swept up in his 'tornado' phase to become the category market share "gorilla".

One corollary of Moore's TALC framework is a *universal strategic marketing path* along which ISVs must adjust strategy, and go-to-market tactics, at each stage of the lifecycle. So that they may successfully capitalize on this seeming multiple personality disorder (visionaries, skeptics, etc.) inherent in tech market adoption.

I'll take issue with Moore's universal marketing path (so-called *'whole products'*, and *'bowling alley'* go-to-market approaches) in Chapter 3---Asymmetric Products, and Chapter 4---Asymmetric Sales Strategy. But for now I'm going to focus on the main issue I am raising here. *The increasingly diminished relevance of the TALC as a market development framework in the age of the superpowers*.

But first a necessary disclaimer.

By raising the issue of Moore's TALC, am I suggesting that under any and all circumstances there are no such carbon life-forms that could be accurately described as 'visionaries' and 'pragmatists'? Or any rational market segmentation model that can dissect emerging markets this way? Absolutely not!

What I'm saying is that I don't find it practical in 2006, on a non-flat landscape of software market superpowers with caged-in customer ecoregions, to debate the issue of abstraction level models of tech market development. I don't see very many ISV 'cargo planes' landing on the runway of abstraction level models.

What does interest me is that unavoidable competitive issue facing ISV marketers. How to effectively compete and succeed in an age of natural monopoly software superpowers. As I pointed out in Chapter One, Geoffrey Moore himself now admits that …

*"The issue is, can you get the technology across the chasm **inside the company that invented it?** The answer historically has been **not very often** (bolding my emphasis)."*

Approached another way, you may decide to pay strategy consultants, or industry analyst firms grounded in chasm theory, hundreds of thousands of dollars to provide you, your CEO, your investors and your board with graphically correct breakdowns of some projected future state of technology adoption in your target opportunity area. *'Here's a nice pie chart segmenting your visionaries and …oh my god.…Just look at the size of that future early majority, Ms. CMO'.*

And here's the rub. You and your team may even execute flawlessly around Moore's TALC model, just as Feynman's tropical cargo cult executed around what they perceived to be the right way to get the planes to land. But as Moore himself now concedes, there is a very high probability you will never end up on the other side of his chasm in the nirvana of his tornado. Want to know why? Here's the answer.

TALC as Laissez-Faire Viewpoint in an Age of Natural Monopolies

TALC theory is an expression of classical *laissez-faire*[3] or 'free market' economics, pure and simple. It is (in Moore's application of the idea) the intellectual offspring of the *'pre-pubescent' phase of the tech buildout*. Seen in its most positive light, it is a romantic notion in an age of software natural monopolies. Seen in its most negative light, it disarms ISV marketers in the face of superpower asymmetry. Here are 5 simple 2006 facts of life for ISVs that support my argument.

1. **Superpower Market Freezing:** The TALC model doesn't account for the ongoing and ever-expanding impact on product adoption of the focused market power exerted by the superpowers, in order to defend the lock-in of their own installed base ecoregions. This asymmetry of natural monopoly market power can *freeze ISV adoption progress and impede ISV success within the superpowers' installed base*--if ISVs do not develop creative counter-measures to cope with it.

Said another way, we're in a market development environment where *software adoption is ultimately driven by the cross-category competitive dynamics of the superpower age*, not broad-brush user psychographics like 'visionary' or 'skeptic'. If you don't believe that ever-evolving, category-extensible superpower agendas can serve as barriers to adoption, ask the folks who used to run Siebel.

Siebel's market share growth in pure-play CRM ultimately bestowed upon them the category leader position. But it wasn't disruptive innovator Salesforce.com that knocked them from their perch. Much of Siebel's forward momentum was effectively halted[4] when superpowers SAP and Oracle placed them in the crosshairs of a CRM category annexation strategy, transforming CRM into a 'feature' of SAP and Oracle's broad enterprise application platforms.

By 'featurizing' the CRM (or any) category, i.e. by making a significant 'good enough' amount of that functionality a 'module' or component of their end-to-end platforms, the superpowers *gradually freeze stand-alone category dynamics*. If I wanted to be charitable to Mr. Moore and describe this in a 'chasmologically correct' fashion, I'd characterize this superpower freezing phenomenon as 'permanent chasm' creation. But if you do decide to think of it as a permanent chasm, then the lifecycle model itself must also fall into it.

In the end, Siebel decided to sell itself to Oracle after having no less than three CEOs inside of one year[5] (including the former WebVan/Andersen Consulting CEO) try to lead them out of this permanent chasm to recapture momentum. But merging with Oracle was the smartest move they could have made in the face of superpower asymmetric marketing that took the form of category-freezing.

I guess one could also argue, in defense of Moore's TALC, that the CRM category had matured and moved into the 'Main Street'[6] phase of his chasm model. But that is insufficient to explain why cross-category superpowers like SAP and Oracle *grew their CRM businesses*, while category market share 'gorilla'[7] Siebel faced increasing adoption resistance within both the SAP and Oracle installed based ecoregions. So the superpowers don't just freeze stand-alone category dynamics, they freeze market progress of the category 'gorilla' benefiting from those stand-alone category dynamics. Picture King Kong frozen in a big block of ice. Exactly. He's not King Kong anymore.

By the way, this same phenomenon of CRM category/gorilla freezing also explains why Salesforce.com, despite its innovative on-demand, Software-as-a-Service (SaaS) approach, continues to have high marketing and sales expense relative to revenue...51% as of Q2 2006...Reflecting their ongoing need to overcome increasing adoption resistance in the superpower-dominated enterprise through pumping up conventional marketing spend on sales people, brand advertising, seminars, etc.[8]

In extreme cases of category gorilla freezing, e.g. Oracle's openly hostile bid for PeopleSoft, not developing effective countermeasures against these kinds of cross-category superpower dynamics can even cost a successful leader his job. In a presentation he made after the Oracle acquisition, Craig Conway, PeopleSoft's CEO, revealed that he was ultimately fired by his board because he supposedly 'lied' to them about the extent to which customers were refusing to place new orders with the company until the Oracle bid had sorted itself out.[9] Conway even had a term to describe Oracle's hostile buyout strategy---He called it the *'twist in the wind'* strategy, and points out that it successfully froze a percentage of his customers from moving forward with PeopleSoft.[10]

By the way, if I were Conway, I'd have repeated that same little half-truth. Because in the face of a superpower category regime change offensive, one man's little white lie is another man's brand messaging countermeasure. It's called *marketing communications in the age of the superpowers*. Unfortunately for Conway, it was not enough of a marketing countermeasure to roll back the asymmetric Oracle strategy.

Ok....let's move on to our second reason why the TALC is losing it's practical relevance as a guide to ISV action in the age of the superpowers.

2. Superpower Contention/Collusion: The TALC model *does not account for the powerful market effects of collusion among the superpowers as well as the contention between them.*

This collusion/contention dynamic of the superpowers is continuously at work impacting the structure of whole markets, eroding emerging categories, and sidelining the success of ISVs who fail to take this dynamic into account. As I mentioned in Chapter 1, Microsoft and SAP have jointly developed Duet, a .NET/Netweaver interoperability strategy[11]. This collusion between Microsoft and SAP is aimed at pre-emptively capturing asymmetric advantage in emerging services-oriented architecture (SOA) markets in general.

But the alliance also targets shared rival Oracle, as it fights to expand its enterprise application muscle through the PeopleSoft, Siebel and other acquisitions. You can see the same contention/collusion dynamic playing out in the search market as well, as Google and Microsoft slug it out, while eBay teams up with Yahoo (and Google) on both search and payments.[12]

When superpowers contend for a promising new (or mature) category, they leverage their asymmetric *never-ending products model* (don't worry, it's in Chapter 3), and *push as much good enough 'beta' technology as possible into their locked-in customer ecoregions, effectively slow-motioning the adoption lifecycle for alternative ISV products.*

Look at the security category, in which Microsoft and emerging superpower Symantec are slugging it out for basic consumer PC protection services. As of August 2006, Microsoft currently has over *25 million 'customers' for it's free Windows Defender Anti-Spyware beta.*[13] And in the run up to the Vista launch, the PC security wars are just beginning to escalate as the superpowers square off with online PC health services---Services that drive higher order user lock-in by virtue of their continuous *'upate-ness'*.

3. Channel Colonization: The TALC model doesn't account for the systematic efforts of the superpowers to 'colonize' their channels, and to control and/or acquire their professional services partners. I've been in more meetings than I can count with ISV folks who thought their hopes for increasing adoption lay in the "channel"---Only to find out that in this age of software superpowers, *the multi-vendor channel is morphing into discrete sets of wholly owned channel colonies*, complete with marketing agendas tied to those of the natural monopolies whose products they service and integrate.

While much of this channel colonization in the after-bubble has been occurring 'under the radar', in 2006 Microsoft's Steve Ballmer has increasingly become up-front about asking his channel and ISV partners to 'choose'...Especially in superpower- contested categories like "search and portal, unified communications and security".[14]

If you want another example, just ask the folks at BEA Systems about the market share battle in application and integration middleware as IBM expands the use of it's M&A-acquired professional services muscle to dominate the market[15] with it's own software.

The ongoing implication of increasing superpower channel colonization is that asymmetric ISVs need to *position themselves as complementary offerings to those of the superpowers*. Since the bread and butter of colonized channel partners is the revenue they receive from providing services around superpower platforms, being perceived as a non-complementary disruptive technology innovator is often perceived as the kiss of death in the channel. Unless you're one of those rare, cash-rich startups prepared to 'pay to play', i.e. effectively subsidize the targeted channel partner's sales effort on your behalf...Or just bite one more superpower bullet and call the expensive headhunter with the database of expensive direct sales guys. I'll expand on my discussion of channel colonization in Chapter 4, Asymmetric Sales Strategy.

4. Superpower 'Non-Strategic' Market Creation: The TALC/ chasm does not shed light on how ISVs can leverage the *new market creation initiatives of the superpowers*---Initiatives that can and often do become the foundation of their future asymmetric advantage.

Superpower-driven new market creation initiatives have historically been the source of rapid ISV adoption success. Just as Microsoft's early attachment to IBM's new market creation activities in the PC industry provided it with the foundation of its future asymmetric marketing advantage, and natural monopoly status, today's ISVs can capitalize on superpower agendas and *supercharge their own adoption dynamics. How? Learn how and where to look for superpower market creation agendas*, and become symbiotic with these target(s) of asymmetric opportunity (TAO).

As I pointed out in the previous chapter, the market territory created by these new market creation activities of the superpowers may be initially perceived as a *'non-strategic' initiative* (as was the original PC to IBM). This is the territory you want to infiltrate...These are the initiatives you want to co-opt. This is the ideal cage for your future cage fight.

These *non-strategic or ancillary initiatives of incumbent leaders, if they are successful, can lift key ISV partners along with them*, and enable those ISV partners to penetrate a new superpower ecoregion with the market permission of the host superpower.

Wasn't Apple's early outreach for desktop publishing printer technology[16] to showcase a 'killer app' for their flagship Macintosh GUI exactly the ancillary initiative by a market leader that gave Adobe their opening to widely market Postscript, and later Acrobat Reader (which now enjoys a natural monopoly in web document viewing)? There is no argument that the Mac GUI was strategic to Apple. But I contend that the wider market for printers was not something Apple wanted to pursue (outside of supporting and showcasing the innovation in the Mac platform). And so the seed of a future superpower called Adobe was planted in the garden of a 'non-strategic' or ancillary initiative of an incumbent market leader.

5. Sea Change in Enterprise IT Adoption Dynamics: Last but not least, the TALC model doesn't really take into account the sea change in adoption dynamics happening inside major IT shop*s* as they institutionalize 'doing more with less'. In the case of IT buyers, everybody seems to drifting in the direction of what Moore describes as a 'pragmatist' or 'skeptic', especially in enterprises with 1000 or more employees.[17]

In 2006, it's fair to say that it has become safe at the CIO level to act as if cautiousness is godliness, and that business software is not a strategic asset, but simply a cost of doing business. The bottom line is this—In many cases, enterprise IT budgets are top-heavy in the direction of maintenance dollars for existing applications, usually superpower applications. I'll pick up on this later in the chapter.

So from where I sit, there are at least 5 dimensions of the after-bubble competitive challenge facing ISVs that Moore's TALC/chasm doesn't account for...Or to be fair to him, was never designed to account for, since his model emerged in what could best be described as the pre-pubescent phase of the tech build-out. Therefore, Moore's admission about the inability of technology originators to cross the chasm, while interesting as a general commentary on how he now sees chasm theory, doesn't go far enough.

For my money, *his observation renders the entire chasm metaphor, as well as the underlying TALC framework, increasingly irrelevant in practical terms* to any ISV facing the challenge of competing effectively in the superpower-dominated software industry.

Sure, if I'm a startup ISV executive responsible for marketing strategy, I may be interested in knowing how markets segment along a lifecycle in an academic sense. But that doesn't mean I'm going to gain access to those segments in the face of natural monopoly market power.

So if not the TALC, what is the way to proceed? Here's my recommendation. ISVs in 2006 and beyond need to begin to teach themselves to *assess the market behaviors of the superpowers as a key starting point for their own product adoption strategy.* This means strongly executing around an asymmetric approach based on symbiosis with one or more of those superpowers.

I'm going to drill down into these issues in the remainder of this chapter, but for now I want to you to stay with me while we find a *working replacement metaphor for the TALC chasm.* Remember what they say in those 12 step recovery groups for Cargo Cult Marketers...If you can't name your problem, you can't deal with it. So let's begin by giving it a name.

How to Think About Market Adoption in the Age of the Superpowers

As rock legend Buffalo Springfield's lyrics suggest at the top this chapter, something really is happening to ISVs in the after-bubble world of 2006. And *'what it is ain't exactly clear'* to many senior marketing and sales executives---let alone to the troops they lead onto the competitive battlefield. If it were clear, you probably would have seen far fewer quarterly earnings warning announcements in the 2001-2005 period from publicly traded ISVs that appear to be having trouble making their number.

So where should today's software marketers turn for straightforward, common sense guidance that can help them make sense of the competitive and market adoption challenges they face in the age of the superpowers? What kind of 'outside the marketing box' insight can help us nail down a new post-chasm metaphor that more aptly describes the challenge facing ISVs in the age of the superpowers? How about the insight of a professional asymmetric warrior?

Here's an observation that helps me set up my next point. It was made by General Peter Schoomaker, U.S. Army Chief of Staff, and a leading thinker on the subject of asymmetric special operations warfare.

*"We must also have the **intellectual agility to conceptualize creative, useful solutions to ambiguous problems** and provide a coherent set of choices to the supported CinC (commander in chief) or joint force commander---more often like Sun Tzu, less like Clausewitz. This means training and educating people how to think, not just what to think.*[18] "

'How to think, not just what to think'...so says one of America's leading thinkers on asymmetric warfare. For me, the challenge of developing a post-chasm-theory marketing strategy for the age of the software superpowers also goes to this question of *how to think...How to think about software marketing as a form of asymmetric warfare...*Not just applicable by the superpowers, but for all ISVs.

This approach, by the way, is consistent with the Microsoft journey that I described in Chapter 1---the journey of a startup company that went asymmetric on its competitors from its earliest days. Evolving from its status as an OEM supplier to IBM, to become the software industry's most respected (and feared) technology brand.

Focusing on the issue of *how to think* about ISV marketing as a form of asymmetric warfare stands in sharp contrast to the whole *'here's what you should think'* universe of cargo cult marketing consultants that have been operating in the tech industry for years. In my experience, many of these consultants appear to be addicted to shoe-horning market reality into graphically correct, abstraction-level adoption models like the TALC/chasm. This 'what to think' subculture of consultants and experts, discredited for a time during the bubble, is still very much alive. And they have exerted an inordinate amount of influence---Influence that has had the net effect of holding back the software industry from taking a fresh look at the marketing challenges facing ISVs.

This *how to think* approach General Schoomaker is recommending can serve as an effective antidote to the 'what to think' strategy industry. It can help point the industry in the right direction as it evolves toward a 21st century post-chasm metaphor that can frame and name the ISV market adoption challenges of 2006 and beyond.

Let me back into this issue of how to think about the challenge of 2006 ISV marketing from an angle near and dear to the hearts of millions of Nasdaq investors (and the marketing folks that try to please them)---The serious-as-a-heart-attack *'Here's why we missed our number'* press release angle.

Here's Why We Missed the Number

The *'here's why we missed the number'* story has become a common one told to investors by more than a few software and web CEOs in the after-bubble. Unless you've been on Mars, I'm positive you've seen the kind of press release I'm talking about. If you're the CEO, CFO or CMO of a Nasdaq company, maybe you've even had to sit up all night editing one before the quarterly earnings call.

Let's look at a few representative quotations from some typically-worded, ISV quarterly 'miss the number' announcements that might help us in naming those *ambiguous problems* (General Schoomaker's term) facing ISVs in the age of the superpowers.

*"While we are unhappy with the shortfall in our forecasted quarterly revenue, this revenue miss was centered in **a handful of large transactions in the pipeline that were forecasted but did not close, and have slipped into future quarters"**.* Market Share Leader Explaining Why They Missed their Quarterly Guidance.

*"The **category in which we compete is changing rapidly and we** are meeting new and intensified price and feature competition from **much larger vendors who have added new functionality to their enterprise application suites.** Going forward, we regret that we will no longer be providing revenue guidance on a quarterly basis."* Emerging Category ISV Leader on Why They Missed the Number.

*"We are **re-adjusting our headcount downward to cope with the continuing softness in IT demand,** and simultaneously announcing the appointment of Vicki Veteran as our new VP of Marketing & Sales replacing Doug Disruption.* Promising ISV Startup on Why They Are Restructuring

You don't even have to try very hard to read between the lines of the PR spin to see that each of these representative sentences suggests that we are in a marketing environment for ISVs in which revenue visibility remains fuzzy. In addition, once 'tornado-capable' growth categories have begun to erode as the ***superpowers systematically expand the scope of the product functionality available to their locked-in customer ecoregions***.

Additionally, more than a few ISV marketing organizations remain woefully ineffective in dealing with these 'ambiguous' problems--- Problems that don't seem to jive with a legacy TALC model that focuses on phases of technology adoption in the abstract. ***Seriously folks... was Moore's TALC/chasm model designed for an age where the R&D budget of a single superpower is larger than the entire U.S. VC investment in all software companies combined?***

The correct answer is capital N capital O period. Moore's 1991 TALC/chasm framework was never designed to function in a software world where asymmetric market muscle and natural monopoly customer lock-in are in-your-face facts of life.

Let me anticipate what you're thinking. *"So Mr. Joe B.... you have some set of marketing cojones on you to badmouth Mr. Moore's chasm metaphor, and try to upset the TALC applecart we all know and love. And despite what they say about us California types back in the 'red states', we do love religion here in Silicon Valley. And the foundation of our religion is the TALC chasm model. So put your symmetric money where your asymmetric mouth is! If you no longer see practical validity in the chasm metaphor, then tell us how you describe the post-bubble, post-9.11, superpower-dominated adoption environment for ISVs"*

OK. Since you asked me so politely, here's my take on it.

The Sandstorm: A Market Development Metaphor for the Superpower Age

Remember the old saying.

"If it looks like a duck, quacks like a duck, walks like a duck - then it is probably a duck."

It looks like a sandstorm.

It quacks like a sandstorm.

It acts like a sandstorm.

How about we just label the challenge facing 21st century ISVs the *sandstorm*, or....more specifically, the ***superpower sandstorm***.

Here's how I break down the ***key elements of the sandstorm as a post-TALC, post-chasm metaphor to describe the challenge of ISV marketing in the age of superpowers***---A metaphor that allows us to zoom in on those ambiguous problems (like missing the quarterly forecast), and make them less ambiguous... By identifying how a superpower-dominated market development landscape looks, quacks, and acts.

Fuzzy Revenue Visibility

Let's begin with the obvious. In a desert sandstorm it becomes difficult to see very far in front of one's own nose. In the superpower sandstorm it has become more difficult for ISVs to gain forward revenue visibility (even within a single quarter) as the underlying market factors driving the sandstorm interoperate. I'm going to get to those factors in a moment, but for now, let's just stick with defining the boundaries of the metaphor.

The sandstorm metaphor helps describe a competitive environment where forward revenue guidance at a wide cross-section of publicly traded and privately-held ISVs, across many categories, continues to be cautious and uncertain (or non-existent in some cases).

So "something is happening here" as that old 60's rock song goes, but it's really not about deals slipping into future quarters. That's just the believable excuse-du-jour, so that the share price of your favorite ISV stock doesn't completely collapse in an after-hours trading session.

So the first chronic issue in the superpower sandstorm is ISV revenue traction in general. And the challenge of how to think about competing, succeeding and locking in your own customers in an age in which cross-category natural monopolies are continually perfecting the art of asymmetric marketing. In other words, a big part of the challenge of revenue growth is not just longer sales cycles for big deals, or soft enterprise IT demand in the abstract. The issue is the *competitive behavior of the superpowers that is fundamentally changing both IT and consumer buying patterns*, transforming the TALC lifecycle into an ISV death spiral. Fuzzy revenue visibility is here to stay in the superpower sandstorm, and you need an asymmetric approach to products, sales strategy and customer management to deal with it. So what's the next aspect of the sandstorm metaphor?

Positional Confusion

In the beginning of the Iraq conflict, American soldiers, at risk of getting lost in desert sandstorms, relied on GPS navigational systems[19] to find their way. This ability to position themselves via GPS in the low-to-no visibility environment of sandstorm confusion become an operational plus. It ultimately allowed them to leverage the desert storm to capture an asymmetric advantage over their opponents.

Similarly, as the software superpowers escalate the practice of regime change and category annexation I described in Chapter 1, and continuously incorporate new capabilities into their platforms, ISVs find it increasingly difficult to position themselves in practical terms (vs. PR hype) within the category in which they compete.

How many press releases have you seen that start off like this: *"Company X, the industry leader in category Y today announced..."* You may see 10 companies, all of which are pretty damn similar, claiming to be the leader in this or that 'visionary magic quadrant'. The fact is, in the superpower sandstorm, category boundaries are blurring (*'what it is ain't exactly clear'* goes the Buffalo Springfield lyrics cited above). So ISVs face new challenges, not just in generating interesting spin to justify their claim of category leadership, but in communicating and marketing their core value propositions to customers, partners and shareholders, an essential pre-condition of marketing success.

Tracking the cross-category market behaviors of the superpowers, and adjusting your own market positioning strategy accordingly, is the asymmetric marketing GPS you will need to navigate the sandstorm market landscape. And then there's.....

Lots of Heat

As in a desert sandstorm, intense heat is being generated in the superpower sandstorm. This heat comes from growing board, investor, VC and regulatory oversight of, and intervention into, the day-to-day operations of CEOs and senior management. This intensified heat has led in many cases to board micromanagement of both marketing and sales executives. In the post-Enron, post-ethics scandal environment, this hands-on board and CEO oversight will only intensify as regulatory agencies impose more and more financial and operational transparency on management teams. For senior marketing and sales leadership facing this intensified heat from the competitive challenges of the superpower sandstorm, there really appears to be *a 'man with a gun over there'*, as the song goes, a man that may pull the trigger and fire you like our friend 'Doug Disruption' in the PR quote above---when you fail to make the number.

This execution heat has *the unintended consequence of increasing the danger of falling into the trap of the cargo cult marketers of the bubble...overspend, overspend, overspend...* in response to that 'man with the gun'. And you can rest assured that the lion's share of overspending will go into cargo cult marketing programs predicated on trying to make the TALC chasm model work in the face of all evidence to the contrary (*"Hey boss, we've got to run all these ads if we want to reach those under the radar early adopters....there's just no way around it boss. You must not read the right books.").*

This sandstorm execution heat intensifies the other sandstorm effects of impaired revenue visibility and positional confusion, and means you may eventually have to dig yourself out of a deeper sand dune, as the 'man with the gun over there' scrutinizes your every move.

Broken Marketing & Sales Machinery

In desert sandstorms modern complex machinery tends to frequently break down, as millions of particles of sand finds their way into moving parts.

In the superpower sandstorm, the moving parts of your marketing organization are at risk. Morale-reducing layoffs and frequent re-organizations have been the order of the day for more than a few ISV marketing and sales organizations in the period since the bursting of the bubble. This has often disrupted the institutional memory of marketing organizations, while creating operating cultures of silence, fear, resentment, timid execution, blame, non-collaboration, risk aversion and paralyzing political correctness disguised as workforce diversity. No wonder CEOs end up micromanaging the marketing and sales function, and so few ISVs have a true CMO role that manages all strategic marketing and sales functions.

I'll address the underlying basis for this in Chapter 6, when I discuss the operating culture of asymmetric marketing. But for now let me describe these symptoms of broken sales and marketing machinery as a sales/marketing execution gap. A gap between a sober vision of market opportunity in the superpower sandstorm, and an execution-ready organization that knows how to capitalize on the specific kind of opportunities the sandstorm creates. It's been my practical experience that this sales and marketing gap is a primary reason for the absence of market momentum for many ISVs, both public and private. The gears connecting sales and marketing just don't engage, and sales opportunities fall into the gap. Investing in the kind of asymmetric or 'tribal' operating culture capable of closing that gap will prove to be a hundred times more fruitful than throwing money at new cargo cult marketing programs designed to make the TALC/chasm work.

Benefits of the Sandstorm Metaphor

I throw myself on the mercy of the marketing court. I'm not a graphics artist. So the sandstorm metaphor is not graphically correct. It's not easy to put on a PowerPoint slide, as is that iconic bell curve with the chasm on the bottom left. But in my defense, let me argue that the *sandstorm is a how to think metaphor* that can serve to immediately focus marketing attention on *the fuzzy revenue visibility, positional confusion, execution heat, and broken marketing machinery characterizing the ISV marketing challenge* in the in the age of the software superpowers.

Rather than take the TALC approach, which focuses on a largely psychographic model of end user and IT adoption dynamics applied by Moore to the tech industry in the early 1990's, the sandstorm metaphor focuses management attention on the actual market, competitive, leadership and organizational issues that must be addressed to achieve consistent, defensible growth in the age of the natural monopoly superpowers. The sandstorm metaphor can serve to shine the flashlight on those seemingly 'ambiguous problems' (General Schoomaker's term) facing ISV marketers in the chronic, on-again/off-again, quarter-to-quarter marketing and sales uncertainty that is the new normal for ISVs as the superpower age unfolds.

Drivers of the Sandstorm: So Where's the Damn Desert?

So what forces are at work driving the superpower sandstorm? Where's the desert that pays off the metaphor? Let's get the no-brainer stuff out of the way first. It comprises the new reality that all software marketers have to deal with on a daily basis.

Let's stipulate to the general-purpose angst and uncertainty that is the new normal in a post-9.11 world. In the wake of 9.11 we all watched as IT spending contracted in step with the overall business downturn in a number of major economic segments---airlines, hotels, retail, etc. Should a second and a third major 9.11-style attack occur on US soil during the course of the global war on terror, look for orders of magnitude more opportunity erosion as IT organizations continue to institutionalize the process of doing more with less.

But as bad as that would be, this alone does not yet constitute a software 'desert'. ISV marketers in the U.S., and around the world, are gradually realizing that they must see terror and war as contextual constants, and teach themselves to think about software marketing more like the Israeli high tech industry, which has thrived in these conditions. How? By coming to terms with them as a source of opportunity, particularly for government-directed marketing programs focused on homeland security and defense applications.

And then of course there is oil fluctuating at, near and above $60 to $70 a barrel. Needless to say, that can't be good for software adoption in industries whose profitability is shrinking because they are oil-dependent, or even in consumer markets hoping to tap into discretionary dollars that are now going into the gas pump. Bad yes.... sand swirling... yes, but still not by itself a software desert.

Then there's what I call the 'new regionalism'. We are witnessing the rise of a European Union that sees itself as an emerging economic powerhouse in its own right, competing head to head with the U.S. in global markets, including software. Hey, Jacques Chirac even wants a Franco-German search engine to compete against Google[20]. Marketing war is, as they say, market politics by other means. Another dimension of this 'new regionalism'— European governments increasingly see Linux as the politically correct alternative to the 'anybody but Microsoft' issue[21]. One more regional attack on Microsoft, a warning to other U.S. software superpowers to embrace Linux, but not yet a desert.

Let's throw in a rapidly expanding China that sees itself as the new hardware superpower, and an India that has similar ambitions in software. Oh, by the way, it wasn't very long after the deal between IBM and Lenovo (sale of the IBM PC division to a Chinese company) was announced, that the head of the Chinese government went to Bangalore India to deliver the message, 'Let's team up' against the U.S. tech industry[22]. Could be a big challenge over the next 10 years, and is a compelling reason why the U.S. government needs to focus on, and continuously re-invigorate, *national high technology industry policy*[23] in the middle of the global war on terror, and the emerging challenge of new regional competition. Clearly, a lot more can be done in this area.

Oh, and did I forget to mention a CIO mindset in major U.S. and global corporations that increasingly sees information technology as a *'commoditized cost of business'*, and not as a strategic competitive advantage. Ok.... now we're approaching the desert.

The 'Desertification' of IT Adoption Dynamics

While sandstorms are usually thought of as purely natural phenomena that occur regularly in arid regions of the planet, what most folks don't know is that they are also fostered and magnified by the factor of human intervention into natural environments, something scientists call *desertification*. Desertification is the process whereby human beings *over-cultivate*[24] *a given landscape* making it even more arid, and more likely to be a place of recurring sandstorms[25], once the right winds start to blow.

It's been my experience that software market landscapes are subject to the same kinds of over-cultivation and desertification effects. There are 2 primary trends driving the desertification of ISV adoption dynamics. They are the:
- IT 'more with less' agenda; and the
- 'No-Fly-Zone Imperative' of the superpowers.

I discuss both of them below.

The IT "More with Less" Agenda

What I characterize as adoption desertification is becoming increasingly evident in the ongoing debate within enterprise IT circles over the current role of information technology as *'cost of business'* or *'strategic competitive advantage'*. This debate, initiated in the Harvard Business Review by Nicholas Carr[26], focuses on his analysis that the IT build-out of the 90's is nearer to the end than the beginning. If you are a software marketer and don't know who Nicholas Carr is, or what he has to say, you need to make it your business to find out...Yesterday.

One practical implication of Carr's analysis is that IT leadership in the world's largest enterprises should do more with less, i.e. focus on executing strategies that bring down the overall cost of information technology, since it is now a universal cost of doing business. Those IT shops that act on Carr's advice can only mean one thing for ISV marketers. Fewer and fewer 'technology enthusiasts' and 'visionaries' will be drinking the Kool-Aid of the next technology marketing spin cycle touting strategic advantage for this or that disruptive technology innovation. This or that new new expression of 'creative destruction'.

With this kind of background debate going on at the highest levels of IT, is it any wonder that CIOs have become more creative and tight-fisted in working with software and technology providers, and are striving to make Carr's point of view pay off for them. So consider it common wisdom that the ***lion's share of IT budgets will continue to go toward maintaining and optimizing existing systems, usually systems based on superpower platforms.***

This can't be a good thing for those cargo cult marketers that remain addicted to an adoption model like the TALC---A model that holds out the promise of an endless summer of 'visionaries' and 'technology enthusiasts' on the hunt for every new disruptive technology innovation. But asymmetric marketers should have a different attitude toward this emergence of a 'more with less' IT operating culture within the world's largest enterprises.

I see the emergence of the 'more with less' culture, and the Carr-inspired debate, as early indicators of a re-invigorated IT *immune system* reacting defensively to the often false and misleading 'value propositions' of many cargo cult marketers. Remember the bubble---a time in which thousands of companies over-hyped every e-widget as breakthrough strategic value. That's cargo cult marketing contributing to the 'over-cultivation' effect I referred to when I introduced the concept of desertification.

The ongoing desertification of IT, this 'more with less' IT culture, requires a continuous re-thinking of how ISVs detect market opportunity, and see market development strategy...How they discover those 'oases' in the sandstorm. Carr's insight, and the ongoing desertification of IT, should be seen by forward-looking ISVs as more nails in the coffin of the TALC/chasm as a practical guide to action for detecting and capitalizing on market opportunity. If you place any credibility at all in the Nicholas Carr vision of the post-bubble IT world (as I do), then assume that over time smart CIOs are migrating into the camp of what Moore calls pragmatists and skeptics.

But there a positive aspect of this desertification and embrace of IT commoditization. It is providing new impetus to a number of emerging opportunities, including the SaaS (software as a service) trend represented by everything from IBM's onDemand initiative, to Google's ad-sponsored applications vision, to CRM poster-child Salesforce.com. Then of course there's the open source movement. As well as the renewed focus by ISVs (and the superpowers) to bring enterprise-grade software functionality to the SMB and consumer markets. These are proving to be emergent opportunity oases within the over-cultivated enterprise IT desert.

And as IT desertification progresses, these opportunity oases will expand. But asymmetric marketers know that they will only do so *in the context of the age of the cross-category software superpowers. Not as the next stand-alone fad-du-jour, and its associated spin cycle.*

One additional point. While it may seem counter-intuitive, this kind of desert-like IT environment actually benefits the software superpowers and their ecoregion lock-ins. Don't forget the simple fact I pointed out above---the lions share of IT budgets remains maintenance dollars for updates from incumbent vendors, usually one or more of the superpowers. But IT's embrace of 'more with less' isn't the only factor driving opportunity desertification. ISV cargo cult marketers themselves are exacerbating this condition.

'Terrorist' Competitors and 'Publates'

In addition to the shift in IT adoption habits, desertification of the software industry in the 2000-2006 period has also intensified as a direct result of the *marketing behaviors of cash-rich bubble survivors* in various emerging categories. These irrational behaviors, e.g. super-aggressive license discounting of complex applications in order to 'buy business' (remember the intensified execution heat to make the number is one element of the sandstorm) are the equivalent of what a leading investment banker calls 'terrorist competition'.

In an after-bubble interview with the Always-on Network, Paul Deninger, Chairman and CEO of M&A banking firm Broadview International, refers to certain companies as irrational or 'terrorist' competitors[27]. Without naming and shaming specific companies, he paints a general picture of terrorist competitors as bubble-era public companies, or well-funded startups, with large cash reserves. Under pressure to perform, the management teams of these companies use their IPO or VC cash to stay afloat, and 'buy' market adoption, as they confront healthier competitors and the IT 'more with less' agenda in the markets they have targeted.

It has been my experience that these irrational or 'terrorist' competitors are often responsible for *downward pricing pressure, reduced profitability, and stalled or delayed adoption in emerging categories.* The net result of terrorist competitors is that they de-stabilize their own categories by contributing to the ongoing desertification of IT.

In other words their bubbleboy cash cocoon allows them to think they are playing hardball, while in fact they are practicing irrational cargo cult marketing. All while having *the unintended consequence of convincing IT execs that if only they keep pushing those new software procurements into the next quarter, the price they pay for new software functionality will keep going down.*

What Deninger describes as terrorist competitors, I refer to as *publates*. 'Publates' is one of those composite words I created for myself to help me think about the well-financed, but irrational, marketing behaviors of hundreds of struggling, publicly-traded small-cap ISVs. ISVs that are often run like private companies by a particular management team or board, but pay lip service to their public status by managing for Wall Street perception, not sustainable growth and market power improvement. *Part public, part private equals publate.* Here's a composite portrait I'll call Publate Company X.

Company X is the market share leader in its established category of enterprise software, yet its revenue has progressively declined to about 50% of where it was at its peak in 2001. It has now gone through consecutive years of cost cutting, laying off almost half its workforce, yet still has not returned to operating profitability. Along the way, the company began to lose the market power it once had with its loyal customers, while the installed base of its flagship product (an offering still considered mission critical by its customers) began shrinking. But what's most relevant for our purposes here--- None of this was the direct result of effective competition within its category, but was instead the result of marketing decisions made by Company X itself.

Under board heat to improve its share price, the default marketing mode that emerged at Company X could be characterized as micro-management of everything by various board committees (surrounded by their coterie of cargo cult-of-the-day 'strategy' consultants). At the instigation of these consultants, Publate Company X began aggressively discounting it's complex software functionality to its own installed base, offering all-you-can eat customer site licenses that ending up having the effect of robbing the company of its future revenue pipeline and visibility.

Publate Company X also made a number of acquisitions of struggling startups, justifying them to its shareholders as the next big thing for the company. Not surprisingly, with line management fighting to hold on to their jobs by working to resuscitate momentum in Company X primary business, none of the acquisitions were effectively integrated into the operating culture of the company (and almost 100% of the staff who came in during the acquisitions left). Since large amounts of cash were used in these acquisition deals, and since none of these acquisitions had even begun to pay for themselves, it was necessary for Company X to carve out and sell a 'non-strategic' product line to raise new capital. Isn't it funny how parts of your business can become suddenly non-strategic when you feel the heat of the superpower sandstorm? Must be another one of those 'ambiguous problems' General Schoomaker referred to.

As the share price continued to drop, Company X then came under a new board/consultant mandate to 'enter the channel', and the management team was compelled to abandon its high-value, premium price customization services model that had been it's revenue meat and potatoes for many years, keeping it close to the long term plans of its customers. The net result---the law of unintended consequences kicked in, and Company X ended up actually creating new competitors. Competitors that now receive the lion's share of its former services revenue on customization deals the company sends them... thereby exacerbating its overall revenue decline.

After not seeing any share price improvement from downsizing, acquisitions, asset sales, channel initiatives, and revenue model changes, the board fell into the trap of adopting a go-it-alone bunker mentality, and began engaging in competitive behaviors in its installed base that alienated its long-term superpower partner, effectively driving that partner closer and closer to competition with the company. While this particular superpower partner chose not to engage in *direct* competition with the company, it did begin supporting smaller head-to-head competitors of Company X, who have themselves begun to make inroads into the Company X customer base by practicing symbiosis with this particular superpower.

So what's the take-away from this little sandstorm parable of Publate Company X? As long as there are publicly-traded, cash-rich ISVs with boards that act like private company owners willing to fund their own ongoing marketing mistakes in the name of improving share price, then both aggressive price-discounting of complex software functionality, and intensified intra-category irrational competition will remain facts of life. In other words, desertification will expand.

Fortunately for those ISVs without sufficient cash to become 'terrorist' competitors, another powerful underlying driver of the sandstorm is operating to mitigate against this form of desertification. I call this market driver the *superpower 'no-fly-zone' imperative*. And understanding and aligning yourself with this no-fly-zone imperative of the superpowers is crucial for ISVs that want to free themselves from cargo cult marketing, and develop an asymmetric product, sales and customer management approach.

As I suggested above in my introduction of the sandstorm metaphor, **think of this no-fly-zone imperative of the superpowers (not the TALC) as the practical marketing GPS.** GPS that will help you navigate the impaired revenue visibility, positional confusion, board heat and broken marketing machinery of the superpower sandstorm.

The Superpower No-Fly-Zone Imperative

As the IT 'do more with less' culture takes hold, and as irrational competitors intensify downward pricing pressure in their categories, the superpowers just smile and smell blood.

They know that the kind of software landscape desertification described above is the best kind of competitive battlefield for them... the kind of battlefield that intensifies their asymmetric market power. A *no-fly-zone* battlefield.

For the military of the U.S. and other modern powers, superiority from above, or air superiority,[28] provides an asymmetric advantage in wartime. The rules are simple. Encroach upon my territory without a note from the principal and you may get shot down. It's referred to as the no-fly-zone approach, and its success in various parts of the world has transformed it into a strategic imperative for 21st century armed forces. A similar kind of *operational asymmetry from above* has become common marketing practice for the software superpowers.

In the age of the software superpowers, there are 4 key elements of the no-fly-zone imperative. I alluded to them at the top of this chapter in describing why Moore's TALC model is out of date. These 4 elements are:

- Control of installed base ecoregions through the use of conventional brass knuckles marketing, and/or kinder, gentler 'stealth containment';
- Collusion between, and contention among the superpowers. This contention/collusion dynamic fosters a continuous category regime change environment for ISVs;
- Colonization of partner networks and channels around superpower agendas;
- Superpower creation of new markets through both R&D-driven and M&A-acquired innovation.

As shorthand, I'll just refer to these as the *4Cs of the no-fly-zone imperative---control, collusion/contention, colonization,* and *creation*.

Control-the 1ˢᵗ C of the No-Fly-Zone Imperative

Uh oh. I can feel my Seinfeld comedy fix from Chapter One wearing off. I think I'm about to go into comedy withdrawal and get asymmetric with another marketing and management guru. Somehow I don't feel like I can effectively address this issue of superpower no-fly-zone behavior without putting my literary finger in the eye of at least one more brand name thought leader. In this case, it's Tom Peters.

Back in the day, as that urban expression goes, I used to be a huge fan of Tom Peters. But with all due respect to the legend of Tom Peters, software companies in the after-bubble period are not engaged in '*A brawl with no rules*', the title of a popular presentation[30] of his that he has frequently delivered to high tech companies. I had the opportunity to experience the "Brawl With No Rules" pitch at an ISV's annual customer conference about 2 years into the after-bubble economic contraction. After digesting it, I reluctantly came to the conclusion that the superpower sandstorm appears to have obstructed the visibility of creative thinkers and management coaches like Mr. Peters.

For you readers who are about to question my sanity, let me answer the obvious question? After 'dissing' Geoffrey Moore's chasmology, why would I be dumb enough to say anything even remotely critical of a walking, talking legend like Tom Peters? Simple.

The software industry is as far as one could possibly get from a brawl with no rules.

And encouraging folks to think that we are in a 'brawl with no rules' means they will definitely fail, when they find out that they have neglected to see the effect of, or broken the rules of.... the natural monopolies that operate in those markets.

In point of fact, we are not even remotely in the vicinity of a brawl with no rules in the software industry. *We are well into an age of asymmetric market rule-makers.* Rule-makers that may overtly, or covertly, shoot you down...If you waltz into their market no-fly-zone without their express permission...or without a strategy based on effective symbiosis.

Here's a simple truth to keep with you and never forget in this age of the software superpowers. While you are dreaming that someday you will cross your category chasm, the superpowers are busy developing a plan to *cross your category border.*

Because crossing category borders is a necessary growth imperative for the superpowers in this age of expanding IT desertification. And understanding *how the superpowers see their own market rules... Aligning yourself with, and co-opting those rules* (not lapsing into hip-sounding market anarchism by fantasizing that there are no rules), *may actually help you keep the superpowers on their side of your category border.* (And here's a little side note for you Seth Godin fans)---What I'm saying here is that consumer markets are not the only permission-driven markets. And the end customer is not the only party granting market permission in the age of the superpowers.

So to illustrate this 1st C of the no-fly-zone imperative, let's continue for a moment using Microsoft history to drive our talking points. As we all know, Microsoft has historically been accused by its competitors of employing various methods of overt control to maintain a customer no-fly-zone. In fact, more than one of these asymmetric marketing approaches became the focus of the DOJ actions[30] against them (at the instigation of their competitors of course). So let's take a walk down memory lane to briefly illustrate the kinds of overt, brass knuckles marketing rules that I am referring to in this first 'C' of the superpower no-fly-zone imperative.

Rule 1--Licensing Rules
Over the course of their rise to superpower status, Microsoft

creatively imposed per-processor Windows OS licenses on PC OEMs. This licensing rule got Microsoft paid by those OEMs whether or not a given system ended up actually running Windows[31]. Now that's an example of asymmetric power for the marketing history books. But the simple fact of the matter is that Microsoft was able to enforce these asymmetric no-fly-zone licensing rules because DOS and Windows had been universally OEM-adopted by *every single cloner on the planet that hungrily wanted a piece of the market pie IBM had baked.*

Had startup Microsoft not been successful in creatively co-opting IBM's market power through the practice of symbiosis, they would never have been able to enforce this particular form of no-fly-zone licensing, something their critics do not give them credit for. As I pointed out in the previous chapter, IBM drove the creation of the market, and created the de-facto 'standard' that the cloners imitated. Microsoft was smart enough to capitalize on this cloner imitation and transform it into a natural monopoly.

The lesson here for asymmetric marketers---If you want to be able to enforce similar kinds of overt no-fly-zone marketing rules, then first succeed at practicing superpower symbiosis---Symbiosis of a kind that allows you to *effectively co-opt the market power of an incumbent market share leader*, as Microsoft did with IBM (and as Google has done with Yahoo and AOL in their 'powered-by' search services deals). Succeed at symbiosis and your product adoption will accelerate, and your market power will grow accordingly. And so will your ability to influence and ultimately set the rules in the markets in which you participate by extending the rules that are already in place.

The takeaway. *Try only getting into brawls where you understand the rules of the dominant players and can make them work for you.*

Rule 2--Developer Rules
Microsoft, over the course of its ascendance, has been regularly accused of holding back internal APIs and undocumented features[32] in Windows---Features that its critics say provided them with a no-fly-zone edge in applications development, or a way to reward and showcase their ISV partners who were doing interesting things with the Windows platform. To this accusation I say---One more asymmetric marketing BRAVO.

Think about it from their point of view, the point of view of an asymmetric marketer. Why should competitors like WordPerfect, Lotus and Netscape have been able to get a lifetime free ride on the Windows platform---a ride taken potentially at Microsoft's expense? What about level playing fields, you say? Of course *you don't want a level playing field if you are an asymmetric marketer*. Sure, it's dangerous to have to fight the U.S. government for years in a court of law---At the behest of your competitors. But I'd argue it's even more dangerous to surrender your no-fly-zone market power to competitors.

Returning to General Schoomaker's comments about Sun Tzu I referenced above, it was none other than Sun Tzu who said *"So it is that good warriors take their stand on ground where they cannot lose, and do not overlook conditions that make an opponent prone to defeat."* The lesson here---Whether you like it or not, stealth, concealment, and even purposeful misdirection have become major factors in software marketing, as they are in asymmetric war. And Microsoft is certainly not alone in embracing this lesson.

In the next chapter, where I cover Asymmetric Product Marketing, I describe this particular practice of stealth in the domain of product marketing as 'darkitecture', one of the key building blocks of asymmetric product 'sharkitecture'...the practice of optimizing product lock-in.

Rule 3--Encroachment Rules
Historically, Microsoft made sure that error messages would appear when competitive products tried to parasitically co-exist with their products without their market permission. For example, during the early explosion in the PC clone industry, Novell tried to sell its Digital Research DOS to various PC OEMs to run underneath Windows. That's just asking for a brass knuckles cage fight from an asymmetric marketer. Redmond's response? Various kinds of error screens would appear[33] stating that Windows detected some kind of incompatibility. Now that's serious no-fly-zone marketing. Definitely not a 'brawl with no rules'.

While Microsoft has come under intense government and competitive pressure over the years to abandon these asymmetric marketing practices designed to resist parasitic competitive encroachment, and has even voluntarily announced their Windows Principles[34] or 12 Tenets to Promote Competition, it's important to underline the fact that *these same kinds of no-fly-zone control practices have not disappeared from the marketing playbook of the other superpowers and rising stars*.

In fact they have been picked up, dusted off, and adopted by other superpowers (even some of the more warm and fuzzy California ones) as a proven means to pre-empt competitive encroachment. For example, even super-hip Yahoo has been known to turn to the 'early-years' Microsoft no-fly-zone marketing playbook, blocking a competitive instant messaging software provider from interacting with its Yahoo Instant Messenger community without it's permission[35].

This proves that these kinds of overt expressions of no-fly-zone marketing exclusively attributed to Microsoft have a shelf life in the software industry far beyond the rise of Redmond. In Chapter 5, where I discuss asymmetric CBM (customer barrier management), I'll go into *ISV no-fly-zone marketing in the open source segment* in discussing how Linux pioneer Red Hat was publicly criticized by Sun CEO Jonathan Schwartz for being 'proprietary'. But for now, I want to stay on point and bring you up to speed on what I describe as the later-years (post-DOJ action) Microsoft playbook, a playbook that includes far more creative lessons in no-fly-zone marketing ...Something I describe as *containment*.

Containment as a Form of Stealth No-fly-zone Control

Since its settlement with the DOJ, there is no doubt that superpower Microsoft has evolved a kinder, gentler form of no-fly-zone marketing. I choose to characterize this kinder, gentler form as containment. Why containment? Because it's a non-confrontational, creative form of no-fly-zone marketing behavior *not primarily aimed at defeating current competitors*, but at *pre-emptively earmarking future opportunity*.

One way to think about containment is to see it as the way a natural monopoly superpower holds an *emerging market in a state of arrested development, until the superpower itself is ready to capitalize on the market's emergence*. You Geoffrey Moore fans can feel free to think of it as a superpower-driven 'pseudo-chasm'.

Just as it did with its early stage, more overt methods of no-fly-zone marketing, Microsoft has begun perfecting this stealth practice of containment. One way containment is carried out---Through the use of *forward-looking industry initiatives* that from the outside looking in appear to be pure technology collaboration with a wide cross-section of other industry participants. But in fact, participating in these initiatives proves to be highly effective and subtle method of temporarily *freezing markets until one's own solution is ready to be launched.*

Let's examine the high profile Next Generation Secure Computing Base (NGSCB) 'trusted computing' initiative by Microsoft as a good example of how Microsoft has creatively (and yes, extremely legally) practiced asymmetric marketing by containing much of the competitive action in the emerging consumer DRM (digital rights management) market for Windows until the release of it's next generation consumer Vista OS in 2007.

For those of you who may not follow this particular technology segment, what has come to be called *trusted computing* is basically a set of ideas that roll up into the simple proposition that a more secure PC can be created capable of addressing the needs of the music and entertainment industry for digital rights management of paid content, while also fighting software piracy.

Additionally, the trusted computing vision holds out the promise of much better enterprise and consumer information security by enabling an IT environment wherein only trusted, authenticated devices (not just authenticated users) are permitted to access enterprise networks, both inside and outside the firewall. In order for the trusted computing vision to become a reality, various semiconductor and software providers have been collaborating since 2002 (and even earlier) to create the building blocks that PC vendors can incorporate into their products.

And while an industry organization called the Trusted Computing Group (TCG)[36] was set up to collaboratively manage trusted computing technical standards, and major silicon vendors did their part by developing a Trusted Platform Module (TPM) chip, very little progress appears to have been made in terms of market adoption of trusted computing-advantaged software applications. In fact, upon doing a search for 'software' the TCG itself lists only one app on their website[37]. And that's against a market background of 50 million PC's conforming to the TCG standard forecasted to ship in 2006. Is this just Moore's adoption 'chasm' between 'technology enthusiasts' and 'pragmatists'?

I don't see it that way from the standpoint of asymmetric marketing. Here's why.

While Microsoft is in fact a leading member of TCG, it also took steps to popularize a parallel vision to that of the TCG[38] that it calls the NGSCB (next generation secure computing base), previously referred to as Palladium. I characterize NGSCB as a competitive vision to TCG not because it doesn't incorporate TCG building blocks---It does. That's the beauty of it. I see it as competitive because the Microsoft NGSCG/Palladium specification sets for itself the broader goal of enabling hardware-based trust for a wide range of applications that need to become more secure. This includes digital rights management or DRM[39], a capability both Hollywood and the music industry would love to see go mainstream on the Windows platform in order to finally fight off the free peer-to-peer file-sharing crowd, while developing more robust online media business models.

But here's the asymmetric rub. NGSCB/Palladium (despite being talked about publicly for years) is not scheduled for delivery into the market until the release of Microsoft's Windows Vista OS. But hey...the online music space has been active all along. It's hotly conflicted over content distribution models. And paid content providers are looking for any commercial solution short of taking P2P downloaders to court.

Some, like Sony, chose not to wait for the launch of Vista, thinking they could capture an asymmetric advantage by dominating the 'early market'. So they went with their own DRM copy protection solution. What happened? They got mercilessly beaten up by the press, *and* the Department of Homeland Security, for placing a spyware-like root kit into the market. A root kit that turned out to be both privacy-invading and insecure. A big market 'scandal'. Hey, it's even listed as a 'scandal' in the heading in the Wikipedia.[40] Somebody needs to tell Sony executives that you can update the Wikipedia. Maybe update it to brouhaha. You're right. It's a scandal.

In my view, the NGSCB initiative represents one way a veteran market superpower creatively builds a 'containment' field, or cage wall, or 'no-fly-zone', around an emerging opportunity they are not yet prepared to capitalize on. Join a forward-looking and widely supported initiative like TCG, and encourage the whole industry to sign on. But make little actual progress in the market until the next major release of one's own platform. The net result of the NGSCB vision relative to trusted computing has been an extremely creative (and completely legal) stealth defense of Microsoft's future DRM media business, as well as one more reason to upgrade to Windows Vista.

These kind of superpower containment initiatives often operate under the competitive radar. Why? Because mature market segments (like the music and film industry) want to profit from the 'digital lifestyle', and do not want to offend dominant software superpowers by fostering a non-superpower or anti-superpower 'standard'. Rather, major media companies would prefer not to rock the boat, particularly if it means going against superpower solutions in a superpower ecoregion. And that's especially true if they see the superpower solution wrapped up in an industry initiative involving more than just that superpower. *'Hey, now we're all part of one big happy DRM ecosystem. Let's just wait until Vista. Nobody wants to end up in a brouhaha like Sony.'*

Let's rewind to my earlier 'dissing' of Tom Peters. These kinds of **containment initiatives illustrate why market competition in the age of the superpowers should never be seen as 'a brawl with no rules'.** For asymmetric marketers, it's all about learning to *see through the sandstorm to the superpowers' market behaviors and market rules.* And making sound decisions about how to profitably engage in symbiosis with these rules.

By the way, isn't that exactly what Apple did with its grand slam home run success called iPod/iTunes. Understanding symbiosis and asymmetric marketing from decades of market combat in the PC segment, they produced their own secure music/video player, coupled it with a paid subscription model, and made the whole thing compatible not just with their own PCs, but with Windows PCs as well.

That's why asymmetric marketers see **the no-fly-zone imperative of the superpowers as their marketing GPS---as an opportunity to practice symbiosis in the sandstorm.** Apple, largely outside the Microsoft ecozone but extremely experienced in Microsoft and other superpower marketing practices, has been a key beneficiary of frozen, pre-Vista DRM market adoption within the Windows PC ecoregion. So while I wouldn't go so far as to agree with the Apple TV commercial that contends 'life is 'random' (a brawl with no rules), I do think Steve Jobs rocks as an asymmetric marketer.

So what is the 2nd aspect of the superpowers' no-fly-zone imperative?

Collusion/Contention: The 2nd C of the No-Fly-Zone Imperative

The superpower no-fly-zone imperative consists of much more than traditional brass knuckles control of installed base ecoregions, or even kinder, gentler pre-emptive containment through forward-looking industry initiatives. The superpowers regularly *collude with each other to direct the path of adoption dynamics in emerging markets*, often targeting for category regime change any ISV or ISVs they perceive to be obstructing the path of those dynamics.

Above and beyond market collusion, the superpowers also overtly and covertly *contend with each other,* to defend their ecoregions from customer defection.

Let's first review superpower contention. As we have seen, database superpower Oracle waged a concerted and ultimately successful effort to acquire Peoplesoft, a leading enterprise applications ISV. Peoplesoft was itself using acquisitions to attempt to capture an asymmetric advantage in enterprise application software markets, having merged with JD Edwards, a competitor. While media pundits often like to point to Larry Ellison's personality as the decisive factor in the year-long fight to acquire PeopleSoft, in the age of the software superpowers Oracle really had few options except to fight for control of this applications competitor. It was not an option. It was an imperative[41].

Oracle's primary foe in enterprise applications is German superpower SAP, which has been consistently growing its top line revenue right through the bursting of the B2B bubble, and even after the economic shock of 9.11. In contrast, Oracle's revenue had been flat to slightly up in the same period. Had SAP (or even IBM) gained control of PeopleSoft, Oracle would have had a very difficult, if not impossible time leveraging it's database natural monopoly into the applications space. Hence the year-long attempt to take over PeopleSoft, and the subsequent acquisition of Siebel in 2005.

And while superpowers contending in mature categories like enterprise applications use M&A to capture (or recapture in the case of Oracle) an asymmetric market advantage, they also collude with each other, practicing mutualistic symbiosis to jointly extend their key ecoregions into emerging markets.

As I pointed out previously, Microsoft and SAP announced Duet, a joint offering that would make MS Office more interoperable with the SAP Netweaver enterprise business process platform. This deal brings benefits to both superpowers. For Microsoft, it means an even wider path into the enterprise through a leading applications superpower. For SAP, it means an army of Microsoft .NET developers capable of extending SAP functionality downstream into SMB markets.

The superpowers even collude with adversaries and former adversaries that may have been experiencing a revenue downturn in the sandstorm, became vulnerable, and subsequently abandoned their public profile of open, head-to-head competitive hostility. These alliances are often temporary, and are based on a mutual interest in seeing disruptive ISVs squeezed out of emerging markets. The settlement agreement between Microsoft and Sun would be an example of this type of collusion by 'former' adversaries.

When long-time competitors Microsoft and Sun settled their longstanding court actions against each other while simultaneously announcing a 10-year technology collaboration agreement, one of the areas of cooperation focused on improved sharing of identity management information between Microsoft Active Directory and Sun Identity Server.[42] Once again, this kind of agreement has the effect of pre-empting emerging category ISVs who have strong domain knowledge in bridging both the Sun and Microsoft infrastructure inside the enterprise.

Traditionally, this kind of gap-filling opportunity between warring superpowers (or in this case, a superpower like Microsoft and a struggling market share leader like Sun) was a lucrative one for 'best of breed" ISVs, e.g. BEA Systems in enterprise middleware. But now best-of-breed and startup ISVs must learn to think asymmetrically, even in relation to emerging opportunities like the identity management space... as the superpowers collude to close these gaps.

Here's an example of what I mean by thinking asymmetrically.

Meet Buck Bootstrap

Let's call the CEO of a startup identity management software company Buck Bootstrap. He's an instinctive asymmetric marketer focused on providing next generation security software infrastructure and services on both the .NET and Sun architectures. His company raised ZERO dollars in venture capital yet rapidly moved to operating self-sufficiency in a handful of quarters. And despite the fact that many non-funded startups face an uncertain future, his company successfully got his solution adopted by about a dozen major global corporations in less than a year.

By the time his company was acquired by a publicly traded security company looking to recapture momentum in a new category, his top line revenue exceeded that of some of those cash-rich but irrational 'terrorist' players left over from the bubble shakeout. How did Mr. Bootstrap and his self-funded marketing team establish this kind of momentum? Simple. He convinced his customers to fund his business... And also to serve as his sales staff. He thought it was just common sense to approach one after another high profile customer of both Microsoft and Sun and explain that the product his company had developed could effectively serve as a connector (He'd laugh and call his offering a 'shim') between Microsoft and Sun identity data. And he would give it to them for free if they paid his team to do the integration, allow him to retain the IP as his own, and serve as a reference for future OEM licensing deals with one or the other leader (or even another contending superpower or market-leading player looking to jump into his emerging category).

So Buck Bootstrap plugged a gap between overlapping Microsoft and Sun ecoregions by solving a problem for those customers who already did business with both companies. All while keeping his eye on a future OEM licensing deal with one or both of them. His outfit became known as those under-the-radar go-to-guys for this particular kind of functionality. No expensive sales VP with a humongous rolodex, no analyst firm telling him what his TALC-based adoption strategy ought to be. Just that highly unorthodox common sense that comes from seeing superpower collusion as a market opportunity for the practice of symbiosis. You could say that *he made superpower collusion his marketing GPS*. On to the 3rd C of the superpowers' no-fly-zone imperative

Colonization: 3rd C of the No-Fly-Zone Imperative

The 3rd C of the superpower no-fly-zone imperative is what I call channel *colonization*. Is colonization too strong a term to use to describe the current state of the solutions channel? No way! Here's a simple example.

According to VAR Business magazine's list of the top 500 channel players, the leader of the solution provider channel is (drum roll please) IBM Global Services[43]. Not surprising in that IBM acquired PWC Consulting to expand its already huge integration and services organization. That's a pure-play example of colonization of the channel, i.e. to become the channel for your own products. But that's only one example of the concept of channel colonization.

In the larger sense of the term, colonization means *increasing symbiotic reliance by superpower channel partners on their natural monopoly 'hosts'* as the foundation of their own market success. In fact, almost half of all solution providers surveyed by VAR Business Magazine are *committed to exclusivity*[44] *with their key superpower vendors*.

One Cisco VAR even told the VAR Business survey folks that if a customer asked for a non-Cisco solution, he'd tell them *"we don't do it because we don't think it's a great solution"*. And he went on to add that for any requirement that Cisco itself does not provide, he'd only go with a 'Cisco-recommended' provider[45]. In other words, colonization plus symbiosis equals channel reality in the age of the superpowers.

These research findings by VAR Business are no accident. The superpowers recognize that they must extend their no-fly-zone imperative to include their solution providers, integrators and channel partners. And to do that they must increasingly 'colonize' them in the form of:
- *Strong financial incentives* to focus their marketing attention on the superpower agenda. These incentives include rebates, bonuses, and other tools that capture the 'share of sales call' of a given channel partner's marketing and sales organizations.
- *Demand creation support* including lead generation, and even 'house account' transfers to select channel partners as a reward for their ongoing loyalty.
- *Co-marketing arrangements involving Market Development Funds (MDF)* that provide increased marketing reach for superpower

partners, including co-branded advertising, partner pavilions at key industry events, etc.
- *Technical training* that transform channel partner staff into virtual staff of the superpowers.

To maintain their market no-fly-zones, the superpowers have no choice but to engage in these kinds of channel colonization efforts. The take-away for ISVs...Start thinking of the channel as mainly consisting of 'wholly-owned' partner networks---kind of like McDonald's franchises. And these wholly owned partner networks will become the main trend over time---Not an independent multi-vendor channel, which like Moore's TALC, is fast becoming a relic of the laissez faire, pre-pubescent phase of the tech build out. That's why it has become increasingly difficult for small and emerging ISVs to capture channel attention in the face of superpower colonization. Unless those ISVs closely align themselves with a given superpower's agenda!

But the good news for ISVs who practice asymmetric marketing and superpower symbiosis is that these kinds of partner colonization efforts can improve their ability to stabilize and grow their business on the superpowers' nickel. Wise asymmetric marketers embrace superpower colonization and even engage in clandestine 'client state' relationships with natural monopolies. They don't go it alone against the monopoly agenda or try to fight for attention in the channel against the agenda of the superpowers.

Instead they 'embrace and extend' (to borrow that phrase made famous by Mr. Gates) their colonial, yet symbiotic, ties to the superpowers. They foster non-disruptive innovation on top of superpower platforms, thereby catalyzing value for the superpowers, while carrying out stealth market expansion around their own agenda. They use *channel colonization and superpower no-fly-zone initiatives as their marketing GPS in the superpower sandstorm*. Here's an example.

'We only look like a VAR, but we're really a software startup'. Meet Ace Emetric.

For ISVs that follow the path of asymmetric marketing in the superpower sandstorm, bootstrapping your business the old-fashioned 'garage' way has once again become a startup alternative. In fact, for more than a few startups in the sandstorm, bootstrapping has become a necessity. Today's ISV startups often face hands-on, metrics-addicted VCs who have sobered up from the intoxication of the bubble period. These VCs often want to see some level of business self-sufficiency and continuous momentum as pre-conditions for their investments at every stage. So it's smart for ISVs to generate revenue as early in their market life as possible, even while still in the development phase of their core offering. To accomplish that, a startup ISV in the age of superpowers is wise to attach to natural monopoly ecoregions, and align with superpower no-fly-zone initiatives as a starting point for their own sales traction. One way to go is to *enroll in the colonized channels of the superpowers and implement projects to products roadmaps*.

I'll call this guy Ace Emetric (pronounced asymmetric). He used to work for Microsoft, but walked away from more than a few of his stock options to found his own company, a Microsoft Solutions Provider concentrating on e-business development on the Windows server platform. Coming from Microsoft he had an instinctive understanding of asymmetric marketing, and symbiotically attached himself to the Microsoft server and tools ecoregion, becoming an early test bed of their bleeding edge and beta technologies. To the world he appeared to be just another VAR or solutions integrator. But he and his close-knit development team understood that the 'component-ware' they would develop to build complex e-business portals would ultimately provide the foundation of a future application software business.

Because the world perceived his value proposition as primarily that of a services company with strong domain knowledge in Microsoft platforms, and because Ace Emetric and his team were lean, hungry and experienced enough to understand how to do fixed price agreements with his early customers, he was able to essentially 'customer-fund' his business and his future software offerings almost from day one. His symbiotic and highly colonial relationship with Microsoft (Ace Emetric's company focused on no other platforms) afforded him both a sales lead pipeline, and positive word of mouth on his team's competence. He had no SuperRolodexMan Sales VP and no formal marketing leadership at the time he did this.

By the time he consulted with me on his strategic direction, he had already developed a working e-business application for a particular category of functionality that ran out of the box on the Microsoft platform. It was at that point in the evolution of his company that he asked me what I thought his strategy should be.

'That's easy', I said. *'You have already developed a powerful strategy (mutualistic symbiosis with Microsoft).'* I simply suggested to him that he and his team start behaving in public more like a software company, despite his absence of resources. I suggested he embrace what I like to call *inverse selling*, i.e., systematically promoting a trialware version of his rapidly evolving product which could be downloaded free from his company's website, or given away on a CD at Microsoft developer conferences. Why 'inverse' selling you ask? Because it flips the adoption model from 'buy/use' to 'use/buy'. While providing real sales prospect pipeline metrics on which to focus resources.

Thousands of product downloads and trialware users later, and without a single dollar of venture capital, his company had the enviable problem of not enough folks to answer the phone and take orders for paid-up licenses (not trialware) of his code. At this point, some local angel VCs happily invested around a million bucks to fund the 2nd release of his code. And around the same time I helped him re-brand his offering, as well as the company itself, since his ongoing success had made it no longer tenable to maintain his stealth VAR/solutions provider camouflage. He was now perceived as a software company with significant traction and momentum in a growing market for e-business applications on the Microsoft platform. Let's sum up what Ace Emetric did.

- He totally **embraced 'channel colonization'** and turned it into something positive through practicing symbiosis with a superpower.
- He began life as services company, but creatively **migrated to ISV status** based on his plan to move from **projects to products**.
- In the absence of VC money, and like Buck Bootstrap, he was **customer-funded**, repeat, customer-funded through the integration projects he was implementing on the Microsoft platform.
- He leveraged an **asymmetric use/buy inverse selling model**, the web itself. Sure he had worked at Microsoft before, but apart from his initial services customers, most of the later software customers came from his download marketing

program. I'll get into this more in Chapter 4 on Asymmetric Sales Strategy.

By the way, he ended up profitably selling his business to a public company for about 25 times what the angels originally invested. He wisely decided not to take a bad deal with some VCs who were messing with his head about valuation, operational control, his ability and qualifications to be an entrepreneurial leader (he had an engineering background), etc. One VC sarcastically told him, *'We don't talk to VARs, only ISVs.'* Now he's well into accomplishing the same thing on his second deal, creatively practicing symbiosis with one of Microsoft's new market creation initiatives in automated speech technology.

Creation: The 4th C of the No-Fly-Zone Imperative

So far I've discussed the no-fly-zone imperative that is driving the superpower sandstorm in terms of *control/containment, contention/collusion* and channel *colonization*. All three of these dimensions of superpower marketing behavior point to the fact that there is indeed a competitively driven 'desertification' of the ISV opportunity landscape. *It is not an adoption 'chasm' or a stalled lifecycle that is the main marketing issue for ISVs today*. Rather, this systematic desertification can and will produce the sandstorm effects of impaired revenue visibility, positional confusion, execution heat and broken marketing machinery...All while eroding the opportunity landscape for ISVs who do not effectively practice superpower symbiosis. Or see these no-fly-zone behaviors as their own marketing GPS.

But the superpower no-fly-zone imperative has a 4th dimension. This is the dimension of market *creation*.

Think of this 4th C, *creation*, as the superpowers long term strategic response to the market sandstorm they themselves are exacerbating. The superpowers need to dig for their own new oases in the midst of an over-cultivated software desert. They need to focus their R&D dollars on co-opting disruptive innovation, while laser-targeting specific forms of that innovation at their own installed base ecoregions and adjacent markets.

Remember, the PC revolution itself was a 'market creation' exercise by IBM in its own installed base. Unfortunately for IBM, it encountered asymmetric marketers from Redmond who successfully practiced symbiosis with them, co-opted their market creation exercise, drove the Windows clone revolution, and rode it to superpower status.

So going back to Redmond's asymmetric marketing well one more time, let's use Microsoft as an example of how a superpower has institutionalized market creation expertise. Understanding this dimension of the no-fly-zone imperative will provide you with the ammunition to engage these market creation exercises in order to grow your own business, just as Microsoft did with IBM. To illustrate my point, here are a few more markets that Microsoft is helping to create by doing one of the things that superpowers are able to do....Think and act *long term*.

Pen Computing: Microsoft has spent more than a decade working on pen-based computing, culminating in the launch of Windows XP Tablet Edition. While tablet PCs have been slow to take off because of their premium pricing, my bet is that 'tablet functionality' will go mainstream within a few years, and even become a must-have feature of notebook systems (even if that functionality is only used part of the time). Microsoft has also rolled out a reference platform for a much lower-priced 7" handheld 'ultra-mobile PC' device (formerly the Origami Project) with full tablet functionality. This device class will ultimately create a very big future market for new kinds of pen-based application software, and Microsoft will not be the only beneficiary.

Xbox connected gaming: Microsoft's Xbox Live service is another example of their market creation activity in the domain of multiplayer gaming over broadband networks. Microsoft sees it as strategic to their long-term broadband strategy and has already signed 2 million subscribers.

Wearable Computing: Watches from Microsoft? No way. But they are here now[46], complete with a wireless service for personalized information, direct to the user's wrist. This initiative, like the tablet's pen computing, and the Xbox Live multiplayer gaming, are all about laying the foundation for whole new markets that will emerge over time---In this case the market focused on wearable computing.

Collaborative computing: Microsoft's acquisitions of PlaceWare (web conferencing) and Groove Networks (virtual office, project management) have positioned them to bring distributed project management to mainstream markets, both IT and SMB. They have even tapped Groove founder Ray Ozzie to take over Bill Gates' role as Chief Software Architect when he steps down.

Search: Microsoft is clearly not ceding the search market to rival superpowers Google and Yahoo. They see search as a core competency, and have decided to become a leader over time. And time is one thing that cross-category, asymmetric marketing superpowers have in abundance. This means that Microsoft search will only get better as Microsoft applies its R&D dollars in this direction. Hey...they even took a temporary hit on their share price in 2006, because they announced that they would be investing more of their profits in this area. It also means that as contention among the big 3 in search (Google, Yahoo, Microsoft) heats up, there will be lots of opportunity for web services ISVs to extend and fine-tune search functionality into more granular, so-called 'vertical' or 'specialty' search markets.

And the other superpowers follow the same path, i.e. market creation as a critical dimension of their no-fly-zone imperative. Oracle in grid computing, Cisco in security infrastructure and software, IBM in open source Linux and 'on-demand' applications, Adobe in rich media publishing, SAP in composite business process applications, eBay in micro-payments and VOIP, Yahoo in rich media services, Google in ad-sponsored applications, Symantec in a new fusion of storage and security. These are all market creation initiatives designed to enable the superpowers to pre-emptively extend their current no-fly-zones into hopeful new areas of innovation.

So One More Time: What is My Marketing GPS in the Superpower Sandstorm?

Let's rewind to the point I made in introducing the sandstorm metaphor? American GI's, blinded by the desert storm, used Global Positioning Systems (GPS) to guide themselves both outside *and inside* their own camps. Without this GPS advantage, there was the real potential to literally get lost in the midst of battle.

The 4Cs of the superpowers no-fly-zone imperative that I have outlined above can become the practical equivalent of your marketing GPS, if you learn how to read them and capitalize on them as have Buck Bootstrap, Ace Emetric and other ISV leaders committed to winning through superpower symbiosis, not disruptive technology innovation.

If you follow the legacy TALC model in 2006, you may just get lost on the sandstorm marketing battlefield, wasting time and money trying to find those technology enthusiasts and visionaries that are becoming endangered species on a landscape of IT "do more with less" desertification.

But learn *how to think* about each dimension of the superpowers' no-fly-zone imperative as a potential business opportunity, and you will place your company in a position to counter the sandstorm effects of impaired revenue visibility, positional confusion, execution heat and broken marketing and sales machinery.

Like an asymmetric special ops warrior, teach yourself how to think outside the TALC/chasm box when it comes to the 4C's of superpower control/containment initiatives, superpower contention and collusion, channel partner colonization and new market creation. Place yourself in a symbiotic relationship with the superpower agenda, as Microsoft did with IBM in the early days of the PC industry, and as Google did when it became the SaaS 'powered by' search provider for Yahoo, AOL and others.

Ok, I think you're ready for the Chapter 2 wrap up. Here it is.

In 2006 and beyond, it's not about the TALC/chasm metaphor... It's about the superpower sandstorm.

In 2006 and beyond, it's not about finding visionaries or pragmatists in the abstract, or a 'brawl with no rules'. It's about leveraging the superpowers' marketing imperative in their own locked-in ecoregions (and beyond) by practicing effective symbiosis.

In 2006 and beyond, it's about an *asymmetric adoption framework for a non-flat age of software natural monopolies, not an age of laissez faire tech market economics*.

So hold on tight to your sandstorm GPS, and let's get busy in Chapter 3 drilling down on the asymmetric approach in the domain of product marketing. And while we're at it, why not peel back the onion on one more core concept in 'chasm' theory.

The so-called 'whole product'.

Chapter 3

ASYMMETRIC PRODUCT STRATEGY

"Now I have a machine gun. Ho, ho, ho."
Message Written on Shirt of Dead Terrorist by NYPD Detective John
McClane in the film 'Die Hard'.

*N*othing personal Joe B. But two chapters of macho talk about software natural monopolies, cage fighters, asymmetric marketing warfare, category regime change, sandstorms, and superpower no-fly-zones is getting me a little depressed. When I bought your book, I was really hoping to read something about on-demand this, open source that, Web 2.0 everything, and the new, new, new, new 'tornado'. I feel like I've fallen into an emotional chasm."*

I can relate, my friend. So why don't we take a little R&R (that's gladiator-speak for 'rest and relaxation') from the sandstorm. In fact, let me treat you to the movies (as long as I get to pick one of those ancient flicks a dinosaur like me can relate to).

In the Hollywood action classic **Die Hard**[1], Bruce Willis plays the role of wisecracking New York police detective John McClane, on his way to LA do some marital fence-mending with his estranged wife. Arriving in time to attend her company Christmas party, McClane begins freshening up in the executive washroom, just as the high-rise office tower is invaded and locked down with military precision by a gang of safecrackers posing as international terrorists.

The 'terrorists' objective--to steal hundreds of millions of dollars in negotiable bonds from the company vault, while holding the party-goers (including McClane's wife) hostage. As gunfire erupts during the initial assault by the gang, our protagonist John McClane races barefoot up the fire escape stairs to collect his wits and figure out what to do next. I hear you thinking 'Yeah, totally cool 80's action flick...must have seen it a dozen times. But what the hell does it have to do with a book on asymmetric marketing?'

Here's the answer.

While certainly different in form (software hasn't yet become a life and death business or so we're told), the scenario our action hero finds himself in is not too far off in substance from the one facing many startups and emerging category ISVs in the superpower sandstorm.

The territory on which McClane must attempt to rescue his wife and the other hostages is **locked down and defended** by his adversaries with the same kind of disciplined precision employed by the software superpowers to manage their installed base no-fly-zones.

McClane is seriously **out-gunned** (he has his service pistol) and **under-staffed** (he has himself), with little prospect for success. Kind of like a startup ISV in an emerging category who wakes up one morning and realizes he is in a superpower no-fly-zone.

Both McClane and the hostages are **caught in the crossfire** between the terrorists and those other 'contending superpowers', the LAPD and the FBI, just as many ISVs are caught in the crossfire between contending software natural monopolies.

So what does Detective John McClane do? Relying on his NYPD streetsmarts, he takes a few moments to begin thinking asymmetrically about the situation in which he finds himself.

Then, as the saying goes, all hell breaks loose.

After fending off, and bare-hands 'neutralizing', the first hostage-taker to cross his path, McClane captures his machine gun and communications device. He then engages in some back-of-the-envelope psychological warfare designed to gain intelligence on his opponents. After all, an asymmetric battlefield is nothing else if not intelligence-driven and feedback-rich. Wanting to understand how his adversaries will react to his dispatching of their comrade and his presence on their high-rise battlefield, McClane places the man's body in an elevator and sends it to his associates.

After provocatively scrawling on the terrorist's shirt... *"Now I have a machine gun. Ho Ho Ho."*

Like a ninja, our hero then conceals himself on the roof of the elevator in order to gather information about the bad guys, while he listens to their reaction to his 'shirt message'. As the hostage-takers freely talk among themselves in the elevator below him, McClane begins to gain more insight into what he is really up against.

In short, Detective John McClane carries out ***stealth asymmetric warfare and intelligence collection against enemies who themselves are asymmetric warfare specialists***. Here are the highlights of his out-gunned, one-man campaign:

- The source of McClane's gathering momentum is based on his ***creativity in capturing and co-opting the assets*** (the machine gun, the walkie-talkie) ***and inside information*** of his better-armed opponent.
- After using the dead terrorist's walkie-talkie to establish contact with a friendly member of the LAPD, McClane builds a practical alliance with the officer, ***effectively bringing to bear the power of another contending superpower***, and forcing his opponents to pay attention to more than just him.
- And let's not forget the ***continuous firing power*** of the captured machine gun. It enables our hero to engage the terrorists on a much more level footing than with his service pistol alone.
- To his machine gun, McClane later adds captured detonators, expanding his own arsenal of options and ***weakening the terrorists' effective control*** of the situation by disrupting their plan to blow up the roof of the building and sacrifice the hostages.

But hey...don't believe me when I tell you that fictional NYPD Detective John McClane is a walking, talking practitioner of asymmetry theory. Let's take a look at how real world experts in military strategy describe asymmetry, and see if a pattern emerges that may be useful for asymmetric marketers.

How Military Scholars Think About Asymmetry

Drs. Steven Metz and Douglas V. Johnson II, respected scholars at the Strategic Studies Institute of the U.S. Army War College, define strategic asymmetry as follows:

"In the realm of military affairs and national security, asymmetry is acting, organizing and thinking differently than opponents in order to maximize one's own advantages, exploit an opponent's weaknesses, attain the initiative, or gain greater freedom of action. It can be political-strategic, military-strategic, operational, or a combination of these. It can entail different methods, technologies, values, organizations, time perspectives, or some combination of these. It can be short-term or long-term. It can be deliberate or by default. It can be discrete or pursued in conjunction with symmetric approaches. It can have both psychological and physical dimensions."[2]

So here's the question. Which 'dimensions' (the Metz/Johnson term) of strategic asymmetry are relevant to software marketers in the age of the superpowers? My view---Here are 5 must-have dimensions to which every ISV should pay attention. Think of them as the optimal foundation for ISV product strategy in the superpower sandstorm.

Dimension 1: Battlefield (Market) Environment: As you develop plans for your products and services, are you prepared to effectively ***capitalize on the asymmetry and built in momentum already at work on the battlefield*** on which your products must compete? Remember Microsoft's creative co-optation of the market momentum of the IBM PC for its own success. Fast forward to now. Thinking like the asymmetric marketers from Redmond would mean developing a product strategy that would make the 4C's of the superpower's no-fly-zone imperative operate on your behalf.

Against your religion to learn from Bill Gates? OK. How about if we back-jump to that asymmetric 'oldie but goodie', legendary Chinese general Sun Tzu. He referred to this critical dimension of asymmetric strategic planning as understanding the *Nine Grounds*[3] of war. The Nine Grounds were Sun Tzu's description of how any successful military strategy must take into account the specifics of the battlefield (read market environment for ISVs), in particular the nature of the terrain and arrangement of contending forces.

If you want to think about Sun Tzu's concept in a practical no-brainer way, picture the Nine Grounds of Software as the locked-in customer ecozones of the 9 leading superpowers, i.e. Microsoft, IBM, Cisco, Oracle, SAP, Symantec, Adobe, eBay and Yahoo. Oops...let's add rising superpower Google as the 10th ground.

And for the sake of argument, let's pretend your business is that of an emerging category ISV and software development partner for a *non-superpower market share leader facing category regime change* in the sandstorm. For example, BEA Systems (under attack in middleware from IBM and others), or McAfee (under attack from security superpower Symantec, as well as Microsoft's entry into anti-virus and anti-spyware services) would qualify. There are more examples I could cite, but these two suffice to make my point. Thinking asymmetrically about how to capitalize on this kind of regime change battlefield would mean answering the following questions.

- Is it your strategy to assist BEA or McAfee to fend off the superpower offensive they face by adding value to, and building applications and solutions that use their products? Or...
- Is it your strategy to attempt to benefit from the category regime change action against them, and capture a part of their market, by being symbiotic with their superpower competitors?

These are unavoidable strategic product considerations in the superpower sandstorm. Maybe your strategy is to do both...Maybe you do neither. Maybe you completely opt out of this landscape. But in the age of the software superpowers, it helps if you learn to think in terms of *leveraging the momentum of those forces already dominant on the battlefield*. Cross-category natural monopolies that are engaged in active campaigns against ISV market share leaders. Campaigns that culminate in category regime change and market restructuring that may benefit your business.

So assuming you do choose to align your offerings with the superpowers in their category regime change campaigns against stand-alone market share 'gorillas', the first basic product marketing implication of strategic asymmetry becomes clear.

Continuous innovation based on the technology foundations provided by the natural monopoly superpowers, not go-it-alone discontinuous or disruptive technology innovation against them, can help jumpstart your product's success.

Now *you* have a machine gun. Ho, ho, ho.

Dimension 2: Justification for War (Value Proposition): In the age of the software superpowers, thinking like an asymmetric warrior means developing a compelling justification for battle (value proposition of your products and services). And it's important to identify a value proposition that expands beyond simple end-customer value, and instead *catalyzes value for the entire value chain in a given superpower ecoregion.* Of necessity, this includes delivering value for the superpowers or other dominant market powers that maintain the market no-fly-zone in your targeted ecoregion(s).

Remember what John McClane does in *Die Hard*. His primary mission is to free his wife and the other hostages (*the end customer value proposition*). But he also calls in the LAPD and attempts to serve as their proxy inside the locked-down office tower (*an extended value proposition that aided one of the contending superpowers*). My point?

Meeting end user requirements alone is not enough to win in the age of the superpowers as they *expand the feature sets of their platforms and enterprise suites to pre-emptively keep disruptive technology innovators in check*. An end-user-only value proposition is what I call a *2-dimensional product strategy*. It helps you and helps your customer---hence it's 2-dimensional.

What you want to do is develop a *3-dimensional value proposition and product strategy*—you benefit, your customer benefits...*and the host superpower in the target ecoregion benefits*. In fact, allying with the superpowers by developing products and services that actually *advance their no-fly-zone agenda* in their installed base ecoregions may be the decisive factor between market life and market death for your products and services.

Dimension 3: Superior Weapons (Core product capability): In asymmetric warfare, superior weapons (like the machine gun in *Die Hard*) can often be the determining factor in the outcome of the conflict. The U.S. military thinks of these as 'force multipliers'. Here's the U.S Department of Defense definition.

"A capability that, when added to and employed by a combat force, significantly increases the combat potential of that force and thus enhances the probability of successful mission accomplishment."[4]

Thinking like an asymmetric product warrior means identifying any and all force multipliers that can be leveraged to help you define and rollout your company's products--Your primary weapons of market combat.

In the domain of product marketing in the age of the superpowers, the ***web itself has emerged as an important force multiplier***, reinforcing and expanding superpower customer lock-in through the practice of ***never-ending product updates***. Smart product marketers imitate this best practice of the superpowers by embedding ***update-ness*** and associated network effects into the fabric of their product and service offerings. This 'update-ness' force multiplier is also a key advantage of the software as a service (SaaS) product model, an approach now widely embraced by the superpowers.

Dimension 4: Defensibility of Position (De-commoditizing your products): Asymmetric product warriors strive to place their strategic weapons in a defensible position, and continuously reinforce that defensible position by making sure that their overall offering is not easily targeted for imitation, neutralization and commoditization. Think of it as ***market hardening*** your products.

Note to my friends in the security software space. I am clearly not using the term 'harden' from an application or network security standpoint, but from the standpoint of ***wrapping one's core offering in a set of related services (body armor)*** that helps that core offering to resist imitation, neutralization and commoditization by attacking competitors.

As the superpowers and the various 'terrorist' and publate competitors I referred to in Chapter 2 drive down the market price of complex software, market hardening your offering becomes a practical necessity. Think of market hardening as the art of delivering a ***compound product*** that creatively integrates code, services, content, communities, commerce, knowledge-bases, intangibles and more...In order to create something that stubbornly resists duplication.

Dimension 5:Precision Targeting (lock-in points): In the 21st century, the preferred weapons are 'smart' weapons that incorporate precision targeting[5]. And impact only those 'high value targets' that serve to expand your momentum into the next round of competitive combat.

Have you identified the effective precision targeting points for your products and services that will enable you to begin locking in customers as rapidly as possible, and capitalize on that lock-in for future engagements?

For example, I'm dumbfounded at how many ISVs in 2006 still think about the trialware version of their product as a development afterthought, instead of the 'path' that provides them with the first opportunity to begin locking in customers.

Additionally, the embrace of **open source by the superpowers has actually served to increase superpower market influence** by enabling them to engage in precision targeting, and actually bring their customers and partners directly into the development process. It's not an accident that Microsoft now has over 1 million folks enrolled in its 'shared source' initiative. Talk about veteran asymmetric marketers creatively capitalizing on an approach that many originally contended was a form of disruptive innovation that would sound their death knell. Microsoft even has a term for this cooptation of open source by asymmetric marketers---They call it the 'move to the middle'.[6] I'll come back to the issue of open source marketing strategy in Chapter 5 when I discuss Customer Barrier Management or CBM.

Summing up the application of strategic asymmetry to the domain of software product marketing--- It helps to begin thinking in terms of 5 critical dimensions of an asymmetric product:

1. Asymmetric products are based on **continuous technology innovation** that leverages the superpowers' investment in R&D. Including their embrace and cooptation of open source. While capitalizing on their market momentum in growing their ecoregions, reinforcing their no-fly-zone agendas, and carrying out category regime change against market share leading ISVs.

2. Asymmetric products deliver value for the entire value chain into which they are introduced, i.e. they have a *3-dimensional value proposition that benefits you, your customer and the superpower 'host'.* That's symbiosis in the domain of product management and marketing.

3. Asymmetric products strive to maximize self-organizing web effects and embed update-ness into the fabric of the offering, i.e. they are *never ending products.*

4. Asymmetric products are market-hardened by wrapping the core technology in *compound sets of services and intangibles* that make the overall offering more difficult to commoditize by both competitors and savvy customers.

5. Asymmetric products strive to embrace, extend and expropriate the superpowers' no-fly-zone imperative. In so doing, they drive a *customer lock-in as early and as often as possible.*

I'm going to build out these 5 key dimensions of asymmetric product offerings in the remainder of the chapter. But before going there, I'd like to spend a few moments getting into Geoffrey Moore's concept of the 'whole product', and contrast that with the kind of asymmetric *'Die Hard'* product approach suggested above.

What's Wrong with the Chasm Theory Notion of 'Whole Products'

The 'whole product' vision, as articulated by Geoffrey Moore, is a key component of the universal marketing path suggested by his TALC adoption model discussed in the previous chapter.

Moore defines a 'whole product' as follows:

"The minimum set of products and services needed to fulfill a target customer's compelling reason to buy, especially important during the bowling alley phase of the technology adoption life cycle."[7]

From this definition one can see that Moore uses the term 'whole' not in any vanilla sense of the word, as in *'Our IT organization needs a whole (end-to-end) solution to our storage management dilemma.'* Moore's 'whole product' is a much more fine-grained concept. Relating to the marketing challenge of how to make a disruptive or discontinuous technology innovation, contingent on its successful progression through a series of 'bowling alley' niches, adoptable by mainstream 'pragmatist' customers.

What's immediately evident from Moore's definition (and I'm not cheating here---this is his 2006 definition) is that Moore's 'whole product' vision does not see *natural monopoly market landscapes and superpower no-fly-zone behaviors* as the primary obstacles to ISV success. Something I have asserted in the first two chapters of this book.

Instead, the 'whole product' vision sees the primary obstacle to ISV market success as an adoption 'chasm' naturally resulting from the *inherent incompleteness* of any product built on the foundation of disruptive or discontinuous technology innovation. Thus, Moore's 'whole product' is essentially the tangible marketing form that must be taken by a disruptive or discontinuous technology innovation in order for it to successfully proceed through a 'bowling alley' of market niches, and overcome pragmatist customer adoption resistance.

I think this is a good time to pay Mr. Moore a compliment before proceeding. No, I'm not all Darth Vader...I still have a little Anakin Skywalker in me.

It is my view that Moore's injection of marketing discipline into the tech product process was a highly progressive contribution in a pre-pubescent, early-1990's tech industry that historically behaved as if salesmen sitting down ad hoc with engineers was the key to defining the next killer app. Moore's 'whole product' contribution is a legacy marketing innovation reflective of the laissez-faire, free market structure of that time. It provided both a rationale and structured approach for entrepreneurs and their financial backers to invest in the discipline of product marketing.

Having paid Mr. Moore this well-deserved compliment, it's my view that in the age of the cross-category superpowers, the whole product notion has outlived much of its earlier usefulness.

Superpower Ecoregions Have Been Ruggedized
From where I sit, the underlying assumptions of the whole product vision do not align well with the reality of a post-bubble,

natural monopoly, sandstorm market environment. Why? Because the superpower ecoregions of the 2006 after-bubble are being progressively 'ruggedized' to *withstand disruption from discontinuous technology innovation.* These customer ecoregions of the superpowers have become dynamic, adaptive environments whose dominant species will go to any length to maintain their market no-fly-zones. Up to and including continuously expanding their enterprise suites and platforms with new 'good enough' product functionality that in many cases pre-empts the need for ISV disruptive innovation, and best-of-breed vendors.

Let's underscore this point about 'ruggedization' by focusing only on superpower R&D investment, leaving out their marketing spend. Using 2006 data, *the combined R&D investment of the top 10 software natural monopolies* (Microsoft, IBM, Cisco (who I think of as a software and software appliance company platform, not a hardware company), SAP, Oracle, Symantec, Adobe, eBay, Yahoo, Google) *is more than $21 billion[8], or about 3X the total U.S. VC investment in all software and internet companies combined.* And if you look at aggregate VC investment in software from the standpoint of Round One startup dollars, the R&D investment of the superpowers is approaching twenty times that amount.

In the context of this overwhelming asymmetric advantage in R&D spending, seeing the superpower agenda as one of status quo defense against disruptive innovation would not be an accurate assessment of the 2006 software landscape. No amount of discontinuous innovation packaged as 'wholeness' and migrating through a pragmatist 'bowling alley' is going to 'disrupt' or unseat these ruggedized software superpowers any time soon.

Instead of seeing product strategy as built around disruptive technology innovation (the 'starting point' of the 'whole product' concept), ISVs need to embrace effective symbiosis with the superpowers, and make *continuous technology innovation applied to superpower ecoregions the starting point of product strategy.* Capitalize on the superpower equivalent of a machine gun. As Detective John McClane does in *Die Hard.*

Ignoring Existing Value Chains: What Napster, Webvan, Govworks and the Bubbleboys Had in Common

Let's take the discussion of 'whole products' a little further. Returning to Moore's definition cited above, a whole product is

"The minimum set of products and services needed to fulfill a target customer's compelling reason to buy...

Consistent with this, the 'whole product' vision is focused on an ***end customer value proposition*** . With a related key requirement for success of a 'whole product' being the construction of an ***entirely new value chain*** to support the disruptive or discontinuous innovation contained in the product. In an age of natural monopolies, this is a notable shortcoming of the whole product vision. And various expressions of this kind of thinking reached their peak in the bubble. Let me give you 3 of the more extreme examples of 'end customer value prop/new value chain' thinking from that period.

It can easily be argued that the first Napster was a 'whole product', as were Webvan and GovWorks. All three having gone bust after pumping virtual fortunes into their respective 'disruptive innovations'. Each company had a strong end user value proposition (free music, convenient internet grocery shopping and home delivery, online parking ticket payment). Yet ***each one failed to embrace the existing value chain in their target markets.*** Believing instead that the cash they had raised from VCs and IPOs would provide them with the marketing war chest to create their own 'ecosystems'. This is what happens when a popular idea, disruptive technology innovation, get romanticized by financial analysts. And when a powerful biological concept like ecosystems gets misapplied.

In practice, the first Napster openly abandoned the pre-existing commercial music industry value chain leading to legal action against it[9], and its ultimate bankruptcy and shut-down. Likewise, Webvan abandoned the vast pre-existing retail grocery industry value chain[10] rather than become a web portal and delivery service for it, as Amazon. com profitably does[11] with retailers like Target, Office Depot and others. GovWorks.com, the subject of the documentary film *Startup.com*[12], had no practical marketing alliances with any incumbent technology or information services providers to the government (although the CEO managed to get a photo op with Bill Clinton). All 3 should ultimately go down in the business history books as pure cargo cult marketing in the realm of product management and marketing.

To avoid going down the same path, ISVs in the superpower sandstorm need to *catalyze value for existing value chains, especially those dominated by the superpowers,* and not delude themselves into thinking that their technology innovation and marketing spend can create a new value chain from scratch. In this sense, Moore's 'whole product' only appears to be *whole* if in the age of the superpowers this specific 'product requirement' is not taken into account.

'Whole Products' Leave Out 'Dotcomplexity Advantage'

So what else is lacking in the 'whole product' vision in the age of the superpowers? How about this simple truth. Moore's 'whole product' vision, a 1991 *pre-web construct,* does not account well for what I call *dotcomplexity advantage.* What is dotcomplexity? Dotcomplexity is complexity science applied to real-time networked markets.

Complexity science should be on the study list of every asymmetric marketer, because it is rich with highly relevant concepts like 'self-organizing systems', and 'increasing returns', that map well into networked software and e-business markets. In the age of the superpowers, asymmetric marketers should make the time to acquaint themselves with these underlying principles and core concepts, especially the writings of Stuart Kauffman[13]. And with all due respect to Mr. Moore's most recent literary endeavor, *Dealing With Darwin,* complexity science applied to tech markets is not the same as 'Darwinism' applied to tech markets.

Complexity scientists see Darwinism as essentially *incomplete,* in that it does not really account for the emergence of 'spontaneous order'. I'll defer to Stuart Kauffman as he explains this in his own words.

"The existence of spontaneous order is a stunning challenge to our settled ideas in biology since Darwin. Most biologists have believed for over a century that selection is the sole source of order in biology, that selection alone is the "tinkerer" that crafts the forms. But if the forms selection chooses among were generated by laws of complexity, then selection has always had a handmaiden (JEB emphasis). It is not, after all, the sole source of order, and organisms are not just tinkered-together contraptions, but expressions of deeper natural laws. If all this is true, what a revision of the Darwinian worldview will lie before us!"[14]

In the software industry, *the 'handmaidens' of future superpowers* have historically come from two distinct sources.

1. Those *incumbent market leaders (e.g. IBM, Yahoo and Apple) that asymmetric marketers like Microsoft, Google and Adobe leveraged as 'catalysts'* during their early period, leading to explosive market emergence on their way to superpower status. That's why, in Chapter One of this book, I began by taking the point of view that the rise of today's superpowers did not conform to the chasm model. But was the result of that *'deeper natural law' of marketing I call 'symbiosis'*. And;

2. Those *path dependent self-organizing network effects found on the web* that ISVs leverage to drive both explosive market emergence, and increasing market lock-in. What I call *dotcomplexity advantage*.

To illustrate this second 'handmaiden', i.e. "path dependent self-organizing network effects found on the web", lets look at a simple, but representative example of superpower dotcomplexity advantage---the Microsoft Windows Update capability. This powerful feature of the Windows platform enables Microsoft to continuously update and patch its customers' operating systems and applications over the web. All while gathering rich anonymous profile information on how Windows and Windows applications are actually used by customers. In fact, by incorporating dotcomplexity advantage and real-time intelligence collection into its core, Windows itself can no longer really be thought of as a 'whole product'.

It's a *never-ending product*.

It's not the service pistol Detective John McClane brought with him from New York. It's the machine gun he captured from his opponents. And in addition, it's McClane sitting on top of the elevator, listening in.

The self-organizing system called eBay is also dotcomplexity in action. This is why I consider it essential to include native web leaders like Yahoo and Google in a book on the marketing practices of *software* superpowers. Software superpowers that ISVs can leverage as *platforms for superpower symbiosis in the sandstorm*.

It's also why I chose to use web companies like Napster, Webvan and Govworks to illustrate my earlier point about the consequences of abandoning existing value chains in favor of creating 'new' ones. ISVs, learning from the best practices of the native web superpowers, can embed similar kinds of self-organizing network effects, asymmetric update effects, and dotcomplexity advantage into their offerings. At the end of the day, this is why the SaaS (software as a service) model, when applied in the larger context of superpower symbiosis, can be so powerful. I'm going to pick back up on dotcomplexity in a moment.

Fighting Commoditization

So what else is out of date in the 'whole product' approach? How about this. The 'whole product' vision is tied to the ultimate onset of commoditization across all categories. In point of fact, *chasm theory sees the attractiveness of commoditization as a marketing strategy*, as products gradually move along the Technology Adoption Life Cycle (TALC) into the tornado.

Here's Geoffrey Moore's associate, Paul Wiefels, explaining this point in *The Chasm Companion, A Fieldbook to Crossing the Chasm and Inside the Tornado*.

"While you may think that actively managing your product to commodity status is marketing heresy, or perhaps, commercial suicide, consider further how customers might be thinking. While you're convincing everyone who will listen that your new widget is guaranteed to save the world, your customer is busily weighing the merits of your new widgets against all the other widgets available during this widget tornado."[5]

As I pointed out in the previous chapter, commoditization of complex software functionality *has become a naturally occurring phenomenon* in the superpower sandstorm, as the superpowers themselves extend the scope of features and capabilities offered by their enterprise suites and platforms in order to more effectively carry out category regime change against market share-leading ISVs. Additionally, bubble-era terrorist competitors with large cash reserves are continuously price-discounting software functionality in order to 'make the number', under intense execution heat from financial markets.

But having said that, it doesn't necessarily imply that one has to help them.

Asymmetric product marketing can assist you in disrupting the march of commoditization. After all, *PCs may be commodities but Microsoft Windows, the key component of a PC, is not.* It commands a premium price in the PC bill of materials, and is a market must-have for almost every successful PC vendor on the planet, save Apple. And who knows. Now that Apple has adopted an Intel-based CPU for the Mac, maybe they'll begin chipping away at Dell with a 'hybrid' system sporting both Mac OS and Windows?

As a general rule, asymmetric marketers seek to forestall the onset of commoditization through the creative packaging of code, content, services, communities, commerce and intangibles into offerings that are more able to resist head-to-head, apples-to-apples duplication. This creative packaging can contribute to hardening or 'body-armoring' the product against attempts by competitors to deconstruct its market value. This approach may turn out to be particularly relevant in the 'do more with less' culture of IT procurement. Why? Because the key asset of any IT organization is the 'human bandwidth' of its staff. Help expand the human bandwidth of the IT staff by creatively wrapping your technology in sets of labor saving services and intangibles, and you are on the way to resisting commoditization.

Groove-in Early and Often

Finally, there is the issue of customer control, the issue of no-fly-zone construction. Asymmetric products systematically design in as much no-fly-zone control of the customer as possible, ***beginning with first user experience of trialware***. Rather than seeing customer dominance as something progressively tied to each given stage in a 'technology adoption lifecycle', asymmetric marketers seek to gain a product ***groove-in*** from day one, and build upon that.

What do I mean by 'groove-in'? It's a concept attributable to Professor Brian Arthur, a breakthrough thinker in the application of complexity theory to economics. Here's the way he puts it.

*'If rain falls on top of a sandy mountain, pretty soon it'll groove a pathway down the mountain and **small events at the start will determine the topography** and what rivers eventually form. It's important to note that the outcome is not completely determined by what's best. The outcome is partly determined by **who gains what advantage when**.'[16] (All bolding JEB)*

Not "what's best"...But "Who gains what advantage when"...that's strategic asymmetry in action.

"Small events at the start"...That's thinking in terms of how to precision target those specific features and capabilities that can help you drive a customer lock-in as early as possible. And don't forget. The important thing to keep in mind about 'groove-in' is that it's not always the 'best of breed' competitor with the optimal 'whole product' that gets 'grooved in'.

OK. Now would be a good time to jump out of the 'whole products' discussion and begin building out the key characteristics of an asymmetric product.

Asymmetric Products vs. Whole Products
Asymmetric products have 5 key characteristics that differ from the legacy 'whole products' vision of chasm theory. These 5 key characteristics are a:

- Foundation of continuous technology innovation on superpower platforms vs. disruptive technology innovation against superpower platforms;
- 3-dimensional value proposition vs. a 2-dimensional value proposition;
- Dotcomplexity-advantaged 'never ending' framework vs. a pre-web framework;
- Hardened or compound orientation vs. consciously driving commoditization; and
- Lock-in early to drive increased control of the customer vs. map your product to each stage of the adoption lifecycle. (Note: In Chapter 5, I'm going to expand on the discussion of 'lock-in' beyond the issue of products, and go into how certain other cargo cult marketing 'thought leaders' (not Mr. Moore) have become increasingly capitulationist on the issue of customer control, actually advocating the surrender of market power voluntarily to the customer.)

I go into each of these 5 key characteristics below.

Continuous Technology Innovation: the Starting Point for Asymmetric Products
Let me get this out of the way up front. Establishing your product strategy on the basis of continuous technology innovation may sound a little boring if you are a CEO with a software development background. So are there exceptions where I advocate disruptive or discontinuous

technology innovation as a foundation for asymmetric product marketing? Maybe if John Doerr or some other world-renowned VC is on your board of directors and has bankrolled your deal, or if you are one of those rare engineering 'rock stars' who can close a term sheet on the back of a bar napkin, then feel free to ignore everything I have to say in this section and go off and build your products based on disruptive innovation.

Just cross your fingers and hope that whatever guru is on your board helps you bring in a bare minimum of $150 million dollars or more in venture capital. Because that's about how much you would need to even attempt to try to establish a discontinuous or disruptive innovation in the age of the superpowers. And then you'll need lots and lots of luck. Because even high-buzz deals like Groove Networks, founded by software rock star Ray Ozzie, raised more than $150 million[17] in VC investment and still ended up deciding to be acquired by superpower Microsoft (terms undisclosed by the way).

But absent having that kind of VC money and a rock star founder (Ray Ozzie is now in the line of succession to replace Bill Gates upon his retirement as Microsoft Chief Software Architect), asymmetric marketers develop their product strategy based on continuous technology innovation on top of superpower technology and customer lock-in foundations. Why? Because it's the fastest and most efficient way to develop market momentum in the sandstorm.

But you said the superpowers are co-opting disruptive innovation. Why can't we? Sure you can. If a superpower itself invests in disruptive technology innovation in order to drive new market creation in the sandstorm, help them and you will profit. By the way, you should still think of that as an exercise in continuous technology innovation because you are doing it in the context of leveraging the superpower no-fly-zone imperative and their R&D spend. Even if you can build a better 'machine gun', you should borrow the machine gun from them and improve upon it.

Here's a little parable that illustrates my point.

The Parable of Rocky Radical
Rocky Radical was the latest CEO at a pioneering disruptive innovator in e-business software that had met with success from its

earliest days. Founded by a group of engineers from one of the software superpowers, and early to market with both B2B and B2C e-commerce capabilities, Rocky's company garnered lots of buzz and was perceived as one of the next 'big things'. The company had also been fortunate enough to go public prior to the bursting of the bubble, so they had money in the bank.

The development team had not only written their own commerce and supply chain applications, but had developed their own built-in middleware and tools for interfacing with the rest of the IT infrastructure of their customers. Most of these customers were global corporations without experience in e-commerce that didn't want to be left out of the 'new economy landgrab'. So providing a turnkey solution and complete software stack worked fine with this set of customers as long as they left it to Rocky Radical's professional services organization to handle the whole project implementation. But then, seemingly overnight, the floor fell out and the orders seemed to stop coming in, or were pushed out into future quarters. Had Rocky's company saturated the early adopter market and fallen into the 'chasm', or was something else at work? Let's see.

Before Rocky Radical's tenure as leader, the previous CEO had vigorously blamed the sales VP for the problem, and needless to say, the company kept losing key marketing and sales people as it moved deeper into the sandstorm effects of impaired revenue visibility and positional confusion. Rocky himself was in a quandary, and was actually on the verge of submitting a plan to the board that would transform the company from a software developer into a pure play professional services firm (implementing his main competitor's platform—a non-superpower 'best of breed' ISV) at exactly the wrong moment in the evolution of e-commerce. Believing the company was on the brink of disaster, one of Rocky's senior marketing folks asked me to come in and provide some independent analysis of the problem of 'declining revenue and poor sales performance in a growth category'. At first I thought it was going to be a tough nut to crack, but it only took me about a day and a half to get back to her with my assessment, after meeting with a representative cross-section of the sales and product marketing teams.

I remember the look on Rocky's face when I told him he didn't have a sales problem at all. He had a *fundamental product problem*. Why? Because despite the fact that he was an execution-savvy executive who paid fanatical attention to his 'sales pipeline metrics', he did not understand the practice of symbiosis with the superpowers. *"Symbiosis you say"*. Rocky Radical looked at me during my presentation like I had just said *Beetlejuice, Beetlejuice, Beetlejuice...* and a dead, larcenous Vegas tap-dancer resembling Michael Keaton jumped out of a miniature sports car on his desk and offered to remove a few ghosts from his building[18].

As I continued my assessment, I explained to Rocky that his problem of declining revenue was not an 'adoption chasm', but superpower containment, pure and simple. Containment directly caused by the fact that at least 3 major software superpowers (IBM, Oracle, SAP) were introducing new pieces of application infrastructure that overlapped with some of the middleware plumbing underneath his e-commerce applications. I then zoomed in on the simple fact that most of the 'leads' he thought he had in his sales pipeline were with large IT shops locked in by IBM. These shops were all in various stages of evaluating or deploying IBM's Websphere infrastructure, and while they were extremely eager to buy new e-commerce application functionality (which IBM did not have at that point), they did need that new functionality to leverage the IBM code. Rocky Radical's sales team was up against superpower no-fly-zone behavior, and there was no 'selling around it'.

So I told him that Phase One of the fix to his 'sales problem' was to swap out parts of his application plumbing in favor of IBM's Websphere. And I also suggested to him that he stop firing any more sales people before all his trade secrets were known by his competitors (who were eagerly snapping up his team).

After his Chief Technology Officer called me an outside agitator, and called the IBM stuff 'buggy unreleased vaporware crap', Rocky looked at me...and then him...and then me again and said, *'I get it. Symbiosis means sometimes less is more'*. I said, *'Exactly. Pulling out some of your own plumbing and temporarily eliminating a few 'killer features' is delivering less from one perspective. But from another, it's more, a lot more, including the opportunity to leverage IBM's momentum around their e-business on demand message to global corporations*. Rocky Radical thanked me and enrolled in the IBM Partner Program the next day. He went on to leverage IBM's global reach by convincing them to promote his set of applications because they showed off the IBM middleware in ways that IBM itself was unable to do. They even put him in their customer newsletter. Within 45 days, the final port to WebSphere was released and the orders started building back up. Three months later another company brought out Rocky Radical's deal at about 12x revenue.

Like NYPD Detective John McClane's expropriated machine gun in *Die Hard*, Rocky Radical had chosen to capitalize on the momentum created by IBM's e-business initiatives in global corporations, and implement a symbiotic product roadmap. Rocky Radical had come to understand that market momentum is an inherent property of superpower ecoregions, and a compelling reason for him to practice symbiosis in the area of product management, not beat up his individual sales folks. Hundreds of years ago, Sun Tzu said it very, very well.

*"Therefore good warriors seek effectiveness in battle **from the force of momentum**, not from individual people."*[19]

Like Rocky Radical, try to see your product marketing GPS as those natural monopoly processes at work in the installed base of the superpowers as they execute their no-fly-zone imperative. These forces of superpower momentum (like their introduction of new products into their own installed base) can help you drive accelerated growth if you practice continuous technology innovation. The takeaway: Quit beating the holy crap out of your sales team and get some strategic asymmetry into your product strategy. Enable your market momentum to accelerate as your product team masters the practice of symbiosis with the superpower no-fly-zone imperative.

And to pacify your rock star CTO, don't forget that superpower investments in R&D and installed base marketing are especially strong in the area of their *new market creation activities,* the 4th C of the no-fly-zone imperative. Since I've already touched on Microsoft's commitment to new market creation, here's a few examples from the other superpowers that are opportunities for breakout asymmetric marketing by ISVs:

- IBM is increasingly a leader in creating and advancing the *Linux market* in the enterprise;
- Oracle is increasingly a leader in creating a market for *grid computing*;
- Cisco (to expand beyond it's legacy business) is co-opting the *security software innovation* of ISVs, and placing it into the

fabric of the network, while simultaneously enabling new services like VOIP and *'application aware networks'*;

- SAP is investing in *services oriented architecture (SOA)* and web services;
- A post-merger Symantec/Veritas is creating a holistic vision of information integrity and *business continuity* infrastructure;
- eBay is innovating in *SaaS (software as a service)* and value added applications for what they now refer to as the 'eBay platform';
- Yahoo is innovating in commerce services for SMBs and sole proprietors, and in *rich media services for consumers.*
- And Google...they're pioneering in creating a market for *advertising-sponsored applications,* in addition to their investments in search.

There are many more examples. Find them and use them as your product marketing GPS.

The Asymmetric Product Requirements Document (APRD)
OK. I think I've made my position clear. Your CTO can still drive market-creating technology innovation by building it out in the context of the superpowers own market creation investments. So let's get practical and jump into the kind of questions you and your product marketing team will need to answer to begin constructing what I call an Asymmetric Product Requirements Document (APRD).

And now would be a good time to remember my earlier rant--- discard the 'What to think' mentality of the cargo cult marketers of the bubble, and embrace the 'How to think' approach of asymmetric marketing. Product marketing is rightfully the first place to begin the practical application of this principle, and seeing immediate payback. Here's an example to illustrate the difference.

Do a search on Yahoo, Google or MSN for 'software product marketing requirements document', or something close to that, and you will quickly discover more than a few cookie-cutter PRD (product requirements document) or MRD (marketing requirements document) Templates that claim to offer a best practices approach to product management. They are very intoxicating... and hey, some are only $6.99. Just pop your 'features' into these templates, ship them off to engineering, and you've done your product marketing job, right? Sure, if delivering six dollars and ninety nine cents worth of product marketing is what you're all about.

While these tools are well intentioned, at the end of the day they remind me of one of those bamboo antennas from Richard Feynman's primitive islander cargo cult in Chapter One. Bottom line---These cookie-cutter Product Requirements Documents templates don't really get you to *ask and answer the important questions* that will help you capture an asymmetric advantage in the age of the superpowers.

What you want to do is create your own APRD (asymmetric product requirements document). An APRD is all about drilling down on those attributes and capabilities that will enable your offering to succeed, not in the laissez-faire world of chasm theory, but in the superpower sandstorm natural monopoly environment. So, Section One of your APRD ought to answer questions that help you get there. Here's a few simple ones to get you started.

- What features and capabilities of your offering will enable you to *capitalize on the momentum of the superpower no-fly-zone imperative* (or other incumbent leader market dynamics) in their installed base ecoregions?
- Is your offering really *based on continuous technology innovation on top of superpower platforms and architectures (including Linux and open source if it's the IBM, Oracle or other superpower-endorsed flavor)*, or like Rocky Radical, do you need to think 'less is more'?
- Have you identified the *specific form of symbiosis* you want to practice with a given superpower, i.e. mutualistic, parasitic, or commensalist, or some combination of these over time? This is an important part of the exercise. Google may be able to get away with popping a search (or other) toolbar onto Internet Explorer, but you may not want to go there if staying friends with Steve Ballmer is part of your long term strategy.

Take some time to discuss these questions internally. What you're doing here is zooming in on a way to avoid making fundamental product management mistakes that will force you into a product re-do later on (and avoid mistakenly firing your best sales folks). Now let's drill down on the issue of 'value proposition' and the next set of questions you will need to answer to populate your APRD.

Asymmetric Products: 3-Dimensional Value Propositions

The importance of developing a 3-dimensional value proposition is a major lesson from the rise of the superpowers. Microsoft's historic value proposition is a great example. The Microsoft natural monopoly today is based first and foremost on MS DOS having served as a *catalyst* for IBM's entry into the PC market, and the emergence of a clone PC industry that competed with IBM. In fact, I'd go so far as to make the argument that *Microsoft's early success was never solely about an end user, or 2-dimensional, value proposition,* as was Apple's.

The path taken by Microsoft in its progression to superpower status ran straight through its creative cooptation of the IBM standard. Both IBM and the no-name cloners needed an off-the-shelf operating system to enable their core business. It was the ticket to the game. Later, it was must-have Windows adoption by hundreds of no-name cloners that transformed the landscape from an IBM compatible world to a Windows world. Windows became the core business enabler that exponentially widened and deepened the PC category itself. Thus Microsoft's value proposition at that time is the classic example of what I mean by a 3-dimensional value proposition. IBM (and later the cloners) realized value, Microsoft realized value, and users realized value.

Fast-forward to now. And you will see that Google's ongoing rise to superpower status (they are well on the way, though evidence of asymmetric product lock-in beyond their paid search affiliates is still a work in progress---their ad-sponsored apps vision, if they execute well, will take them all the way to a user-level no-fly-zone) corresponds closely to the Microsoft playbook of asymmetric marketing.

In 2000, Google succeeded in getting superpower Yahoo to use its technology[20] as the Yahoo search engine. Even as Google itself continued expanding its own web presence via Google.com. Google smartly developed this 3-dimensional value proposition by practicing mutualistic (and later parasitic) symbiosis with its future competitor Yahoo. Google delivered value for Yahoo, value for search users, and value for itself. When Yahoo management had their epiphany and realized that Google was in fact a long-term competitive threat, they gave them the boot in favor of acquiring Inktomi[21] and Overture[22]. But it was too little, too late to pre-empt Google's ongoing rise to superpower status, as they had already leveraged the market power co-opted within the overall Yahoo ecozone (and later the AOL ecozone) to create powerful market momentum.

Catalysis — A Key Aspect of the 3-Dimensional Value Proposition

A 3-dimensional value proposition is powerful because it is *catalytic* and enables an ISV to build its business with *permission inside a superpower ecoregion* (remember it's not a 'brawl with no rules'), as Microsoft did with IBM, and Google did with Yahoo. The dictionary defines a catalyst in this fashion:

"A catalyst permits reactions or processes to take place more effectively or under milder conditions than would otherwise be possible."

The milder condition in these cases---less resistance and implicit permission from the host superpower, because it sees value in your 3-dimensional value proposition.

Let illustrate this concept of *catalysis* with a 'how NOT to think' example from the bubble period, the height of cargo cult marketing in the tech industry. Remember B2B marketplaces and marketplace infrastructure...One of those segments that was supposed to be 'the next big thing'? In fact, so-called independent *net marketmakers* were universally hailed by many financial analysts as the preferred form to bring together buyers and suppliers in B2B electronic commerce. But now most of the net marketmaker pioneers (Chemdex/Ventro, VerticalNet, etc.) have closed up shop, or rebooted as completely different businesses. And I don't know any VCs that will return your call if becoming a net marketmaker is part of your business plan. Why? Because the net marketmakers didn't understand this notion of a 3-dimensional value proposition. They were not catalytic.

But their suppliers did understand the concept. Many suppliers had toiled for years to cultivate locked-in 'preferred supplier' relationships with their customers. But the independent B2B marketmakers promised auction-driven, commodity pricing for buyers at the expense of destroying preferred relationships that were key to business success for many suppliers. So despite paying lip service to complexity theory and self-organizing systems models, much of new economy cargo cult marketing theory (of which the 'B2B marketmaker' was one form) did not really understand that *value has to be catalyzed for an entire value chain* if you are going to have an asymmetric offering.

If you are developing products for the enterprise this is the only way to go. As IT executives continue to focus their annual spend on optimizing existing systems, many of which fall into the installed base ecozones and ecoregions of the superpowers.

The issue of 3-dimensional value propositions is also closely related to how you publicly position and communicate value to potential customers in today's 24/7 market conversations. Don't be afraid to aggressively weave into your story how you deliver value to the superpowers and their ecoregion installed base customers. Tell the market that your application is optimized for a '.NET world', or for 'Oracle's grid initiative' or 'leverages SAP's Net Weaver *applistructure*'. Why would you not want to systematically capitalize on the massive marketing spend of the superpowers (as Microsoft did with IBM, as Google did with Yahoo) and communicate your value proposition in the context of their new initiatives? I'll go into this more in Chapter 7, Asymmetric Brand Messaging.

OK. Let's get back to building out our APRD (asymmetric product requirements document). Here's 3 more questions that you might find helpful.

Have you developed a *3-dimensional value proposition* that clearly articulates value to your users, value to yourselves, *and* value to the host superpower in whose ecoregion you are conducting marketing operations?

Is your value proposition optimized to *capitalize on the marketing spend of the superpowers* as they carry out their installed base marketing programs designed to reinforce their no-fly-zone imperative?

Is your value proposition optimized to practice *mutualistic symbiosis with a superpower, and later evolve* into an effective form of parasitic symbiosis that co-opts their market power (Microsoft, Google)?

Dotcomplexity Advantage
Let's review before moving on.

Continuous technology innovation on top of superpower platforms. Check.

3-dimensional value propositions that benefit you, your customer and the host superpower. Check.

Which brings us to what I call *dotcomplexity advantage.*

Leveraging dotcomplexity advantage begins with the simple understanding that the internet and always-on network connectivity have changed software product management and marketing forever. *'Whole products' are morphing into 'never-ending' products that incorporate constant feature updating, network effects, and loose-tight coupling of 'platform and service'.*

I see 4 flavors of dotcomplexity advantage in the domain of product marketing that are being leveraged by the superpowers and other asymmetric marketers:

- Self-updating advantage, e.g. Microsoft Windows Update, Symantec security offerings, etc.;
- SaaS (software as a service) advantage, e.g. IBM or Oracle on-demand applications, eBay, Yahoo, Google web services, etc.;
- Services-coupled platform advantage, e.g. RIM Blackberry, Apple iPod/iTunes, Akamai Edge Platform
- Player-coupled platform advantage, e.g. Adobe Acrobat, Microsoft Media Player.

Let's jump into these one at a time.

Never-ending Products: The First Form of Dotcomplexity Advantage

The first flavor of dotcomplexity-advantaged offering takes the form of the *never-ending product*. Never-ending products leverage the always-on nature of the web to deliver a stream of continuous updates of features and capabilities. This self-updating model helps drive an asymmetric customer groove-in, while enabling the superpowers and other ISVs to capture *critical user information that drives the next wave of 'never-ending-ness'.*

As I indicated above, Windows Update is a representative example of this first form of dotcomplexity advantage. Another would be Symantec's anti-virus, intrusion protection and related security software.

Because Symantec's products are dependent for their operation on the latest 'attack signatures' and security policies, they require ***continuous content infusions*** to remain effective. But this also gives them expanded market power and makes it more difficult for customers to exit these products.

In speaking with a CMO at an application security startup focused on disruptive technology innovation, he related to me that he was having a difficult time getting his technology adopted because this update practice of Symantec and others had become a real barrier to entry. Even though major publications and analyst firms had validated his company's 'non-update-centric' technology as more effective in preventing malware attacks. That's superpower dotcomplexity advantage in operation---Continuous updates pre-empting a disruptive innovator. That's the kind of situation complexity science is referring to when it uses the term 'path dependent' market lock-in.

On-Demand Products & Increasing Customer Visibility

The second form of dotcomplexity advantage is derived from delivering products based on the SaaS (software as a service) model, i.e. the increasingly popular on-demand approach. IBM, SAP and Oracle on-demand initiatives, eBay, Yahoo and Google's web services 'platforms', Symantec's managed security services offerings, and Microsoft's Live Meeting are representative examples of this approach, as is SaaS poster child Salesforce.com.

But I'd like future asymmetric marketers to note that Salesforce.com is experiencing high sales and marketing expense (50%) relative to revenue. Why? Because the company has chosen not to capitalize on the kind of symbiosis or 3-dimensional value proposition that Google did, when it infiltrated the Yahoo ecozone. Hence Salesforce.com is increasingly relying on expensive conventional sales approaches like telesales, seminars, advertising etc. to grow its business, rather than leveraging the 'powered by' or SaaS OEM model popularized by Google, which closely links symbiosis with dotcomplexity advantage.

One more thing. The power of dotcomplexity-advantaged SaaS for asymmetric marketers is not simple 'customer feedback' but the promise of ***real-time actionable product intelligence---Increasing visibility into how the end customer uses your offering***. Remember our Die Hard hero John McClane. He sat on top of the elevator to listen in on the conversations of his adversaries. By capturing this kind of user intelligence from one customer you can *roll in new features and capabilities on a continuous basis for all customers*. It also allows you to get more creative with your selling model, your revenue model, your pricing model and your customer retention model.

The Services-Coupled Platform

The third form of dotcomplexity advantage takes the form of what I call a 'services-coupled platform'. You can see this approach being taken by companies who are not yet superpowers, but are seeing consistent growth in the sandstorm. Research In Motion (RIM), the Blackberry folks, have leveraged this form of dotcomplexity to *expand their business from a device model into an integrated device/platform/ software/services business.* The device becomes one component of the compound product 'hardened' against commoditization by blending all components into an integrated, connected offering.

Apple also leveraged this model to great success with the iPod/ iTunes platform/service offering. Akamai, a company that was initially hurt by the bursting of the bubble and the death of many content and e-commerce websites is also a good example of an ISV that is leveraging this form of dotcomplexity. Their Edge Platform and associated network service have allowed them to move through the bursting of the bubble into steady customer and revenue growth, and inclusion in the Nasdaq 100.

The Player-Coupled Platform

The fourth form of dotcomplexity advantage is what I call a 'player-coupled platform'. The free Adobe Acrobat reader coupled with their paid 'Engagement Platform' is a powerful combination that has driven their rise to superpower status. Adobe's acquisition of Macromedia and its ShockWave technology is in the same vein, leveraging a web-downloadable player to drive a paid software business.

Real Networks also leverages this form of dotcomplexity advantage. As a result of their success with Real Player (downloadable alone or bundled with streaming content), they faced a protracted category regime change campaign by Microsoft's Media Player. This head-to-head battle was one element in the European Union's actions against Microsoft, and ultimately a settlement between Real and

Microsoft leading to new forms of mutualistic symbiosis between the two companies.[23]

What ISVs need to do is get creative with how various flavors of dotcomplexity advantage can interoperate in their overall product strategy. The bottom line is that the more dotcomplexity you design into the fabric of the offering, the more you can leverage the web in the age of the superpowers, and the more rugged your overall offering will be.

OK, back to our APRD questions.
- How many of these 4 basic forms of dotcomplexity advantage are you designing into your offerings?
- Have you designed your offering to be natively deployed in a SaaS (software as a service) form, or real-time updatable?
- Are you considering how to capitalize on the implications of dotcomplexity advantage in your sales approach, revenue model, and customer retention programs? I'll come back to this in Chapter 4 on Asymmetric Sales Strategy.

De-Commoditizing Your Products: Process-to-Product Re-incarnation

Long before complex software functionality became increasingly commoditized in the sandstorm, other industries with their own superpowers provided a roadmap on how to begin 'market hardening' their products by transforming them into compound asymmetric offerings.

Fedex/Kinkos: Nobody can argue that the output of a copying machine is anything other than a 'commodity'. But Fedex/Kinkos changed that in their network of 24/7 print-on-demand services. What did they do? They wisely decided to productize their own internal workflow and document management processes, and offer their 'FILE, PRINT Fedex Kinkos' service over the web. That's a compound asymmetric offering model that leveraged dotcomplexity advantage to re-incarnate a 'commodity' business, and resulted in 1 in 4 printing orders being submitted over the web[24]. Here's another one.

UPS: Package delivery is definitely a commoditized, price-competitive market. But what did UPS do? UPS decided to leverage decades of experience delivering millions upon millions of packages to global markets and capitalize on its worldwide logistics networks by entering the supply chain management business. UPS, aided by some strategic acquisitions, has effectively *'re-incarnated' itself into a 24/7/365 global supply chain management solution* for other companies seeking to cut costs, outsource internal operations and improve business processes. UPS outsourced supply chain operation is now a multi-billion dollar 'synchronized commerce' business. Both Kinkos and UPS are examples of what I call *process to product re-incarnation*. Learning from an in-house process and re-tooling it for outside customers.

Starbucks: How about a cup of coffee. That's got to be a 'commodity'. But not for Starbucks. Starbucks is fighting the coffee wars using WiFi hotspot technology, becoming a temporary office for mobile knowledge workers. Currently Starbucks boasts thousands of 'Wireless Internet Stores" providing high-speed broadband connectivity based on T-Mobile services.

That's how asymmetric marketers in mature industries deal with commoditization---Market hardening and body-armoring their increasingly commoditized offerings by wrapping them in sets of high-value related services.

Sun Tzu and 'Formlessness' in Product Strategy
The superpowers also understand this concept and market harden their products. When Microsoft wanted to take on WordPerfect and Lotus, it integrated its competitive offering into a multi-product bundle it called MS Office, now the standard. Now software suites and bundles are common practice. When IBM wanted to re-invent itself, it became a services-oriented business that provided integration services, not just for IBM products but for Microsoft and others.

And a new breed of asymmetric competitor in the open source Linux movement is following suit, e.g. Red Hat. Red Hat has packaged a host of compound services into its enterprise Linux offering. How else do you make money on enterprise software perceived as *free*. The Red Hat 'product' is not simply the open source code, but the blended offering of support, education, maintenance updates, management platform and more. It's an asymmetric approach to product management. And it's success in the market is why Red Hat was referred to as 'proprietary' by the leader of a company 40 times their size[25]. Look for more on Red Hat in Chapter 5, Asymmetric Customer Barrier Management or CBM.

Ancient Chinese military strategists like Sun Tzu referred to this kind of thinking as *'formlessness'*[26]. Formlessness in the software industry means presenting your product to the market in a way that provides as few attack points as possible for your enemy to drive commoditization. Always keep your product on the level of an ***apples to oranges*** product comparison with your competitors (no matter what your VCs tell you before they hand you a check). Think of it as using product stealth to conceal your actual formation and level of preparedness. Here's a few more questions for your APRD.

- Is your product team focused on the issue of commoditization and how to deal with it?
- Are you wrapping your core technology in sets of services, training, support, community interaction, content, commerce and more to make them increasingly resistant to commoditization?
- Are there internal processes in your own organization that can be productized to make your overall offering increasingly non-duplicatable?

Asymmetric Products Embed Best Practices in Customer Lock-in

As I look at the market behaviors of the software superpowers, I often find that the English language really doesn't really provide me with the precise terms I need to communicate complex forms of asymmetric advantage, and their underlying processes and practices. Or sometimes a common term or phrase I want to use carries a lot of unhelpful baggage that has accumulated over the years. The phrase 'customer lock-in' is one of those that historically has carried a lot of negative baggage. Why? Because ISVs who go head-to-head with the software superpowers have regularly attacked 'lock-in' as a kind of Darth Vader-ism, at odds with the 'noble' mission of the software industry to bring technology to the masses (while still making millions of course).

In their efforts to attack the notion of 'lock-in', some have often chosen to describe themselves and their solutions as 'open', hoping that by condemning the evil Darth Vader to potential customers they will effectively differentiate themselves.

I choose not to get into a political argument about what is really open and what is not. Even Linux open source provider Red Hat was called proprietary by an executive at Sun. So the line between lock-in and open is blurring fast, and is often a competitive marcom exercise.

I find it more practical to create new terminology that helps me deconstruct and describe the underlying best practices of 'customer lock-in'. Practices that can be freely applied by all ISVs in their own interests. And an appropriate level of lock-in, whether you like it or not, is something every commercial software vendor needs to be concerned with as a core condition of business stability.

For me, the most fun comes from taking common words and fusing them, thereby conveying a greater meaning. The term *publate* I used previously is an example. 'Governator', now a popular term to describe Arnold Schwarzenegger....one part governor, one part Terminator, is an example of the form I strive for. So to provide a more asymmetric terminology to think about lock-in best practices, let's work with a word that is one part architecture and one part shark......... *'shark-itecture'*.

Shark-itecture: Optimizing Customer Dominance
Shark-itecture is the overall product strategy implemented by asymmetric marketers to maximize customer dependency and pre-empt competitive encroachment.

It is the product strategy of the cross-category software superpowers developed over the life of their offerings. A product strategy that over time, allows them to 'eat' their competitors, and carry out category regime change. Shark-itecture in the domain of product marketing is how the superpowers anchor and defend their ecoregions, migrate their installed base of customers to their new products, and achieve multi-generational product dominance.

Relative to ISV product strategy in the superpower sandstorm, sharkitecture should be thought of as the systematic practice of *embedding precise targeting points of asymmetric advantage into the fabric of your offering.* So that your business becomes competitively defensible, and increasingly symbiotic with the agendas of the superpowers.

In my investigation of superpower best practices in product strategy, I've isolated 4 basic building blocks of shark-itecture that all ISVs can begin implementing in order to improve the quality of their customer dominance and competitor defense. I'm going to keep having fun with these fusion terms and describe these 4 building blocks as follows:

Building Block One--Quark-itecture: As in quark, a subatomic particle. Quark-itecture means thinking in terms of the *smallest piece of your overall offering you can get adopted in the shortest amount of time to begin driving and/or expanding a customer lock-in.* Or groove-in, to use Brian Arthur's concept of 'small events at the beginning' from complexity science referenced earlier in this chapter.

Quark-itecture implies a *less is more approach*, based on continuous innovation on top of superpower platforms, as in the Rocky Radical example above. It means putting a lot of work into how you think about your trialware, or player-ware, because that's your first opportunity to begin driving a customer groove-in.

The free Adobe Acrobat reader is a good example of quark-itecture in action, driving ubiquity and market power for Adobe's platform products. Yahoo's free email service is also quark-itecture in action. The joint SAP/Microsoft Duet technology, that brings a new level of interoperability between Microsoft desktop apps and SAP enterprise apps, is thinking in terms of quark-itecture. The Google Toolbar that installs on top of Internet Explorer is also quark-itecture in action. The Salesforce.com free trial period is quark-itecture in action. The Skype VOIP client is quark-itecture in action.

Building Block Two--Bark-itecture: As in tree bark, not the sound a dog makes when it hears the mailman. Bark-itecture means having a clear roadmap for marketing your products on an OEM, 'powered by', or private-label basis by embedding them in superpower or other market leading offerings. It means *designing in OEM-ability* and easy customization so that the external 'bark' of the tree may be another company's branding, user experience, etc., but the substance of the tree is yours.

Microsoft's early relationship with IBM, and Google's relationship with Yahoo are examples of thinking in terms of bark-itecture. As service-oriented architectures and web services mature, thinking in terms of bark-itecture may mean designing in customization for your on-demand offerings, as Salesforce.com does with its CustomForce capability.

Building Block Three--Narc-itecture: Here the term 'narc' has a dual meaning. First...what you must do to make your user experience more addictive, as in narcotic. Second meaning---if you have teenage kids who watch way too much cable TV you may have heard them say something like this. 'I wasn't talking in class, Dad...That little snitch Ashley 'narc-ed' me out to the teacher'. Or even better---Your next door neighbor has been busted by a 'narc'. Figuratively of course.

Narc-itecture means systematically designing in dotcomplexity, in the form of *update-ness that increases customer dependency, while providing you with continuous feedback and user profiling.* Narc-itecture in action is Windows Update, Symantec anti-virus and security product updates, Yahoo's MyWeb personal page, or Google's new 'search history' capability. They drive addictive use and continuous feedback that can help you fine-tune your overall shark-itecture.

In an on-demand software world, narc-itecture is also key to precisely identifying those new features and capabilities you want to incorporate into your SaaS offering. You may see a handful of customers using your application in a specific way, and from that data, decide to expand the scope of functionality to all customers.

Building Block Four--Dark-itecture: Dark, as in the other guy cannot see what you are up to. Dark-itecture is the conscious incorporation of stealth into your product strategy. Dark-itecture is what you hold back in the form of *undocumented features and APIs* that can provide your company with asymmetric advantage, as it copes with the ongoing positional confusion of the superpower sandstorm.

Smart dark-itecture is how the young Microsoft leveraged its OS into the applications business. For ISVs seeking to lock down their customers and lock-out the competition, dark-itecture is critical. Don't ever forget that the Godfather of Asymmetric Embrace and Extend, Mr. Bill Gates, was an avid poker player in college. And the first rule of poker is *not to show your cards to the other players.*

Another form of dark-itecture is what I described above as market hardening your product, i.e. delivering a compound offering that 'bodyarmors' your core technology in a set of related services. SaaS (software as a service) can also be implemented as dark-itecture in action. How? Deliver part of your solution as an on-demand application that provides limited visibility into your overall product strategy, and turn on new features based on your competitive circumstances. Later, offer a hybrid product roadmap, including an on-premises edition of your offering that incorporates all of the enhanced capabilities you identified via your initial on-demand offering.

Ok. Let's close out this section with our APRD questions.

- Are you thinking in terms of driving product lock-in as early and as often as possible, i.e. *are your thinking in terms of product shark-itecture*?
- Are you thinking small, i.e. thinking in terms of the smallest unit of your overall offering that can leverage web dotcomplexity advantage, and be packaged for ubiquitous distribution, i.e. *do you have a 'quark-itecture'*?
- Are your products OEM-able and easily customizable, or 'powered by' ready (the form a software OEM approach takes in an age of web services and SaaS), i.e. *do you have a 'bark-itecture'*?
- Are you implementing a *'narc-itecture' that incorporates both regular user feedback and user dependence* (product addiction)? In an age of web services and on-demand SaaS, narc-itecture will allow your customers to effectively design your products for you.
- Are you *holding back something in order to drive follow-on products, i.e. implementing a dark-itecture*? Are you effectively masking your overall roadmap, i.e. incorporating stealth and 'body-armor' into your product strategy?

Sun Tzu on Music: Product Strategy is About Combinations

Let's sum up before moving on to the next chapter. In the Art of War, Sun Tzu writes the following:

"There are only five notes in the musical scale, but their variations are so many that they cannot all be heard. There are only five basic colors, but their variations are so many that they cannot all be seen. There are only five basic flavors, but their variations are so many that they cannot all be tasted."[27]

In this chapter, I've identified 5 basic building blocks of an asymmetric offering that today's ISVs would be wise to incorporate into their product roadmaps.

1. The starting point of asymmetric products is ***continuous technology innovation*** on top of superpower platforms.

2. Asymmetric products have a ***3-dimensional value proposition*** that catalyzes value for you, your customers and the host superpower in your targeted ecoregions.

3. Asymmetric products embed ***dotcomplexity advantage*** in an always-on internet age.

4. Asymmetric products are wrapped in ***compound sets*** of services (content, commerce, community) and intangibles designed to resist commoditization in the superpower sandstorm.

5. Asymmetric products capitalize on ***shark-itecture***, i.e. designing in customer and user dependency or 'groove-in' as early and often as possible.

In combination, these 5 foundational elements can create, in the words of Sun Tzu, more 'variations' of an asymmetric offering than can be heard, seen, or tasted.

It is up to you to think creatively about how to apply these elements to your product/service roadmap, and capture a superpower machine gun, as our fictional hero John McClane does in Die Hard.

By so doing, you will place your company in position to implement the kind of asymmetric sales strategy I will discuss in the next chapter.

Chapter 4

ASYMMETRIC SALES STRATEGY

The Tao gives birth to the One,
the One gives birth to Two,
and from Two emerges Three,
and the Three gives birth to the Ten Thousand things.
Lao Tzu, Tao Te Ching

I hear you thinking out loud.... *"From Die Hard to the Tao... I'm actually starting to like this guy...But what the heck does ancient Chinese philosophical and spiritual tradition have to do with asymmetric sales strategy?"*

Let's review a little superpower history and see if a pattern emerges.

The Tao of Microsoft

Microsoft closes the DOS OEM agreement with IBM. That's IBM, Microsoft's target of asymmetric opportunity, or TAO, giving birth to 'the One'...The one big deal that bestows real market power on a young startup.

The OEM relationship creates the opportunity for Microsoft to progressively co-opt more of IBM's market power. They execute similar deals with hundreds of no-name and bargain basement PC cloners seeking to compete with IBM. That's the One giving birth to the Two.

Microsoft's PC OEM ubiquity enables them to up-sell their desktop applications on the Windows platform, and subsequently carry out category regime change against WordPerfect's word processor and

Lotus' 1-2-3 spreadsheet. That's the Three (cross-category dominance) emerging from the Two.

This experience enables Microsoft to successfully enter the server, database, web portal, gaming, media, handheld, search, online conferencing, security, CRM and (name your own) multiple other categories with a proven formula for capturing asymmetric market advantage. That's the Ten Thousand Things.

Need a few more examples of what I'm describing as the 'Tao' of asymmetric marketing? I would hope so. After the first three chapters of this book, you've probably begun to detox from cargo cult marketing, and demand more from me than a few well-worded bamboo antennas to support my thesis. OK... let's look at Adobe, a company nowhere near the size of Microsoft, Oracle, SAP or the other superpowers, but possessing strong asymmetric market power.

The Tao of Adobe

Adobe markets its PostScript and PDF technology to, and through, Apple at the time Apple was seeking to develop a killer app (desktop publishing) to showcase its Macintosh PC. That's Adobe's target of asymmetric opportunity, Apple, giving birth to the One. The one asymmetric deal that enables Adobe to begin accumulating category-extensible market power.

The Apple deal provides Adobe with the opportunity to capture similar agreements with other laser printer providers focused on the wider, non-Apple market for Windows PCs. That's the One giving birth to the Two.

Adobe, capitalizing on what I refer to in the previous chapter as 'quark-itecture', creatively re-purposes its foundation technology into the Adobe Acrobat reader, for free distribution to hundreds of millions of digital document users on the web. That's the Three.

On the strength of its Acrobat ubiquity and lock-in, Adobe consolidates its market power and ascends to superpower status with its engagement platform for print, web and multimedia authoring markets. That's the Ten Thousand Things.

Still not convinced. OK... let's do Oracle.

The Tao of Oracle

In its formative years, Oracle successfully piggybacks its relational database technology onto the hot minicomputer market led by Digital Equipment Corporation (DEC), a 1980's pioneer that grew to become the second largest computer company (behind IBM) in the world[1]. That's the One for Oracle, their target of asymmetric opportunity.

Based on its success in the exploding DEC market, Oracle delivers a cross-platform database[2] that will run on other non-DEC 32-bit minicomputer systems, as well as on IBM mainframes, in a successful attempt to widen the market their DEC momentum created. That's the 'Two' proceeding from the One.

As the Windows PC age takes hold, Oracle leverages its minicomputer and mainframe market power into the emerging client/server computing opportunity. Its technology becomes the key platform enabling a new generation of database-driven enterprise applications from hundreds of ISVs and integrators. That's the Two giving birth to the Three.

Oracle consistently capitalizes on its database ubiquity, and moves into web and e-commerce computing, grid computing, application middleware, Linux, as well as its own family of home-grown and acquired enterprise applications. That's the Ten Thousand Things of cross-category market dominance.

'Ok Joe B. So far, so good.'

But are there any *non-superpowers*, or better yet, *emerging superpowers* following this path you call the Tao of Asymmetric Marketing?' So glad you asked. Let's fast forward to Google.

The Tao of Google

As the bubble bursts and banner advertising collapses[3], Google closes a *"powered by Google"* paid search agreement with Yahoo in 2000. 'Powered-by' is the SaaS or on-demand equivalent of the kind of OEM deal Microsoft originally struck with IBM. That's 'the One' for Google, their target of asymmetric opportunity.

Google expands beyond Yahoo to sign the same kind of "powered-by" agreements with AOL and other leading portals. That's the 'two' emerging from the 'one'.

Based on its strength with leading portals like AOL and Yahoo, the company builds the Google Network of paid search affiliates accounting for 40% of its revenue in 2006[4]. That's the 'three' arising from the 'two'.

Google's search advertising success enables the company to enter the desktop software and enterprise search markets, mobile markets, email services, mapping and more. Including a compelling vision for a new generation of advertising-sponsored, cross-category, web applications. That's the 'Ten Thousand Things' of Google.

Here would be a good time to do an instant replay from Chapter One.

"While a traditional starting point for ISV marketers has been the identification and quantification of the market opportunity represented by the 'target end customer', asymmetric marketers who want to build their businesses on the basis of superpower symbiosis first identify what I call the TAO (targets of asymmetric opportunity). Targets of asymmetric opportunity are the installed base ecozones and discrete ecoregions of the superpowers, as well as the gaps and overlaps within, between and among ecozones and ecoregions. These ecozones and ecoregions can be thought of as the 'host' to which you can attach your business in order to develop market momentum. By concentrating on both openly embracing and/or secretly infiltrating installed base ecozones and ecoregions in multiple forms, asymmetric marketers harness the asymmetry of superpower success and failure for themselves. Within the framework of a symbiosis-advantaged strategy, asymmetric marketers at every stage of their evolution have the potential to transform their own relative weakness into absolute strength."

The TAO of Asymmetric Marketing

Let's drill down on my opening metaphor for this chapter, the Tao? The literal translation of 'Tao' is *the way*. More specifically the Way is *'the basic, eternal principle of the universe that transcends reality and is the source of being, non-being, and change'[5]*. Based on studying the rise of today's superpowers, I'm suggesting that the 'basic, eternal principle' of asymmetric sales strategy...a strategy that will enable you to successfully navigate the sandstorm, is *'the Way' of leveraging the market power and asymmetric advantage of incumbent category leaders.* As did Microsoft, Adobe, Oracle and Google during their rise to superpower status.

Indulge me for a moment. Let's pretend that only taxes are inevitable (as opposed to death and taxes).

More specifically, that we are all capable of *re-incarnation*.

But instead of being re-incarnated as another legendary wise man, Lao Tzu decides, for some strange reason known only to him, to re-incarnate as the Chief Marketing Officer of an emerging category ISV.

Perhaps in that context he might re-write his famous passage as follows:

The TAO (targets of asymmetric opportunity) gives birth to that one major OEM, SaaS 'powered by', or co-marketed partner deal that enables your team to begin progressively co-opting the market power of an incumbent leader as your foundation for future competitive advantage.

That first OEM or 'powered by' deal with an incumbent leader (e.g. Microsoft with IBM for the PC, Google with Yahoo in paid search) gives birth to similar kinds of deals with competing players seeking to grab a slice of the market your incumbent leader, or first 'target of asymmetric opportunity' has created.

This second wave of success enables a third wave of follow-on cross-category market opportunity based on your own gathering asymmetric market power, which you have successfully accumulated by progressively locking-in your customers (MS expansion into desktop apps).

This third wave gives birth to the so-called Ten Thousand Things, i.e. a broad range of sales and business development options, including future category regime change opportunities and a path to natural monopoly status.

Seems like common sense when you put it in the words of Lao Tzu, re-incarnated CMO. That the real strategic sales lesson that emerges from the history of the superpowers is simple. Today's ISVs can begin their own journey to superpower status by embracing a go-to-market strategy focused on *sales symbiosis with incumbent market leaders---Leaders who represent Targets of Asymmetric Opportunity.*

For it is these targets of asymmetric opportunity that possess the potential to trigger a chain reaction of ongoing growth and market power for your products and services---If you practice creative symbiosis with them. The 'One' deal giving rise to the 'Ten Thousand' deals. But I would hazard an educated guess that the conclusion reached by CMO Lao Tzu does not yet rise to the level of common wisdom in our industry. In fact, anyone paying close attention to recent history would have seen thousands of companies in the bubble (as well as in the after-bubble) moving in exactly the opposite direction.

Bubbleboy Sales Strategy Revisited

The overwhelming majority of now-extinct bubble companies did not follow what I have characterized as the TAO of asymmetric marketing, i.e. develop and implement a sales strategy based on coopting the market power of targets of asymmetric opportunity. In fact, a significant contributing factor to the rapid death of many bubble-era startups (even those that went IPO) was the sales and marketing equivalent of the not-invented-here (NIH) mentality, a mentality that stubbornly refused to apply the sales best practices of the superpowers.

Unfortunately, the VC industry and investment bankers of that time provided 'the dope' (the easy money) that artificially sustained NIH thinking by an entire generation of entrepreneurs, enabling them to temporarily entertain the illusion of go-it-alone sales grandeur. It is my view that this illusion, and the refusal to study and apply sales best practices from the rise of the superpowers, ultimately sent thousands of them into spasms of capital withdrawal, and an inevitable death spiral.

But even years later, in today's after-bubble environment, it's not hard to see why more than a few ISVs continue to end up with a sales strategy based on the cargo cult sales mentality of the bubble. One moment, talking heads, analysts and pundits promote their 'advisory' services to ISVs by declaring that a new bull market for this or that category of software may be just around the corner. A bull market for on demand this, open source that, and Web 2.0 everything. But despite these passionate prognostications, we see no general bull market in software emerging. Only a select group of streetsmart ISVs and emerging superpowers continuing to capture market power in the post-bubble, post-9.11 period of on-again/off-again economic uncertainty.

For the majority of ISVs, there remains the persistent challenge of navigating a sandstorm competitive landscape characterized by impaired revenue visibility (and quarter to quarter 'deal slippage'), positional confusion within drifting categories, intense board and investor heat, and broken sales and marketing machinery. Not really a very pretty picture. And the swirling of the desert sands appears to be most intense for those ISVs whose sales organizations have not begun to develop a *go-to-market strategy based on creative symbiosis with the installed base ecoregions of the superpowers*.

Empty Spaces (Superpower Market Gaps) and the TAO

So how about a little more practical sales, marketing, and business development wisdom from Lao Tzu (the real one, not my re-incarnated CMO)? In the passage below, he identifies the underlying reason why there is asymmetric opportunity in *comprehending the fundamental duality inherent in superpower dominance of today's software landscape*. And why the one deal that can start you on 'the Way' is not simply some mythical history of this or that superpower, but a practical asymmetric sales imperative you ignore at your own peril.

> *"We put thirty spokes together and call it a wheel;*
> *But it is on the space where there is nothing that the usefulness of the wheel depends.*
> *We turn clay to make a vessel;*
> *But it is on the space where there is nothing that the usefulness of the vessel depends.*
> *We pierce doors and windows to make a house;*
> *And it is on these spaces where there is nothing that the usefulness of the house depends.*
> *Therefore just as we take advantage of what is, we should recognize the usefulness of what is not."*[6]

'Recognize the usefulness of what is not'. So what are these 'empty spaces'... those *'what is not'* segments... that potentially constitute targets of asymmetric sales opportunity for today's ISVs? Glad you asked. It is the superpowers' own natural monopoly, no-fly-zone marketing approach.

Why? Because the no-fly-zone approach of the superpowers often has the *unintended consequence of continuously creating 'opportunity spaces' and ISV oases*. But you can't sell into these opportunity oases if you don't know how to recognize them. So let's pick back up on our discussion of the 4 C's of the no-fly-zone imperative from Chapter Two, and see if we can begin teaching ourselves how to detect these 'empty spaces'.

Superpower Control/Containment Imperative: To maintain their customer control and lock-in, the superpowers are continuously adding new functionality to their enterprise suites and platforms. But despite their asymmetric investment in R&D that far outpaces VC investment in ISV startups, *short-term and medium-term functionality gaps (spaces) remain a fact of life* for the superpowers as they attempt to carry out category regime change against 'best-of-breed market share leaders. Smart ISVs that focus on *selling to or through the superpowers on an OEM, SaaS powered-by, or 'co-branded' basis* are optimized to fill the vacuum, even if only for a time. And that's OK. Remember, you want that 'one' deal that will get you inside the superpower ecoregion with permission, not a lifetime welfare check from the superpowers.

These open spaces regularly appear when there is an attempt at containment (the freezing of a market until the next superpower major product release or update can address the gap). Remember my Chapter 2 discussion of Microsoft's containment strategy in the security and 'trusted computing' segment---Containment strategy that contributed to freezing the Windows DRM market until the release of Microsoft's next generation Vista OS? Smart ISVs like RSA Security took advantage of this 'empty security space' created by Microsoft's containment strategy around an emerging security standard (as well as Redmond's overall market creation efforts in security markets). They packaged a symbiotic offering for strong authentication of Windows server environments, made sure they articulated a 3-dimensional value proposition that was directly in Microsoft's interests[7], and got the Redmondistas to sign on to help them promote it. Hey, they even got Bill Gates to provide a keynote address at their annual customer and partner conference...and hold up the RSA authentication token to the assembled audience[8]. That's the Tao of asymmetric selling.

On the strength of this symbiotic initiative into the empty market spaces around Windows security, RSA's annual sales grew significantly in 2004, allowing them to launch new initiatives that continued to capitalize on their relationship to the Microsoft ecozone (while attracting the attention of other incumbent market leaders like storage provider EMC). Clearly, *these kinds of empty spaces do not stay open forever* (Microsoft, 18 months after doing the alliance with RSA, made an acquisition of its own in the strong authentication category[9]). That's why asymmetric sales strategy dictates that you capitalize on these openings while you can.

The key here is to begin to think of the no-fly-zone imperative as an opportunity to embrace the kind of selling practices that enable you to close that 'one deal' that can eventually trigger or re-trigger the 'Ten Thousand Things'. That's what RSA did. That's got to be a big reason why storage leader EMC, seeing both RSA's symbiotic success in the Microsoft ecozone, and competitor Symantec's integration of security and storage functionality, decided to acquire RSA[10] to bolster it's own software portfolio.

Superpower Contention/Collusion Imperative: As the superpowers go head-to-head, and openly contend among themselves, temporary market space is inevitably created into which ISVs can sell. For example, since Oracle's acquisition of Peoplesoft, Siebel, JD Edwards and Retek, SAP has been systematically targeting their customers with a 'Safe Passage'[11] campaign. Oracle has countered with its own "5 Questions You Should Ask SAP"[12] campaign. ISVs who are nimble enough to sell into this superpower contention, and articulate 3-dimensional value propositions that 'take sides' will benefit.

Some best-of-breed ISVs, understanding category regime change dynamics, take the bold position of seeing superpower contention as an opportunity to practice in-your-face parasitic symbiosis. For example, BEA Systems Aqualogic or 'liquid computing' service oriented architecture (SOA) initiative is designed to capitalize on the IT silos[13] of superpower contention as SAP, IBM, Oracle and Microsoft slug it out. BEA's sales strategy is definitely high risk/high reward, designed to directly capture business from the ecoregions of not one, but four contending superpowers (IBM, SAP, Oracle and Microsoft). But taking this approach, it will be a challenge for BEA to develop the kind of 3D-value proposition that benefits one or more of the superpowers (unless they submit to an acquisition by a superpower, as did PeopleSoft and Siebel). As I explained at the top of this chapter in providing examples of the Tao (targets of asymmetric opportunity) approach, asymmetric marketers prefer to *practice parasitic symbiosis from the inside*, as Microsoft did with IBM, and Google did with Yahoo. This is why

OEM and 'powered by' selling approaches are critical for ISVs in the superpower sandstorm.

Beyond the issue of superpower contention, there are opportunity spaces that open up when the superpowers *collude with each other*. Take the joint Microsoft/SAP Duet product. Duet is a new offering co-developed by Microsoft and SAP to build a bridge between SAP's enterprise applications and Microsoft's Office Desktop applications, used by hundreds of millions of information workers around the planet. Within days of the Duet announcement, both SAP and Microsoft ISV partners were holding conversations in an online developer community on Duet.com[14], exploring ways to grow their businesses in the context of the new MS/SAP co-created solution.

Superpower Channel Colonization Imperative: As the superpowers leverage their marketing spend to increasingly 'colonize' their key distribution and partner channels, a target of asymmetric selling opportunity for symbiotic ISVs is created. ISVs that understand how to think about the channel in the age of superpowers know that a given *superpower's key channel allies are increasingly focused on meeting the sales objective of their superpower host* (a key indicator of colonization). In this kind of channel environment, superpower channel partners will drop certain vendors that are not symbiotically aligned with the agenda of that host, while they *simultaneously look for incremental revenue from new ISVs whose products are clearly aligned* with the agenda of the superpower (and openly articulate a 3-dimensional value proposition).

Thinking asymmetrically about the channel and *segmenting your own channel programs by superpower ecoregion*[15] will enable you to capitalize on the empty space that opens up as colonized channel partners search for incremental revenue and complementary products. Understanding superpower channel colonization can also help you extend the reach of your marketing spend. It's now commonplace for me to be able to save my clients big bucks in misplaced channel marketing spend. How? By symbiotically aligning their spend with the agenda of the particular superpower ecoregion they are targeting. Without this superpower alignment, ISVs can end up spending a small fortune on 'VAR and solutions partner training', market development funds, lead generation activities, etc. that do little to drive traction for their offering.

Superpower New Market Creation Imperative: By this point in the book it should be engrained in your marketing DNA that the superpowers are not simply engaged in a classic industry consolidation exercise, but are investing in creating new markets that capitalize on their asymmetric cross-category market power, and customer lock-in. Let's review again.

- Microsoft in Windows Live services, search marketing, security, pen computing, wearable computing, gaming, SMB applications, etc.;
- Oracle in grid computing, content management and on-demand applications;
- SAP in enterprise business process services;
- Cisco in network security and 'network-aware' applications;
- IBM in open source and business transformation;
- Yahoo and eBay in consumer and business e-commerce applications based on their respective 'platforms';
- Symantec/Veritas in business continuity and information integrity;
- Adobe in 'engagement suites' that enable publishing of every media everywhere.
- Google in enterprise search, desktop search, mapping, local services, desktop utilities and ultimately...a new generation of ad-sponsored web applications.

To help make these market creation efforts successful, the superpowers need ISVs that embrace these innovations, and fill the 'empty space' by creating symbiotic value on top of them. In fact, think of IBM's entry into the PC business in the early 1980's as a market creation initiative and you see the point I am making. As I indicated earlier in the book, IBM marketing staff at that time thought that there would only be a worldwide market for a few hundred thousand PCs, and so they cut what they perceived to be a *'non-strategic' deal* with a little known startup. An asymmetric marketer from that little known startup saw it differently, knowing PCs would not be 'non-strategic' for very long. And so they became the principal software beneficiary of IBM's market creation investment.

From a day-to-day selling point of view, where do we take this discussion of the TAO as targets of asymmetric opportunity? How about this. At a fundamental level, there are *3 building blocks of an asymmetric sales strategy* that ISVs can rely on to begin co-opting the market power of incumbent market share leaders and natural monopolies. They are as follows:

The Asymmetry of OEM or Powered-By Selling

Creating and fine-tuning an OEM sales program targeting the superpowers as both customer and go-to-market partner is a must-have in the sandstorm. And in 2006, creative OEM selling isn't just something ISVs think about doing with hardware suppliers like the PC manufacturers, or appliance providers like Cisco. The potential exists to embed your software into hundreds of applications marketed by the superpowers into their installed base ecoregions.

And if your products are delivered over the web via the SaaS or on-demand approach, a *powered-by selling model* of the type Google employed with Yahoo in 2000 is the functional equivalent to the TAO giving birth to that one big OEM deal that leads you to the 'Ten Thousand Things' later on. Even superpower Yahoo temporarily filled a gap in Microsoft's MSN ecoregion by providing them with a paid search platform (the Overture acquisition) on a powered-by basis. While Microsoft clearly had its own plans to make search technology a core competency[16], having a powered-by deal with the MSN ecoregion was positive for Yahoo as it went head-to-head with Google in paid search.

All on-demand ISVs should think the Yahoo way, practicing opportunistic sales symbiosis and offering applications and infrastructure to the superpowers in exchange for a piece of the action. And this recommendation is even more to the point in conventional enterprise software. Depending on whose research you choose to believe, up to 80% of IT spending is maintenance revenue for incumbent vendors[17], mainly the superpowers and other market leaders. If you want to get to that 80%, the fastest and least costly way to go is through the superpowers themselves.

The Asymmetry of Colonial Selling

Your indirect channel sales programs can benefit by thinking of them in a *colonization-centric fashion,* i.e. carefully segmenting your channel targets of asymmetric opportunity by superpower ecozone and ecoregion. I'm amazed at how many companies I interact with still approach the challenge of building an indirect sales organization of channel partners from a point of view that does not take into account this simple reality of channel colonization. The facts are clear. Post-bubble representatives of the channel are focused on *selling, integrating and installing superpower platforms and applications*.

One more sobering truth. The channel is not in business to 'make a market' for your offering. They are looking to capitalize on the commitment they have already made to their superpower partners, in exchange for the discounts, sales leads, market development funds, early releases of new technology, and other tangible benefits they receive from these partners.

Once you focus in on this, you can see that what I refer to as a 3-D value proposition (benefits you, benefits your customer, and benefits the superpower host) is the smart way to approach the channel... excuse me... the Microsoft channel, the Oracle channel, the IBM channel, the Cisco channel etc. One startup asymmetric marketer I know even placed his paid telesales team members *on-site at key superpower channel partners* to capitalize on their colonial status...And like Detective John McClane from the previous chapter, gather intelligence on superpower marketing programs.

The Asymmetry of Inverse Selling

Remember my discussion of the 4 building blocks of product 'shark-itecture' from the previous chapter, i.e. designing in as many lock-in points as possible into the fabric of your offering. Here's where thinking in terms of shark-itecture helps you sell.

In today's markets, a 'sales prospect' for most ISVs should be defined as a *completed trialware evaluation of your offering*. 'Inverse selling' is the term I created for myself to think about this trialware-advantaged *'use/sell'* sales model, versus the pre-web *'sell/use'* model. Use/Sell simply means that the end customer has been working with your product in some form, and on some free or trial basis for some time. In other words, you only really 'sell' to those prospects already familiar with the benefits of your offering, and have *invested their own 'human bandwidth' into conducting and documenting a formal evaluation* (even if it's a business manager evaluation as distinct from the ultimate IT owner/decision maker evaluation).

I'm going to use the remainder of this chapter to expand on these 3 basic elements of an asymmetric sales strategy (OEM/powered-by, colonized superpower channels, inverse selling). But first, I'd like to take a few moments to contrast the TAO approach (outlined above) with the 'chasm theory' go-to-market model referred to as the 'bowling alley'.

What's Wrong with Chasm Theory's 'Bowling Alley' Go-to-Market Approach?

Let me set some background by recapping what I've said so far about the first 3 pillars of chasm theory that are closely connected to the 'bowling alley' model.

1. Tornadoes

Market 'tornadoes' of disruptive technology innovation (the underlying eyes-on-the-prize vision of chasm theory) are being co-opted and harnessed by the software superpowers to reinforce and expand their own asymmetric market power. Today's superpowers are not stand-alone category 'gorillas'. They are 21st century software natural monopolies with *category-extensible market power*.

Thus the superpowers are fully capable of carrying out 'regime change' against market share leaders in adjacent categories. Geoffrey Moore himself concedes as much when he states that:

"The issue is, can you get the technology across the chasm inside the company that invented it? The answer historically has been not very often."

For me, the practical implication of Moore's observation is that ISVs should toss the 'chasm' as a strategic marketing path, and instead concentrate on *practicing marketing symbiosis* with the superpowers. Not engage in exercises of disruptive technology innovation against the superpowers in the name of getting inside the mythical tornado.

2. TALC

The TALC (technology adoption lifecycle), of which the chasm metaphor is one component, is no longer a reliable market development framework for ISVs facing the superpower sandstorm effects of impaired revenue visibility, positional confusion, execution heat, and broken marketing machinery.

ISVs in 2006 are not crossing an adoption chasm characteristic of the 'laissez-faire' tech market environment of the early 1990's. They are *navigating a competitive sandstorm in today's natural monopoly market environment.*

Focusing solely on the psychographics of visionaries and early majorities in an age of an increasingly pragmatist, 'do more with less' IT culture is not the way to spend marketing time and attention in the age of the superpowers. The foundation for ISV success is an asymmetric marketing approach designed to *capitalize on the superpower sandstorm and its underlying driver, the superpowers' no-fly-zone lock-in/lockout imperative.*

3. Whole Products

Chasm theory advocates so-called 'whole products' based on disruptive technology innovation, and 2-dimensional value propositions (benefits the customer, benefits the provider). This 'whole products' approach needs to give way to asymmetric offerings, based on continuous technology innovation on top of superpower platforms, and 3-dimensional value propositions designed to *align with and benefit superpower initiatives.*

Moreover, since the superpower practice of 'never-ending products' (update-ness) is quickening regime change in categories traditionally led by 'best of breed' ISVs that compete head-to-head with the superpowers, marketers must adapt accordingly. Update-ness and never-ending product approaches are best practices of asymmetric marketing that can be implemented by all ISVs regardless of size and stage of development.

The takeaway. *Study the 'shark-itecture' (groove-in architecture) of the superpowers and apply it to your own product roadmap.*

Now if I wanted to be a cheapskate, I'd just wrap it up here and say, "OK gentle reader, it's my belief that the underlying assumptions of chasm theory (tornadoes, TALC, whole products) are no longer practical in the age of the superpowers. Therefore, any selling or go-to-market model based on those foundations is also impractical.

But hey, this is a chapter on sales strategy. And I want you to get your twenty bucks worth. So let's explore the bowling alley model. And we'll even throw in a few choice words from Paul Wiefels, Geoffrey

Moore's colleague, and the author of *The Chasm Companion* (the 'Field Book to Crossing the Chasm and Inside the Tornado').

Moore's Bowling Alley

The 'bowling alley' go-to-market model advances the notion that in order to move a 'whole product' across an adoption 'chasm' into a category 'tornado', marketers must first attempt to dominate a series of market niches. In practice, usually a vertical or industry specific segment, but in fairness to Moore and Wiefels, it could be any 'self-referencing' market subset.

Using the game of bowling as a metaphor, tech marketers are encouraged to see each niche segment as a bowling pin that must be knocked down, beginning with the head pin, or first pin. So why do the advocates of chasm theory propose a niche or segment-driven model as the path across the chasm and into the tornado?

Because one basic premise of the TALC is that a given ISV's 'visionary' or early adopter customers not only dry up (creating the chasm on the way to the tornado), but are ***not perceived as credible and authoritative references*** for later-stage-TALC 'pragmatist' customer prospects, who are risk-averse relative to disruptive technology innovation.

Hence the recommended go-to-market path in chasm theory is to advance from pin to pin, segment to segment, in order to have credible pragmatist sales references from one niche vouch for your solution in the adjacent niche.

I must admit...It sure sounds logical for ISVs to follow this approach. But here are 4 reasons why, in this age of the superpowers, the 'bowling alley' model will not take you where you want to go, can trigger costly restarts if you pick the wrong headpin, will significantly drive up your marketing and sales expenses, and negatively impact your marketing culture.

1. Self-Referencing Segments vs. Self-Evaluating Customers

Once again, the bowling alley approach, like much of chasm theory, suffers from being (through no fault of its own) a pre-web construct. What's important for asymmetric marketers to understand is that the web has not only enabled an age of on-demand computing in a general sense—It has also enabled *the practice of always-available software evaluation by enterprise customers, SMBs, and consumers.*

As I indicated above, I think of this practice as *'inverse selling'*, i.e. an inversion and transformation of the sell/use customer model into a *use/sell customer model.* In other words, free product trialware is made available as either a download, or time-limited trial usage of a SaaS (software as a service) or on-demand application.

But even ISVs camouflaged as appliance providers (commodity hardware configured with special purpose software, i.e. the Cisco model) have begun providing free trial periods of full-featured devices to kick-start adoption by fostering self-evaluation.[18]

Inverse selling and on-demand evaluation are rendering the chasm theory argument, i.e. that 'pragmatists don't reference visionaries' (the case for the 'bowling alley') a moot point. *Self-evaluation, not pragmatist self-referencing*, is fast becoming the principal driver for adoption of ISV products in the superpower sandstorm.

Inverse selling models also obviate the need for 'a-priori' selection of segments in bowling alley-driven go-to-market model, while enabling you to develop a real data-driven sales program by watching where the downloads and trial subscriptions actually go. In fact, if you want to define 'sales lead' for the software industry, it is a successful product evaluation, not a name on a call list from a market research organization, or even an RFQ that comes over the transom. I'll expand on this later in the chapter.

But the bottom line is this. You want to make sure that the starting point for your sales program is *qualified* lead generation, not from a segment-based abstraction model, but from actual users who invested their scarce *human bandwidth* to self-evaluate your offering.

2. Headpin Selection Issues
Even if you reject my defense of inverse selling as the first argument against the 'bowling alley' model, there are at least 3 other areas in which to take issue with the 'bowling alley' component of 'chasm' theory. How about the inherent problem in the selection of the 'headpin' or first niche segment, the starting point of the bowling alley go-to-market model?

Here's what Paul Wiefels, Moore's colleague, and the author of *The Chasm Companion,* has to say about the headpin selection decision.

*"Just pick the right customer segment to start with. You can recognize them by their **compelling reason to buy your product** (this condition, by the way, should not be confused with your compelling reason to sell the product) and by **the absence of any other vendor making a concerted effort to serve the real needs of that segment.**"*[9] *(Note: the emphasis is Wiefels'.)*

But in the real world of software sales, isn't it more likely that you will pick the wrong headpin as your starting point if all you have to go on is 'a compelling reason to buy' and the 'absence of any other vendor' as your segment selection criteria? Sorry Paul. Nothing personal. But I see this kind of 'field' advice as pure bubblegum marketing...pure abstraction. And in a model largely dependent on dominating your original pragmatist segment, or headpin, isn't that the equivalent of *'go to jail, go directly to jail, do not pass go, do not collect $200'*, as that infamous card reads in the board game Monopoly[20]?

But I'm probably one of those guys that just doesn't 'get it'. I guess the point is that if an ISV follows Wiefels' suggestion, they simply have to keep fine-tuning the pinhead....oops headpin... model over time (Sorry Paul, I couldn't help myself. Too many cage-fighting head butts.). But all joking aside...Isn't this just a formula for continuous marketing restarts until that 'compelling reason' is identified?

If after all these years (*The Chasm Companion* is a 2002 work, more than 10 years after the original *Crossing the Chasm* was published), this non-specific, non-data-driven approach is the best field advice available on picking a headpin, or initial bowling alley market segment...well... Maybe it's time for a different way to think about segment targeting.

My suggestion, as I've indicated since Chapter One, is to look at market niches from the standpoint of their **pre-existing segmentation by those superpowers that already have some level of market lock-in and dominance**---i.e. identify segments first by superpower ecozones and ecoregions. This is an asymmetric marketing segmentation approach that is not abstract and a-priori, but based on the quantifiable, measurable commitment by customers to superpower platforms, in the form of both dollars and human bandwidth investment.

It's why my 'TAO' summation of the history of the superpowers at the top of this chapter has relevance for today's ISVs. But if it helps you to apply my approach in terms of the 'headpin' metaphor, then target the locked-in superpower ecoregion you have selected for sales symbiosis as your first segment to begin knocking down.

3. Expense Model Issues

It's been my experience that ISVs trying to apply a bowling alley go-to-market model usually pick some vertical or industry specific market niche as their headpin. This usually translates into hiring key elements of your sales team from a targeted industry segment (of that headpin as well as from adjacent pins). This can get very expensive. Why?

Because you are screening and selecting qualified candidates based on domain specialization, e.g. banking, health care, government, etc. It also inevitably leads to increased selling expense as your horizontal promotional material, web content, presentations, white papers, etc. (from your 'early market') will need to get 'verticalized' to tell your bowling pin 'industry' story. If it's not, the sales team will just blame the marketing team for not effectively supporting them, and lobby the rest of the company that 'marketing just doesn't get it'.

Above and beyond these factors, verticalizing elements of your sales team and marketing materials at an early stage of development can also *deflect your attention from thinking creatively about how to capitalize on the superpowers' own marketing and sales spend*. And since the bowling alley model means you have to dominate each segment on the way to the 'tornado'...Wow, that's a lot of specialized talent on your team.

This can also have the unintended consequence of driving expenses even more out of control in terms of vertical or segment specific 'feature requests' to product marketing and management. I say, stick to the download or *on-demand evaluation model that provides you real preliminary data on your evaluation customers*. Data that can help you build a manageable and intelligence-driven expense model. Stay away from crystal ball verticalization approaches that will force you to incur additional expense, not just in sales, but in your entire marketing organization. Or if your analysis tells you that a given superpower ecoregion is highly deficient in a given vertical expertise, then go vertical, and stay vertical. But don't see verticalization as a temporary base camp on the way to the 'tornado'.

4. Operating Culture Issues

In Chapter 6, I'm going to go into detail about the culture of asymmetric marketing and the importance of embedding what I call 'kernel values' into your marketing and sales organizations in order to drive a more tribal, cross-silo, special operations (Navy Seals, Army Rangers, Green Berets) execution mindset. But the bowling alley go-to-market approach holds the potential to almost ***autonomically pull your sales and marketing culture in the opposite direction.***

It's been my experience that the more 'bowling pin-centric' a given ISV's focus becomes, the more the operating culture of that ISV may manifest symptoms of increasing organizational silo-ization and fragmentation. Questions like these often come up.

- Are we spending too much time, and paying too much attention, to researching and debating specific industry segments, and not focused on the ***competitive landscape dominated by the superpowers***?
- Do we adopt the culture of the specific industry into which we are selling, or do we adopt ***best practices in asymmetric marketing*** in the software industry?
- Do we ***go deeper*** into our targeted industry vertical, or do we move on to the next pin?
- Will our vertical or ***segment focus help us or hurt us*** if we seek being acquired by a superpower?

Remember, those key sales executive hires you make because of their specialized industry experience are invariably going to bring with them their embedded operating values. And these values may end up shaping your overall marketing and sales culture. Keeping you in one 'pin' or segment and rendering your culture ineffective in migrating to the next one.

OK. Before closing my critique of this aspect of chasm theory, let me make one final (and highly sarcastic) observation that the only real asymmetry in the bowling alley approach is the bowling alley metaphor itself. Hit the head pin, and knock down the adjacent pins...That *is* a metaphor for asymmetry in action. But to develop and execute a real asymmetric sales strategy in the superpower sandstorm, it takes more than a good metaphor.

You need real asymmetry in your lead generation programs, channel approach, and powered-by or OEM strategy.

Paying Respects to an Asymmetric Sales Warrior

Before proceeding, I need to stop here and pay my respects to a departed mentor. Vince Caracio, a natural born asymmetric marketer, passed away in late 2004 after a rich and rewarding career. Over the course of his life, Vince was involved in Xerox' early sales training approach, sat on the advisory board of the original Comdex Expo during the explosive rise of the PC industry, and was President of the Houston, Texas chapter of the National Association of Corporate Directors[21]. Not to mention providing sales and marketing training to countless of his students who will always carry his sense of humor and infectious optimism around with us.

Vince came to the world of business from the United States Marine Corps (and it's true---there are no ex-marines). As a consequence, he instinctively embraced the idea that sales and marketing were not just about competition in a general sense, but were specific forms of business warfare to be systematically studied and mastered.

Vince and I met while I was working as a marketing manager for the pre-divestiture, early 1980's AT&T. He helped our small 'skunk works' group (AT&T 'bell-shape headed' marketing types and Bell Labs engineers) define a strategy for the sales launch of what we then called 'videotex', i.e. pre-internet online services[22]. At that time, AT&T was providing the platform to enable videotex as a subscription service, in partnership with content providers like the Knight Ridder newspaper chain, and the Los Angeles Times. While Vince didn't use the term 'asymmetry', he used to say things like *'It's all about finding the leverage'*... or *'strategy is applying your strength against their weakness'*. I credit Vince with being my first teacher in the practical foundations of what I now refer to as asymmetric marketing.

So in memory of my first marketing drill sergeant, Vince Caracio, let's take off those chasm theory bowling shoes, lace up a pair of Marine corps combat boots, and pick up where we left off above. Drilling down (this time in reverse order) on the 3 key elements of the leverage underlying an asymmetric sales strategy, i.e.:

- Asymmetric Lead Generation Strategy Based on Inverse Selling,
- Asymmetric Channel Approach to Superpower-Colonized Partner Networks, and
- Asymmetric OEM or 'Powered-By' Selling to Superpowers & Incumbent Leaders

Asymmetric Lead Generation Strategy

In a significant percentage of client engagements (often involving a turnaround or re-launch), it's not unusual for me to be proudly presented by an ISV's marketing leadership with a 'sales lead pipeline' that essentially consists of a CRM system crammed full of prospect names from conferences, trade shows, print advertisements, opt-in email lists, white paper requests, etc. It's also par for the course for sales management to have engaged a telesales firm of some kind to proactively smile and dial into these tire-kicker 'leads' in order to 'qualify them', and set face-to-face appointments for a direct sales rep or channel partner.

It's also commonplace for me to see my client's sales reps 'working' these 'leads' by spending an inordinately large percentage of their time *selling inside the company*, lobbying for this or that product feature or enhancement that will help a particular rep close a particular deal with a particular prospect. Usually it takes the form of a rep engaging in a lot of arm waving and dramatic claims that 'this is what the customer wants'. Hey, without a doubt, the superpower sandstorm is clearly an arm-waving environment for many sales reps, and I know I'm definitely not alone in reaching that conclusion.

According to post-bubble, post 9.11 sales performance research conducted by management consulting organization Accenture[23], 56% of senior executives described the performance of their sales organizations as *"average, worse than normal, or catastrophic"*. While the Accenture study did look into a wide cross-section of industries above and beyond software, the study's remarkable findings can and should serve as a wake up call for ISV marketing and sales professionals.

Insights contained in the Accenture study point to a basic problem identifying and engaging targets of opportunity, as well as why CRM systems chock full of 'leads', and sales folks lobbying inside the organization for the feature-du-jour, are not going to sustain you in the superpower sandstorm. Here's just a few of the Accenture findings.

- 58% surveyed in the study commented that their sales organizations were *'stuck in the past'*;
- 55% found it difficult to assess *which leads were 'qualified'*;
- 47% said sales leads often *'fell through the cracks'*.

The Accenture findings are highly relevant to ISVs battling to stay competitive in the superpower sandstorm, while working to develop a pragmatic, actionable, sales and business development strategy. Sales and marketing organizations 'stuck in the past', who can't identify a 'qualified lead' or who allow leads to 'fall through the cracks'----these are the kind of **broken machinery sandstorm effects** that absolutely must be addressed, before they send you into the kind of death spiral experienced by thousands of companies in the bubble.

What Constitutes a 'Qualified Lead' in the Sandstorm?

Let's begin with one of the core issues raised in the study---55% found it difficult to assess which leads were qualified. So let's put a line in the sand and define a qualified lead. Remember Ace Emetric from Chapter 2, the ex-Microsoft manager who founded, built and successfully sold his application software company at a premium valuation. A big part of his value to the acquiring company was that he had no problem understanding which of his leads were qualified. And so he was able to present the prospective buyers of his company with a clear, un-fuzzy pipeline. His entire lead generation program was based on what I earlier referred to as *inverse selling,* i.e. the use/sell model described above.

For Ace Emetric's team, an actionable sales lead did not even come into existence until a download of his application had been *installed and formally evaluated by a prospective customer.* Later, Ace raised the bar on his own working definition of an actionable lead by offering an online community for information sharing among those prospects conducting ongoing evaluations of his downloadable product. If they posted something positive on the community message boards about his offering, then he really knew that a sales rep should invest the expensive 'human bandwidth' to follow up with a phone or face-to-face conversation.

Remember Rocky Radical, our CEO from Chapter 3. Same story. After he aligned his product roadmap with the marketing agenda of his superpower target of asymmetric opportunity, his sales and marketing team launched an on-demand trial version of Rocky's offering. Rocky's team would even run an extended 'live pilot' of the on-demand edition, with actual prospect data for any prospect willing to commit the 'human bandwidth' to develop a formal evaluation summary that Rocky could later use as a sales tool. So he and his team knew the definition of a 'qualified' lead. And it drove his successful turnaround and acquisition.

Both Ace and Rocky *leveraged an inverse selling model based on user self-selection and self-evaluation* of their respective offerings, in order to effectively pre-qualify where their companies should direct their precious sales resources.

Leads Falling Through the Cracks, or the Alignment of Marketing and Sales

Back to the Accenture study---47% of respondents complained about *leads falling through the cracks*. One underlying issue in making sure your overall sales strategy doesn't contribute to leads falling through the cracks is the alignment of product marketing and sales. Remember--- both Ace Emetric and Rocky Radical had adopted product strategies that were grounded in asymmetric marketing:

- Continuous technology innovation on top of superpower platforms;
- 3D value proposition---Ace focused on Microsoft, Rocky focused on IBM;
- Dotcomplexity advantage in the form of a never-ending, update-centric, offering model—they knew when their products were being evaluated---they had visibility in the sandstorm;
- Tightly-coupled 'compound product' services, including user communities that shared best practices with each other: and
- Shark-itecture that enabled them to undertake an early groove-in at the trial use stage and beyond.

Because they had this product foundation, they were able to naturally leverage an inverse selling or asymmetric lead generation model. Downloads and on-demand trial subscriptions gave them visibility into when their trial prospects were ready to be closed as paying customers. And they creatively used their own evaluation community as an extended sales force.

Let me get at this point another way by underlining what my other favorite 'Tzu', not Lao Tzu, but General Sun Tzu said:

"Therefore good warriors seek effectiveness in battle from the force of momentum, not from individual people." [24]

How is this relevant? Simple. It means js that ISV leaders like Ace Emetric and Rocky Radical put in place a lead generation strategy that leveraged the on-demand nature of the web to pre-qualify all sales leads. On the basis of the target prospect's investment in the time and energy to self-evaluate their trialware, i.e. *on the basis of the force of momentum of web-advantaged inverse selling.*

They didn't rely on their 'individual people', i.e. highly skilled sales veterans with a fat rolodex from years in the industry, to create a base of qualified prospects. They focused on creating an environment of momentum, not just a sales force of individuals with 'contacts'.

Additionally, inverse selling and an asymmetric lead generation approach can enable you to implement a truly metrics-driven sales strategy. The metrics are well known.
- How many downloads or trial subscriptions did we get today?
- Have they been installed and used?
- Have the users enrolled in our community?
- Did we send them an email telling them about the community?
- Are they being incentivized to post a favorable evaluation?

You get where I'm going with this. Anymore would be overkill.

OK. By now you see right through me. I'm into overkill.

So how about this as the takeaway. Business folks used to say "Nothing happens until somebody sells something'. Here's my suggested replacement slogan---*'Nothing happens until somebody downloads something.'*

So if your lead generation strategy is not optimized for trailware, or SaaS trial subscription-driven adoption, that's got to become priority number one. When I look under the hood of a quarterly announcement from an ISV that missed their revenue forecast, and fired the CEO or sales/marketing VP, I invariably find the absence of an inverse selling approach, and the non-alignment of product marketing and sales. Or as my sorely missed mentor Vince Caracio would say, *'Son, they got no sales leverage'.*

Asymmetric Channel Strategy

The second leg of the kind of TAO-based asymmetric sales strategy I outlined above is an indirect sales effort targeting the specific channel partners of the superpower or superpowers with whom you are practicing symbiosis. And this is nowhere near the same thing as having a general purpose 'channel program'. Here's a parable to illustrate the point.

It's not unusual for me to participate in meetings with representatives of various 'channel' publications who are working hard to sell advertising programs to one of my clients. During one such meeting (in late 2005) I felt like I had entered my time machine, and been transported back to 1991, as this particular team of ad sales reps kept repeatedly referring to the 'channel' in the abstract. I asked them if their particular publication had developed any targeted lead generation programs that my client could actually use. Programs that were segmented by 'dominant vendor'- -or 'superpower'. The head honcho looked at me like I was from the future and said, "Uh........no'. What do you mean by that?"

So I briefly launched into my concept of 'channel colonization', i.e. that natural monopoly market leaders work to progressively lock down and effectively cage or colonize their channel partners, just as they work to lock-in their customers. And that's why successful channel companies (VARs, integrators, solution providers) are invariably focused on *leveraging the marketing spend and partner programs, i.e. the tangible evidence of channel colonization,* of one or more superpowers that they embrace as their biological 'hosts'.

I elaborated further that a given channel company's *commitment to implementing the superpower agenda for a given category of technology* was for me the defining aspect of whether or not that specific VAR, integrator or solutions provider should even be targeted by my client, a potential advertiser for their publication. Why advertise for channel partners if they were not in bed with the target superpower with which an ISV wants to practice symbiosis? In other words, *why pay to play if the game isn't being played on your 'home field'?*

The assembled reps all gave me one of those *"that hurts my head'* looks. And then immediately switched gears into a pitch about their 'advertorial' model, i.e. an ad model where they insert a seemingly neutral Q&A into the middle of their magazine, with a given advertiser's questions and answers. And at the top of the page it says 'advertisement'.

All I could do was smile, grind my teeth, and say 'Ah...that's sounds...really compelling. But please....Can we backtrack a little so you tell me about your specific focus on the different subsets of the Microsoft channel, for example---I'd really find that valuable'. 'Well... our editors and publishers don't think about the channel that way. We see the channel as *independent*,' was the answer. 'Thank you for your time. I'll definitely explore your advertorial thing', was mine.

The point I was trying to make to our good friends, the channel magazine sales reps, was that an asymmetric channel sales strategy in the sandstorm is one front in the practice of superpower symbiosis. An extension of thinking about and segmenting markets in terms of superpower ecozones and ecoregions. And that channel programs in general are not what you want.

What you want are *specific programs that allow you to capitalize on superpower asymmetry in the channel.*

So here's a simple 3-item checklist on how to get started with the development of an asymmetric channel approach for the age of the software superpowers.

1. Identify all superpower ecoregions and their associated channel partners that align with your product strategy.

For example, the Microsoft server ecoregion, the Cisco ISP ecoregion, the Oracle grid ecoregion, the Google Network affiliates ecoregion, the eBay payments ecoregion. You get the point. And I'm also a big believer in doing this partner identification on a bottom's up basis, vs. buying research from a publisher or analyst firm (which I find to be a lot like driving while looking through the rear view mirror). The data is rarely as fresh as the certified partner list on a superpower's own website.

In a recent re-launch project where I and my associates were helping migrate a client from a direct sales model to an asymmetric channel approach, we literally built our channel 'TAO list' of potential VAR and solutions provider partners right off the names listed on a superpower website... as our starting point. We had our client's channel team search by zip code and identify our universe of certified partners. Only then did we begin segmenting the list by potential attractiveness to our client's products, which fell into the network security segment. Then we filtered our channel target universe even further based on the appearance of at least one security product in the VAR's portfolio. So what's point two in an asymmetric channel approach?

2. Own demand creation as the way to lock-in your channel partners.

And let your channel partners own demand fulfillment. The kind of lead generation strategy I described above as 'inverse selling' can and should be optimized for channel fulfillment. When your inverse selling model produces a qualified prospect that has conducted a trail evaluation, make sure your solution provider partner or partners in that geography have that lead within 24 hours or less via email or some other means.

It's been my experience that ISVs who send a box of 'leads' to a solution provider partner often end up wasting that partner's time and resources, no matter how many 'market development fund' dollars or sales training programs they throw at the channel partner. Whereas ISVs who provide their fulfillment and customization partners with the names of prospects that have successfully completed an evaluation of their offering create locked-in channel relationships that pay off for years.

Remember the words of the Hyman Roth[25] character from the classic film series, 'The Godfather'. I quote from the film, *'Hyman Roth always made money for his partners.'* By the way, Roth was a knock-off of famous real-life mob entrepreneur, Meyer Lansky. Make money for your partners by owning demand creation, and strive to provide them with actionable, pre-qualified, short-sales-cycle leads generated via inverse selling.

3. Make sure your channel programs and channel communications revolve around a '3-dimensional value proposition'.

Don't hesitate to tell your channel targets that your offering is positioned as complimentary to the agenda of their primary superpower host. And that's why the lead pipeline you are providing them with is based on real product evaluations conducted by the existing customers of their superpower host. Don't be afraid to trumpet the fact that your channel program is for the 'best of the best' Microsoft solutions providers, or Cisco network integrators, or Google paid search affiliates. Here's why.

In the superpower sandstorm, smart channel companies, while strong on technical competence, also make sure they capitalize on 2 key benefits of their 'colonial' status relative to the superpowers:

Superpower Marketing Spend: Superpowers are tending to drive an ever larger portion of their marketing spend through their partners. And they increasingly focus on those partners that are focused on them. And it pays off in revenue for both. For example, according to Dan'l Lewin of Microsoft, *"96-97% percent of Microsoft revenues are generated with other people making $7-8 dollars per every dollar that Microsoft makes."*[26] With this kind of leveraged model being practiced by the world's leading software superpower, ISVs targeting the Microsoft ecozone need to make sure that they systematically align their own marketing spend with Microsoft's.

For example, if you are an emerging ISV your trade show booth may get tons more traffic if it's in a Microsoft Partner Pavilion, not stand-alone. Your web advertising would be on MSN, not Google. Your print advertising would be in a Microsoft-specific section of a general publication or in a superpower-focused publication like Redmond Partner Magazine. Your dealer program would have tiers targeted at finding partners with high Microsoft-based revenue. You get the point.

You can apply the same kind of thinking to the partner networks of all the superpowers. It's anticipated that the Microsoft marketing spend will be at an all time high during the launch[27] of Windows Vista in late 2006 and early 2007. So if Microsoft is your TAO (target of asymmetric opportunity), don't forget to laser-target your 3-dimensional value proposition in the context of the Windows Vista rollout.

Borrowed Brand Association: I just finished sending an email to the CEO of a Nasdaq ISV that has just had a significant quarterly miss, despite spending a ton of money on his company's attempts at jumpstarting a 'channel'. I recommended to him that he begin seriously re-thinking how he communicates the value of his offering by simply refining his message with the word 'for', which was missing from his brand messaging campaign. What do I mean by *'for'*? Here's a simple formula. 'My Product *for* My Superpower Target'.

In other words, ***always borrow brand association from your target superpower.*** Even Oracle, a superpower in anyone's book, when displaying its products at a Windows TechEd Conference in China, symbiotically positioned its core database offering as the Oracle database *for* the Microsoft environment[28]. Oracle understands channel colonization and is targeting specific Microsoft partners for its offerings by invoking Microsoft brand equity. You'll know that your 3-dimensional value proposition is resonating with your targeted channel partners when they call you up, and want to walk you into their best accounts.

A corollary to 3-Dimensionality---Most successful channel companies may not even make time to read your sales promotional material if they don't see the name of their superpower host screaming at them from the headline.

Asymmetric OEM or 'Powered-By' Strategy
OK. Let's circle back to the beginning of the chapter.

It's a historical fact that, as I indicated at the top of this chapter in my discussion of the TAO (targets of asymmetric opportunity), many of today's most powerful software superpowers have captured their asymmetric market advantage by closing an OEM or 'powered by' deal with an incumbent market leader. I used Microsoft, Oracle, Adobe and

Google as examples. So too for today's crop of startups and emerging category leaders---Having an OEM or SaaS powered-by approach as part of your sales strategy can provide the revenue visibility and market power needed for the next stage of your growth and business momentum in the superpower sandstorm---'The TAO giving birth to the 10 thousand things", per the wisdom of Lao Tzu, CMO.

And let me underscore one more time that really interesting little asymmetry I've observed over a number of years in deconstructing the sales and marketing lessons from the rise of the software superpowers. While in certain cases, the motive of an incumbent leader in working with an emerging category ISV is strategic---In other cases, the ISV (and future superpower) offering was in fact perceived to be ***non-strategic to the incumbent leader that was adopting it!***

So.......that's why....

Asymmetric Marketers Hunt for 'Non-Strategic' Deals
What do I really mean when I say that the motivation of an incumbent market leader that enters into an OEM or powered-by deal with an emerging ISV may be non-strategic? Let's return again to Microsoft and Google as examples.

When in the early 1980's, IBM went searching for an operating system for their PC division, one could make a strong argument that they themselves didn't even believe that the PC was strategic to their business. After all, as I cited in Chapter One, their worldwide market forecast was for only a few hundred thousand PC units over 5 years. So their original OEM deal with Microsoft for MS DOS was probably not perceived as a strategic deal for IBM by many among IBM's top management[29]. Many even saw a PC through the filter of the past. It was more like a 'smart terminal' back in those days.

Only later, as the business PC market rapidly and dramatically expanded around the new IBM standard, and a universe of PC add-in boards and desktop apps emerged, did the PC division become strategic in the eyes of IBM. And that's when their reliance on Microsoft as an OEM partner evolved into something they wanted to significantly limit through their advocacy of OS/2.

IBM management could see that Microsoft had successfully leveraged the IBM PC OEM deal to become a powerhouse in its own right. And so IBM needed to clip Redmond's wings (if only a little). Unfortunately for IBM, the symbiosis strategy practiced by Microsoft was too powerful to defeat, as hundreds of IBM clones embraced the Microsoft OS to pursue the market IBM had created.

I can't prove it beyond anecdotal evidence, but I'll also wager that the Yahoo/Google 'powered by' paid search relationship, a relationship which Google leveraged to capture much their early market power, was initially non-strategic from Yahoo's point of view. After all, in 2000 the bubble was bursting, easy banner advertising revenue from a generation of VC-funded startups was drying up, and the paid search market opportunity was not perceived by many folks as one that would rival and overtake conventional web ads. So it was natural for Yahoo, a web services portal with many flavors of services in a hybrid revenue model, to partner with a high-buzz Silicon Valley startup like Google. Had they known that Google would morph into their most significant competitive threat...Well maybe then they would have gone in a different direction. Since the company they kicked out (Overture) in favor of Google was a company they ended up buying anyway.

While We're At It...2006 Model Year Geoffrey Moore Also Gets It Wrong on Google

It is critical for the new generation of on-demand or SaaS ISVs to see this convergence of sales strategy between both Microsoft and Google. A strategy based on leveraging the market clout of an incumbent leader via OEM or 'powered by' relationships. But this point is obviously not a 'no-brainer'. Because as recently as February 2006, in an opinion piece on SandHill.com titled *Top 10 Innovation Myths*, Geoffrey Moore takes the exact opposite point of view to the one I am advocating here.

He describes his Myth 7 as follows:

"7. We need to be more like Google. Not on your life. Google is a once-in-a-decade phenomenon, a company riding a wave of adoption so powerful that not only is the first derivative of its growth curve positive, but so is the second derivative."[30]

You could not be more wrong Mr. Moore. All SaaS ISVs need to be more like Google.

The relevant point is that the management team at Google executed a go-to-market model that enabled them to capture the asymmetric advantage inherent in their "powered-by" customer's business. Google has applied best practices in asymmetric sales strategy by attaching first to Yahoo and later to AOL. And *systematically capturing their customers' traffic and customers' customers from within*. That's sales symbiosis in action. That's asymmetric sales strategy.

Additionally, through it's download strategy, Google has even had the marketing audacity to attach symbiotically to arch-nemesis Microsoft (via the Google ToolBar that installs on Internet Explorer, and the Google Pack of software utilities). So as to expand their market footprint based on Microsoft's own ubiquity. That's conscious symbiosis at the product and sales levels. And that's why Google is anything but the kind of *market exceptionalism (Google is a once-in-a-decade phenomenon)* you are attributing to them.

For Moore to take the position, *"We need to be more like Google. Not on your life"*, is to do ISVs a disservice. By *not focusing on those best practices in Google's go-to-market approach that future asymmetric marketers can learn from and emulate*.

Remember—Overture, not Google, was first in category with paid search solutions. Had they stayed in place in 2000 as Yahoo's provider, maybe it would be a different story in search today. Maybe they'd be riding that 'wave of adoption' Moore refers to. It most definitely would have been a different story relative to Google's top line revenue in its critical pre-IPO period. So it's not just about the *'wave of adoption'* of paid search in the abstract, as Moore contends.

Much of Google's success is solidly based not on a 'wave of adoption', but on better execution of an asymmetric sales strategy (a more effective groove-in, a better path to increasing returns) in a post-bubble environment than was Overture's.

And here would also be a good time to underline the point that *market 'Darwinism' and complexity science-based asymmetric marketing are two completely distinct strains of thought in the software industry*. Two 'forks' in the road of marketing strategy code.

In fact, this 2006 Sand Hill commentary on Google demonstrates that *Moore's new marketing 'Darwinism' is not really new at all. But is explicitly designed to be 'backwards-compatible' with 'chasm' theory.* If I were you, based on this misinterpretation of Google's success, I'd take a really, really, really close look at both, before you make them the foundation of your 2006 go-to-market strategy. But that's just me.

After all, from Geoffrey Moore's point of view, I'm what you would describe as a marketing disruptive innovator. I've still got an adoption chasm to cross. I've got some marketing pragmatist bowling pins to knock down. On the way to creating a tornado of asymmetric marketers.

The bottom line for ISVs seeking to practice asymmetric marketing is this. While it's great to pursue those rare opportunities in which one of the superpowers sees your offering as something strategic that they want to OEM-license, or plug into their services platform on a powered-by basis, it's equally as great to find the *'empty spaces' in the superpowers' no-fly-zone imperative that they may perceive as non-strategic.*

Certainly Microsoft and Google, during their rise to superpower status, leveraged the empty spaces of market leaders with whom they cut OEM and powered-by sales deals. You can too. The key is to tune your marketing GPS to detect those potential 'non-strategic' empty spaces that you can then target for OEM or powered-by selling.

Here's a few empty spaces that I see as continuously recurring opportunities to practice an asymmetric sales strategy. I think of it as detecting asymmetric urgency.

Some Indicators of Asymmetric Prospect Urgency

1. *The CEO of a superpower or other market leader has opened his or her mouth and made a public announcement committing the company to some new milestone.*

CEOs of all technology companies, especially the superpowers, are now under the microscope to perform and out-perform (Hey...even respected industry pundit John Dvorak has written an opinion piece stating that Microsoft is 'dead in the water'[31]). These superpower leaders will require new kinds of support that your company may be in a position to provide on an OEM or powered-by basis.

For example, as I indicated above, watch for broad Microsoft market initiatives around the rolling launch of Windows Vista. In addition to Vista, Wall Street is constantly complaining that Microsoft is not growing fast enough for its tastes. So expect Microsoft to expand the number of non-strategic web services relationships it develops with emerging category and on-demand ISVs, some of whom it will actually buy outright.

2. *There is evidence of some kind of time pressure driven by superpower contention.*

For example, as the battle between SAP and Oracle heats up in the enterprise, expect to see rapid escalations of 'dueling announcements' in this or that category of capability. Be ready to approach them with your offering as a way to rapidly fill the empty spaces created by their superpower battle.

3. *There are multiple 'development pilots' inside a superpower or other market leader because of turf wars and silo battles between competing parts of the organization.*

A while back I undertook a consulting assignment with a multi-billion dollar technology company that wanted to organize a new e-business initiative around enterprise self-service, and standardize on a single platform that they would procure from an ISV. Part of my role was to set up a cross-organizational working group to capture the internal requirements for the project. When I got deep into the assignment it became clear to me that many of the various silos inside the company had *dueling projects* going on, and many of them had no intention of abandoning their silo roadmaps to participate in the company-wide initiative. Two years later the silo leaders were still slugging it out, and more than a few application software companies had reaped the benefits of their internal duel by selling hundreds of thousands of dollars of pilot licenses and professional services into their warring silos, and using the street credibility from those deals to capture new customers.

4. *Somebody sold something and can't deliver without you.*

A client and I once walked into the offices of a gigantic systems integration market leader that had to develop an end-to-end e-commerce and e-community portal for a household consumer brand name. The integrator had sold the deal without having a vendor for the particular type of functionality my client had to offer. They were particularly interested in my client's offering because he had been referred into the deal by one of the superpowers after attending a developer conference. He walked out with his first $500,000 PO for a one-time use, private label OEM license for his code. Later he turned it into a corporate-wide deal worth much, much more.

5. *A superpower's customer is in the middle of what Ed Yourdon calls a 'death march' project*[32].

If you are not familiar with the term, I'd recommend that you read his book titled *Byte Wars, The Impact of September 11 on Information Technology*. Yourdon's death march projects are based on a sense of extreme urgency inside a corporation, or government agency. An urgency that translates into the whole IT organization being focused on a single objective. And while the project from the point of view of the end customer may be seen as strategic, *it may not be strategic for one or more superpowers providing parts of the project*. And that can be a way for you to wedge your technology into a superpower ecoregion on a customer-by-customer death march basis. Later you may be able to expand it into a full-fledged OEM agreement, if it suddenly becomes 'strategic' to the superpower technology provider.

Let me add that when you pursue a sales strategy of embedding all or part of your product set into superpower offerings through OEM or powered-by deals, there are benefits even if the up-front dollars to your company are small. Here are a few of those benefits to wrap up this chapter.

With up to 80% of all IT spending going to incumbent vendors, why not sell through a superpower, and let a superpower create demand for your products within its own ecoregions.

And there is always the opportunity to create natural 'add-ons' to the products you license to a superpower...Add-on products that can allow you to create your own symbiotic brand visibility inside a superpower ecoregion.

There is also the benefit of going global from day one, through your relationship with a superpower, as opposed to attempting to build out your own worldwide sales force. And then there is the *'one giving birth to the two'* TAO effect I cited at the opening of this chapter. An effect in which other superpowers or market leaders see you doing business with their competitor, and line up for a similar deal. Didn't Google leverage it's Yahoo deal to close it's AOL deal.

In closing this chapter let me underscore one final point. The TAO of asymmetric sales strategy I've described above is even more powerful when you add one more ingredient. The ingredient of strong, systematic *customer dominance*.

So before Geoffrey Moore calls the Godfather's Hyman Roth, and 'makes me an offer I can't refuse', let's jump to Chapter 5 and explore the next aspect of asymmetric marketing. The issue of customer lock-in and competitor lockout.

Something I describe as CBM, or customer barrier management.

Chapter 5

ASYMMETRIC CBM
(CUSTOMER BARRIER MANAGEMENT)

**"Sun Insists Red Hat Linux Is Proprietary, But Red Hat and
Experts Disagree"**
Headline of eWeek[1] Article

C all me crazy folks. But isn't this exactly the kind of news headline
that still makes it fun to work in the software industry? It's this
kind of in-your-face PR combat that gets me day-dreaming.
Day-dreaming that the industry held the equivalent of a world boxing
championship title bout, complete with a tuxedoed ring announcer,
bellowing and blustering for all to hear:

*'Let's get reeaaaddddy to ruuuuuumble![2] In this corner, weighing in at
around $12 billion dollars in annual revenue, it's network computing hardware/
software giant Sun Microsystems. And in the far corner, weighing in at a lean,
mean but highly respectable $300 million in sales, it's the plucky open source
Linux challenger Red Hat.'*

Thank you Mr. Announcer. This would be a good time to put on
my color commentator[3] hat, rest up a bit from my climb out of the
marketing strategy chasm, and grab a ringside seat at this software
smackdown. In order to explain what it all has do with asymmetric
marketing. So back to the action.

The opening punch in the bout was thrown by none other than
Mr. Jonathan Schwartz, President and CEO of Sun, who is quoted in an
eWeek article making the following statement:

"Sun's definition of proprietary is behavior which defeats the customer's **ability to compete vendors against one another,** *or choose from among many 'compatible' implementations'."* Schwartz further adds *"Some open* **source can be proprietary—if it defeats this competition and defeats interoperability by erecting barriers."**[4] *(bolding my emphasis)*

Aha. So the 'proprietary' behavior our plucky challenger Red Hat appears to be guilty of, in Mr. Schwartz' view, is that they dared to *'erect barriers'* to competitors, and had the audacity to try to retain the existing customers for their Red Hat Enterprise Linux (RHEL) operating system by purposefully restricting these customers' *'ability...to choose from compatible implementations.'*

My first bit of color commentary. Let's all put our hands together in rousing applause, and cheerily thank Jonathan Schwartz for doing the software industry an invaluable service. What invaluable service you ask? The invaluable service of focusing the industry's collective attention on what is, of sheer business necessity, a critical component in any ISV's asymmetric marketing strategy in the superpower sandstorm. Something I call *customer barrier management* or CBM.

And the importance of this particular brawl over the issue of competitive barriers goes far beyond whether one side or the other won or lost this little public debate. In fact, I personally don't care whether or not Sun and Red Hat are still slugging it out, or may have kissed and made up after the bout. Perhaps vowing to work more closely together against those perennial 'Darth Vaders of proprietary', the Redmondistas.

What's really important here, from the standpoint of the ISV marketing community, is whether both parties to these verbal fisticuffs have contributed to educating their peers in the art and science of effective customer management. And Mr. Schwartz, by sucker-punching Red Hat in plain sight for all of us to see, has made such a contribution. A contribution well worth learning from. So allow me to do a little more round by round commentary on Mr. Schwartz' critique of Red Hat.

Fork Me, Fork You
No. I'm not referring to the names of the make-believe Japanese twins[5] that super-spy comedian Mike Myers had on his hilarious checklist of 'things to do before I die' in the film *'Austin Powers, Goldmember'*. I'm

referring to what Jonathan Schwartz characterized as the underlying proprietary element of the Red Hat customer management and market power strategy. Something apparently so objectionable that it would compel the operating leader of a $12 billion dollar company to publicly throw a PR punch at a competitor less than 1/40th his company's size. The open source folks refer to it as 'forking'.

According the Internet.com Webopedia, forking is defined as follows:

*'To split source code into different development directions. Forking leads to the development of **different versions of a program** (JEB emphasis). Forking often occurs when the development of a piece of open source code has reached an impasse. The project is forked so that the code can be developed independently in different ways with different results.'[5]*

Back to my color commentary. Here is how Jonathan Schwartz characterizes Red Hat's alleged practice of forking in the eWeek story cited above:

*"ISVs and customers don't simply qualify to the (Red Hat Linux) kernel—they qualify to the **distribution** (i.e. what Red Hat actually delivers to customers as a commercial product-JEB). To that end, Red Hat's **forked kernel+distribution disables ISVs from moving from one Linux vendor to another**. RHEL (Red Hat Enterprise Linux) is available only through Red Hat. This erects a **proprietary barrier.**"[7](all bolding JEB)*

If I worked at Red Hat, I'd proudly process the Sun CEO's remarks not as an indictment, but as a ***big time compliment for smart marketing in the open source segment of the software industry***. Why?

Is Open Source Red Hat Embracing Asymmetric Product Shark-itecture?

Because Red Hat, while most definitely taking a different path to an asymmetric product than the one I recommend in Chapter 3---(Red Hat is not an ISV engaged in continuous innovation on top of a superpower platform, but rather is an ISV that has embraced the potentially disruptive innovation of free open source as their technology foundation)---Does however, appear to have wisely decided to embrace proven asymmetric marketing best practices, to help them grow and stabilize their enterprise Linux business in the superpower sandstorm.

Specifically, Red Hat appears to have embraced and applied a property of asymmetric products I discussed in Chapter 3, i.e. shark-itecture. I repeat:

"Shark-itecture is the overall product strategy implemented by asymmetric marketers to maximize customer dependency and pre-empt competitive encroachment. It is the product strategy of the software superpowers developed over the life of their offerings, i.e. a product strategy that over time allows them to 'eat' their competitors and carry out category regime change. Shark-itecture in the domain of product marketing is how the superpowers anchor and defend their ecoregions, migrate their installed base of customers to their new products, and achieve multi-generational product dominance."

At a bare minimum, shark-itecture means defending yourself from competitive attack by designing into your products some kind of **effective customer barriers, especially if you are an open source provider**. And this is really all that is happening when Red Hat 'compels' (Schwartz' term) its customers to qualify to the RHEL distribution.

So in my self-appointed position of color commentator for this bout, I hereby declare Red Hat guilty of creatively applying one of the asymmetric marketing practices of the software superpowers in the domain of product management. This is a very good lesson for other ISVs to learn, open source or otherwise.

And despite my magnanimous Thank You to Mr. Schwartz for the gift of his PR sucker punch, this commentator awards Round One in our David/Goliath match-up to Red Hat for thinking and acting like asymmetric marketers. But as reported in the eWeek story, Schwartz does not cease and desist his anti-Red Hat invective simply with his comments regarding 'forking'.

Does Red Hat 'Market Harden' and 'Body Armor' It's Offering?

In fact he expands on his critique of Red Hat's asymmetric product marketing practices in the context of focusing on the Red Hat Network systems management platform.

"They (Red Hat) tether their systems to the Red Hat Network. Customers that want to retrieve information contained in Red Hat's database

can't— the system is not open to enable customers to move to another support provider's network. This erects a proprietary barrier.[8] *(all bolding JEB)*

Once again, I must declare Red Hat guilty of the Jonathan Schwartz indictment. Just like an emerging ISV leader in the Linux market would be expected to, Red Hat appears to be studying and applying more than one of the best practices of the software superpowers in order to capture an asymmetric customer advantage, and defend their installed base. Here's how I describe this particular best practice in Chapter 3.

"Asymmetric products are market-hardened by wrapping the core technology in compound sets of services and intangibles that make the overall offering more difficult to commoditize by both competitors and savvy customers."

In this case, the compound sets of services and intangibles that provide the asymmetric product body armor revolve around the Red Hat Network. No doubt perceived correctly by Red Hat as a complementary, high value-add, systems management platform for their core open source Linux offering. In other words, the Red Hat Network is **not something any sane marketing executive would want to open up willy-nilly to his or her competitors** (unless he or she wanted to go out of business overnight, but be fondly remembered by Jonathan Schwartz as the Mother Teresa[9] of software).

So once again, Round 2 goes to Red Hat for defending their hard-won market gains by incorporating elements of asymmetric marketing into their customer management strategy, and using their systems management platform to capture a market advantage. But our fight is not yet over.

Is Red Hat Price Gouging, or Behaving Like a Future Linux Superpower?

Like a bruised and bloodied prize-fighter who instinctively senses he is losing on points in a title bout, Schwartz battles on and attempts to go for the knockout punch.

*"As their (Red Hat's) control increases, so does their price. If Red Hat was free, customers wouldn't have to pay—so clearly it's not, or Red Hat wouldn't be so aggressively raising prices. Open source doesn't equate to free— witness that Red Hat also requires customers to **pay for all servers on which***

Red Hat is running. Blessed by the FSF [Free Software Foundation] or not—customers know full well that Red Hat is far from free."[10] *(all bolding JEB)*

Driving price *increases* in the superpower sandstorm. Is that supposed to be a bad thing for an emerging category ISV?

Driving price increases in an enterprise market environment where an estimated 80% of the total IT spend goes to incumbent vendors, usually the superpowers. That's supposed to be a bad thing for an up-and-coming ISV to do?

And a software licensing model bold enough to require payment for *all servers*. That's bad? If that's bad, then so is applying any marketing lesson learned from the rise of the software superpowers.

It's pretty apparent to me that the particular set of criticisms that Schwartz makes against Red Hat are not really about the issue of proprietary this, or proprietary that. Rather, these criticisms go to the issue of Red Hat's emerging **market power vis-à-vis it's customers and competitors**, including Sun. That's why I choose to see the Schwartz critique of Red Hat as an opportunity for a little tutorial on the positive marketing benefits than can be reaped by an ISV, when they creatively strive to capture an asymmetric advantage over their customers in a tough enterprise market.

Red Hat Definitely Not a Cargo Cult Marketer

Now would be a good time to do a rapid rewind to the question I pose at the beginning of this book. It was right up front that I introduced renowned physicist Richard Feynman's notion of 'cargo cult science', and his little parable about the friendly WWII Pacific islanders who appeared to be missing 'something essential' in their attempt to get the cargo planes to land.

"And is it conceivable that "something essential" actually is missing from the marketing strategy of those under-performing, cargo-challenged ISVs? Perhaps a practical grasp of the marketing science necessary to win...In this age where software natural monopolies move the bulk of the cargo."

If Schwartz' criticism is any indication, Red Hat is definitely *not* missing that something essential, and has in fact begun to develop its own set of marketing countermeasures to compete effectively as an open source-based ISV in the superpower sandstorm.

On the basis of who landed the most punches, this commentator scores a Round 3 TKO (technical knock out) for Red Hat in our make-believe championship bout. But the lessons of this fight are far from complete. It's important to take another look at the underlying cargo cult science that contributes to Mr. Schwartz comments about the 'proprietary' nature of Red Hat.

And in the spirit of debunking more cargo cult marketing science, I think this would be a good time to recall the advice given by sitcom legend Jerry Seinfeld to his perennially combative and 'in crisis' friend, George Costanza. At the very moment when George's life seemed to be falling apart. I quote, *"If every instinct you have is wrong, then the opposite would have to be right!"*[11]

Translation, if every instinct cargo cult marketers have is wrong.........well..........you can figure out the ending for yourself.

Customer Barrier Management (CBM) vs. Digital Political Correctness

As evidenced by the Schwartz critique of Red Hat, one of the continuing legacies of bubbleboy thinking and cargo cult marketing in the software and internet industries (even years after the bubble burst) is a kind of creeping digital political correctness. The exact opposite of how you want to behave vis-à-vis customers and competitors in the market.

What Jonathan Schwartz sees as a scathing indictment of Red Hat's proprietary nature, should be seen by asymmetric marketers as evidence of Red Hat's *embrace of marketing best practices.* All ISVs can benefit from understanding the importance of applying these practices in the superpower sandstorm.

And here's why I choose to see the Schwartz critique as a form of digital political correctness. From his lofty perch as the president of a $12 billion dollar systems company with its own legacy customer ecoregions (Sun has been around since 1982), Mr. Schwartz nevertheless chides Red Hat for not being good little open source purists. He also chastises them for doing really horrible things like commanding a fair value for their offering (raising prices), a fair licensing model (for every server), and a competitor-defensive support structure and customer retention approach (the Red Hat Network). It's no wonder that one of Red Hat's defenders, is quoted in the eWeek article stating the following in relation to Mr. Schwartz' critique:

> *"In other breaking news, war is peace and freedom is slavery. Mr. Schwartz has a lucrative career waiting at Orwell's 'Ministry of Truth' after Sun goes belly-up, something I'm back to thinking it will do shortly with a mind like this at the helm."*[12]

As a British friend of mine is fond of saying *'Now I wouldn't have been that harsh myself'*. But if you take the time to boil down the Schwartz argument to its essence, here's what you get. If an ISV chooses to build it's offering on the basis of open source, while simultaneously attempting to capture an asymmetric advantage over customers and competitors, that ISV is some kind of proprietary digital 'evil-doer'. That's what I'm characterizing as digital political correctness. And yeah, maybe it is just a little Orwellian[13].

I would hope that thousands of marketing professionals working for emerging category ISVs will join me in concluding that while we are eternally grateful to Mr. Schwartz for raising the issue of barriers in such a public way, we think that his remarks are inappropriate criticisms for the president of a $12 billion dollar hardware and software systems company to make, against a much, much smaller software-only competitor.

And what is really important to take away from the Schwartz critique of Red Hat, regardless of whatever tactical coopetition or market truce the two sides may declare in order to paper over Mr. Schwartz' critique, is this. ISVs need to come to terms with, and ultimately embrace the proposition that they have a ***right to reject anti-price-increase, anti-market power, and anti-customer dominance thinking,*** especially if it comes from a vendor 40X their size. You could get away with digital political correctness during the bubble, when money was cheap, business models were often imaginary, and a shared new economy utopia was just around the corner. But not in the superpower sandstorm.

Rather, ISVs have a right to learn and apply the primary lesson of the rise of the software superpowers. That even small, poorly funded startups have the potential to evolve into software natural monopolies. And that the path to this end means *locking in one customer at a time*. That's why ISVs have a responsibility to themselves (and their investors) to learn to practice customer barrier management (CBM).

If ISVs Had a 12 Step Program for Digital Political Correctness

Let's have a little more fun with this notion of digital political correctness and try approaching the subject another way. Assume for a moment that the software industry has developed some kind of 12-step support group to help ISVs who appear to be 'hitting market bottom' because they bought into the kind of thinking contained in the Schwartz critique of Red Hat. Hey, let's even call the group Digital Political Correctness Anonymous.

And at your first meeting of Digital Political Correctness Anonymous, here are the kinds of questions that the 'ISV old-timers', those sages of marketing sobriety, would include on their little intervention brochure to see if a particular ISV qualifies to go to their self-help meetings:

- If your company is pathetically weak, and has no real competitive market power, is that really good for your customer, or a sign that your customer should look elsewhere?
- If you have permitted your company's products to be commoditized by your competitors, and as a result, you have no pricing power, and no sustainable profitability, is that really beneficial for your enterprise or consumer customers who may be building part of their business or part of their life around your products?
- If your company goes out of business, goes bankrupt, or gets de-listed by the Nasdaq, for failing to build competitive barriers around your business, is that good for your customer who is now forced to look for an alternative?
- If there is a continuing cloud of uncertainty hanging over your business because it is not perceived as a serious commercial venture (despite your heartfelt commitment to open source, the Sierra Club and Birkenstock footware), is that good for your customer?

I think you can see my point. The right answer for serious ISVs to all these questions is NO!

What you ought to do, as Jerry Seinfeld advised George Costanza, is take the antidote to the digital political correctness drug (*especially* if you happen to be a commercial open source provider), and ***do the opposite***. What you want to do is leverage asymmetric marketing principles to create as much locked-in, forward revenue visibility as possible. What you want to do is build effective barriers to competitive entry, barriers to customer exit, and barriers to product imitation.

And from here on out, what's critical to glean from our little Schwartz/Red Hat PR boxing match is that in the software industry, various 'forks' of bubbleboy thinking did not die when the bubble burst. Bubbleboy thinking is alive and well, and when you encounter it...Say it with me.

Do the Opposite.

Bubbleboy 2.0: Impotent Thinking on the Issue of the Customer

As I pointed out earlier in the book, bubbleboy thinking in it's Version 1.0 incarnation took on various blatant, now laughable manifestations like 'capture the eyeballs and the revenue will come later', or 'net market makers will defeat the brick and mortar leaders', or 'new rules for the new economy', or my favorite, 'free peer-to-peer music file sharing is a sustainable business model'.

Likewise, in today's superpower sandstorm, bubbleboy thinking has taken a new, much more slippery form of digital political correctness. A kind of ***intellectual elitism that opposes and attempts to invalidate the key strategic marketing lessons of the rise of the software superpowers***. And it is precisely the marketing lessons of the superpowers that need to be applied by emerging ISVs to provide the revenue traction and expanding market power needed to grow your business.

To hammer this point into stone, I want to turn to one of my favorite examples of Bubbleboy 2.0 thinking, as creatively articulated by none other than (drumroll please) Jonathan Schwartz' old boss, Scott McNealy, the founder of Sun. In his promotion of what he calls the *Participation Age*.

Note to my more 'pacifist' readers. I am absolutely not picking on Sun because I'm some kind of undercover marketing shill for Microsoft.

I have nothing but respect for Sun's immense technical contribution to network computing. But since my target audience is a new generation of ISVs seeking to win on a landscape of natural monopoly superpowers, it's incumbent upon me to call a spade a spade when it comes to what I perceive to be laughably fallacious marketing theory. *Especially* when it is promoted by a pioneer of McNealy's stature.

So I quote Mr. McNealy as follows:

"Information Age thinking says, "Control the creation and distribution of information and you dominate markets." Participation Age is the antithesis of that. It's all about access. That access allows for value to be created through networked human beings who share, interact and solve problems. Because of participation, meaningful content, connections, and relationships are created like never before. In the Participation Age, there are no arbitrary distinctions between passengers and crew, actors and audience. Be one, be both, be everything in between. Welcome to the revolution."[14] *(all bolding JEB)*

Who wouldn't agree with McNealy that the web and network computing have introduced a bottoms-up, many-to-many, participatory network or '*n*' effect into commercial markets. And even facilitated a multi-role nature for customers, i.e. both buyer and seller ('be one or both'). The eBay marketplace and trading platform is the most stunning example of this web dotcomplexity effect.

But '*No arbitrary distinctions between passengers and crew, actors and audience*'. That's not even Web 2.0. It's Bubbleboy 2.0 in Wide Screen High Definition Technicolor.

Wait. I'm not differentiating myself enough here. This is a marketing book. Must draw clear lines. So let me take another crack at it.

In terms of cargo cult marketing-speak, McNealy's Participation Age mantra is the new 2006-model-year version of the San Francisco Bay Area ELECTRIC KOOL-AID MARKETING TEST[15]. And that's the point I want to pick up on.

Passengers and Crew, Customers and You, Let's All Sing Cum-Ba-Ya

But let's clarify terms before continuing. For the purposes of this chapter let's stipulate to the fact that the 'crew' or the 'actor' in McNealy's Participation Age metaphor may perhaps be an emerging category ISV. And that the 'passenger' or the 'audience' in the metaphor refers to the ISV's customer.

So I ask you this one simple question. If you're an on-demand, open source, Web 2.0, or 'Enterprise 2.0'[16] startup that tried pitching a line like *'no arbitrary distinctions between passengers and crew'* to a venture capitalist that wants to know why you and your team have confidence in your revenue forecast, and why he or she should plow $10 or $20 million dollars into your startup, what do you think his or her reaction would be? How about this one, *"Come back and see us when you're old enough to be a member of the crew!"*

But seriously, all kidding aside, *the distinctions between passenger and crew are non-trivial and non-arbitrary, and baked into capitalist economics.* Despite the fact that Scott McNealy seems to want us all to sing cum-ba-ya while digitally holding hands in the Participation Age. And here's the primary distinction.

The passenger *pays to fly on the airplane while the crew gets paid.* The audience pays to see the movie, the actor gets paid.

My conclusion from this new example of Bay Area Electric Kool-Aid Marketing Test thinking is simple. For ISVs facing the competitive landscape of the superpower sandstorm, the only real outcome of buying lock, stock and barrel into McNealy's Participation Age message, which creatively blurs the critical distinction between *paying and getting paid*, is easy to predict. There will be *no execution emphasis placed on gaining market power relative to customers and competitors.* In other words, it's the theoretical basis of what Mr. Schwartz recommended to Red Hat.

Nothing Is More Important Than The Distinction Between Passengers & Crew

This new Electric Kool-Aid Marketing Test will ultimately lead to business failure for ISVs that chug-a-lug and 'trip' on this particular flavor of Kool-Aid. Nothing, I repeat, nothing.... is more important to an entrepreneur and emerging category ISV than the distinction between 'passengers and crew' or 'actors and audience'. Nothing is ever more important than having an asymmetric framework for relating to the customer. And nothing is more important than, as Jerry Seinfeld urged George Costanza, "doing the opposite" of what McNealy recommends.

In fact, If I wanted to be a really sarcastic color commentator, e.g. the Dennis Miller or Chris Rock or Margaret Cho of software marketing punditry, here is where I'd take a little poetic license with Karl Marx and Frederick Engels famous first line of the *Communist Manifesto*[17] which, if re-written by Scott McNealy in the context of his Participation Age newspeak[18] might go something like this,

'A spectre is haunting the software industry, the spectre of the Participation Age. All the natural monopoly market superpowers of the old information economy have entered into a holy alliance to exorcise this spectre.'

Doubtful, dude. Not really bro!

The superpowers will probably just ignore Mr. McNealy's digital political correctness, which their leaders know is designed primarily not to increase access for emerging ISVs, but to increase 'access' for Sun as it faces a tough server market, and asymmetric competitors like Dell and IBM. The software superpowers long ago grasped the critical importance for business strategy in the distinction between 'passenger' and 'crew', customer and vendor. It's the new generation of post-bubble ISVs that need to learn these lessons well. And inoculate themselves against Bubbleboy 2.0 thinking.

Hip 'Revolutionary' Messaging, or the Real ISV Revolution

Just as I applauded Mr. Schwartz for publicly raising the 'proprietary' issue in relation to Red Hat's innovative marketing, I don't actually blame Mr. McNealy for coming up with his 'Participation Age' manifesto. On one level it's just good messaging strategy. Why wouldn't Scott McNealy and Sun opt to have a really cool-sounding, super-hip, very Web 2.0 Bay Area messaging platform to attack the underlying asymmetric market power of Microsoft, Dell, IBM and others, while gaining increased access for their own products and services? And the 'participation' mantra vs. 'information age control' most definitely works in certain circles as an attractive cargo cult messaging candidate to accomplish that objective. But don't let yourself get fooled into thinking it's a real *'welcome to the revolution'* (McNealy's punchline) for ISVs.

As I've maintained from the beginning of this book, the real 'Welcome to the revolution' for ISVs is to become successful in the age of the software superpowers. The real revolution is achieved by seeing the ISV mission as symbiosis with the superpowers, not disruption against them.

The real revolution is achieved by studying and applying superpower best practices in the domain of products, sales approaches, competitive strategy and customer management. That's the only way to capture any kind of *sustainable* competitive advantage in the sandstorm. And that's why it's doubly important not to buy in to any kind of thinking, even from an industry pioneer and network computing visionary like Scott McNealy, that muddles the key distinction between you and the customer. Or obfuscates your need for effective customer management and control.

That's the way to begin to detox from the Bay Area Bubbleboy 2.0 Electric Kool-Aid Marketing Test, and digital political correctness. So if an open source pioneer like Red Hat can embrace certain elements of an asymmetric marketing approach, so too can a new generation of ISVs attached to the Microsoft, Oracle, Cisco, SAP and other superpower ecozones. Which brings us to the issue of customer barrier management (CBM).

Customer Control 101: What I Learned Long, Long Ago in a Universe Far, Far Away

Early in my career, I was fortunate to have a boss (let's call him Bob) who served as both mentor and role model, and made a point of coaching me on some of the finer points of 'black belt ninja' customer control. Here's a story from that time that illustrates the lesson I learned from this particular mentor.

The company that Bob and I worked for was a pioneer in electronic publishing software and related customization services. They had set the pace in enabling telecommunications companies to migrate their lucrative directory publishing operations (Yellow Pages Advertising, White Pages, Special Directories) from hot metal typography to database-driven computerized photocomposition and pre-press services, and had rapidly become the early category leader.

It would also be accurate to say that at that time, our company's solution was a true 'disruptive or discontinuous technology innovation' and had the effect of driving a classic industry game change in pre-press services. The company had clearly differentiated itself by rolling out a compound asymmetric offering that included directory database infrastructure, professional integration services, hosted application services, and a team of experts that served to drive business model and process transformation for our customers. Bob and his team were the first folks to really enable the Regional Bell Operating Companies (RBOCs) to dramatically cut their costs, while simultaneously becoming more agile, by launching new Yellow Pages directory products based on the content contained in the digital warehouses we were creating.

Long Ball Hitter Goes to Batting Practice

I had been hired by Bob to develop and execute a plan to expand the company's business into new non-telecom markets in commercial and government publishing, based on the systems we were building for the Bell companies. As part of my training, he told me I needed to hang out with him and some of the company's strategic customers in order to make sure I really understood how to become a 'long ball hitter'. Long ball hitter was his code phrase for somebody who could market and manage big deals (since Bob's division of the company had a profile of only pursuing profitable 7-figure and 8-figure projects).

So one night after work, Bob invited me to go with him to meet a couple of customer representatives from the telecom market segment at a local restaurant (they flew in to see us by the way). They turned out to be the two top guys from the business decision-making team assigned to one of our newest and largest projects. As we pulled into the parking lot, Bob told me not to freak out if the 'fur started flying', meaning if there was open friction with the customer. *"Just sit tight, shut up, sip your drink, listen and learn...Because there's going to be a test later"* was exactly how he put it to me.

After some pleasantries in the restaurant lounge, where I was introduced as the 'new guy', one of the two customer representatives (let's call him Jim) quickly cuts to the chase and asks, *"How's it going with our project, Bob"*?

Without missing a beat, my boss scrunches up his face and says, *"Lousy Jim, really lousy."*

Needless to say, Jim, the senior guy, gets that 'deer in the headlights' look in his eyes. But before he can respond, my boss Bob re-scrunches his face and continues on. *"The team you have assigned to the project are just not that technology-literate, Jim, and frankly, if you ask me, they don't want to be. So if you're going to hold our feet to the fire to meet the deadline for the launch of your new database-driven directories, we're probably going to need a bunch more people on our side of the equation... and about a 35% price increase."*

At this point Jim glared like an NFL center whose mother was insulted by the opposing team's linebacker, right before the snap of the ball. I made a mental note to myself to shut up, pushed my chair back a few more inches from the table, reached for my drink, watched and waited.

"I Wouldn't Blame You If..........."

"But, Bob, we have a fixed price contract for this project", Jim replied, and took a big gulp of his extra dry vodka Martini. I waited for the fur to fly as my boss and mentor calmly stated, *"Look Jim...I understand you're upset, but the fact of the matter is that I'm not set up to lose money on this deal just because your guys are not used to the processes we all agreed on up front. If price is a big issue for such a strategic project, we can always stretch out the delivery schedule, and I'll find some other way to make up the difference in lost revenue to us. Joe over there is tasked with bringing in new commercial and government accounts, and I've been stalling him on the start date of one of his hot projects... because of my commitment to your success. I needed to make sure I have enough development capacity to get your job done right."*

My boss then added, *"Personally, I wouldn't blame you if you decided to pack up and take the work someplace else. But that would end up being even more expensive. Your team would still have a big learning curve with a new vendor, and your people would still be stuck in the old business processes and mentality relative to publishing automation."*

Up until that point, Jim's companion, let's call him Hal, had been quiet. But then Hal jumped in looking at Jim, who, as I indicated above, was his boss. *"Jim...Here's another way to go. We can forget all about this computer database stuff, and I can get our old hot metal pre-press provider to do the directories"*, said Hal, appearing to cut my boss Bob off at the knees. *"But then we can't get the new database driven spin-off products that these guys can deliver for at least another year or more. And that's a lot of revenue that won't be in our pockets...Revenue that we put into our budget plan. And we would still have startup costs with a new vendor....and they'd still have to come up the learning curve and modify the software we've already paid for. But I understand that money is money, and so we do have an option,"* concluded Hal.

Jim excused himself to ponder Hal's comments, claiming he had to go and use the men's room. My boss looked at him as he got up from the table and chimed in, *"I'll order another round of drinks, and when you come back we'll decide what to do".* As Jim walked over to the men's room, what happened next surprised me. My boss looked at Hal, smiled, and said, *'Are you and Mary still coming to my house for the Super Bowl party?'* Hal looked back at my boss and said, *"I wouldn't miss it for the world."*

When Jim came back from the men's room Bob smiled at him and said, *"Jim, would you mind if I hire this guy Hal. He just talked me down to about a 22% increase if we agree to discount some of those new projects you were gonna ask us to quote on next quarter. And Hal also suggested we get creative about your team's learning curve, and set up some of our new digital page composition workstations at your shop, so your folks can update the advertising content and graphics themselves, remotely."*

Jim breathed a sigh of relief, picked up his drink and said, *"Are we having dinner or what.............and you're picking up the check after this little surprise."* My boss looked at me, grinned ear to ear and said, *'No we'll let Joe here pick up the check. He claims he wants to be a long ball hitter, and there's no better training than picking up the check.'*

"I Told You There Would Be a Test"

The next day at the office I saw Jim and Hal running around happily meeting with our project team members as if it had been their idea all along to increase both the scope and the price of the project. The boss called me in and said, *"I told you there would be a test young man. So what did you learn."*

Here's what I told him.

- You established the principle with the customer that *we don't do unprofitable business*, and that we were prepared to walk away from their contract in favor of new commercial accounts.
- You were successful at *raising the price*, even with a fixed-price contract already in place.

- You got the customer to **commit to new business** and to new software development, which we will end up owning and selling to other customers.

- You displaced some of our costs by placing the new digital photocomposition workstations at their offices. This also raises their switching costs, and **locks them in to our systems and our processes at a deeper level**.

- You showed me the importance of having a **customer advocate internally**, i.e. Hal, as part of your strategy in achieving you objective. Hal, at your coaching, purposely painted a worst-case scenario for his boss, which frightened his boss even more than your price increase. And you engaged in stealth by complimenting Hal for negotiating you down on the price increase you originally quoted to Jim.

- You demonstrated **effective working management of the customer in a way that benefited us, and them**.

"You Missed The Most Important Thing"

I asked him if I missed anything. My boss smiled and said, *"Only two things...Number one: I got you to pick up the check for dinner."* I laughed and said, *"OK, what's number two?"* He answered, *"You missed the most important thing. Since at this point, as a result of our multi-year investment in creating a team of domain experts in computerized pre-press services, we actually know more than our customers do about how to make their businesses more successful. Therefore my price increase was nothing more than a fair value exchange. And since it was only in the course of deploying our systems with their team that we realized exactly how much value we were bringing to their new business, it was my responsibility to our shareholders to push for a price increase. So in the context of delivering exceptional value to the customer, my pushing for a higher price, more projects, and increasing customer control will, in the end, provide our customers with even better opportunities to leverage our technology. It's in the very nature of the software industry."*

At the time, I was way too green to see my mentor's Bob's lesson in the larger context, i.e. as an exercise in asymmetric customer management. But looking back, it was worth a drawer full of Ph.D.'s in a 2006 software industry where we are consistently invited to drink lots of new Kool-Aid around the issue of the customer.

So for the remainder of this chapter, I'm going to expand on the lesson provided by my mentor, and outline 3 basic tips in developing an asymmetric marketing-based CBM approach. And should Jonathan Schwartz criticize you in public, or Scott McNealy invite you to join hands in his Participation Age, these tips should help strengthen your marketing immune system, while allowing you to feel no guilt or shame about your company's right to practice customer barrier management in the domain of products, business models and overall strategy.

3 Tips to Help You Develop an Asymmetric CBM Strategy

CBM Tip 1: Don't Drink the 'Customer Economy' Kool-Aid

It's important for ISV marketers to understand that the kind of thinking expressed by Schwartz and McNealy, thinking I've characterized as Bubbleboy 2.0 digital political correctness, thinking that I believe sets up ISVs to fail....Did not originate with them.

And definitely not with Geoffrey Moore who, to his great credit, introduced the testosterone-drenched metaphor of the dominant category 'gorilla' into marketing nomenclature.

Rather, Bubbleboy 2.0 thinking has a different pedigree. It is essentially the continuation of one 'fork' of new economy theory in the realm of the customer, i.e. so-called 'customer economy' theory. Here's a representative sample of customer economy thinking from Patricia Seybold, one of its originators.

"You're no longer in control of your company's destiny. Your customers are. Thanks to the Internet and to mobile wireless devices, customers are now armed with new, more convenient tools with which to access our businesses (as well as those of our competitors) around the clock and around the globe. Business and consumer customers are challenging and disrupting the standard practices in virtually every industry. They're demanding that we change our pricing structures, our distribution channels, and the way we design and deliver our products and services to them. They won't be denied. They have the power and they know it. Companies that don't "get it" will be out of business soon. Like most revolutions, this can't be stopped. We can't turn our backs on it. We have no choice but to surrender gracefully."[9] (all bolding JEB)

Earth to Patricia Seybold, Earth to Patricia Seybold!

It's one thing to acknowledge the transformation of business processes as a result of a feedback-rich web. It's another thing altogether to embrace the viewpoint that customers are *'in control of your company's destiny'*, *'have the power'*, and that marketers have no choice but to *'surrender gracefully'*. I see this kind of thinking as representative of an entire marketing theory of the customer that led to the bubble. Let's not forget that Seybold used the first Napster as one of her proof-of-concepts. But you pick your own characterization. Call it customer co-dependence, ...customer appeasement...hey, wait a second. I believe in giving credit where credit is due. Ms. Seybold's term is the better term---*surrender*.

Simply put, in a superpower sandstorm where the adoption of ISV products is significantly impacted by the no-fly-zone imperative of the superpowers, where category regime change offensives that target best-of-breed ISVs are an ongoing fact of life, and where impaired revenue visibility, positional confusion, execution heat and broken marketing machinery are often the norm---You do not want to continue to drink the customer economy Kool-aid, no matter how hot it gets in the desert. You want to develop as much asymmetric customer advantage as possible. And if you've over-dosed on this particular flavor of Kool-Aid, get into recovery fast.

In fact, it may be helpful to think of the issue of customer surrender as one of those Seinfeldian aha moments you want to carve into the side of your cubicle. *'Surrender---I will do the opposite'*.

For those of you who were smart enough or lucky enough never to have been swept up in the customer economy fad...For those of you who have no problem with my macho mantra that marketing in the software industry is a form of asymmetric warfare, then let's return once again to Sun Tzu, who got the opposite of surrender just about perfect.

'Feed Off the Enemy'
Here's something he wrote many, many centuries ago that underlines why it's so important to have a programmatic approach to customer barrier management.
"Therefore a wise general strives to feed off the enemy."[20]

"Whooooooooaaaaaaaaaaaa Nelly, I hear you thinking. This time you've gone too far Mr. Joe B. Slow this asymmetric predator drone down. It's one thing to joke about Scott McNealy... and as a Tom Wolfe fan I can relate to the Electric Koolaid Marketing Test....But is what you're implying...Heaven forbid....That we should see the customer as the enemy?"

I'm not *exactly* stating that. But then again, what the hell. I guess in one way that's exactly what I'm suggesting. Why?

Because, out of practical necessity, asymmetric marketing acknowledges this seeming paradox of the *multi-role nature of the customer.* And you need to acknowledge it as well, in order to develop an effective CBM strategy for the specifics of your business. But it's definitely not Mr. McNealy's 'passenger and crew' that are the multiple roles. It's *partner* on the one hand, and *adversary* on the other. The partner part we've all heard before. It's the minimum price of admission to the game. It's that adversary part where folks get into trouble.

So to 'feed off the enemy', for any ISV bold enough to apply either Sun Tzu's Art of War, or my old boss Bob's Art of Cocktails, means having a CBM approach that dominates the customer in a practical way. Effectively *driving the customer to profit-fund your opportunity.* Thereby providing you with the follow-on initiative you need to compete in this age of the superpowers.

For asymmetric marketers, seriously acknowledging the multi-role nature of the customer means having both an *orthodox and unorthodox customer strategy, i.e. orthodox in terms of the striving to achieve the highest level of customer satisfaction, and unorthodox in terms of striving to achieve the maximum amount of customer control.* Those are not exactly my mentor Bob's words to me years ago, but that is in fact the spirit of his words.

So here's my challenge to you. If you've begun applying the ideas in this book, then by all means stay focused on delivering on your 3-dimensional value proposition, and improving the asymmetric nature of your offering. And be confident that you are on the way to practicing symbiosis with one or more of the superpowers, while implementing an asymmetric sales strategy. And if you're doing those things, then be my guest and do one more thing.

Place your customers between the rock of your product barriers and the hard place of your CBM strategy.

Push Back Hard on Customer 'Power'

Never "surrender". Rather, focus on mitigating the growing customer power Seybold references by creatively working to take back control. Don't embrace a point of view that passively enables customer power to increase in the name of customer satisfaction. Don't allow your customer management approach to lead you into becoming some kind of digital doormat to customer power. Creatively resist it. That's how the superpowers do it. That's how your own lock-in will begin. And that's how to evolve the customer relationship on your terms.

And that is exactly what Jonathan Schwartz criticized Red Hat for...Not proprietary software (it's open source Linux for heaven's sake). But for *exercising power over the customer that progressively pre-empts competitive encroachment.*

Detoxing from the customer economy Kool-Aid, and embracing Sun Tzu's 'feed off the enemy' guideline for asymmetric warriors, can take different forms and have a different emphasis depending on your stage of development.

For startups, detoxing from the customer economy Kool-Aid, and executing around an asymmetric marketing CBM approach would mean focusing on bootstrapping your deal. And *creatively customer-funding your products and services* in order keep the initiative in your hands. This path has been almost instinctively followed by many ISVs in the post-bubble software economy, i.e. focus on a 'projects to products' customer-funding model, grow a little of your own power over the customer, and only then seek outside capital. Don't get stuck in the trap of those cargo cult startups that never maintain any consistent market initiative, because they are in perpetual fund-raising mode. Don't focus on feeding off the VCs (as did the bubbleboy crowd). Feed off the customer.

For small cap public company turnarounds that still have money in the bank, it means stopping the bleeding now. Not in three or four quarters, simply because you have 'sufficient cash to fund ongoing operations'. Don't you just love those guys posting on the Yahoo Finance message boards who talk about how much cash a company has. As if that was the same as having an asymmetric advantage in the market. Bleeding in the name of customer satisfaction is just marketing masochism. Look at your customer approach, and if you're not happy with the amount of customer control you are currently exercising, then make focusing only on profitable customers, and re-capturing an asymmetric customer advantage, the most important issue at your executive team meetings.

For market share and other best-of-breed category leaders facing regime change action by one or more superpowers, detoxing from the customer economy Kool-Aid often means having to deal with *the impact of the superpowers' own asymmetric marketing strategy on your customers*. Remember what I pointed out earlier in the book— One of the more extreme examples of superpower asymmetry relative to an ISV's customers in recent history directly led to the firing of Craig Conway, former CEO of PeopleSoft, during the year-long hostile takeover bid by Oracle. In describing why the PeopeSoft board of directors fired a high-caliber CEO like Conway who had consistently grown the company's revenue, one news reports stated that:

> *"PeopleSoft fired Conway after the board learned about a deposition in which he admitted to **lying to analysts by telling them that Oracle's offer was no longer chasing away customers**. (JEB emphasis) In the deposition, Conway said the statements were 'promotional, not true, absolutely not true'."*[21]

In the same news article, Conway described Oracle's hostile takeover bid as having an intentional 'twist in the wind' effect on his customers, driving them to postpone both new and expanded purchases until the takeover drama played out.

Unfortunately, Conway and the PeopleSoft Board of Directors did not have sufficient countermeasures in place to deal with the impact of the Oracle bid on their customers' willingness to do business with them. And high levels of customer satisfaction alone were not enough to deal with Oracle's asymmetric 'twist in the wind' strategy.

CBM Tip 2: Think in Terms of Building 3 Specific Kinds of Barriers

Marketing Defense-in-Depth
Ok. You've raised your right hand, put your left hand over your heart, and taken a solemn vow to refuse to surrender, and stop drinking the customer economy Kool-Aid. So what's the next tip. Simple. Start

thinking in terms of 3 legitimate customer and competitor barriers, specifically:

- Barriers to Exit
- Barriers to Entry
- Barriers to Imitation

And here's a metaphor that works for me on how to think about the 3 kinds of barriers---*marketing defense-in-depth.*

I'm shoplifting this metaphor from the security software segment where 'defense-in-depth' is a popular concept. It means that no single 'point solution' (firewalls, intrusion prevention systems, authentication systems, anti-virus, etc.) will work to secure a network on its own. So you build a layered defense model driven by your information security policy.

Applying the idea in a marketing context means this. You build a *layered customer defense, or CBM system based on your asymmetric marketing policy* in order to protect your hard-fought market gains one customer at a time. So let's look at the three most common barriers.

Barriers to Exit

Building a barrier to customer exit is essentially what Jonathan Schwartz accused Red Hat of doing, right? And he accused Red Hat of following two approaches that I refer to in my Chapter 3 discussion of asymmetric products, i.e. a so-called 'proprietary' or non-duplicatable product implementation (the RHEL distribution) that has effect of driving customer dependence. And a 'compound', 'hardened', 'body-armored' offering approach' in the form of a high-value management platform (the Red Hat Network), that makes their core Linux OS easier to deploy, provision and manage. These two approaches should find their way onto the CBM short list of every ISV.

There are many approaches beyond these two that you can leverage in an asymmetric CBM strategy. My favorite, and the most graceful and frictionless to implement relative to customer perception, is *information dependency,* i.e. continuous 'updateness' designed into the fabric of the product. Earlier I used Windows Update as a representative example of this approach in action. An approach that can be highly effective in reducing customer exit for all classes of customer---from enterprise IT, to the SMB, to the consumer.

The security software segment is a good example of this 'information dependency' approach to building a barrier to customer exit. Anti-virus software requires incremental updates to function properly, as do spam firewalls, intrusion prevention systems, etc. This information dependency serves as a continuous 'high touch' customer interaction, and has the effect of producing a more locked-in customer. Other ISV market segments beyond security are now beginning to imitate this best practice of high touch information dependency.

In the asymmetric marketing playbook I follow, it's a general rule of thumb to assume that a well-constructed barrier to exit is less about raising the switching *cost*, and more about **raising the perceived switching pain**. We've all heard software sales professionals talk about detecting business opportunity by looking for IT 'pain'. What I'm talking about here is the opposite. Getting creative about your CBM approach, so that any exit from reliance on your continuously updated product, and subsequent migration to a competitor, **creates pain**. Pure and simple pain. So that the customer surrenders...to you.

Barriers to Entry

For my more squeamish readers, let me re-assure you that when I advocate creating barriers to competitive entry, it is not the same thing as advocating breaking anti-trust law[22]. I'm simply advancing this idea— That it's in your interest to forcefully insist that potentially competitive ISVs entering your customer ecoregion receive explicit and/or implicit market permission from you to do so. I'm advocating that you begin thinking like the superpowers, and work on creating your own no-fly-zone CBM approach over time. So the question is, over the years, how have the superpowers implemented their barriers to competitive entry?

They have a few 'oldies but goodies' they turn to. For starters, they have demonstrated a willingness to systematically and creatively **deny interoperability** to non-permissioned market entrants practicing in-your-face parasitic symbiosis. A classic example from the history of the rise of the superpowers mentioned earlier in the book—When Novell's Digital Research group tried to sell DR DOS as an OS to run underneath MS Windows, Microsoft made sure a potentially 'incompatible' or 'error' message appeared to the user. That's denial of parasitic interoperability in spades, because clearly, Digital Research was the 'predatory' party in the equation (according to any honest, practical definition of the term 'predatory').

But in the main the superpower's primary barrier to entry has been to foster interoperability. And drive the ultimate emergence of a large number of 3rd party applications that support their customer ecoregions.

Even if your deal is a startup or emerging category player with limited or no market power, you can begin to do the same thing by effectively attaching to superpower installed base ecoregions and *leveraging their no-fly-zone activities.* To underscore this point, let me add that one of the other criticisms Schwartz leveled against Red Hat was that Oracle 'exclusively' supported Red Hat's Linux distribution.... and that somehow that was a bad thing.

Obviously it was a very good thing for Red Hat, as well as for Oracle customers that wanted to go to a Linux OS. But wanted the blessings of a superpower, prior to making the move to a potentially disruptive technology. In other words, practicing effective symbiosis with a superpower, as Red Hat did with Oracle, became an effective barrier to competitive entry. So effective that Schwartz criticized them for it. And even after Oracle began supporting other Linux providers, e.g. Novell, the time period in which Oracle supported Red Hat served as one of those 'empty space' periods in which Red Hat was able to make significant market gains.

Barriers to Imitation
The mother of all barriers is the barrier to imitation, i.e. make your customer experience as non-commoditizable as possible. Easier said than done, but that's why they pay you CEOs, CMOs, and marketing VPs the big bucks. Here's how the superpowers and other leading asymmetric marketers are doing it.

With the convergence of software, web services, content, and tailored devices, we are seeing some very creative approaches that drive an asymmetric barrier to imitation by creating virtually *non-duplicatable customer experiences.*

eBay leverages the network effect of its trading community and trading platform to create a virtually non-duplicatable customer experience for small and home-based businesses that want to go global.

Apple has combined the iPod device platform and iTunes content service experience to rapidly emerge as a leader in paid music and video. The RIM folks also follow this model with their tightly-coupled Blackberry device and email services.

Akamai has combined its EdgePlatform network, with its EdgeControl and EdgeComputing technologies to create a virtually non-duplicatable customer experience for delivering on-demand computing.

The important thing to realize is that building a barrier to imitation is not a 'what to think' thing, i.e. some cargo cult script you can follow. It's a *how to think* thing. How to think about creatively combining multiple technologies and services into winning experiences that are more difficult to copy, clone and commoditize in the superpower sandstorm.

At every opportunity, look at feature/function issues as ways to build these 3 kinds of barriers. It's a creative effort that will yield powerful benefits. However, even if your product strategy needs work from the standpoint of asymmetric marketing, don't worry just yet. The good news is that developing and implementing a CBM strategy is not just about using your product or product experience as barriers. Good CBM can also leverage your company's *business model* to defend you against customer defection and competitive encroachment. So let's begin by looking at how 4 popular ISV business models can be used (and multiplexed) to reinforce your CBM initiatives.

Tip 3: Work Your Business Model from a CBM Point of View
From the standpoint of CBM, I like to lump software business models into 4 distinct clusters, each of which has its own advantages:
- Universal or traditional models,
- Utility or on-demand models, i.e. subscribing to Software-as-a-Service (SaaS), e.g. Salesforce.com, or Webex;
- Ubiquity models, i.e. a virally distributed piece of 'quark-itecture' into which you plug a revenue business, e.g. the free Adobe Acrobat Reader and the Adobe Acrobat Professional authoring platform;

- Unorthodox models, i.e. pure dotcomplexity-driven businesses, e.g. eBay.

I'll begin with the universal model.

To Improve Your CBM, Make the Universal Model All About Flexibility

The universal or traditional software business model has historically been about engaging the customer across 3 streams of revenue---licensing fees, maintenance/update dollars, and professional integration and customization services. And for years, continuing growth in the licensing fees component of this model has generally been perceived by industry analysts as an indicator of your business vitality.

But for many ISVs facing the challenge of surviving and thriving in the superpower sandstorm, license fees have often barely grown at all, or have declined. This is a direct result of both ISV pricing pressure in the face of the superpower no-fly-zone imperative, as well as delayed IT procurement cycles (the desertification I talked about in Chapter 2). Desertification that often forces ISVs to reduce prices in order to close a deal in a given quarter.

In fact, many 'revenue misses' by publicly traded ISVs, and their subsequent downgrading by analysts, have often been interpreted as evidence of the continuing erosion of the universal software model, and the declining market power of the specific vendor with the 'miss'. As a consequence, more than a few ISVs get hung up on focusing only on how to improve the license revenue component of the universal model. But that's not how asymmetric marketers see things. *They work the whole model*, not just the license component...from the standpoint of CBM or customer barrier management.

Here's a great metaphor from Sun Tzu that makes the point.

"So a skillful military operation should be like a swift snake that counters with its tail when someone strikes at its head, counters with its head when someone strikes at its tail, and counters with both head and tail when someone strikes at its middle."[23]

Applying this metaphor, think of the head of the snake as your licensing revenue, the tail as services revenue, and the middle as maintenance revenue. When the license component of your model is attacked by intense price competition, counter with the services and maintenance components. In other words, see the universal model as a flexible weapon in the arsenal of your CBM strategy. For asymmetric marketers that want to improve revenue visibility in the superpower sandstorm, the key consideration is how to *leverage the model as a whole* to drive higher levels of customer lock-in. This is particularly true for open source ISVs whose license component may be free.

Back to Publate Company X

Remember my Publate Company X example from Chapter 2. One of the mistakes they made was to walk away from lots and lots of services revenue because an influential 'marketing expert' on their board pressured the CEO to 'focus only on the license line'. As a result, they not only left money on the table, but also missed the opportunity to use services to increase their market power relative to their biggest customers.

In point of fact the reverse happened---they lost market power and opened the door to new competitors. The outsourced services providers that Publate Company X originally saw as their implementation and customization partners ended up becoming their competitors. How? By creating more value in the application 'connectors' they built to deploy Publate Company X' e-business software at complex enterprises, than Company X had built into it's platform. The lesson of this parable---See the universal business model through the prism of CBM, and don't get hung up on conforming to some financial analyst vision of the model.

Learn From Company Y

Here's another example from Company Y, a 'best-of-breed' ISV that faced a regime change action from an adjacent *hardware* superpower seeking to annex their small, but stable, category. How? By attacking their license revenue with a free open source alternative.

Company Y went on the offensive and temporarily *cannibalized its own license revenue* by selling all-you-can-eat volume purchase agreements. Agreements that served to build a temporal customer barrier against the superpower's entry into their category. Locking in their customers and locking out their opponent. Until Company Y figured out Plan B.

Fortunately for them, they did figure out Plan B, and ended up actually growing their overall revenue 15% in the year they were facing the attack, as well as building up a large deferred revenue number. They created a suite of new add-on products that redefined the category the superpower wanted to commoditize and annex. They did category 'regime change' against themselves.

By seeing their universal business model from the standpoint of CBM, and temporarily driving the commoditization of their own licensing revenue, they turned the situation around. Ultimately, the hostile hardware superpower relented, and collaborated with them on its future roadmap, realizing it was foolhardy to try to beat them down in a market Company Y had created. OK, on to the utility model.

To Improve Your CBM, Make the Utility Model All About Invisibility

While the universal model is all about business model flexibility as a barrier, the utility or on-demand model is about invisibility, i.e. the construction of barriers to entry, exit and imitation that are invisible to the customer from day one. As practiced by pioneering ISVs like Webex and Salesforce.com, the on-demand subscription model, a.k.a. utility model, easily lends itself to a CBM agenda, and has been instrumental in helping both companies exceed $300 million in annual revenue in 2005. These CBM best practices, open to application by all ISVs, include:

The Hook-Them Trial Period: An easy to subscribe free trial evaluation, in which prospective customers become familiar with your user experience, and become ***increasingly invested in your product through expending 'human bandwidth'***, i.e. placing their data into the platform, or integrating the product into their day-to-day business process.

The Conversion Phase: An easy to convert, affordable fixed or variable subscription payment plan, that tends to ***'groove-in' the customer for some initial time period***, from a month, to a year, or more.

The Customization Phase: Under competitive threat from the superpowers, Salesforce and Webex, both on-demand pioneers, have begun to adapt their subscription business models in order to ***provide*** *the kind of flexibility traditionally found in the universal model, i.e. customization and 3ʳᵈ party services.*

The Diversification Phase: Here's what I mean by diversification. Salesforce has decided to morph from primarily a CRM application provider into a broad, on-demand platform provider, via their AppExchange OS. Their goal---To enable their revenue model to reach across categories into new application segments, as well as to *power customer-developed and 3ʳᵈ party applications.* This increases the strength of their customer barrier in the face of the superpower sandstorm in CRM, in which Oracle, SAP and Microsoft are all placing Salesforce in the cross-hairs of an on-demand CRM category regime change. In addition they have developed something they call AppExchange, a community of 3ʳᵈ party developers whose applications plug into the Salesforce on-demand OS. This is a smart move. What this means in practical terms is this. *Going around the superpower's IT lock-in to get departmental and business line users to write apps* that they want to run on the AppForce infrastructure.

Driving Down Sales Expense Can Also Be Part of the Barrier

Webex has diversified as well, and has also innovated in another direction. By marketing their platform via an *OEM powered-by model* to companies likes Global Crossing, MCI and other telecom providers seeking to add online conferencing revenue to their services mix. By leveraging the marketing spend of its "powered-by" customers, Webex has achieved a much lower level of sales and marketing expense (around 33% of revenue) than Salesforce (around 50% of revenue). But both the Salesforce and Webex approaches (3ʳᵈ party on Salesforce, Webex on 3ʳᵈ party) are solid examples of innovative practices that leverage the SaaS/on-demand/utility model to create a strong barrier to imitation in the market.

To Improve Your CBM, Make the Ubiquity Model Connect the Free & the Un-Free

The ubiquity model is most associated with those companies that deliver some kind of platform, application, tool, player or service, *for free.* And then deliver a closely connected paid product or service that leverages the free offering. The widespread availability and use of the free ubiquitous distribution becomes the immediate competitive barrier to overcome. While the *relationship between the free offering and the monetized offering* comprises the barrier to imitation.

The Adobe Acrobat Reader is a great example of the ubiquity model in action. It's so ubiquitous that if you do a Google search on 'PDF' you will get 2,290,000,000 references (as of 9/06). By contrast, 'Windows' only gets 1,610,000,000 and more than a few of those are for the actual windows you have in your house.

More than 10 years ago, in his 1995 call to action to the Microsoft troops titled 'The Internet Tidal Wave', Bill Gates acknowledged the CBM impact of the ubiquity model when he wrote:

"Once a format gets established it is extremely difficult for another format to come along and even become equally popular."[24]

That's a pretty powerful endorsement of the ubiquity model as contributor to a CBM approach. And on the shoulders of Acrobat Reader and PDF ubiquity, Adobe has built a robust publishing platform business for both creative professionals and the enterprise that is second to none.

Emerging category players are also demonstrating that they understand the CBM benefits of the ubiquity model---Lavasoft, for one, in the fast growing anti-spyware category. As of September 2006, Lavasoft's Ad-Aware free spyware removal tool has been installed on over 200 million machines. And this privately held Swedish company has introduced a higher end enterprise edition, complete with a management console and enterprise deployment tools. That's an asymmetric startup working out of the Adobe playbook. No wonder Google included Lavasoft's Ad-Aware in their 'Google Pack' bundle of free software. And the Google pack itself is designed to leverage the ubiquity model into new software markets beyond web search.

Ubiquity and 'Sponsored Apps'
In this age of SaaS and on-demand apps, Google has already accomplished something similar to Adobe, using the ubiquitous application of free web search to grow a multi-billion dollar advertising business. This has led to a lot of discussion within the software industry around the whole notion of sponsored applications. In other words, if you can offer search, or web-based email as a free application based on advertising, why not word processing, spreadsheets, small business applications, 'Enterprise 2.0' capability, and more.

And you know that there may be something to this idea when Bill Gates jumps into the market conversation. Here are his comments from an internal Microsoft memo titled 'Internet Software Services' dated October 30, 2005.

"The broad and rich foundation of the internet will unleash a "services wave" of applications and experiences available instantly over the internet to millions of users. Advertising has emerged as a powerful new means by which to directly and indirectly fund the creation and delivery of software and services along with subscriptions and license fees. Services designed to scale to tens or hundreds of millions will dramatically change the nature and cost of solutions deliverable to enterprises or small businesses."[25] (all bolding JEB)

OK. That's Microsoft once again preparing to co-opt a potentially disruptive innovation to their Windows franchise. And jumping in with both feet to engage in new market creation.

But even if all the Microsoft hoopla about sponsored application services is simply a no-fly-zone containment move vs. Google, and not an attempt to transform their existing applications business, it still means that Microsoft will begin implementing and evolving the services version of the ubiquity model in ways that allow them to build higher barriers to entry by Google into Microsoft ecoregions.

My reading---the Gates memo on software services is not simply containment or market freezing. It is an early shot across the Google bow that could potentially turn in to a full-blown 'browser wars' category regime change campaign against Google in paid search. After all, while Google is a very strong, very innovative company, and a darling of Wall Street, it is still early in the process of demonstrating that it can drive a defensible market no-fly-zone of its own. But I can't wait to go ringside at that cage fight. Because Google gets asymmetric marketing. And will be a formidable foe in developing marketing countermeasures to resist regime change.

To Maximize CBM, Begin Applying the 'Unorthodox' Model

Unorthodox models are those that cluster around what I have earlier referred to as dotcomplexity advantage. The successful leveraging of a web-based platform that enables customers to *self-organize and spontaneously catalyze value where previously there*

was none. The many-to-many marketplace based on the eBay trading platform is a standout superpower example of the unorthodox model in action. eBay is in fact the poster child for the application of self-organizing systems theory to e-business, i.e. dotcomplexity advantage. It's why eBay's market capitalization continues to be high relative to other internet commerce companies, providing it with public currency for major diversification acquisitions like PayPal and Skype.

How About an 'Unorthodox Model Description Language'

Using eBay, and others, as my reference examples of self-organizing business models, I developed an Unorthodox Model Description Language (UMDL) that I apply in my consulting practice to advise companies seeking to maximize CBM via dotcomplexity-advantaged asymmetric marketing.

I even have a name for this Unorthodox Model Description Language. I call it **'N-glish'**.

In N-glish, the 'N' is my *'how to think asymmetrically'* descriptor. It serves to modify common English words in order to better describe the various levels of CBM that can be achieved in the many-to-many, dotcomplexity-advantaged unorthodox model.

Here's a few examples of **N**-glish terms, and how they describe the various stages of development of CBM in an unorthodox dotcomplexity model:

Stage 1: N-formations---As a result of the asymmetric, many-to-many nature of the eBay platform (the **n**-gine or catalyst), a self-organizing systems market model emerged. I call this self-organized market phenomena an 'n-formation', i.e. a market formation based mainly on '**n**' or network effects that cluster around the **n**-gine.

Stage 2: N-stitutions---As **n**-formations mature and coalesce, a stable, reputation-rich community evolves, i.e. an **n**-stitution. These **n**-stitutions evolve rules, conventions and practices that participants live by, e.g. the banning of the sale of Nazi memorabilia on the eBay website, and or the 'outing' through peer reviews of **n**-stitutional auction participants who don't pay, or sell damaged goods. If you want a non-eBay example, think of an **n**-stitution as the 'Safety Tips' section on social network MySpace.com, designed to protect children against pedophiles in an open, self-organizing n-formation.

Stage 3: N-dublicatability—In order to compete against the barriers inherent in the unorthodox, dotcomplexity-based model, the competing company *must equal or surpass the related network effect at each stage of evolution.* Which in the real world of n-formation-based businesses is a virtual impossibility, no pun intended. In other words, to beat eBay at the eBay game, you would literally have to duplicate the n-formations, the n-stitutions and the other many-to-many, member-driven market effects. Not just have a better auction platform, lower fees, cheaper products on the website, etc. That's why, at a certain stage of maturity of the unorthodox model, the business becomes literally n-duplicatable.

Is My Dotcomplexity or 'N' Metaphor Just Another Way to Say 'Participation Age'?

Is my 'n-glish' metaphor, designed to depict the discrete stages in the development of self-organizing web markets, simply another way to describe the 'participation age' Scott McNealy refers to? No! It is not.

Because all unorthodox models that succeed in catalyzing value where no value previously existed lend themselves to *high levels of market lock-in*. Real n-gines drive n-formations, which lead to n-stitutions, which catalyze n-duplicatable businesses, and a powerful asymmetric advantage. Hey, maybe these business models are not really unorthodox.

Maybe they are simply... 'n-orthodox'.

On the other hand, Mr. McNealy's Participation Age approach criticizes the lock-in agenda entirely. Even attributing it to that dusty old 'information age'. In point of fact, **dotcomplexity advantage makes the notion of 'lock-in' more alive than ever**. It's just that the 'shark-itecture' of the lock-in is *co-created by the n-formation participants*, and triggered by the market platform (the n-gine of n-formation) of the asymmetric marketer.

You can see the n-orthodox model emerging in many places that have been tagged 'Web 2.0'. For example, in the open source community, as well as in many emerging social networking applications like

MySpace, YouTube, Meetup, FaceBook, and others. In fact, anyplace where a web-native, many-to-many network effect can be unleashed, e.g. Match.com in the online dating service segment, LendingTree in loans, CraigsList in classifieds, etc.

But if the n-orthodox model does not successfully mature through each stage (n-gine to n-formation, n-formation to n-stitution, n-stitution to n-duplicatability), then it can and usually does unravel. As did many bubble era startups claiming to harness 'virtual community', or 'participation'.

Cellularity in Unorthodox or n-Orthodox Models

Dotcomplexity and n-glish are derived from what I like to think of as the customer phenomenon of *cellularity*. A characteristic of self-organizing markets that almost seems to be built in to the unorthodox or n-orthodox model. No, I don't mean cellular as in cellular phone.

I mean that in a living, complex adaptive system, like those based on n-orthodox web and open source approaches...The customer *cells* live, the customer cells die, and the customer cells are continuously replaced, in an effort to make the overall body (the business) stronger. The financial analysts often refer to the surface expression of cellularity as 'customer churn'.

Cellularity or 'churn' is a phenomenon also found in biology. Every day, for reasons that are still in many ways a mystery to biologists, certain human cells commit suicide. Some, such as those that have been infected by a virus, kill themselves to preserve the health of the body as a whole. Others self-destruct simply because they sense that a threat to their survival or merely something unfamiliar is lurking nearby. This process, called apoptosis[26], or programmed cell death, is a normal biological occurrence that can promote proper organ development and help to prevent cancer. This is the underlying science that drives how to think about customer barrier management (CBM) for unorthodox or n-orthodox models, in which a high degree of 'customer churn' is normal.

My concept of *cellularity assumes cell death, the natural 'end' of a customer relationship*. Living right alongside cell birth, i.e. the creation of new customers and the re-capture of returning customers. Think of it as 'customer *life* theory' as opposed to 'customer *for life* theory'.

Myth of Lifetime Customer Relationships for n-orthodox Models

With this concept of cellularity as my foundation, the notion of a customer barrier is not the same as the notion of *lifetime customer relationship*. Unless your company is a software superpower with the long-term practice of asymmetric marketing in place, then the 'lifetime' concept probably carries a lot of baggage with it. It implies that your job as a marketing professional at an ISV with an n-orthodox model is to keep and hold the customer at any cost. When this may be a fruitless task.

What one wants from the 'cells' (customers) is to contribute to the overall health of the business organism of which they are a part. In other words, what you really want to focus on is the *effective life of the relationship,* and what is your strategy to manage that effective life, profit from that effective life, and *leverage a temporal "effective life" lock-in to advance to the next stage of market power.*

Your n-orthodox TAO giving rise to the Ten Thousand Things.

What's Up Next?

OK. You've made it this far in the book. And thankfully, you have chosen not to report me to the Society for the Prevention of Cruelty to Geoffrey Moore, Tom Peters, Patricia Seybold, Jonathan Schwartz and Scott McNealy. I appreciate that. I really do. Despite receiving those flame emails of the 'Quit sucking up to Bill Gates and Larry Ellison variety.

So here's where I begin to go out on an asymmetric limb, and take the fact that you've managed to plow through the first 5 chapters to mean the following:

You're right there on the asymmetric edge, still deciding whether or not to toss the chasm, and develop a marketing strategy based on symbiosis with the software superpowers.

But you do see merit in understanding how to successfully navigate the superpower sandstorm, co-opt and leverage the superpower no-fly-zone imperative, and gain market access to their installed base ecoregions.

You'd also like to implement a roadmap for asymmetric products, and design in more than a little shark-itecture of your own. In order to provide yourself with forward revenue visibility in the sandstorm... from your own locked-in customers. And you see value in building your shark-itecture based on continuous innovation on top of superpower platforms. Or through creatively attaching your open source offering to superpower platforms (as did Red Hat).

You want to support your sales team by developing and executing an asymmetric go-to-market strategy that incorporates inverse selling, OEM/powered by selling (like Microsoft and Google), and attachment to superpower-colonized channels.

And you're beginning to get motivated to stubbornly refuse to surrender to customer power, and instead practice customer barrier management (CBM), to defend your hard-won market gains against your competitors.

Well... if that's the case, then here's the one thing you absolutely need to do in order to 'get ready to rumble'. The one thing that will provide you with the consistent *ability to execute these kinds of asymmetric marketing practices*.

You need to foster and grow a *culture of asymmetric marketing* inside your organization.

Chapter 6

ASYMMETRIC MARKETING CULTURE

Perhaps you have already seen memos from me or others here about the importance of the Internet. I have gone through several stages of increasing my views of its importance. Now I assign the internet the highest level of importance. In this memo I want to make clear that our focus on the Internet is critical to every part of our business. The Internet is the most important single development to come along since the IBM PC was introduced in 1981. *Bill Gates, "Internet Tidal Wave". Internal Microsoft Memo, May 26, 1995*[1]

Let's start off this chapter with some good news for ISVs seeking that asymmetric competitive edge. Your *marketing culture* is that special, one-of-a-kind thing that will help you capture a sustainable advantage in this age of the software superpowers. Even better. It's something over which *you have 100% control*.

The not-so-good news. Your marketing culture, if neglected, or based on the toxic, cargo cult values of the bubble, is also the one thing that can set you up for continuous marketing self-sabotage.

In order to avoid marketing self-sabotage, and build a marketing culture that will enable you and your team to implement the kind of asymmetric product, sales, and customer barrier management thinking presented in the first five chapters of this book, it's important to know where to look for your cultural role models. Where to look to *identify best practices in marketing culture management*. And it helps if you have a simple metaphor for how to think about building a culture of asymmetric marketing.

Here's one that works for me. Organizations that foster a culture of asymmetric marketing often resemble *tribes*. And their leaders often play the role of tribal *chieftans*.

Tribal Leadership: What Can ISVs Learn from 'The Internet Tidal Wave' Memo?

Let's get this out of the way right up front. Is the quotation from Bill Gates at the top of this chapter just one more unabashedly shameless attempt on my part to cozy up to Microsoft by paying them one too many compliments in this book? While simultaneously criticizing their historic competitors like Scott McNealy. Hey, between you and me, I'd love to get cozy with Bill Gates now that he's going to become a full-time philanthropist. However, unlike the big Kahuna[2] running China, I'm not expecting a dinner invite to the Gates lake house anytime soon.

But I do know healthy marketing culture when I see it. And the quote I've referenced above, and many others from Gates' now 11-year old internal memo, strike me as being *more relevant than ever to any ISV seeking to win big in the superpower sandstorm*. Seeking to capture an asymmetric marketing advantage in an age of software natural monopolies. I'd further argue that the content of the Gates memo is proof positive that Microsoft, while being a complex, multi-divisional, global corporation (like all superpowers) remains an organization with a historically strong... very strong indeed, tribal culture and tribal leadership model.

This tribal culture has helped to set Microsoft apart. And for that very reason, the Internet Tidal Wave memo can and should serve as instructional material for every asymmetric marketer seeking to rise someday to superpower status. *By unleashing the power that may be lying dormant in their operating culture*.

What is tribal chieftanship? First, let's clear up what it's not.

It's nothing at all like that tribe of primitive islanders described in Richard Feynman's cargo cult science commencement address I refer to at the beginning of this book. *"But hey Joe B, isn't it logical to assume that the blindly imitative cargo cult islanders were organized into a tribe?"* Of course they were. Was it the kind of tribal leadership one can catch a glimpse of by reading the Gates memo? Not in a thousand years.

Tribal chieftanship of the type we get a snapshot of in the Internet Tidal Wave document, is leadership in which one's corporate executives are not simply outstanding managers, but exceptionally strong *contributor/doers* who play a very hands-on, critically indispensable role in actual value creation within the business.

They are able to play this role because, within their own organizational cultures, these tribal leaders have accumulated rich repositories of lead-by-example *reputation equity* (a.k.a. street credibility or street-cred). This street-cred enables them to drive self-correction and rapid response in times of technology change and competitive challenge. When these tribal leaders speak, both the formal and informal cultures of the company listen.

Here I go again, dating myself with the following little rant. The kind of entrepreneurial tribalism I'm talking about used to be the norm during the early waves of innovation and growth in Silicon Valley and other centers of U.S. high tech innovation. But in many ways, we departed from this norm as a cultural operating model during the bubble period. In fact, it wouldn't be a stretch to say we subjected entrepreneurial tribalism to 'creative destruction'.

In the bubble period many leadership teams were not really all that tribal in nature, having been hand-picked by VCs and bankers to take their companies into a rapid IPO environment. The bubble management agenda was often a 'liquidity event' agenda, and did not place a very high premium on the construction of rugged, fiercely competitive tribal cultures capable of enduring and adapting for decades (as have the cultures of Microsoft, Oracle, Adobe, SAP, IBM and others). As a direct result of departing from the kind of tribal leadership model that made our industry great to begin with, this bubble-era liquidity event agenda did more than a little *damage to the culture of software and web entrepreneurism as a whole*. And for that reason I'm going to come down hard on the underlying dysfunctional bubble values in more detail later in the chapter.

Thankfully, today's startup environment appears to be more focused on investing in experienced tribal leaders who possess street-cred, and play a hands-on role in the value creation of their business. This change is directly related to the VC industry experiencing the death spiral of a wide cross-section of portfolio companies in the bubble period. That 'eternal' principle kicked in. No pain, no gain.

And from the standpoint of cultivating a new generation of asymmetric marketers capable of creating the next software superpower...pain is good. Hopefully the memory of that pain might even help prevent 'Bubble 2.0' from happening. But don't bet on it.

With the hype machines for 'Web 2.0', 'the On-demand tectonic shift'[3] and 'Participation Age' startups in 5th gear, and a tech IPO market that hasn't seen much action in 5 years outside of Google and Salesforce. com, thinking we will not see some form of Bubble 2.0 is probably just wishful thinking on my part. That's why understanding tribal culture and tribal leadership is more relevant than ever for ISVs that want to win. And keep winning, in the age of the software superpowers. Not end up as digital road kill in the new, new, new, new bubble.

Tribal Leadership: "You Are the Message"
Tribal leadership, as a role within software and web companies, has historically been the function of a founder, co-founders, or turnaround leaders, who carry not just the institutional memory, but the market mythology and actual *values* of the company. As a result of having helped create or re-create (in the case of IBM's Gerstner) tribal values and mythology, tribal leaders are more able than others to inspire higher levels of performance throughout the organization.

Tribal leaders don't just craft a message. *They **are** the message,* to paraphrase the title of a book by Roger Ailes[4], CEO of the Fox News Network, and former presidential speechwriter for Ronald Reagan. *('Oh my God, this guy doesn't just admire those predatory pirates up at Microsoft. Now we find out he digs Roger Ailes and the Fox News network. I knew there was something fishy about a guy who references asymmetric warfare theory and American army generals in a business book.')* I throw myself on the mercy of the marketing court your honor.

But seriously folks, the relevant point here (despite the fact that I am a card-carrying, out-of-the-closet panderer to that vast right wing conspiracy run by Rupert Murdoch) is that tribal leaders lead, not just through management mandates. But through a combination of ***example, creative thought leadership and internal evangelism.*** They become the message.

That's why, as one of the software industry's pioneering asymmetric marketers, I see Microsoft as a role model for other ISVs. A role model in how to create and systematically foster a tribal culture of *self-correction and rapid response to both competitive threats and emerging opportunities*. Exactly the cultural skills ISVs need to master in the age of the superpowers.

By any measure, the Microsoft journey to superpower status is a compelling testament to what a startup ISV can accomplish with a *strong tribal culture and tribal leadership model applied to an asymmetric marketing strategy*. So using a few more timeless excerpts from the Gates *Internal Tidal Wave* memo as my course material, let's get started on our cultural journey by taking a quick look at the evidence. That tribal leadership helps facilitate asymmetric marketing strategy and execution.

Competitive Sobriety: The Tribal Chieftan Can and Does Change His Mind

For my money there was one, and only one, blockbuster benefit to software marketers that came out of the DOJ's anti-trust actions against Microsoft. It was the declassification and public availability of the *Internet Tidal Wave* memo.

For those willing to temporarily put aside their *'Bill Gates is the software anti-Christ'* mentality, and take the time to look at its content with fresh eyes, the memo provides amazing insight into the thinking of an asymmetric marketing pioneer. While shedding light on the critical elements of a culture of asymmetric marketing. First and foremost is the memo's remarkable *sobriety* in relation to Microsoft's competitive strategy for the web.

In the memo, Gates confesses to having gone through *'several stages of increasing my view of it's (the internet's) importance'*. In other words, Gates admits to his tribe in real time that its *tribal chieftan was changing his mind*. And not just about small things. But about the entire strategic direction of Microsoft's business in relation to the internet build-out and emerging web competitors of the mid-90's. And if the company Gates co-founded was going to keep being successful in its core and new businesses, his tribe needed to know exactly, and specifically, just how much their chieftan was changing his mind.

To set up the points he wants to impress upon his tribe, Gates even goes so far as to say that the internet was even more important than the arrival of the *'GUI'*[6]. This from a man who made a fortune on the GUI, and leveraged the GUI to dislodge IBM from the standard it had created. That's certainly a not very shy way for a tribal chieftan to grab the attention of his team. Tell them you've found an even more significant business than the one that enabled you to unseat Lotus, WordPerfect, and Novell and begin your rise to superpower status.

In the memo, Gates engages in what strikes me as an unabashedly sober and humbling act of competitive assessment, commenting that *'Browsing the web (circa 1995) you find **almost no Microsoft file formats'**[7]*. Translation: Hey guys we're missing the boat! He then drills down into the competitive meat of the matter. He points out that Netscape (then the category-definer in internet browsers, possessing overwhelming market share leadership) is *'pursuing a multi-platform strategy where they move the key API into the client **to commoditize the underlying operating system.'**[8]

Aha moment. Here's the tribal call to action for the soon-to-commence 90's browser wars against Netscape. Because commoditization (especially if you're the one being commoditized) is not just a marketing no-no. It is the kiss of death for an asymmetric marketer focused on customer barrier management.

Gates soberly perceived the competitive opportunity that the web presented to companies like Sun, Netscape and others to potentially marginalize Microsoft products. So he rallies his tribe not to stand still for it. Not to rest on their laurels. Not to wallow in the glow of past market victories. Not to become intoxicated by prior successes.

He even underscores the *'scary possibility'*[9] that some day there would be a scenario in which there were devices *'far less expensive that a PC which is powerful enough for web browsing.'*[10] In a culture of asymmetric marketing, the ***first steps of sober competitive assessment*** often take the form of ***getting out of denial by acknowledging any asymmetric market power held by competitors.*** Gates doesn't sugarcoat it, and he doesn't stop there. As the memo continues, one can see the second key attribute of the tribal culture of asymmetric marketing---the importance of ***getting real.***

Getting Real: Praise & Respect for Competitor Best Practices

A culture of asymmetric marketing acknowledges best practices no matter where they come from. Or whom they come from. Including your competitors. It's something akin to the post-game ritual that an NFL head coach goes through every Monday morning. He, his staff, and the team, reviews the game-day film, studying both the good and bad plays that were made on both sides of the ball. By his team and the opponent.

In the *Internet Tidal Wave* memo, Gates candidly compliments[11] Yahoo, Adobe, Apple, Sun, Lotus, Netscape and others, stating that these competitors were doing some things better than Microsoft. In particular, Gates praises them for investing in and leveraging their corporate websites to drive marketing communications, software downloads and tighter customer relationships. And Gates continues to 'get real' by acknowledging other asymmetric marketers and emerging natural monopolies when he sees them.

In referring to Adobe, and its Acrobat technology, Gates acknowledges the role of path-dependent, increasing returns. And its ultimate asymmetric effect of creating a natural monopoly player in the software industry. He writes, *'Once a format gets established, it is extremely difficult for another format to come along and even become equally popular'*.[12] In short, Adobe's free Acrobat Reader grooves in, and it's a whole new ball game for everybody eyeing that space.

The implication is clear. There is no foolproof strategy for an asymmetric marketer except to pre-empt one's competitor *before* they activate a market lock-in, and become established as a de facto standard. The corollary is also clear. Software category regime change happens, but against other asymmetric marketers it's tough, even for Microsoft. The cultural lesson... ***Getting real is all about complete internal candor and nothing but complete candor***. Even if it means that your tribal chieftan temporarily appears to eat crow in front of his tribe, by acknowledging the market power of others.

Empower Team Self-Organizing: 'Go Overboard'

In his *'Next Steps'* section of the memo, Gates points out that he was *'not alone'*[13] inside Microsoft in stressing the importance of the web, and references others inside Microsoft who did focus on its critical importance---Thereby empowering them to keep doing what they were doing. By acknowledging those who exhibited *stick-to-it-iveness* in pointing out the potential vulnerability of the company in the face of its web competitors, Gates as tribal chieftan was laying a foundation for an even more rugged culture of continuing asymmetric marketing innovation at Microsoft. One expression of this---he urged his product teams to *'go overboard'*[14] on web features. As we now know...........they appear to have done exactly that.

Despite the fact that this internal Microsoft document is more than a decade old, and has been declassified and available to the ISV community for years, tribal leadership of the *Internet Tidal Wave* variety has not been embraced by software executives in the period before, during and after the bubble.

One telling symptom of this lack of the study of best practices in marketing culture is the ongoing fragmentation of the marketing, sales and partner leadership functions at many publicly traded and private tech companies. This fragmentation has been relatively pervasive. So much so that when surveyed by the *Always-On Network* almost 4 full years after the bubble burst, only 6% of online poll respondents indicated that their company actually had a true Chief Marketing Officer (CMO) role[15]. So why pay attention to the arguably unscientific results of a snap web poll like this? Because at that stage of development of our industry, the number should have been closer to 95%. Why? Because the CMO role is essentially a tribal leadership role, one that is responsible for integrating the full spectrum of all sales and marketing functions across the whole marketing tribe.

Without this tribal role in place a gap between strategy and execution is often the norm. So how does this gap between strategy and execution play out?

It's a Case of 'Big Hat, No Cattle' Syndrome

In my day-to-day work, I regularly witness the negative consequences of the absence of a tribal leadership approach. It's almost the norm to encounter ISV sales and marketing leadership that want to enthusiastically discuss and capitalize upon a perceived market gap, while remaining deafeningly silent about the *ever-widening execution gap* inside their own organizations. A colleague from Texas has a great way to describe this. He calls it ***'Big Hat, No Cattle' Syndrome.***

Grandiose talk about market opportunity and strategy (the Big Hat part). Anemic marketing execution in the sandstorm (the No Cattle part).

Big Hat, No Cattle Syndrome manifests itself in lots of different ways. One new symptom can be seen in the behavior of those who choose to echo the 'Participation Age' ideology I criticized in Chapter 5. They seek to create customer 'communities', and hold market 'conversations', without *creating and empowering internal marketing communities, and holding the candid, get-real internal conversations* that always precede effective market conversation.

Many of these same executives correctly advocate collaborating across enterprise boundaries with partners and customers. But appear to be clueless about collaborating across departmental boundaries with each other.

They launch promotional programs to reward the customer for buying. But don't know how to reward the whole organization for selling. ISVs plagued with Big Hat, No Cattle Syndrome, despite seeing value in asymmetric marketing strategy, are simply not culturally prepared for asymmetric marketing warfare in the superpower sandstorm.

To recover from Big Hat, No Cattle Syndrome, to lay the foundation to win in the age of the software superpowers, today's ISVs need to begin embracing the kind of tribal leadership model, and its underlying values, highlighted above in my commentary on the *Internet Tidal Wave* memo. And for startups it's probably not even an option. For them, having a tribal leadership approach has become an operational necessity. As more than a few ISVs are compelled to bootstrap or customer-fund their businesses in the absence of the easy venture capital of the bubble years.

I see this as a healthy trend for the software industry as a whole. A trend that may ultimately produce a new crop of potential superpowers and asymmetric marketing warriors. Marketing warriors that are *culturally rugged and able to turn on a dime* to capitalize on any new opportunities presented by the no-fly-zone imperative of the superpowers.

Culture is also a domain where asymmetric marketers can learn a lot from asymmetric warfare strategists. In fact, what students of asymmetric warfare can teach students of asymmetric marketing about Big Hat, No Cattle Syndrome is this!

A healthy operating culture and its underlying values have for centuries been a critical foundation for any winning strategy.

It was none other than Sun Tzu who suggested that *'the Way'* (the Taoist philosophy and values of his day) was the foundation for the victories of the 'wise generals' who followed his "art of war".

So in 2006, what would be a comparable 'ISV Way'? *How about the core process values of traditional bootstrapped or 'garage' entrepreneurism.* As distinct from the intoxicated cargo cult cultures of the bubbleboys. I'd submit that this rugged 'garage' legacy constitutes the *way,* or positive cultural heritage, for the challenges ISVs face in overcoming Big Hat, No Cattle Syndrome, and winning in the superpower sandstorm. So for the remainder of this chapter I'm going to expand upon my discussion of tribal leadership and tribal culture. And go deeper into what I see as the *constituent components of that 'way', describing in detail the underlying tribal values of asymmetric marketing culture.*

But writing makes me hungry. So let's eat.

My Over-Cooked Rubber Chicken Epiphany
I call it my over-cooked rubber chicken epiphany. That seemingly insignificant synchronicity that got me focused on investigating the underlying building blocks of asymmetric marketing culture. And the importance of marketing organizations migrating to a more tribal, *values-driven* approach to marketing strategy and execution. It happened like this.

About one month after the 9.11 terrorist attacks, I was, like many Americans, defiantly eager to get back into more friendly skies, despite the long security lines. As I was sitting in a business class seat on my favorite airline, the flight attendant delivered the meal service...You know, the decent meal you get when you are lucky enough to lock in one of those precious upgrades to business class. Not the meal you buy in a box for 5 bucks.

As I looked down at the tray, I glanced at the airline rubber chicken I had been served (in my attempt to be a good Atkins diet fan). Then I saw *it*. That totally out-of-context, post-9.11 plastic airline knife sitting next to the stainless steel fork and spoon.

I thought to myself, plastic knives—One more new post-9.11 airline reality. But OK, I know I can do this. I can cut this dense, over-cooked rubber airline chicken with this little plastic airline knife. Chop, chop, chop, nothing. I dented it a little, cursed Bin Laden under my breath, and wished I had ordered the high-carb, non-Atkins ravioli, as had the guy in the next seat. Frustrated, hungry, and without an ounce of pride, I improvised. I picked up the chicken in my hands gaining a clear but unorthodox asymmetric advantage over my hunger. Trust me when I say that eating chicken in your hands is not generally perceived to be business class behavior, and I saw a few passengers in the cabin cringe as I did it.

While I ate the chicken with my hands, red-faced in my business class shame, I thought about the turnaround assignment I was on at that time. It suddenly occurred to me that the cargo cult marketing culture of my ISV client was a lot like that little plastic out-of-context airline knife trying to cut through the tough, intractable rubber chicken of the superpowers' locked-in customer ecoregions. A little denting, a little splatter on the shirt, a lot of regret about the ravioli, but very little protein gets consumed, unless you get your hands dirty, unless you approach things in an unconventional way.

Rubber chicken epiphany translation. For ISV marketers trying to survive and thrive in the age of the software superpowers, the first asymmetry a marketing organization needs to leverage is the asymmetry of tribal will, of organizational values, of operating culture. And to do that, you need to be prepared to *'go back to the 80's' to transform your 'business class' values into more unconventional, bootstrapped, 'coach class', tribal, garage*[16] *values*. So let' define and describe those values.

Kernel Values Drive Tribal Culture: Let's Call It 'Marketing by Garage Values' (MBGV)

At the end of the day, a tribal marketing culture of the kind you see in the *Internet Tidal Wave* memo is all about **values-driven culture**. What do I mean by values-driven culture? When I use the terms values, I am *not* referring to the often lofty, always politically correct, chronically abstract Corporate Values statements (e.g. We Believe in Innovation, We Believe in Standards, We Serve the Community) you often see pinned to cafeteria walls up and down the Silicon Valley. Rugged, self-correcting marketing cultures of the Internet Tidal Wave type are not primarily the direct expression of these kinds of 'values' statements.

And I'm also not talking about the kind of corporate culture the supermarket magazines want to focus on in their 'Life in the Googleplex' stories[17]—All about the lava lamps, free gourmet lunches, and the massages. Very 'Bay Area', yes—but not what I mean in this case by culture or values. I'm talking about something I describe as *kernel values* (as distinct from higher order values like 'innovation', 'customer satisfaction', 'leadership', etc). But why distinguish between 'values' of various types?

In the face of the marketing challenges confronting ISVs in this age of the superpowers—— a go-to-market background of sandstorm-limited revenue visibility, broken organizational machinery, positional confusion and investor heat—A kernel-values-based orientation (call it Marketing-by-Garage Values or MBGV) can work to spontaneously and continuously transform your culture and drive healthy execution. While traditional MBO (management by objectives) or MBI (management by instruction) often has the unintended consequence of band-aiding over broken cultural machinery. Enabling internal cargo cults to flourish. Fostering Big Hat, No Cattle Syndrome.

If we take as our 'laboratory sample' the kind of tribal, asymmetric marketing culture I cited above, i.e. the Internet Tidal Wave experience at Microsoft, I've isolated *4 basic underlying kernel values that appear to be organically embedded in tribal marketing cultures that outperform in the software industry*. I see these kernel values as the basic components or *tribal process building blocks of a Marketing-by-Garage Values (MBGV) approach*. They are:

Kernel One-Operational Sobriety: No. I don't mean abstinence from alcohol. I mean sobriety as in a non-dysfunctional approach to the challenge of marketing strategy and execution in the sandstorm. Why raise the issue of cultural sobriety in marketing organizations beyond my earlier reference to Bill Gates 'sober' assessment in the Internet Tidal Wave Memo? Because the intoxicated cargo cult legacy of the bubble, not traditional garage, or bootstrapped entrepreneurism, is in many ways still the dominant culture inside many ISV marketing organizations. But how can that be? That was then. This is now.

Call me crazy, but my own day-to-day working analysis of the effects of the tech bubble, five plus years after it burst, proceeds from the viewpoint that the bubble was essentially not a financial markets event.

The bubble was mainly a cultural event. The largest epidemic of mass gambling addiction and dysfunctional business behavior in modern tech industry history. Those who participated in it know that the bubble was all about non-sober and non-self-sufficient marketing cultures. Capital-intoxicated marketing cost structures. And 'WebVans' full of other dysfunctional behaviors that were in fact 'radical' departures from the values of traditional garage entrepreneurism.

Against this kind of historical background, operational sobriety must of necessity be the first critical kernel value to embed in a tribal marketing culture. It helps to not only drive effective (sober) competitive assessment (the Gates example I referenced), but is the general foundation for a non-bubble, non-intoxicated execution approach. I'll expand on marketing 'sobriety' later in the chapter.

Kernel Two-'Get Real' Candor: The second kernel values component of an MBV-based tribe is what I call the 'get real' or candor component. In the *get real culture* of asymmetric marketing, you don't shoot the messenger for internally discussing your company's competitive vulnerability. You don't silence your troops for that big idea that may be just a little outside the cultural box. You don't send them to an organizational gulag for pointing out that there may be a gigantic gap between strategy and execution in your marketing organization.

Rather, *in an MBGV-driven organization that seeks asymmetric marketing dominance, you reward him or her for getting real.*

Getting real, like all of asymmetric marketing, goes to the issue I've raised throughout this book— The issue of *how* to think, not simply *what* to think. Much of conventional MBO-driven marketing culture has been about *what* to think. "Are we systematically following the chasm TALC model, and engaging in disruptive technology innovation?"

On the other hand, unconventional or asymmetric marketing culture is about *how* to think. "What can we do to effectively prepare for marketing warfare in the superpower sandstorm, an age of natural monopolies? Are we systematically studying and applying the best practices of the software superpowers? Are we analyzing their no-fly-zone behaviors, their cage-fighting prowess... and using those behaviors and that prowess as our 'marketing GPS' in the sandstorm?"

Marketing cultures that focus on how to think vs. what to think tend to foster the emergence of high reliability 'marketing armies of one', i.e. responsible, experienced, hands-on tribal warriors who can execute effectively. Even in a 'no-huddle offense' environment. Those marketing armies of one were the folks Bill Gates was praising in his *Internet Tidal Wave* memo for having persisted in keeping Microsoft's pre-1995 web competitive deficit in his face. *Before he changed his mind.*

Kernel Three---Self-Organizing: Culture possesses the potential to become what people in the military call a 'force multiplier'. A *cultural force multiplier is created when your kernel values drive individuals to 'swarm' on a problem*, as the folks at Microsoft did after the Internet Tidal Wave memo.

In many ways, conventional organizational structures like sales, marketing, partner development, etc. are like having discrete, stove-piped armies, navies and air forces. And stove-piped structures rarely catalyze force multiplier, tribal organizations. And for this reason, are insufficient for the marketing challenges of the superpower sandstorm.

By contrast, modern asymmetric warfare often relies on multi-disciplinary, special operations teams (Rangers, SEALS, Delta Force, etc.) that are empowered to 'self-organize' around a mission. While also practicing 'joint war fighting', in concert with the conventional military organizational structure.

Similarly, marketing and sales organizations can foster the emergence of tribal leadership, enable dynamic team building, cross-stovepipe collaboration, and higher levels of organizational agility in demanding and uncertain market environments if their kernel values empower self-organizing. Self-organizing means 'swarming' 'mobbing' or 'concentrating superior force' on sales and marketing problems by *first mobilizing the markets inside your company*. In Gates' message to his troops, the self-organizing kernel was evident when he stated unequivocally that he wanted all product teams to 'go overboard' on internet features.

Kernel Four---Ownership: In healthy marketing cultures, positive execution momentum is palpable. You can feel it in the air and it seems to be owned by everybody. One thing all marketing professionals can agree on is that market momentum is definitely not created, and shared tribal ownership is not in place, when sales leads fall through the cracks, or confusion as to what constitutes a qualified prospect is the general state of your sales and marketing culture. As the Accenture study I referenced in Chapter 4 uncovered. Your marketing culture will grow healthier if what you *measure and compensate* reinforces *shared tribal 'ownership' behaviors and kernel values* that drive positive momentum in the sandstorm.

And a culture of shared ownership in an MBGV (marketing by garage values) orientation may need to be rewarded differently than traditional MBO-driven sales rep quota-defined cultures. It will also need conscious board support to succeed, especially in an era where incentive stock option programs are changing at many companies. Shared ownership reward systems work to dynamically reinforce the 'sobriety', 'get real' and 'self-organizing' kernel values you want to embed in your MBGV-driven marketing organization. They become the glue in the complex adaptive system that is your company.

How Do We Embed this MBGV Appoach? Tribal 'Attractors' & Culture Management Systems (CMS)

The plain truth is that differentiation based on culture and values has always served as a key attractor for corporations, politicians and media personalities. Bill Clinton playing his sax on MTV is one kind of political cultural attractor. George W. Bush landing a plane on the deck of an aircraft carrier is another kind of political cultural attractor. CNN's Larry King pitching softball questions to friendly Hollywood guests is one kind of media cultural attractor. Fox News' Bill O'Reilly confronting hostile guests in a 'no spin zone' is another kind of media cultural attractor. A well-funded Napster (not the new one, the original) seeking to overthrow the music industry is one kind of marketing cultural attractor. Akamai refusing (in the immediate aftermath of 9.11) to provide services[18] to the Al Jazeera network, perceived by many as a pro-terror propaganda machine, is another kind of cultural attractor. Akamai founder and CTO Danny Lewin, a passenger on the American Airlines flight that hit the World Trade Center, was a victim of Al Qaeda terrorists on September 11th, 2001. So Akamai, in this instance with Al Jazeera, chose to reject political neutrality in its customer marketing approach.

As I pointed out earlier in the book, modern complexity science (as distinct from 'Darwinism') is one of the key theoretical foundations of asymmetric marketing. Complexity theory is a way to understand not just powerful web self-organizing market processes, like the unstoppable momentum of the many-to-many eBay trading community. It's also a way to think about how kernel values get embedded into an organization. One of the more relevant ideas in complexity theory for MBGV-driven marketing tribes is the concept of 'attractors'.

From the standpoint of fostering a high-performance tribal culture, ***attractors are those seemingly invisible rituals*** (the Friday night beer bash), shared company artifacts (the departmental message board or blog), and day-to-day tribal mythmaking (the Bill Gates home page on Microsoft.com), ***that serve to spontaneously catalyze cultural order and facilitate self-organized tribal execution***.

And since only a few ISVs have a multi-decade operating history like Microsoft, what you want to do in the beginning is systematically create and cultivate attractors inside your organization. One short cut I've seen work, is to use a combination of bottoms-up technologies like weblogs, message boards, social networking software and other collaborative applications, closely combined with the ritual of continuous cultural self-assessment. I'll get into this more in a moment.

In any case, I'm definitely not alone in seeing kernel values as important drivers of market success. In their popular book, *'Execution, The Discipline of Getting Things Done'*, authors Larry Bossidy and Ram Charan make the following point:

> *"Most efforts at cultural change fail because they are not linked to improving the business' outcomes. The **ideas and tools of cultural change are fuzzy and disconnected from strategic and operational realities** (JEB emphasis). To change a business' culture, you need a set of processes---**social operating***

mechanisms (JEB emphasis)---that will change the beliefs and behavior of people in ways that are directly linked to bottom-line results."[19]

Let me build on this by suggesting that Bossidy and Charan's valuable concept of social operating mechanisms can be further crystallized to take the form of tangible *culture management systems (CMS)*. These culture management systems will serve as a kind of asymmetric marketing OS, designed to embed and reinforce tribal, kernel values one day at a time. (Quick note to my readers: Culture management systems are not the same thing as an EMM or Enterprise Marketing Management system that augments your SFA or CRM system. EMM is great, and it can be that much more effective if your culture is mobilized via a CMS.)

But before describing a CMS in more detail, let me stay for one more moment on this subject of attractors.

The 'No Huddle Offense', the 'Chow Hound' & Other Attractors

Tribal attractors need to be not only tangible---they need to be downright *sticky,* and *tied directly to emotional reality*. This is what will give tribal cultural attractors the power to drive self-organized marketing execution. Here's an example.

As I write these words, I am wearing a rugby shirt with the slogan *No Huddle Offense*. The shirt was a gift from a client, a CMO working to turn around an ISV facing asymmetric market attacks from a much larger competitor. The shirt became a highly visible, cultural artifact that allowed his team, as well as the rest of the company, to embrace the concept of a dynamic, self-organizing marketing tribe. A tribe that can *deal with competitive threat and uncertainty as the norm*. To this particular CMO and his team, the shirt was an organizational attractor. It said "The superpower no-fly-zone imperative is our marketing GPS. To stay one step ahead, we need to think 'no huddle offense'". That's what the shirt meant to those who wore it. Which brings me to some personal history.

My earliest experience with the power of cultural artifacts (like the no-huddle-offense shirt) as 'internal market attractors' came from my father. A guy who has never believed in life inside a safe, secure, germ-free plastic bubble. My dad is not one of those guys fortunate enough to graduate from an Ivy League b-school, or any university for that matter. Instead he chose to drop out of North Catholic High School in Philadelphia at the age of 17 to enlist in the Army Air Corps during World War II. Why? Because like most of the other kids in his neighborhood, he thought it was important to lay a little asymmetric justice on the Nazis.

In Jimmy Doolittle's 8th Air Force, he served as a top turret gunner on a B17 bomber, the *Chow Hound*[20] (painted on its side was a picture of Walt Disney's Pluto character, Mickey Mouse's dog). As a member of the crew of the Chow Hound, he flew 30 combat missions over Germany, including the very first allied raid on Berlin itself. Through his simple storytelling and mythmaking of those days, my father imprinted on me his cultural heritage. A heritage of what life can be like in times of quantum uncertainty, e.g. WW2.

The cultural artifacts displayed at home, pictures of the Chow Hound and it's crew...the grainy, black and white photo of a young, straight-backed GI saluting fierce-eyed as the Distinguished Flying Cross was pinned to his chest...the toy models of American war planes (and the enemy planes that were shot down)...All these became components of the 'culture management system' of our family. These artifacts served as effective attractors catalyzing the internal 'market' within the family that pulled me, organically and over time, into my father's culture.

And there were regular rituals as well. I remember being the only 10 year old on the block who could sing the Air Force Anthem, *Wild Blue Yonder*[21], on key. Always remembering to keep in mind that the right ending (according to my dad's culture) was 'Nothing can stop *the Army Air Corps*', the only 'legitimate' name of the U.S Air Force for those who had experienced it's 'startup' culture during WW2.

Like the kernel values I absorbed from my father, the 4 components of an asymmetric marketing culture are not embedded overnight, or imposed on a marketing organization with top-down management mandate or HR guideline. *Asymmetric marketing culture is catalyzed by similar kinds of 'Chow Hound' attractors, i.e. symbols, rituals, artifacts and social software-enabled tribal interaction* that can serve to provide your marketing team with the equivalent of a 'B17 flying fortress' of cultural stability in the chaos of everyday marketing warfare.

For this reason, asymmetric marketing organizations don't need more abstract, cafeteria-wall cultural values statements.

They need 'sticky' artifacts, regular rituals, market mythmaking, and internal systems that foster a marketing culture of execution.

Modules of a CMS (Culture Management System)

'OK Joe B. I want to learn more about MBGV (management by garage values) and these 4 kernel values of asymmetric marketing culture. And I get the whole 'No Huddle Offense' and 'Chow Hound' things. But what the hell do you mean by an asymmetric marketing 'culture management system' (CMS) if you're not talking about EMM systems?' Glad you asked.

Think of a CMS as a set of knowledge and social software-enabled tribal attractors that serve to progressively embed the garage kernel values described above (sobriety, candor, self-organizing, ownership) into your organization one day at a time.

Remember---The basic goal of your CMS is to shine a big, bright flashlight on Big Hat, No Cattle syndrome, and focus tribal attention on those least common denominator kernel values that are the foundation values needed to systematically create an *asymmetry of execution will*. In keeping with this, a culture management system (CMS) should include 4 basic modules as follows:

- Culture Self-Assessment
- Internal Tribal Weblogs
- Cross-Stovepipe Social Networking
- Ownership Management

So let's get into them one at a time.

CMS Module 1: Culture Self-Assessment---Identify the Symptoms of Big Hat, No Cattle Syndrome

Conducting periodic culture assessments is the first step to systematically uncovering a Big Hat, No Cattle culture gap---The gap between strategy and execution in your organization. Your initial (or zero-day) assessment should provide you with a working execution snapshot of your entire marketing tribe, including sales, product marketing, partner development, marcom, etc., exposing both the *formal and informal* operating cultures that are driving marketing behavior.

For example, in a zero-day assessment, you may want to ask the following kinds of questions:

- What are our kernel values? Do we place value on competitive and operational sobriety, candor, self-organizing, and tribal ownership? Or is our operating culture politically correct, ass-covering, fearful of speaking out, risk-averse, and stovepiped?

- Do we see the bubble as primarily a financial markets event, or as evidence of the 'creative destruction' of entrepreneurial culture in the software industry? Do we place value on the traditional approach of garage entrepreneurial self-sufficiency?

- Does our operating culture really acknowledge the competitive realities facing ISVs in an age of software natural monopolies? Or, Are we happy to remain in denial, and keep our fingers crossed, hoping to get swept up in the next category 'tornado'?

- As a culture, do we place more emphasis on what to think or 'how to think'?

- Do we embrace tribal leadership on the model of the Internet Tidal Wave memo, or not?

These are a few examples to get you started. What's important in your zero-day, or first culture assessment, is to look at the main underlying assumptions driving your marketing activity. And it's absolutely critical not to sweep the past under the rug in the name of marketing optimism. False optimism, a common character defect of many sales and marketing professionals brought up on the *'power of positive thinking'*, can become the invisible enemy of asymmetric marketers. What you want to do is identify each and every symptom of cargo cult marketing you can, and then tie it back into any Big Hat, No Cattle execution behaviors.

It's also critical to look at the role of dysfunctional industry culture, i.e. bubble-culture, in fostering what I call the *3Ds*, i.e. ***dependence, denial and desperation*** in the perpetuation of non-sober marketing and sales activities. Your first culture self-assessment, when completed and published for open discussion on your internal marketing weblog (a critical starting point and key attractor of any culture management system), will jumpstart the process of embedding the garage kernel values of operational and competitive sobriety. So what's the next CMS component?

CMS Module 2: Getting Real---Fostering Creative Conflict on Your Internal Weblog

To lay the foundation to 'go overboard' (Gates term in the Internet Tidal Wave) in your target market, the *whole marketing community inside your company must be mobilized to participate in everyday get-real dialog, and healthy creative conflict*.

But for more than a few ISVs, the marketing community, or tribe, is not really a *community* at all. Being locked up in functional stovepipes or silos (sales, product marketing, channel marketing, field marketing, alliance development), where it is often difficult to get real, or activate creative conflict, because of the political allegiances inside each silo. So what's the fix?

In addition to your self-assessment, your CMS needs to incorporate *technologies that can help propagate candor*, e.g. employee weblogs, team discussion boards and other collaborative intranet applications, thereby creating a persistent tribal artifact, or digital attractor, where the best ideas *and the best tribal reputations* in the company can emerge.

Internal weblogs can also help to overcome the frequently negative cultural effects of email as a weapon of toxic corporate shunning. Or as a means of building divisive factions within the informal culture of the company. I have seen more good ideas killed by flame email than by any other means. And you can always tell who the most candid folks in the tribe are. They're the ones who get mysteriously 'dropped' from an email distribution list right before it goes 'toxic'.

What you want from your internal weblogs, discussion boards, and other collaborative intranet apps, is to make *creative conflict the norm,* not the exception.

In other words, when you publish your own version of the *Internet Tidal Wave* memo to foster cultural transformation at your company, make sure it's posted for comment by the whole marketing tribe. And that the whole tribe can help embed the kernel values of candor, and getting real, in order to chip away at Big Hat, No Cattle behaviors.

CMS Module 3: Internal Social Networks: To foster a self-organizing, collaborative environment, you need to build internal social networks. With functionality like MySpace---Only for the internal use of your marketing organization. Internal social networks can enable self-organized teams to create marketing dress rehearsals. Or what I call *marketing war games*, i.e. collaborative, pre-launch or pre-campaign rituals that test-market and *shake out your products and programs internally*. This helps to get as many folks as possible on the same page, surfacing objections, probing competitive vulnerabilities, and showcasing the really good ideas that may be locked up inside departmental silos.

Enabling internal social networks is a powerful way to prepare the whole marketing team for external market warfare while unifying your tribal culture. In the regular social networking rituals of the pre-launch or pre-campaign process, people will learn how to think, not just what to think. And they come to feel that their fingerprints are on the offering or program being launched. This produces more marketing team members who collectively and collaboratively are prepared to *own the revenue goals of the company*.

With internal social networks, it also becomes easier to self-organize to address the challenges of the superpower sandstorm (the no huddle offense). And even introduce new 'special ops' marketing functions that bridge departmental silos, and serve as attractors for new ideas and initiatives.

CMS Module 4: Ownership Management: Big Hat, No Cattle Syndrome often rears its ugly head in the absence of tangible (and intangible) compensation models that appropriately reward marketing tribalism. Within the context of a culture management system, it's critical not just to reward the rolodex warriors in the sales department, but also to *disproportionately reward* those members of your marketing tribe responsible for creating momentum in the areas of asymmetric product marketing and customer barrier management. Over time, this approach is markedly different than reinforcing and rewarding the traditional ownership roles within the discrete silos of your company. It's about rewarding cross-silo execution. It's about rewarding the eradication of Big Hat, No Cattle Syndrome. It's about rewarding asymmetric marketing.

Next generation EIM (enterprise incentive management) technologies, and a sense of what I call 'higher mission', can also be incorporated into this component of your CMS. What you want to do is to build tribal incentive programs that *reinforce shared ownership, as well as the day-to-day expression of the kernel values of sobriety, candor and self-organizing.*

So that's a compressed introduction to the 4 basic modules of a CMS. For the remainder of the chapter, I'm going to go into more detail on the 4 underlying kernel values of an asymmetric marketing (MBGV) culture, and also expand on this notion of Culture Management Systems. So stay with me, because this tribal cultural model I'm advocating will provide you with the organizational foundation to carry out asymmetric marketing warfare in the superpower sandstorm.

Marketing Sobriety: Recovering from the Creative Destruction of Garage Culture

When I take the position that *sobriety is a necessary values component of an asymmetric marketing culture*, am I talking about outlawing the Friday night beer (or espresso) bash? Absolutely not. I'm talking about something else. I'm talking about *systematically recovering from the negative consequences of the cargo cult marketing culture of the bubble*. I'm talking about keeping you out of the death spiral.

In fact, anytime you want make culture a competitive advantage, it helps to begin by making your own candid assessment of the *culture of the industry in which you compete*. If you begin from this perspective, you will inevitably conclude that many ISVs (despite having elaborate HR programs tied to MBO and MBI) already operate in what I call a MBGV or marketing-by- garage values 'default mode'. What do I mean by that? Simple. When tough and uncertain times arrive in the superpower sandstorm, folks tend to *revert to their core process or kernel values*. The question is: Do folks speak out candidly, focus on what's real, and succeed in the face of a marketing challenge? Or stay silent, cash one's check, and protect one's posterior.

During the bubble (and well into its aftermath), the default values mode of an entire generation of marketing professionals was anything but sober. In fact, the default values mode often got them *marketing drunk and capital dependent.* How? Through actively participating in a web-of-wealth-entitlement that hooked large parts of the software industry in the United States (and elsewhere).

The Bubble & the Web of Wealth Entitlement

What do I mean by the phrase 'web of wealth entitlement'? Let me use modern addiction treatment theory as a guide to explain this concept. Why addiction theory? If you study the decades-long experience of the U.S. treatment industry in helping addicts, you will find that all addicts (drug, alcohol, gambling, food, shopping etc.) tend to believe they are 'entitled' to their fix, i.e. their drug or addiction of choice. In the case of the bubble, many 'IPO addicts' felt they were entitled to major financial returns simply for participating in the 'new economy land grab' (both real and imagined). Let's look briefly at the co-addictive roles played by the key parties to this web of wealth entitlement.

First there were the entrepreneurs themselves—Many of whom (as we now know) should have never been funded or gone public to begin with. Having been funded, many grew comfortably *dependent on invested capital* to support their ongoing market existence, as they functioned in an atmosphere of speculative business models and spurious economic theory, re-spun 'on demand' to gain new funding. This is why I often return to the metaphor of the 'bubbleboy', who lived in a protected cocoon, and could not survive in the real world.

This atmosphere of *capital entitlement is the exact opposite of bootstrapped garage entrepreneurism, the healthy tribal cultural legacy of Silicon Valley*. Is this still an issue today? You tell me. Could 'capital dependence' be one reason why 75% plus of all VC dollars invested in US software companies are still going into 'later stage deals'? If these 'startups' had been executing out of a culture of operational and competitive sobriety, i.e. 'Marketing by Garage Values', would they not be further along the road to self-sufficiency? I'll let you answer that for yourself.

Another role in the bubble web of wealth entitlement was played by the VCs. During the bubble period, as the entrepreneurs grew dependent on the VCs, the venture capital industry grew dependent on a steady stream of IPO's to recapture many times their original investments. Absent this steady stream of IPO's, the industry contracted. Today, many VCs are more hands-on with their portfolio companies, contributing to the execution heat in the sandstorm. But if another window of opportunity emerges to fast-track scores, or even hundreds of new IPOs (perhaps a Web 2.0 bubble, or an 'on-demand' bubble, or an 'open source' bubble), expect to see the erosion of tribal entrepreneurism all over again.

And finally there were the investment bankers. The bankers became dependent on the individual gambling addicts, i.e. the retail investors and day traders looking for a rapid run-up of value for various tech and web stocks. Without the gambling addicts in large numbers, it's hard to hold a web of entitlement together.

Remember what I said in Chapter 2 about the over-cultivation or desertification of enterprise IT opportunity? This desertification of IT markets by thousands of non-self-sustaining startups was accelerated by wholesale mass gambling addiction—Gambling addiction that over-cultivated any so-called new economy business model that appeared to be floatable on the Nasdaq.

From where I sit, it appears our industry has still not come to terms with the idea that the bubble was an episode of mass gambling addiction. In many respects, the industry is still stuck in the blame game, rather than trying to draw the relevant cultural lessons. Sure, folks like investment banker Frank Quattrone[22] have had to go before the courts for their actions in the bubble. But how many CEOs and management teams said, 'we are not going to cash out on those options'. Not many. How many VCs said, 'No, we are not ready to cash out on that IPO yet, that deal is not fully cooked'. Not many.

And how many companies decided not to build a big war chest of cash just in case their original business model and market opportunity were dead on arrival. Say it with me... Not many. The bubble and the web of wealth entitlement were a lot like the plot of the novel 'Murder on the Orient Express'[23]. Everybody on the new economy train conspired to over-cultivate the tech industry landscape. And everybody on the train, not just a few high-profile IPO bankers, needs to share the responsibility for the wreckage that followed.

3Ds:Dependence, Denial and Desperation-A Starting Point for Cultural Sobriety

I know my characterization of the bubble as a web of wealth entitlement may sound a little preachy, even disingenuous. Especially for a guy who takes the point of view that software monopolies are both good for, and the natural state of, the industry. But stay with me for a minute more. Allow me to continue down this line of thinking about the bubble as an episode of mass addiction.

When an individual has an addiction problem, and ends up someplace like the Betty Ford Clinic, or contemplates attendance at a '12 step' self-help recovery group, he or she is often handed a list of Addiction Assessment Questions. Questions like these for example.

- Do you find yourself becoming more and more dependent on the drinking, the drugging, the pint of Haagen Daaz, those gambling excursions to Vegas? Do you find yourself losing control, become intoxicated, or spending more time and money than you can afford pursuing your habit?
- Do you lie to yourself, rationalize, justify, or in any way engage in denial of the impact of these behaviors by thinking, *"I'm in control. I can stop whenever I choose to stop. My behavior is normal because everybody does it"*.
- Have you engaged in acts of desperation to maintain the addictive habit, e.g. lying, cheating, stealing, covering up, or worse?

There are a lot more questions on your average 'Am I an addict' assessment list. But these are a few examples of questions that shine the spotlight on what I call the *'3D's of addiction assessment—Dependence, Denial and Desperation. These same 3Ds became a big part of the cultural legacy of the bubble and after-bubble.* Prospective asymmetric marketers need to examine the impact of these 3D's on their current marketing culture, as a necessary step in fostering cultural sobriety in their organizations.

What Do I Mean by Dependence? 'Money for Nothing and Your Clicks for Free'

If you needed a name for a song parody to sum up the culture of capital dependence that characterized the new economy bubble, here's my suggestion. Call it *"Money for nothing and your clicks' for free"*. What better song title would be historically appropriate for a company like WebVan that burned through over $1 Billion of invested capital selling bags of groceries for $1.00 that cost $2.00 to produce and deliver to your home. What kind of 'new rules/no rules' marketing culture thinks that's a sober idea? Too many to mention would be the honest answer. Here's why it's important today.

In the beginning of all addictive processes there is always one particular kind of 'drug of choice' in evidence. A drug of choice on which the addict becomes completely dependent. So too with the cargo cult companies of the bubble. The drug of choice was *capital*.

The result of using the drug called capital was often toxic dependence. A culture of dependence on capital is the opposite of a culture of sobriety, or bootstrapped self-sufficiency. One of the traditions of technology garage entrepreneurism in the U.S.

Many companies born during the bubble never really equated success with business self-sufficiency, but with this essentially dependent relationship to capital. A dependent relationship validated for them by an army of analyst enablers. I know dozens of CEOs who, when asked how their business was doing, would describe success as, 'We've raised $25 million from some tier 1 VCs?' Not, we've built a symbiotic alliance with Microsoft, Cisco, IBM, Oracle or SAP that is driving more new business than we can handle.

The now historic Barron's article by Jack Willoughby, exposing the timeline around which many publicly-traded internet companies were running out of invested cash, blew the whistle on the epidemic of capital dependence, and triggered the first wave of the sell-off of tech and internet stocks, as well as the boom period for new IPO's.

One article in one major financial publication was all it took to blow the whistle on capital dependence and begin to tank the web of wealth entitlement.

When you see a mass episode of capital dependency like the bubble, it means that sober self-sufficiency (as a values component of marketing culture), was not very high on management agendas. So why does that matter? Here's why. What chronic capital dependence does (like a drug) is progressively weaken the initiative of marketing and sales organizations in *marketing their way out of their problems*.

In my experience, when you actually make it a priority to do a culture self-assessment focused on capital dependence and self-sufficiency issues, it will quickly reveal many things. Including *expensive overlaps in marketing and sales functions, duplication of effort due to non-collaboration, wasteful or poorly targeted spending...and even those 'terrorist competitor' behaviors* I referenced in Chapter 2. Now let's continue with our bubble culture addiction assessment, and move on the 2nd of our 3Ds, *denial*.

Second D: Denial Justifies Dependence

It's a sad fact of life that on their own, many addicts seem to be incapable of self-correcting their behaviors. Why? Because of strong denial and rationalization systems that often go hand in hand with dependence. The denial is often so pervasive, and takes so many different forms, that most addicts end up needing a recovery process grounded in simple reality-based values to even begin to get better. I have found that the same is true of marketing organizations.

The pervasive marketing denial of the dominant culture of the bubble is still with us. And it continues to take 3 important forms that run counter to sober marketing practices. These 3 forms of denial are as follows:

- Denial of Best Practices,
- Denial of Competitive Dynamics,
- Denial of Actual Demand.

Let's take them one at a time.

Denial of Best Practices: Embrace of 'New Economy/New Rules' Belief Systems

Remember what I said earlier in the book. The dominant marketing culture of the bubble justified capital dependence, intoxicated overspending on marketing and sales, and outright squandering of money...Under the pretext that we are operating according to the 'new rules of the new economy'. So why do I consider 'new rules' a form of marketing denial?

In retrospect, we know that many of the so-called new rules were embraced by a small army of now extinct e-strategy companies and media outlets, often as self-serving justifications for spending millions with them on advertising, analyst validation, and marketing at 'internet speed'. It was a brilliantly self-serving 'pay to play' ploy...Until reality set in. But that was then, and this is now, right? We'll never do that again...Right!

Unfortunately, this 'new rules' flavor of thought leadership is still floating around inside many ISV and web companies. Companies where the systematic study of the proven best practices of dominant, winner-take-all players (asymmetric marketing) has fallen by the wayside. One blatant form cargo cult marketing denial has taken in the after-bubble, as I pointed out in the previous chapter, is a co-dependent interpretation of the 'customer economy' concept.

The 'customer economy' concept replaced the 'new economy' concept, in justifying weak, politically correct, 'surrender to the customer' approaches that teach sales and marketing professionals how *not* to practice customer dominance. One key attribute of an asymmetric marketer. Getting out of denial means studying the best practices of the superpowers in customer barrier management, not going fishing for the newest, newest, newest, newest rules.

Denial of Competitive Dynamics: Category Fragmentation
When you deny the best practices of the superpowers in favor of some new rules, why stop there. Why not also re-write the general rules of competition in the tech industry as a whole. This was the case with those that advocated that 'brick and mortar' and the 'legacy tech' businesses were not competitive with the 'new economy' companies. This kind of thinking led to sloppy competitive analysis by ISVs, as well as category fragmentation all along the line, that is still with us in the superpower sandstorm.

You can see the aftermath of this thinking in many fragmented categories that continue to have four, five or more ISVs with comparable annual revenue and no clear winner-take-all player on the horizon. Take the ECM or enterprise content management category as an example. You tell me why pioneering ECM ISVs like Vignette and Interwoven haven't merged yet. I don't get it. Especially in the wake of EMC's acquisition of Documentum, and IBM's acquisition of FileNet? Both Vignette and Interwoven are relatively comparable in terms of annual revenue and market cap (as of September 2006 both are slightly above $400 million dollars in market value). And both appear to have burned through significant cash (read capital dependence) over the four-year period from 2002 to 2005.

Seriously, I am not trying to criticize or beat up on these two companies. I really don't get it. But one simple explanation may be this. A persistent culture of dependence and denial is at work in more than a few 'emerging categories' intoxicated by the mythical lure of the 'tornado'. This denial of actual category dynamics in the age of the superpowers appears to foster a go-it-alone marketing mindset that keeps pioneering companies from merging, and creating a potential 'winner-take-all' scenario. Instead of opening the door to stronger players to come in and cherry-pick the category to death. Absent being snapped up by a superpower, Vignette and Interwoven executing a merger of equals would be a very good thing for their category and for them.

As a general rule, asymmetric marketers get out of category denial, and pro-actively undertake 'merger of equals' consolidation activities that can lead to a winner-take-all, pre-emptive category leader. Exactly what the Symantec/Veritas combination is doing in their creative fusion of security and information management. You may want to look at this issue in your own culture assessment if you are in one of these highly fragmented categories where the tornado is not coming to a theater near you... anytime soon.

Denial of Actual Demand: Non-Existent 'Market Opportunity'

Hey, I just realized I've been really, really serious in this chapter, and that it's been more a few pages since I hyped a movie. So here goes.

If you didn't see *Wag the Dog*[24] with Robert DeNiro and Dustin Hoffman, you missed a 2-thumbs-up flick. Funnyman Dennis Leary plays the role of the 'Fad King', a kind of folk-marketing anti-hero who identifies emerging cultural trends upon which his clients can capitalize. In the movie Leary uses his findings about specific fads within the popular culture to divert the nation's attention away from a presidential sex scandal by creating a phony war in Albania, complete with phony heroes.

In the age of the bubbleboys, the marketing departments of many companies tended to be run by this kind of fad king. For example, many bubble-era companies hijacked Brian Arthur's concept of 'increasing returns' as a strategic fad to justify eyeballs-based business models built on top of markets for which there was little or no demand ('money for nothing, clicks for free').

When a chronic absence of demand became self-evident, the *fad king marketers abandoned increasing returns and instead made increasing 'u-turns', swapping out the model-du-jour for an even newer fad.* I still get calls like this. *'Enterprise software is out of style. Our investors want us to re-position ourselves in the consumer space in order to gain new funding. Hey, maybe you can help spin us as the next big 'on-demand' company... or maybe a Web 2.0 company'.*

Like the alcoholic who thinks his problem is whiskey, not vodka, or the addict who thinks his problem is heroin, not crack cocaine, many fad king marketing teams switched poisons by 'morphing' and re-positioning, without getting to the root of the cultural problems of dependence and denial, and the fundamental absence of demand for their offering.

I laugh at the lengths to which the fad kings went to deny the fact that there was no actual demand for their products or services. Often times their denial of actual demand was disguised thusly: *'We've gone through all our early adopters and we're in the chasm now'...'once we get into the 'bowling alley' we will be OK.'* Riiiiiiiiiiiiiight!

The Third D: Desperation
Taken together, denial of best practices, denial of competitive category dynamics, and denial of real demand, can end up becoming what the treatment industry calls a 'set up'. *A set up to practice desperation behaviors.*

These desperation behaviors end up poisoning organizational culture, while widening the gap between strategy and execution that I call Big Hat, No Cattle Syndrome. In extreme cases of capital dependence and denial, sales and marketing teams under pressure to perform may do or say anything to deal with declining revenue.

During, and in the aftermath of the bubble, desperation behaviors have included:
- Questionable revenue recognition practices that inflated revenue. Thats why Sarbanes-Oxley now forces CEOs to sign income statements;
- Bartering, or non-standard exchanges of technology that companies booked as revenue;

- Channel stuffing, or the over-shipping of product into your partner network while calling it revenue, knowing full well it's going to come back to you.

One major after-bubble form of desperation behavior is known as 'click fraud'[25], in which a network affiliate of Google, Yahoo or other search engine artificially inflates the number of click-throughs to a particular advertiser, thereby pumping up its own (and the search engine's) revenue. It's even gotten to the point where class action law suits were filed against the search engines on behalf of advertisers, and the search engines have begun incorporating fraud detection technology into their systems. So desperation behavior didn't end with the bubble.

Once More on Self-Assessment: Some Sobriety and 'Big Hat, No Cattle' Questions

A tribal culture of garage sobriety recoils from the desperation behaviors listed above. In contrast to the 3Ds of dependence, denial and desperation, *a marketing culture with sobriety as an embedded kernel value is all about fostering bootstrapped entrepreneurial self-sufficiency as a spontaneous behavior*.

Marketing sobriety is also about detoxing from the various denial systems of the new economy thought leadership, the 'new rules' and 'no rules' in favor of a culture of best practices of the software superpowers.

Keep in mind that I've only scratched the surface with the 3Ds above. That's why it's important to go into this in depth in your ongoing Self-Assessment...Something that needs to become an integral part of your culture management system. *Doing the opposite of the 3Ds is a continuous 'one day at a time' process, not a mental exercise*.

To borrow a phrase from the addiction and recovery industry, *'You have to live yourself into a new way of thinking, you can't think yourself into a new way of living.'* In other words, beginning anywhere is the way to tackle this subject. There is no wrong way to get started assessing your own culture. So don't procrastinate.

But here's an analogy that may help you jumpstart the process. Readers knowledgeable about IT security practices are familiar with the concept of 'vulnerability assessment', i.e. a continuous and ongoing scan of your entire network to detect areas that may be undefended in a hostile attack by a hacker or insider. *Marketing self-assessment is like an ongoing vulnerability assessment for your tribe, focused on how values and beliefs impact strategy and execution.*

You'll want to begin with a few simple questions, for example:

- Has our dependence on invested capital in any way undermined our resolve and creativity in marketing our way to self-sufficiency and profitability? Is dependence on invested capital contributing to symptoms of Big Hat, No Cattle Syndrome?
- What form is marketing denial taking? Are we focused on studying and applying superpower best practices, or are we up all night searching for the blogs of the latest fad kings?
- Is there any evidence of short cuts and desperation behaviors in our efforts to 'make the number' in the superpower sandstorm?

The time and resources you invest in this assessment will create a *cultural baseline* that tells your organization where you are now, what values are actually driving your current behavior, and where you need to focus in order to improve marketing and sales performance. A work in process, the first or zero-day draft assessment should immediately be published inside the organization as a first step in fostering the 2nd core kernel values component, *candor*.

More on the 'Get Real' or Candor Values Component of MBGV

Having begun walking down the path to marketing sobriety and completed a first draft Big Hat, No Cattle Assessment, the second kernel values attractor you want to embed in your marketing culture is what I call the *Get Real or candor* component. Getting real sounds like a no-brainer, but it's not as simple as it seems. *We have a business culture in the U.S. (and it's worse in other countries) that doesn't think twice about celebrating corporate whistleblowers on the cover of Time Magazine, but refuses to listen to them in time to fix the problems of the company.*

Learning from the Culture of HROs

Psychologist Karl E. Weick, a respected thought leader on the subject of organizational performance, points to high reliability organizations (HROs) as leading examples of what I call 'get real' cultures. HROs operate in 'market' environments where Big Hat, No Cattle Syndrome is not an option, e.g. nuclear power plants, air traffic control systems, hospital emergency rooms, special operations units in the military (SEALs, Rangers, Delta Force, Green Berets, etc), first responder units like the Fire Department of New York, etc.

In an interview in the Harvard Business Review, Weick makes the point that:

"The big difference between HROs and other organizations is the **sensitivity or mindfulness** *with which people in most HROs* **react to even very weak signs that some kind of change or danger is approaching** *(JEB emphasis)."*[26]

This concept, **mindfulness of vulnerability**, is a powerful idea that ISV marketers need to embrace in the superpower sandstorm as a foundation for developing competitive strategy and patching internal vulnerability. It is what I mean by a 'get real' culture of asymmetric marketing. Weick continues.

"Everyday problems escalate to disaster status very quickly when people don't respond appropriately to signs of trouble. HROs distinguish themselves by being able to **detect incredibly weak warning signs** *(JEB emphasis) and then taking decisive action."*[27]

Contrast Weick's advocacy of pre-emptive mindfulness with the kind of risk-averse marketing culture in which various aspects of market vulnerability are not discussed internally because of the blame game. It's a companion disorder to Big Hat, No Cattle Syndrome I call the *'tiger inside/pussycat outside syndrome'*. It's a syndrome where team members (and even management) blame and shame their own people for raising important issues (tiger inside), while letting customers walk all over them in the name of the 'customer economy' (pussycat outside).

Asymmetric marketers foster marketing cultures that embrace candor and creative conflict, and organize themselves around **behavioral rituals and cultural artifacts that serve as early warning signals**. This is a legacy characteristic of traditional garage entrepreneurism. It was best captured in a sound bite by retired Intel CEO Andrew S. Grove in his observation that *'only the paranoid survive'*[28]. In the superpower sandstorm, all ISVs must learn to be a lot more paranoid... a lot more 'mindful'.

Companies that are not paranoid, or do not practice 'get real mindfulness', tend to get competitively punished, even if they are market-share leaders. As I pointed out earlier, I can recall having a discussion many years ago with a marketing executive at one of the desktop application companies eventually defeated by Microsoft. I asked him if he had an OEM marketing program to counter Microsoft's own desktop apps effort, which at that time of our discussion was just getting off the ground. He said something like *"We don't need that. We are the overwhelming market share leader in our category of software, we have 'top of mind' brand equity, and we command premium prices. Why would we want to do that?"* In hindsight, it's clear he could have used a little more paranoia.

Marketing Weblogs, Discussion Boards, and Collaborative Intranets: Embedding Candor and a Get Real HRO Attitude

What I recommend to embed the 'get real' or candor principle, and reinforce it (on an hour by hour basis) is a marketing intranet with both weblog and discussion board functionality. In this way you can capture the creative conflict, informal conversation, and mindfulness of your marketing, sales and partner development knowledge workers, while allowing them to grow their own personal 'reputation equity' and street-cred.

Weblog and discussion board functionality is especially helpful in marketing cultures that use email as a divisive tool of organizational factionalism. In extreme cases, I've seen email become the digital version of the Pennsylvania Amish tradition of *shunning*. *'You've been bad. You went off the reservation and said something complementary about our competitors at the product review meeting. Nobody will talk to you until you repent'.* Soon you're not copied on the important emails. You're not part of the marketing 'in crowd'.

Collaborative intranets with internal weblogs and message boards hold the potential to serve as a more effective alternative to email in terms of *fostering a persistent conversation that can uncover and fix Big Hat, No Cattle Syndrome.* In many cases, a critical mass of discussion board comments, or weblog postings, can serve as a powerful cultural artifact to drive the emergence of your *get real* marketing tribe.

In terms of fostering emergent leadership within the marketing tribe, marketing weblogs also build *personal reputation equity* for those highly 'mindful' contributors whose blog entries, message board posts, and cumulative institutional memory are there for others to 'swarm' or 'mob' around.

These systems also provide visibility for board members or VCs into the day-to-day operations and mindfulness of the company, and serve as an alternative to canned or filtered management presentations and reports. This direct visibility into your marketing culture can only improve board, investor and stakeholder governance.

More on the Kernel Value of Self-Organizing: Bureaucracy to Special Operations Teams

Not surprisingly, many ISVs that have non-sober, capital-dependent marketing organizations, as well as operating cultures that have difficulty 'getting real', are also highly 'stovepiped' or 'siloed'. In plain English, they are bureaucratic, and not run like a mindful, high reliability organization. Embedding and fostering the kernel values component of 'self-organizing' is the best way to root out this bureaucracy, while preparing for the on-again/off-again market uncertainty and competitive challenges of the superpower sandstorm.

Sorry, with all this heavy duty culture talk, I can't resist giving myself a comedy 'fix' with least one more movie comparison. Perhaps late one night, on some obscure cable channel, you may have seen the sophomoric but hilarious 80's comedy *Stripes*[29], starring Bill Murray and Harold Ramis.

In the film, 2 cultural misfits join the army in order get some self-discipline. While undergoing basic training their platoon leader, the grizzly Sergeant Hulka, gets injured, effectively leaving them leaderless in the middle of basic training. But Bill Murray and his buddy Harold Ramis actually save their platoon by 'self-organizing' and training their unit for the final boot camp graduation drill. As a reward they are then promoted to a secret special ops unit, and even end up rescuing their comrades from some Iron curtain-era bad guys. The whole movie is basically a tongue-in-cheek look at how the discipline of getting real, and being mindful, transforms itself into the discipline of self-organizing.

Since September 11th, 2001, and the emergence of high media visibility around the global war on terror, many ordinary American citizens have become increasingly aware of the concept of 'special operations' forces, i.e., teams of specialists from different branches of the military that come together to address the threat of modern asymmetric warfare by clandestine terrorists against open societies. Marketing professionals can apply spec-ops thinking by focusing on 4 basic aspects of Self-organizing Culture. They are:

1. Create 'Doer' Management: In the traditional corporate organizational model, a leader is primarily a manager, whereas self-organizing cultural leadership sees the leader as a 'doer' with personal reputation equity. Bill Gates organizational shift from his old role as COO to his current role of Chief Software Architect is an example of an organizational decision that re-enforced the asymmetric culture of doer leadership at Microsoft. Keep in mind that Gates decided to make this shift at a time when the company was betting the future on its web initiatives, and was embroiled in the Department of Justice court actions. *The leader as doer is the best cultural insurance policy an organization can have*. It provides a role model artifact that is powerful, and drives imitation of the best kind. I wouldn't be surprised to see Bill Gates continue to dip his big toe back into this role (maybe through his home page) even after he retires in 2008.

2. Foster Non-Interchangable Parts: Bureaucratic organizational forms assume that people can be reduced to interchangeable parts, a mechanical model. Self-organizing tribes practice a more organic model, and have a higher percentage of *non-interchangeable parts, i.e. key people with reputation equity who are relied on in both good times and bad to add value to the culture and provide direction.* Much of the sandstorm-broken organizational machinery inside many marketing departments is based on the assumption that restructuring is restructuring, and people are people. This belief has a high price attached to it. In my consulting practice, I've noticed that much of the overspending and duplication of effort that widens the Big Hat, No Cattle execution gap is directly related to the downsizing or elimination of individuals who were true non-interchangeable parts, i.e. *culturally key people* who may have been seen as outside the norm, and were forced out during episodes of cost cutting.

3. Relevant Experience with Failure: In a culture of self-organizing, relevant experience matters more than title. This is something everyone should have become painfully aware of during the bubble meltdown when hundreds of companies run by just-out-of-b-school CEOs simply self-destructed, and continued their college education on the investors' nickel. And as anyone who has been around the tech industry for a long time knows, ***experience with failure is just as important as experience with success (if not more so).*** Relevant experience with market downturns, periods of uncertainty, and superpower marketing practices, is highly valuable. It produces enhanced levels of market mindfulness inside a marketing culture.

4. Word-of-Mouth Traditions & Urban Legends: Bureaucrats draw up abstract, committee-driven 'Values Statements'. Corporate tribes rely on cultural traditions passed down by word of mouth (mythmaking) over the course of the company's history. This allows an organization or company to become a self-organizing system. A system that self-directs and self-corrects based on the traditions of prior campaigns, business victories, and defeats, not abstraction or political correctness.

The right traditions can ***even keep groups of highly inexperienced and behaviorally dysfunctional people on track.*** This simple truth has been known to self-organizing groups for many decades. Look at the *12 Traditions of Alcoholics Anonymous*[30] as an example. They are simple set of 'group guidelines' that keep thousands of alcoholics culturally self-organized in the face of persistent obstacles to a new life free from addiction.

Here's an example of word-of-mouth 'tradition' that takes the form of a Microsoft urban legend. Over 10 years ago, a mentor of mine, the CEO of the US branch of an Asian PC OEM, told me this story. My mentor was one of those rare marketing warriors who loved to stir up creative conflict. So to this day, I honestly don't know whether the story is true, or was simply word-of-mouth mythmaking designed to motivate me. In either case it's a powerful cultural attractor. The story goes like this.

Long, long ago in a PC industry far, far away, Bill Gates (before he became one of the most successful asymmetric marketers in the world) used to make regularly-scheduled 'vendor day' visits to the office of the president of a major PC retail chain (who in our urban legend shall remain nameless). The retail chain president, resenting the must-have nature and asymmetric market power of Microsoft's operating system, used to schedule Mr. Gates in at 9AM...And then make him wait in the reception area all day!

In the meantime, the CEOs of other PC software vendors (Lotus, WordPerfect, Novell, Borland, Corel) would be ushered past Mr. Gates into the office of the retail president to conduct their business. This would go on all day long until the retail president thought he had made his point. According to my mentor, this systematic and intentional 'dissing' (disrespecting for those of you who don't have teenage kids) had the exact opposite effect. It helped to bestow on Mr. Gates an iron-willed competitive personality, and a steely resolve to rise to the very top of the PC software business. The point here is this. True or not true, traditions-based tribal cultures produce this type of word-of-mouth legend. Legends that attract imitation and self-organizing. Legends that serve as cultural catalysts to drive action. So what are some additional benefits of fostering a bias toward 'self-organizing' in your marketing tribe?

Some Additional Benefits of Self-Organizing as a Cultural Value

In addition to fostering a spec-ops-type, cross-stovepipe orientation, here are some not-so-obvious benefits to following through on the commitment to build a marketing culture that promotes self-organizing.

Crisis Response: In the superpower sandstorm, crises can come out of nowhere. A missed quarter, an SEC inquiry, a dismissed CEO, a social network or web chat room with child predators, a deal with a foreign government that doesn't play well in your home market, your core OS stolen by hackers, etc. *Cultural conditioning becomes the foundation for how quickly and effectively you respond* to these crises. Fostering a culture of self-organizing is like having a crisis 'immune system' that can react to crises in real time.

Stronger Brand Reputation Equity: Organizational culture is the foundation for reputation in the marketplace. And *reputation equity is becoming the key ingredient in brand equity*. For example, try to imagine eBay without its reputation management system for the millions of participants who trade with each other having never met face-to-face. We've also seen the opposite——a rapid loss of reputation equity tied to bureaucratic cultures that don't get real and don't foster self-organizing. The corporate accountability scandals rapidly imploded reputation equity at companies like Enron and Andersen, resulting in a quantum loss of brand confidence and business failure.

M&A Stealth: Asymmetric marketing teams in head-to-head market combat need to practice stealth relative to competitors and customers. With a strong and healthy culture you can do this. Without one, *loose lips sink marketing ships*. Stealth often comes to the fore in an acquisition or merger situation. With a self-organizing culture that fosters doer leadership, the breakdown of silos, and reliance on key people with high reputation equity, acquisitions are easier to negotiate and integrate, and people are more likely to succeed in executing them with stealth and speed.

More on Self-Organizing via Internal Social Networks

As I pointed out earlier in the chapter, the 3rd module of your CMS, designed to foster self-organizing behaviors, is the use of social network software to facilitate the discipline of internal self-organizing. One way to enable a culture of self-organizing is to *internally launch all your products and programs in a dress rehearsal or war games setting*. This unifies your tribe, surfaces get-real objections, fosters candid creative dialog, and prepares people to swarm or mob around the real market-based launch events. Social network software can help the individual marketing-armies-of-one in your tribe weigh-in quickly on a launch, and organically align strategy with execution. Social software *unleashes dotcomplexity advantage inside* your organization. In addition to social network software, conferencing tools (e.g. Webex, MS LiveMeeting) commonly used for regular customer contact and sales presentations can also serve to be effective in embedding a culture of self-organizing into your organization, while breaking down silo behaviors. In focusing this technology internally you can begin to *reinforce what I described above as 4 attributes of self-organizing teams, i.e. doer leadership, non-dublicatable people (armies of one with tribal street-cred), relevant experience, and word-of-mouth cultural traditions.*

More on 'Ownership' as a Kernel Values Component of MBGV

What do I mean when I say that 'ownership' is a core values component of an MBGV approach to building an asymmetric marketing culture? Simple. What I mean is that every individual in the organization will answer the question "Who owns the challenge of creating revenue momentum" with the same answer...."I do." Not he does, or she does, or the sales guy with the fat rolodex who rarely comes into the office except to process his expense report.

From a revenue execution standpoint, working to embed the ownership values component is the best long term approach to eliminating 'leads falling through the cracks' or confusion over 'what constitutes a qualified prospect', two of the major culture gap symptoms I use as examples from the Accenture study referenced in Chapter 4.

Shared ownership of revenue creation, not complete reliance on your 'rolodex warriors' in the sales team is the smartest path to asymmetric advantage in the superpower sandstorm. As Sun Tzu pointed out (and as I've cited multiple times in this book),

"Therefore good warriors seek effectiveness in battle from the force of momentum, not from individual people."

Translation. Creating sales momentum is not just the job of the sales organization. It's a challenge and mission for the whole sales and marketing culture. And this is the way creative ISVs are actually finding success with IT organizations in the sandstorm.

Sun Tzu describes it this way.

*"Getting people to fight by letting the force of momentum work is like rolling logs and rocks. Logs and rocks are still when in a secure place, but role on an incline; they remain stationary if square, they roll if round. Therefore **when people are skillfully led into battle, the momentum is like that of round rocks rolling down a high mountain---this is force."*[31]

Creating momentum, skillfully leading your tribe into battle, means *fostering deep, embedded ownership behaviors across the whole marketing organization*, including product marketing, partner marketing, field support, call center customer support, etc. How does this play out?

Let's return to what we covered in Chapter 3 and 4. In the superpower sandstorm, IT organizations considering new projects are increasingly demanding that technology sales and marketing organizations (both new and incumbent vendors) *pre-prove ROI* not simply to invest budget dollars, but to invest the finite 'human bandwidth' of their staffs.

In fact, if we take the enterprise software segment as an example, a 'qualified sales lead' in today's world does not even exist without shared ownership by:

Product Marketing: In order to pre-prove ROI, IT organizations expect software products to be highly evaluation-ready via either a downloadable trial version of the product, or an on-demand instance of the software available as a subscription web service. Without this, the sales force is not really operating with the force of momentum, but as 'individuals' attempting to convince the customer prospect 'a priori' of their value proposition. I don't care how many 'relationships' your newly hired VP of sales has, how many names are in his rolodex, or how many contacts he has on the latest and greatest business social network. Without pre-proving ROI through the execution of best practices in asymmetric product marketing (trialware editions), how can you ever really know if you have a qualified prospect? Product marketing organizations with a culture of shared ownership take pains to design easy evaluation-readiness into products upfront and do not see it as a development afterthought.

Partnering/Distribution: If our hypothetical ISV markets the software product via a network of partners, it is expected by IT organizations that these partners will not simply have evaluation-ware, but have access to a standard version of the product deployed in their shop and available to run full customer pilot programs, or extended trials, that may involve customization by the partner. This is especially true in vertical market situations with highly specialized business logic and data dependent applications.

Customer Service/Support: Asymmetric marketers know that up-selling and locking in existing customers is the key to establishing revenue momentum, and a long term asymmetric advantage relative to these customers. Support and service organizations are critical in providing customer insight and competitive intelligence on how to make that happen, and what product changes need to occur. Without embedding ownership values in the support organization, up-selling and emergent opportunity detection are less likely to happen.

Summing up, marketing tribes working to embed the kernel values component of ownership strive to **deconstruct, reconstruct, and most importantly, re-incentivize the selling process across all stovepipes, and don't rely on sales heroes.** But they also go one step further and reward behaviors that extend the concept of tribal ownership through a sense of **intangible higher mission.**

Intangible Incentives---A Sense of 'Higher Mission'
Many in the high tech industry have historically embraced a sense of higher mission to super-charge their operating cultures. For example, the open source movement has a market power greater than the sum of its parts for this reason. Without the culture of collaboration as an embedded principle, the open source movement would not exist.

Many 'white hat hackers' in the security space also see it as their higher mission to expose software vulnerabilities through highly publicized system break-ins.

And while some may find it controversial to acknowledge, those of us in the post-9.11 software marketing profession have left behind that period of history where expert B-school panels held interesting cocktail party discussions around concepts like 'creative destruction'. Instead we are living in a time of **extremely uncreative real destruction** that threatens the very existence of individuals, businesses, and civilization itself.

So while the bubble and the 'web of entitlement' were all about rapid personal enrichment, and anything it took to get there, a growing number of business leaders are turning to **higher mission or higher purpose as part of their reward systems, their intangible incentives in dealing with this threat of extremely uncreative real destruction.**

For example, asymmetric marketers are starting to see that one important aspect of their role in society is to create and market technology products that foster homeland security. As in Israel, a nation that has dramatically grown it's software exports during a 30 year, terror-induced sandstorm of market uncertainty, *conscious asymmetric marketers are part of what I call the 'eFront', i.e. the high tech front in the war on terror.* One of the key reasons behind the growth in the Israeli technology industry, as well as its ability to pioneer in the creation of new categories of capability (security, instant messaging, electronic warfare, optical processors) has been its symbiotic relationship to the Israeli government. This has fostered a sense of shared ownership of national survival in the face of decades of terrorism.

Like their counterparts in Israel, software marketers in the U.S. are aligning with government IT initiatives, and adopting new government partnering models, sensing instinctively that the September 11th terrorist attacks in New York and Washington altered the relationship of US tech companies to the US government for the foreseeable future.

Against this background, embedding a sense of higher mission in your marketing and sales organization may best be accomplished by *turning your 'government marketing' team into a values attractor*, an engine of self-organizing activity, and a hotbed of rich dialog within the organization as a whole.

Here are a few representative examples of what I mean by 'higher mission statements' created by government marketing teams:

- Mobile Services Network Provider: 'This organization is dedicated to providing mobile technology and connectivity to first responders on the frontlines of homeland security. No fire or rescue professional need face additional risks for lack of robust mobile communication.'
- Vertical SW Provider Higher Mission: 'We provide business intelligence and analytic software to target Al Qaeda and other terrorist funds. Part of our reward system is wanting to play our part in defeating terror.'
- E-security Managed Services Provider: 'Our company is proud to defend corporate networks and critical infrastructure against cyber-terrorism. Part of our reward system is in knowing, despite uncertainty outside our control, we can help to foster business continuity.'

Embedding Ownership via EIM Technology

As I suggested above, the 4th module of your asymmetric marketing CMS is optimized by incorporating enterprise incentive management (EIM) technology in order to reinforce the 'ownership' values component across the organization, while rewarding a sense of higher mission.

EIM will place you in position to implement *'pay for team performance'* strategies that can be managed directly by specific 'no huddle offense' business managers. With EIM as a component of your culture management system, you can begin to design sales and marketing *compensation models that reinforce the 'sobriety', 'get real' and 'self-organizing' tribal values components* described above, while simultaneously facilitating market momentum.

You can also use EIM as an internal catalyst to begin *eliminating barriers to collaboration,* i.e. those legacy compensation programs that reinforce only your departmental silos. In other words, you can use your incentive programs to laser target Big Hat, No Cattle Syndrome, make it the job of the entire marketing tribe to close the gap between strategy and execution, and encourage 'garage' culture to blossom.

I'm not going to hype a specific EIM vendor here, but do a search on Yahoo, Google, or MSN and you will find these folks. I suspect the best among them will soon be getting gobbled up by the superpowers, as I believe complex global enterprises are going to embrace Culture Management Systems big time.

Wrapping Up, Moving On to the Last Chapter

The culture of asymmetric marketing in the superpower sandstorm is about *capturing market advantage based on the strength and flexibility of your embedded kernel values.* And the tribal processes that emerge from those embedded values...sobriety, candor, self-organizing, and ownership.

When *market superpowers like Microsoft get real about their vulnerability* (*The Internet Tidal Wave* memo), and don't shoot the messenger for blowing the whistle in advance of a potential market meltdown, that's the culture of asymmetric marketing in action.

When a new, post-bubble generation of startups and emerging category leaders, *in the tradition of garage entrepreneurism, avoid the mistakes of bubble-era ISVs*, and foster an internal marketing environment focused on bootstrapping their businesses to self-sufficiency, that's the culture of asymmetric marketing in action.

As you have seen throughout the course of this chapter, my framework for assessing healthy marketing culture is drawn from an eclectic bundle of sources. But principally from the Spartan, pre-bubble cultural legacy of high technology entrepreneurism in the United States. I also draw upon 'recovery theory' as practiced by the professional addiction treatment industry, and related self-help groups. As a way to make meaning of the mass phenomena of business dysfunction called the bubble, and to *expose the toxic business values passed down from that period to today's marketers*.

I also integrate complexity theory into my approach, *particularly in terms of understanding why some operating cultures are dynamic, self-organizing, and capable of coping with uncertainty*, while others appear to be static and paralyzed in the face of uncertainty. My advocacy of social software technologies *inside* organizations, as a key element of *Marketing by Garage Values (MBGV) and Culture Management Systems (CMS)*, is also based on understanding the power of self-organizing, and the infrastructure catalysts (the **N**-gines, to reference my **N**-glish language) that enable complexity-advantaged processes to emerge and grow.

Finally, my advocacy of higher mission in the context of the global war-on-terror, while perhaps controversial to some, is simply practical for today's marketing warriors...Because *to win this protracted conflict, it is my view that the U.S. high technology industry must remain '2nd to none'*. This will not happen if the dysfunctional marketing values of the bubble are not replaced with the kernel values of a culture of asymmetric marketing.

OK....enough cultural overkill. On to the last chapter. It's about answering a simple question.

In the age of the software superpowers, what's the most effective way for an ISV to practice messaging symbiosis, i.e. participate in today's 24/7, superpower market conversations in order to showcase their products, services and operating culture.

In other words, how do you develop an asymmetric brand messaging strategy?

Chapter 7

ASYMMETRIC BRAND MESSAGING

"Don't be evil." *Google Corporate Motto*[1]
"Google don't be evil." *Placard Held by Tibetan Protester*[2]

Talk about a sober, candid, self-organizing asymmetric culture. How about this for your consideration? Peaceful Tibetans protesting. Right on! Who doesn't love to see self-organizing democracy in action?

But hold on a minute. Peaceful Tibetans *protesting against Google*...The web search superpower voted the most influential brand[3] in the world in 2005? Come again. Did I hear that right?

Could it be that Google, like some red-caped, high-flying, big screen super hero, has been weakened by 21st century brand kryptonite[4]? Maybe even trapped by a villainous media in some kind of brand Bizarro[5] world...Where everything is *backwards* (As in--- Google's *live* web apps are really *evil* web apps).

Or is the explanation simply this. The software superpowers, in the normal course of contending with each other and striving for market dominance, appear to have developed the knack for *spontaneously generating brand heat all over the place*. And I don't mean warm and cozy by the fireplace heat. I mean 24/7, always-on, sandstorm-intensity, *'Keep your hands off the stove kid or you'll get burned'* heat. So pray tell, how in the world did things become so hot in 2006 for Google, the 2005 influential brand of the year? Here's my take on it.

As a condition of expanding it's business in the Peoples Republic of China (i.e. playing by that government's new 'dotcommunist rules' for the web), Google's leadership made the decision to blacklist search references to Mr. Lhamo Thondup. *'Who the heck is Lhamo Thondup... I've never heard of him',* you exclaim. Forgive me. He happens to be best known to his followers by his official name, His Holiness the 14th Dalai Lama[6], a world-class spiritual and political thorn in the side of the Chinese Communist Party bureaucracy.

As the tale is told, Google censored His Holiness by redirecting keyword searches for the Dalai Lama to pre-sanitized (and definitely unholy) government-sanctioned websites. But as they're known to say in New York's Little Italy, *"It wasn't personal your holiness...It's just business".* Because apparently, Google did precisely the same thing to keyword searches for the Tiananmen massacre[7], the Falun Gong movement, the Republic of China (aka Taiwan), and that perennially problematic search phrase 'human rights'. Personally, I wouldn't consider it all that much of a stretch to characterize Google's business strategy in regard to its expansion into the dotcommunist China market as *Embrace/Extend/ Expunge*.

Let me spell that out.
Embrace...as in embrace the Chinese government's web policy for content filtering and information suppression.
Extend...as in extend Google's global search ecozone into the world's fastest growing market as a reward for playing by the government's dotcommunist rules.
Expunge ...as in expunge from your search results all record of the existence of any political or religious movement that the Party of Mao may find offensive.

Sorry...You're probably too young to remember the Party of Mao. So a quick flashback is in order. They're those lovable, huggable folks that brought you the 'Great Proletarian Cultural Revolution', during which grandfatherly college professors were perp-walked in dunce caps[8] on their way to forced 're-education' at the good old collective animal farm. And I'll bet your English lit professor told you Orwell was only writing *fiction*.

Not surprisingly, as one inconvenient piece of 'customer feedback' regarding Google's *'embrace, extend, expunge'* dotcommunist web policy, the 2005 Influential Brand of the Year met with vocal opposition from exiled Tibetans proudly displaying *'Google Don't Be Evil'* placards. And as

2006 unfolded, the brand-bashing fun was only just beginning for those well-massaged, gourmet-mealed marketers in the Googleplex. As those rowdy Tibetans turned out to be just one among many disgruntled market segments spinning the Google brand prayer wheel in reverse!

Passionately anti-communist, Chinese pro-democracy advocates, arm-in-arm with politically conservative American media commentators, all jumped in to blast the Google brand, welcoming the opportunity to throw a multitude of other perceived sins into the mix. One influential-and- highly-trafficked-on-the-right web editor/ talk radio personality flat-out called Google an 'enemy of freedom'[9]. While the neo-conservative (read influential at the Bush White House) Weekly Standard online edition was a little more forgiving, running a parody of Google with the results for the search term 'human rights' returning links to the 80's synthesizer rock group Human League. As well as the *'Despotipedia'*[10], an imaginary dotcommunist version of the Wikipedia.

But that was just the beginning. Faster than you can say *'word of mouth,'* an avalanche of Google's other perceived brand sins became sound bites in an ever-loudening market conversation.

From refusing to turn over search records to the U.S. Department of Justice in connection with proposed new internet child protection legislation[11], to Authors Guild charges of copyright infringement in connection with Google's online book service[12], to more accusations (this time regarding Google News) of censoring as 'hate speech' any militant opposition to Islamic terrorists and Jihadists[13], to complaints and lawsuits by advertisers connected to 'click fraud' in their affiliate network[14], to legal notices to media organizations not to use their brand name as a 'verb'[15], Google's '2005 Influential Brand of the Year' cup was definitely running over in 2006.....*with negative reputation equity*.

Not to be outdone, even the President of India jumped into this widening Google sound bite sandstorm, opining that their mapping service was too detailed[16], exposing sensitive locations (including the President's own house) to potential terrorist attacks. My favorite anti-Google commentary---Prime Minister Jacques Chirac is backing a native 'French' search engine[17] as a matter of national and cultural pride. Hmmm! Based on Chirac's entry into the disruptive innovation business, one could safely surmise that Liberte and Egalite are good things on the web...But to hell with the Fraternite when it comes to superpower competition in the European search market. Unfortunately for Google, Chirac wasn't the end of the sound bites.

Throw in the fact that in the 2004 U.S. presidential elections, 98% of Google employees' partisan political contributions went to the Democratic Party[18], and you can see how even an ascendant brand superpower like Google may begin to feel like one of those 'sure winner' *American Idol* contestants voted off the show to the strains of *'You've had a bad day'*.

So it was not surprising that after all the brand dust began to settle, one of Google's celebrity founders wisely decided to order a little marcom crow from the gourmet menu at the Googleplex. He wisely chose to issue a mea-culpa to the press, indicating that the company he co-founded may have 'compromised' it's principles[19] in the course of it's business expansion into China... and would be re-considering its current policy.

Then he washed down that 'compromised' brand crow with a tall glass of 2006 vintage Washington Lobbying Firm...Some folks with close connections to those Republican politicians[20] who failed to get their fair share of Google election contributions. And a month or so later, it sure didn't hurt for Google to cut a 900 million dollar ad deal[21] with Rupert Murdoch's MySpace.com...Who, by the way, also happens to have a little something to do with that 'neocon' Fox News Network.

The Sound Bite Sandstorm--- Just Background Noise or Something More?

Rising superpower Google is merely the most recent high profile example of a technology company that managed to get stuck inside a sound bite sandstorm. A sound bite sandstorm that on the surface appears to resemble some rapidly mutating strain of tabloid tech journalism. But Google is far from alone in the sound bite sandstorm. Their brother and sister software superpowers have faced, and continue to face, the brand messaging challenge of grappling with persistent, polarizing reputation conflict that may at any moment turn into the lead story on the nightly news.

Google's arch-nemesis Microsoft has for years been the poster child of this type of high-profile polarizing reputation conflict, beginning with the widespread media coverage of the DOJ anti-trust actions, and most recently with the European Union continuing to accuse and fine the Redmondistas for 'unfair competition'. Define 'unfair' from the European Union perspective you say. As best as I can determine, it appears to mean *any new Windows functionality* that in *any way* and at *any time* competes with *anybody else* in *any market* on the planet. Kind of makes you wonder how the European Union defines *fair* competition. But I'll leave that for Microsoft's well-compensated barristers to sort out.

Even hip, always-trendy Yahoo has had to come to terms with negative and polarizing brand reputation conflict when it was forced by the Attorneys General of New York and Nebraska to close 70,000 web chat rooms[22] that had apparently been infiltrated by sexual predators seeking to entrap and do harm to children. No, I'm not making that number up. Seventy thousand Yahoo chat rooms sporting names like *"Kiddies Who Love Sex"* to *"Teen Girls for Older Fat Men"*.

Superpower eBay has also had to deal with reputation conflict in it's many-to-many marketplace, when it bans the sale of all kinds of brand-polarizing items. From Nazi memorabilia, to human embryos, to the endangered smalltooth sawfish[23]. Don't ask me what a smalltooth sawfish is---Look it up on Google---the American version that is, not the Chinese one. Some Beijing bureaucrat may think it's a disparaging nickname for the Party Chairman, and redirect your search to the secret police.

Superpower Oracle has also had to deal with its fair share of polarizing reputation equity as news reports negatively spun the thousands of layoffs[24] of PeopleSoft staff in the wake of it's acquisition by Oracle. And then there was that world famous 'Unbreakable' brand advertising campaign[25], which...(I'm searching for the most diplomatic term designed not to offend Larry Ellison)...*broke.*

Even Cisco, *'the self-defending network'* company has had to cope with negative sound bites when its flagship IOS platform software was reported stolen, and a sample made public on a Russian website[26]. Oops, that's gotta hurt. Ask your brand communications team to try 'self-defending' against that.

As instructional material for future asymmetric marketers, there is one really interesting conclusion you can draw from this near-perpetual sandstorm of negative superpower reputation sound bites in the media.

The sound bite sandstorm has little to do with whether or not a given superpower's technology or user experience is innovative or embraced by customers.

Does this observation mean that I see these negative reputation sound bites as a kind of permanent *background noise* against which all other ISVs have to fight for attention? Sure. All ISVs *are* compelled to compete for attention in the broad context of superpower-dominated, locked-in, 'attention deficit' markets. So from that point of view the superpower sound bite sandstorm would qualify as a kind background noise that ISVs must learn to rise above in order to attract eyes and ears to their brand message. But what I'm here to tell you is that the kind of superpower sound bite sandstorm I've described above is more...Much more than that.

When you boil it down to its undiluted essence, the tabloid tech sound bites illustrate that the challenge of superpower brand messaging has moved *beyond the traditional issues of head-to-head product competition most agencies and brand managers spend their time dealing with.* Instead, the overall market conversation in the software industry is now tending to cluster around whether or not a given superpower (as defined by some specific segment of the overall market) is a *good corporate citizen.*

So as the first practical consideration in developing an asymmetric brand messaging strategy, it's important to recognize that the sound bite sandstorm is more than background noise. Instead, think of the sound bite sandstorm as the *brand price the superpowers pay for maintaining and extending their natural monopoly businesses.*

Seriously folks...What enterprising reporter, blogger, industry pundit, or tech columnist wouldn't want to grab her 15 minutes of fame by taking the superpowers' positive brand perception down a notch? While along the way, furthering her own career. That's why asymmetric marketers correctly see the superpower sound bite sandstorm as an important new fact of life on the software messaging landscape.

Feature Wars to Reputation Wars, Value to Values

Let's take this observation one step further. In the U.S. and around the world, the kind of software superpower tabloid headlines we are now witnessing are the most recent indicators of a *brand messaging shift* that has been underway in the software and web industries for some time now. Which shift is that, you ask? It's the shift *from narrowly-focused brand feature wars to broadly-focused brand reputation wars*. So what's driving this shift? Let's begin with the obvious. The media environment in which superpower brands live and breathe has changed.

The 24 hours a day, 7 days a week news cycle that brought you the OJ Simpson and Michael Jackson trials, the Clinton impeachment, the 2000 Presidential Election vote counting free-for-all, and the Iraq war Abu Ghraib coverage is now alive and well in the software, web and larger tech industries. Sure, sure, sure... Software industry trade publications, websites and email newsletters are still important factors in the overall mix of industry information consumed by both B2B and B2C software buyers. But in this connected age in which the software superpowers have prevailed and become household names, anybody and everybody from weblog 'citizen journalists', to the Drudge Report, to talk radio, to 24/7 cable news...Are equally likely to showcase tech industry sound bites and headlines as a feature story. Hey---tell me who hasn't published some kind of Bill Gates 'retirement' piece? That's why....When a media-juicy, global brand fracas like Google's dotcommunist search policy (or for that matter Microsoft's entry into *any new category* of software) breaks out, you can be sure that the winds of the sound bite sandstorm will howl louder by the minute.

Another factor driving the emergence of 24/7 tech tabloidism in the U.S. is the so-called Red State/Blue State culture clash. The culture clash, while seemingly restricted to non-tech markets, is fast evolving into the latest brand 'wild card' that will begin manifesting in tech markets in many ways. So it's only prudent that this issue of 'culture clash' remain consistently on the radar of every ISV marketer responsible for communications strategy. One no-brainer way it manifests---Sales of many major American newspapers have been trending down[27], increasingly driven not just by competitive threats from online advertising, but also by customer polarization around partisan political issues. So if a particular political point of view doesn't read a given newspaper... Then they are never going to read your major product launch PR announcement (or paid advertisement) in it. On the other hand partisan blog readership and talk radio audiences are growing by leaps and bounds, reflecting a widening customer preference to restrict news consumption to 'trusted sources' (translation 'I already agree with your political or cultural point of view').

The 'culture wars' have also spilled over into Hollywood. Attendance at studio-created feature films (where tech and web companies historically like to do 'product placement' deals) has been on the decline[28]. On the other hand, culturally or politically partisan 'indies' like Michael Moore's "Fahrenheit 9.11", or Mel Gibson's "Passion of the Christ", benefit from growing audiences.

And in American cable television news it's more of the same, as Fox News Network with its 'Fair and Balanced' Red State audience has beaten ratings holy hell out of CNN[29], the Blue State cable channel of choice. Even the Bush administration's communications director Tony Snow, a former Fox News commentator, was brought in to an embattled, low-poll-numbers White House[30] for his asymmetric marketing streetsmarts in waging the unconventional good fight against the 'MSM' (mainstream media).

So one more brand lesson for ISV marketers and their brand communications agencies in the superpower sound bite sandstorm— In politically-polarized and culturally-charged markets, against the background of 24/7 news cycles---*Everything about your business reputation is on the table for brand conflict.*

Not just your product features and benefits, cool user experience, or lack thereof. Hey, if you think my observation is a stretch, go talk to the folks at MySpace.com. Nobody in the press appears to be paying very close attention to the 'innovation' in their social network infrastructure and web applications---It's those sexual predators[31] and 'members behaving badly' within their online social network that continue to capture the lion's share of media attention.

Asymmetric Product Plus Brand 'Credibility Gap' Intensifies Reputation Conflict

And here's another related observation. While traditional *brand value* remains a necessary battlefield for software marketers, it is no longer the only one. *Brand values* are emerging as a new battlefield on which asymmetric marketers can carry out ongoing messaging campaigns in this 'everything on the table' setting.

And against this background of polarization-driven 'everything on the table' reputation conflict, you would be wise to expect both the size of the 'everything'... as well as the size of the 'table' itself... to grow. Why? Because for all practical purposes, values conflict is designed into the very fabric of superpower and other customer-dominating asymmetric offerings.

Let's rewind for a minute to explain this point. In Chapter 3, I described the characteristics of never-ending, non-duplicatable, dotcomplexity-advantaged asymmetric products built from the *creative fusion of software, content, community, commerce and intangibles*. All well and good. But these offerings, while more market-rugged, also have higher levels of potential brand conflict *built in*.

Let's return to my discussion of the Google China sound bites at the top of this chapter to explain the point. In Google's case, the overall market conversation shifted from the virtues of search-as-cool-technology, to *search as a mechanism of content and community censorship*. Whether the brand management at Google sees it this way or not, users experience 'search' as a Google *application*...But they see the web links and content delivered into their browser by a given search as the actual Google *product*.

That's why any intentional suppression of content at the behest of a government in a given regional market (let alone the Chinese government) represents a major league product marketing, corporate ethics, and brand reputation issue. An issue that is *fair game for journalists and competitors alike*.

The takeaway. If your total asymmetric offering incorporates content as one differentiator, then it is wise to consider potential polarization and reputation conflict built in to your messaging challenge. And my conclusion is not Google-specific. It's true for other superpowers and asymmetric marketers as well.

With eBay, for example, *any* market conversation can rapidly shift from the benefits of the commerce platform and marketplace itself (**n-gine**), to the banning of specific products that discrete customer segments in the eBay community (**n**-stitution) find to be objectionable. The takeaway. If your blended asymmetric offering incorporates peer-to-peer, many-to-many, dotcomplexity-advantaged commerce as a differentiator, then you are wise to consider polarization and reputation conflict built in to your messaging challenge.

Same story with Yahoo. In their case, the market conversation did not revolve around some kind of competitive war over the features of their chat software. Rather it was the perception that Yahoo's chat community system was facilitating the behavior of sexual predators. The takeaway. If your total offering incorporates community interaction or social networking as a differentiator, consider potential polarization and reputation conflict built in to your messaging challenge.

And here's the really big brand lesson for future asymmetric marketers. Look for the decibel level of negative brand sound bites to reach the ear-busting threshold if there is in any way, shape or form a *perceived credibility gap between your company's stated values* (e.g. Google's Don't Be Evil brand promise) *and actual market behaviors* (i.e. getting into bed in the name of market expansion with a government more than a few folks on planet Earth see as evil).

In rising superpower Google's case, any brand professional worth their paycheck will tell you that their *high visibility corporate motto actually invited the backlash* of Tibetan protesters carrying 'Google Don't Be Evil' placards. To put it in the context of a point I made in the last chapter, the Google motto became a self-organizing cultural 'attractor' for the Tibetan protestors. Google's motto became the 'no huddle offense' shirt the Tibetan protestors wore to the game.

And where you're positioned in the market power pecking order also turns up the volume. Sure, sure, sure...Everybody knows that Yahoo and Microsoft made similar 'compromises' with the Beijing dotcommunists in relation to competition in the highly coveted Chinese search market. It's just that superpowers Yahoo and Microsoft are *not perceived to be the leader in search*. And above and beyond that, their respective *brand mottos didn't invite the same kind of media sandstorm* as did Google's. Their brand mottos did not morph into brand kryptonite.

OK, I think that's enough setup for what comes next. After all, this is the final chapter (before offering a few designed-to-vault-me-to-asymmetric-pundit-status predictions). And I'm assuming that at some point you do want to put down this book and get busy going asymmetric on your prospects, customers and competitors.

So that said, let's step through *10 practical, brand messaging implications* of my introductory observations about the superpower sound bite sandstorm. These observations, if you heed them, may keep you from having to chow down on brand crow, or hire those really expensive Washington lobbyists in the future. So here goes.

1. The software superpowers, while dominant natural monopoly brands, *generate significant reputation conflict* based on their ongoing market behaviors in the normal course of doing business.

2. This persistent state of brand reputation conflict stems from the fact that the software superpowers are increasingly being *judged as good or bad corporate citizens*. It's the brand price they pay for being natural monopolies.

3. When judged through this corporate citizenship filter, *everything about the superpowers' market behavior is on the table for brand warfare*, not just their technology innovation, or user experience, traditional focus areas of brand marketers.

4. In particular, the *use of their market power, and natural monopoly, in a given category or regional market* can trigger a negative reputation sandstorm that gets louder with each new sound bite or headline in today's 24/7 always-on media setting. This is an important new 'asymmetry' on the software brand messaging landscape.

5. These recurring sound bite sandstorms *intensify market polarization* both inside and outside the superpowers' locked-in customer ecoregions. Polarization on which both competing and symbiotic ISVs can capitalize.

6. This polarization shines the media and customer *spotlight on corporate values, not just product value*.

7. Additionally, the very nature of *asymmetric products* as creative fusions of software, content, community, commerce and intangibles can have the unintended consequence of *intensifying values vs. value*

polarization. Any blended element in the mix may become a polarizing product 'hot spot' under the right circumstances.

8. *Positioning yourself as the leader turns up the volume* on the polarizing sound bite sandstorm. As leaders are held to a higher standard of market behavior.

9. Messaging a *brand promise that is perceived by key segments to be at odds with market behavior* drives the volume of the sound bites to the ear-busting threshold. And can trigger brand 'back-pedaling' and embarrassing brand flip flops.

10. From the standpoint of brand messaging strategy, asymmetric marketers approach these frequently recurring superpower sound bite sandstorms as *persistent market conversations that can serve as brand messaging opportunities.* Opportunities to promote themselves and their products in an age of natural monopoly market power. Think of this as the opportunity for brand messaging strategy based on *conversational symbiosis.*

For the remainder of this chapter, I'm going to step you through the 'deconstruction' of a representative example of one of these persistent superpower market conversations. And then draw some practical conclusions about how to practice conversational symbiosis. Additionally, I'm going to make some basic recommendations on *how to think about your positioning and your brand promise within today's superpower market conversations.*

Conversational Symbiosis: Deconstructing the 'Messaging Mashup'
Before we get down and dirty deconstructing a specific market conversation, it helps to be able to answer the following question.

Question: Why did God give human beings two ears and one mouth?

Answer: So they can listen twice as long as they talk!

This is the first step in understanding how to think about conversational symbiosis. To pro-actively train your asymmetric marketing ear to learn to listen to these ongoing superpower market conversations... *before* you jump into them. Because once you learn to listen to them closely, you will be able to *detect their underlying messaging dynamics.*

Dynamics you can leverage to build your own brand in superpower-dominated markets.

And when you listen to enough of them, it will be come increasingly clear that superpower market conversations are actually *composite* conversations. On the one hand they are many-to-many market dialogues focusing on *conventional 'value' issues of product competition within a given category* of capability. But they also bleed over into *highly polarizing 'values' dialogues that magnetically attach themselves to cross-category superpower market behaviors in general.* Behaviors that can provide you with a messaging opportunity.

One additional point. These market conversations often tend to be dominated by the *superpowers' own active brand contention with each other.* As well as by those specific market forces within a given category that *oppose the very existence of natural monopoly superpowers.* Or at a bare minimum, will use every natural monopoly marketing behavior as a brand messaging weapon against a particular superpower. Here's a descriptor I use to think about these composite superpower/category conversations. I call them *messaging mashups.*

Note: Those of you who follow Web 2.0-speak are familiar with the term 'mashup'. For those of you who are not, the Wikipedia defines a mashup as *"a website or web application that seamlessly combines content from more than one source into an integrated experience."* For the purposes of making my point, I'm shoplifting the mashup concept, and applying it to describe this phenomenon of composite, cross-category superpower conversations

Think of a messaging mashup as a many-to-many market dialogue containing multiple competitive, and complementary, 'threads' and 'brand storylines'. Within a given mashup, a specific *superpower or multiple superpowers' ongoing messaging tends to serve as an anchor thread.* Or focal point for brand warfare within the broader product category conversation.

Upon 'first listen' to a given market conversation from this messaging mashup standpoint, one might erroneously conclude that they (and the superpower sound bite sandstorms these mashups give rise to) appear to be *random*. But you'd be missing out on a major opportunity to get your own brand message out to a broader audience if you think about these composite conversations simply as some kind of random or unstructured mix of communications. You would not be able to effectively leverage them on your behalf.

It's when you listen below the surface of these messaging mashups that your asymmetric marketing ear will detect an underlying structure, or **mashup framework,** around which a given composite conversation evolves in the age of the superpowers. Once you successfully deconstruct this mashup framework, you will be able to more effectively **develop your own positioning and brand promise,** two 'must get right' elements of your asymmetric brand messaging strategy. So let's dig deeper into the structure of composite market conversations or messaging mashups.

In today's superpower-dominated markets, messaging mashups are structured around 4 basic conversational threads that comprise the brand communications landscape in any category in which the superpowers are active, or plan on being active.

These *4 framework threads* are as follows:

The Superpower Thread: As the name implies, this thread consists of the **basic brand story** (key executive speeches, ongoing PR, brand advertising, website copy, product white papers, email newsletters, marketing webcasts, etc.) **told by a specific superpower or contending superpowers** within a given category of market contention (e.g. the Symantec and Microsoft brand stories slugging it out within an increasingly contested category, e.g. PC security software.)

The Anti-Superpower-on-Principle Thread: This thread consists of the anti-superpower messaging of one or more trade groups or industry associations, alliances, coalitions, media pundits or tech gurus (and the 'word of mouth' of their followers). This thread tends to be **consistently critical of natural monopoly market power in general,** as well as any specific ecoregion lock-in maintained by a particular superpower for a given category of capability, e.g. Microsoft in PC operating systems. This thread can be co-opted by one ISV to attack another, and often contains messaging in defense of 'open-ness', 'platform diversity' or 'customer choice'. Referring back to Chapter 5, the messaging smackdown engaged in by Sun's CEO Jonathan Schwartz against Red Hat's so-called 'proprietary' Linux is an example of this kind of messaging in the open source segment.

The Best of Breed Pragmatist Thread: In this thread of the composite conversation, an innovative ISV (or ISVs) often focuses its brand messaging around a specific product or service, in head-to-head opposition to that offered by either the dominant *or* regime-changing natural monopoly superpower in the category. But unlike the folks driving the 'Anti-Monopoly on Principle' thread within the overall conversation, *these ISVs do not criticize customer lock-in or natural monopoly market power per se*. Apple's funny TV commercials touting their Mac systems as inherently more secure than Windows PCs would be an example of this thread. So would a *'best of breed' brand story* told by a company like McAfee as it fights to defend and grow its PC security business against the background of superpower contention between Symantec and Microsoft.

The Asymmetric Emerging ISV Thread: This thread consists of the brand storylines and messaging initiatives of startup or emerging ISVs that have chosen to practice some form of strategic symbiosis with a given superpower or superpowers, or other incumbent leader in an adjacent space. *ISVs participating in this thread piggyback on the marcom spend and brand messaging of a given superpower*. And within the context of the sound bite sandstorm, attempt to 'come to the messaging rescue' of a given superpower or other incumbent leader facing competitive conflict. How? By *touting their own offering as a 'complementary solution'* to a polarizing problem faced by the superpower's installed base customers.

So let's try our hand at listening to, and deconstructing, a representative example of this 4-thread messaging mashup framework. And let's see how it plays out in a specific category conversation. And we'll do it in a category in which there is both escalating superpower contention as well as an in-process category regime change campaign by one of the contending superpowers.

At the end, we'll sum up and identify a few more practical messaging guidelines, especially in relation to positioning and brand promise, two critical ingredients of messaging success in the superpower sandstorm. (Unless of course you actually enjoy the taste of crow, or get turned on from the experience of having your own messaging come back and bite you in the ass). I'll also make some recommendations on how the parties within the specific conversation we are about to deconstruct could do a better job participating in this messaging mashup by *capitalizing on the polarization and values issues identified above*. Since it's a high profile and timely example, let's stay with the conversation I alluded to previously, i.e. the messaging mashup raging in the hotly contested PC security category.

The PC Security Category Messaging Mashup

You're right. To set up the points I want to make, I could have selected many other superpower- contested categories (e.g. search, CRM, database, VOIP, enterprise infrastructure, content management, payments) for our conversation-listening pleasure. But in 2006, the PC security market conversation possesses all the essential characteristics of the kind of messaging mashup that will serve as sound instructional material for every ISV. Seeking to develop an asymmetric brand messaging strategy based on conversational symbiosis.

Let's summarize those 4 representative characteristics as they apply to the PC security category.

1. In the well-established PC or 'endpoint' security segment (anti-virus, anti-spyware, personal firewall), brand contention between two superpowers[32] (Symantec/Microsoft) is on the rise. *Understanding the major differences in the messaging of both superpowers as they contend with each other is critical for ISVs* seeking to effectively promote their own brands, and leverage the PC security category conflict to further their own agenda.

2. In the PC security category there is a well-articulated 'anti-monopoly on principle' thread within the overall market conversation. Specifically, this *'anti-monopoly on principle' thread* is laser-focused on skewering Microsoft as they add more security capability to the Windows platform. In fact, the explicit purpose of this thread within the PC security messaging mashup, as articulated by its proponents, is to prevent Microsoft from having any legitimate market permission to succeed in the security category itself. While driving increased government oversight of the category. In the PC security category messaging mashup, this thread *serves as the 'everything on the table', 'judge them as corporate citizens', 'values-polarizing' wild card.*

If effectively co-opted, it can serve as a rich source of asymmetric messaging material for both pro-superpower and anti-superpower ISVs. But only if 'effectively' co-opted.

3. As I alluded to above, there are more than a few direct and indirect 'pragmatist anti-superpower' players participating in the PC security category messaging mashup. Most are going head-to-head with either Symantec or Microsoft or both. Usually based on the ***classic 'best of breed' storyline***. A competitor like McAfee would fall into this thread.

4. In and around the category, there are literally scores (if not hundreds) of startup and emerging ISVs of all sizes practicing ongoing market symbiosis with the superpowers, delivering complementary products, and seeking to ***gain 'share of ear' based on some form of brand association with the superpowers.***

In other words, the PC security category market conversation is a rich, well-structured messaging mashup. As such, it will serve as a good reference example of the points I want to make. So let's begin deconstructing the threads and storylines within the overall messaging mashup, to better understand how the dynamics of these 4 basic structural threads actually play out.

And don't forget that these four basic structural threads can be found in any category in which the superpowers are active.

Thread One: The Superpower Thread in the PC Security Messaging Mashup

Part One: The Symantec Storyline within the Superpower Thread

Let's set up the conversation with a little background info for those of my readers who may not be familiar with the security category itself. If we take annual revenue in both consumer and enterprise PC security as the main indicator, Symantec (through it's Norton brand) is the incumbent leader in the space[33].

Additionally, it helps to point out that Symantec (seen through the lens of this book), can accurately be characterized as a practitioner of asymmetric marketing in a number of key dimensions of the marketing challenge, including:

- Asymmetric Products: Symantec leverages an asymmetric 'never-ending' product model, providing continuous code and virus file updates, delivering real-time protection to both consumer and enterprise PC users. And along with this never-ending product model, comes a high level of customer groove-in for its overall business.
- Asymmetric Sales Strategy: In the highly contested consumer security segment, Symantec relies on 50 OEM and 150 ISV relationships[34], thereby leveraging the market reach and market power of others (including superpower Yahoo). And the web itself. Additionally, Symantec is adept at leveraging trialware and trial subscriptions to drive market momentum. A marketing practice I characterized in Chapter 4 as a 'use/sell' asymmetric sales approach.
- Asymmetric CBM: Symantec's revenue model is continuing to evolve in the face of rising superpower contention in the consumer category. They are migrating to a 'multi-year subscription' approach[35] thereby driving higher order customer barrier management, while improving forward revenue visibility in the sandstorm.

Additionally, Symantec (under CEO John Thompson, an IBM veteran) has systematically and creatively annexed new market segments via M&A, including it's cross-category merger-of-equals with storage leader Veritas. While the product synergies of this merger are still coalescing, the merger with Veritas holds the potential to create a unique fusion of security and storage management capability Symantec refers to as 'information integrity'[36].

This may be one reason why, in 2006, storage systems market share leader EMC made the move to acquire application security pioneer RSA. Symantec's overall 'information integrity' message fusing storage and security must be perceived as having 'legs' by its competitors.

But despite Symantec's successful execution of asymmetric marketing best practices in the area of products, sales and business models, the company's future status as the revenue and market power leader in PC security is in no way a done deal. Symantec's continued leadership will ultimately depend on how effectively the company succeeds in defending its broad PC security customer ecoregion against the category regime change campaigns of a contending superpower. You guessed it, Microsoft[37].

One effective counter-measure for Symantec against Microsoft's category regime change campaign is to **progressively dominate the composite conversation, or messaging mashup, in the PC security category.** How? Through the persistent presentation of its story to it's own customer ecoregions, including effective counter-arguments to the Microsoft story.

In particular, it must succeed with two critical elements of its story:

1. Where Symantec continues to **position itself within the overall conversation**, and

2. What kind of **'zero credibility gap' brand promise** it makes to existing customers and partners, as well as to new prospects.

So where can we turn to get a quick, compressed version of Symantec's overall brand messaging, positioning and promise. How about if we listen to their leader, John Thompson, as he participates in the messaging mashup by laying out Symantec's **'market leader'** story to his own customer base at their May 2006 annual Symantec Vision conference.

When future asymmetric marketers review the webcast (or transcript) of Thompson's talk at his company's annual customer conference, two things immediately jump out relative to his company's approach to brand messaging. The first would be Thompson's **strong, fact-based assertion of category leadership** (his brand positioning) by Symantec in every conventional sense of the term 'leadership'.

The second thing that jumps out is his effort to **creatively re-define the nature of the security problem facing businesses and consumers,** and Symantec's evolving brand promise relating to those problems. Let's begin with his consistent positioning of Symantec as the category leader in PC security.

In his speech Thompson states unequivocally that *"We (Symantec) pioneered the idea of protection...In fact, we protect more people from more online threats than anyone in the world."*[38] Additionally he supports his category leadership assertion by pointing out that, *"We track vulnerabilities in more than 30,000 technologies...operating systems...and application product versions from more than 4000 vendors. We track emerging threats with a network of more than 24,000 network sensors in 180 countries worldwide. We see more than 25 percent of the world's email. Our insight and intelligence around the connected world is unsurpassed."*[39]

Within the overall 4-thread messaging mashup, Thompson's brand story represents a clear, unambiguous assertion of category leadership in every conventional sense in which that term is used in the software industry. But Thompson doesn't stop there. Based on his fact-based assertion of category leadership, he then ***redefines the nature of the problem facing his customers***, as well as his brand promise going forward.

Here's how he puts it. *"The main threat to information these days isn't necessarily a large-scale, fast moving virus or worm. From 2002 to 2004 there were almost 100 medium-to-high risk attacks. Last year (2005) there were only six. We've made significant headway in containing these types of threats. But those are **yesterday's problems** (JEB emphasis). Today, we face a bigger and perhaps more insidious challenge."*[40]

Thompson continues. *"Sophisticated criminal elements are now behind many of today's attacks---and, unlike the hackers of the past, they are much more interested in anonymity than in notoriety. Today's threats are silent and highly-targeted. What these criminals are searching for is personal and financial information---and they are looking to use it for <u>serious</u> (Thompson's emphasis) financial gain."*[41]

So what has Thompson done here? Asked another way, why shift messaging focus to a new problem if you are already the category leader in solving the old problem? Because champion marketing cage fighters like Thompson understand there is value in;

(1) ***laying the messaging groundwork for his company's future solutions*** as one way to defend the Symantec customer ecozone against regime change by another superpower, and

(2) *providing the brand argument for cross-category expansion into new markets* more suited to the merged Symantec/Veritas 'information integrity' company.

In short, in this 2006 speech to his customers, Thompson has taken the first steps to *drive the next phase of the market conversation* by redefining the PC security category itself. Toward this end he invokes new messaging he rolls up in the phrase *"Security 2.0"*, which he describes as a *"broad set of solutions designed to protect your infrastructure... your information....and your interactions."*[42]

Later on, I'm going to give you my color commentary on how effective Thompson's approach may prove to be as he goes head-to-head with an experienced regime-changing superpower. But before I get to that, let's listen in on CEO Steve Ballmer, the post-Gates leader of the Microsoft tribe, lay out Redmond's story within the PC security market conversation, at their July 2006 Partner Conference. From Ballmer's comments, we will catch a telling glimpse as to how a contending superpower, one historically successful at asymmetric marketing and software category regime change, participates in the messaging mashup.

Part Two: The Microsoft Storyline within the Contending Superpower Thread

Here's the first big messaging lesson about superpower brand contention, Microsoft style. At no time, even in a major speech to his own partner network, does Steve Ballmer ever assert category leadership in security. Or even openly challenge an assertion of leadership by others. Why?

Because he doesn't have to.

What he does instead is articulate his company's security messaging in the context of re-iterating the classic and compelling 'Microsoft-as-underdog' story. That security needs to become an ever-more-important *'feature'* of Microsoft products. Then he builds on that. Quoting Ballmer: *"We focused a lot in the past on improving the core security in our products...This year (2006) we will enter the security market in full force."*[43]

He continues, " *The next opportunity I want to talk to is another broad horizontal market opportunity that we're trying to build this year, and that's* *in the area of security. We've introduced our Forefront product line, and really what we're saying and what we're doing with Forefront is **moving beyond just this notion of improving the security in our core products.** Yes, Vista is the most secure release of Windows we've ever done; yes, Longhorn Server, the next release of Windows Server, will be the most secure release of our server infrastructure. But we made a concrete choice under the umbrella of this People Ready software to say we need to provide an end-to-end solution for security, which really means clients, server and edge protection."*[44]

He goes on to underscore the often-repeated point that Microsoft's entry into the security market is not simply customer-driven, but in fact is **customer-demanded.** *"I think this is an exciting opportunity, I think it's one **customers push on us hard** (my emphasis)."*[45] In other words, Ballmer has chosen to **position his company's offerings not in relation to category competitors, but first and foremost in relation to his own customer ecoregions.**

I underscore this point to illustrate that this is **qualitatively different than Thompson's positioning of Symantec** as a **legacy category leader relative to its historic security competitors.**

Ballmer then gets down to the real issue of superpower contention in the PC security category as he makes a simple, basic marketing argument that justifies category regime change. Quoting Ballmer: *"They (Microsoft's customers) want the **kind of integration that Microsoft uniquely can provide in the security world** (JEB emphasis). And while there's going to be very healthy coopetition in the security business, I think having a rich and complete security offering from Microsoft will provide incredible value to our customers and give you incredible new alternatives to build business."*[46]

Note here that Ballmer's message takes the form of *a direct monetary appeal to his base of hundreds of thousands of business partners*---Partners that may benefit from new Microsoft security offerings, as well as the ongoing 'featurizing' or embedding of security functionality within the Windows platform (*'the kind of integration that Microsoft uniquely can provide'* is how he puts it).

So let's sum up 2 major points within the category regime change story that Ballmer has told here, and briefly contrast it with the Symantec category leader story told by John Thompson. My comparison goes to the issue of fundamental strategic messaging decisions about brand positioning and brand promise that I will expand on in a moment.

1. Despite his company's status as a market superpower, Ballmer chooses to position Microsoft within the security category conversation as a new entrant. A new entrant demanded by his customers. In fact, he positions the company as the brand underdog. Thompson, on the other hand, positions Symantec in the messaging mashup as the technology pioneer, and the legacy leader in the category.

2. Ballmer's brand promise focuses on the 'featurizing' (embedding) of security within the Windows platform, as well as on his partners' financial gain by participating along with Microsoft in the security category. Thompson's brand promise redefines the very nature of cyber-threats, as one basis to introduce new *'Security 2.0'* messaging. Messaging he hopes will make his offerings more relevant to the enterprise and the consumer in an age of organized criminal cyber-attacks. It's also significant that in his annual keynote to his own customer ecoregion, Thompson appears to make his case for Security 2.0 from the point of view of a 'single-source' vendor, and does go into much detail about the role of his ISV and channel partners. Significant during a major speech to his own customer base.

OK. Let's move to the second thread in the PC security messaging mashup.

Thread Two: 'Anti-Monopoly on Principle' in the Security Messaging Mashup

Since 2003, one of the loudest voices represented within the security messaging mashup has been the voice I characterize as the *'Anti-Monopoly on Principle'* thread.

So what is the core story within this thread? Simply put, this thread is dedicated to the proposition that the Microsoft PC *'monoculture'* is the primary source of most security problems faced by corporations and consumers.

This storyline is best represented by a white paper titled *'Cyber Insecurity: The Cost of Monopoly'*, authored by a group of prominent security folks[47], and published by the CCIA (Computer & Communications Industry Association). Let's listen to them in their own words.

"Most of the world's computers run Microsoft's operating systems, thus most of the world's computers are vulnerable to the same viruses and worms at the same time. The only way to stop this is to avoid monoculture in computer operating systems, and for reasons just as reasonable and obvious as avoiding monoculture in farming. Microsoft **exacerbates this problem via a wide range of practices that lock users to its platform** *(JEB emphasis). The impact on security of this lock-in is real and endangers society. Because Microsoft's near-monopoly status itself magnifies security risk, it is essential that society become less dependent on a single operating system from a single vendor if our critical infrastructure is not to be disrupted in a single blow. The goal must be to* **break the monoculture. (JEB emphasis)"**[48]

Consistent with this goal, the paper's authors also take the position that even if Microsoft succeeds by 'integrating' more security into its products---That would be a bad thing for its customers! Why? Because then they would become even more dependent on Microsoft.

"Efforts by Microsoft to improve security will fail if their side effect is to increase user-level lock-in. Microsoft must not be allowed to impose new restrictions on its customers – imposed in the way only a monopoly can do – and then claim that such exercise of monopoly power is somehow a solution to the security problems inherent in its products. The prevalence of security flaws in Microsoft's products is an **effect** *of monopoly power; it must not be allowed to become a* **reinforcer.***"[49]

In plain English, this thread in the PC security messaging mashup takes the position that Microsoft's efforts to improve security are a bad thing. So what is the solution recommended by the authors?

Not surprisingly, increased government intervention into software markets.

"Wise governments are those able to distinguish that which must be tolerated as it cannot be changed from that which must be changed as it cannot be tolerated. The reapportionment of risk and responsibility through regulatory intervention embodies that wisdom in action. If governments are going to be responsible for the survivability of our technological infrastructure, then **whatever governments do will have to take Microsoft's dominance into consideration**[50] *(JEB emphasis)."*

Now would be a good time for me to point out the following. If you've been awake up until this point in the book, you know by now that I don't have a problem with Microsoft's expertise in asymmetric marketing. I see it as a highly creative form of unconventional marketing warfare that has directly led over time to their increasing returns-advantaged, cross-category natural monopoly.

But *that doesn't mean I think that this 'monoculture' (or anti-monopoly on principle) thread in the messaging mashup can be dismissed or discounted out of hand.*

It's a critically important storyline for asymmetric marketers to understand, within the overall PC security conversation. My evidence. How about 441,000 links returned in a Google search on the expression *Microsoft monoculture* (as of September 2006). But why is this thread so critically important to pay attention to? Good question. Here's the answer. Because the monoculture thread *opens the door to the 'values' and corporate citizenship issues* I talked about in my introduction of Google's sound bite sandstorm at the top of the chapter.

'But Joe B…Are you saying here that ISV asymmetric marketers should embrace the authors' call for more government regulation of software markets?' Not at all!

In fact, the messaging asymmetry, the messaging power, in the 'monoculture' story breaks down at the point of it's open appeal for government regulation. Why does it break down? Because this appeal ignores 3 practical realities facing ISV marketers seeking to successfully practice symbiosis in Microsoft ecoregions:

1. Microsoft *customers have businesses to run and lives to live.* For that reason, they do want improved security within Windows, despite their dependence on it.

2. Microsoft *business partners have an unprecedented opportunity* to grow their own top line by participating in Microsoft security initiatives, and see this kind of 'more government regulation' messaging against Microsoft as an argument against themselves.

3. ISV marketers want to *grow their own customer lock-in* based on some form of asymmetric CBM (customer barrier management)

practices they have gleaned from the market success of the superpowers. Hell, even smart open source Linux ISVs seek to defend their hard-won customers, and do not hesitate to turn to the asymmetric marketing playbook (as I pointed out in Chapter 5 in discussing Red Hat).

But that doesn't mean asymmetric marketers in the security space should not see a 'monoculture' white paper like this as an opportunity to advance their own messaging agenda---A ready-to-wear anti-Microsoft 'monoculture' storyline on which to piggyback their own participation in the messaging mashup. So they should select those specific arguments that work.

Moreover, asymmetric marketers should *see any 'monoculture' storyline as simply one more reflection of the superpower sound bite sandstorm and the brand measurement of software superpowers as corporate citizens.*

As such, the 'monoculture' arguments hold a lot of potential for creative messaging co-optation by ISV marketers (Who wouldn't want a built-in market villain complete with it's own negative sound bite sandstorm for every marketing story you want to tell?) Surprisingly though, no brand professionals in the security industry or their agencies seem to have figured this out. I mean none. Why am I so sure of this assertion? Because when you search on Google for 'Microsoft monoculture', there are Zero...I repeat...*Zero sponsored ads or links next to those 441,000 plus search results.*[51] (As of 9/06).

And you thought I was being too hard on the cargo cult marketing industry.

But wait...Asymmetric messaging lives! Because the monoculture story has proven valuable to contending superpower Symantec. In fact, Symantec actually acquired a company run by one of the authors of the monoculture white paper, and CEO John Thompson has used the term 'monoculture' in analyst-sponsored panel discussions[52].

As a general rule, *look for similar 'anti-monopoly on principle' (monoculture) messaging to emerge in some form in all markets Microsoft enters, and increasingly...in markets dominated by other superpowers.*

Why? Because the same 'monoculture' messaging logic can be used against Oracle in database systems, Adobe in electronic documents, eBay in commerce, Cisco in networking, and SAP in European regional markets, to name a few.

And from a practical point of view, *the basic messaging logic contained in the values-based 'monoculture' story is identical to that used against Google, in criticizing their brand missteps related to the government-sanctioned 'monoculture' of web search in the Chinese market.*

Same story, different market. Values, not value. Everything on the table for brand warfare. Ecozone polarization. You get it.

Thread Three: The Best of Breed Pragmatist Thread

The third thread in the messaging mashup is based on those brand stories told by ISVs that have decided, out of business necessity, to go head-to-head with the superpowers in a given category. However, their messaging takes the form of a more pragmatic story, a story not based on opposing superpower monopoly or monoculture in principle, but *critiquing various market effects of monoculture.* The humorous Apple TV commercial[53] comparing PC security to Mac security is one high profile example of this thread. Just *opt out* of the monoculture is the basic message.

But in the main, ISV messaging in this thread of the mashup tends to cluster around the classic 'best of breed' positioning and brand promise. In a nutshell, the classic best of breed story is this. *'There is no way in hell that Superpower Product X is better than Best of Breed Offering Y' because....* In the PC security messaging mashup under discussion, a competitor like McAfee best represents this thread.

As I did with Symantec, let's review a few background facts about McAfee, and its embrace of various aspects of asymmetric marketing. While Symantec's overall security-related revenues are around 3 times the size of McAfee's, McAfee continues to grow at 20 plus percent a year (50% in the consumer segment of their ecozone per their annual report[54]). And is the number two in market share[55] behind Symantec in anti-virus software and services.

The company has also broken through the $1 Billion dollar annual revenue mark in 2006. No shabby accomplishment, while simultaneously divesting itself of all non-security business under the leadership of its CEO, George Samenuk. So unlike Symantec and Microsoft, 100% of McAfee revenue is in consumer and enterprise security products.

But very much like security revenue leader Symantec and regime-changing superpower Microsoft, the astute observer can see McAfee creatively practicing asymmetric marketing in a number of key areas of their overall marketing challenge:

Asymmetric Products: Packaged as a continuously updated '8 in 1' (anti-virus, anti-spyware, etc.) security suite, delivered online as a web service, creatively blending code, vulnerability assessment and security content (anti-virus files), the McAfee offering leverages many best practices in asymmetric product management. And for this reason drives a high order 'shark-itecture' groove-in, especially for consumers. Hey, in the interest of full disclosure, they've got a lazy pragmatist like me locked in to their offering via my Dell notebook. (Until John Thompson or Steve Ballmer makes me an offer I can't refuse.)

Asymmetric Sales Model: Their veteran CEO has also led the company in eliminating dependence on a direct sales force. In favor of a highly leveraged, partner-advantaged selling model[56]. Like the early Microsoft, they appear to be laser-focused on their TAO (targets of asymmetric opportunity), and symbiotically capitalizing on the market power of incumbent leaders. They currently have deals with AOL (still the number one dial-up ISP), Comcast (the leading cable internet provider), Dell (the number one PC company) as well as with eBay's Skype subsidiary, now touting 100 million VOIP users.

Asymmetric CBM: McAfee's subscription revenue model (in close concert with its asymmetric product model, and leveraged reliance on sales partners who are dominant in their respective categories) has provided them with a high level of customer groove-in expressed in terms of almost $750 million in deferred revenue from subscriber accounts at the end of 2005. This provides them with outstanding forward revenue visibility[57] in the superpower sandstorm.

So without a doubt, McAfee has an outstanding brand story to tell. Conceivably one that would allow them to insulate themselves from, and even benefit from, the Symantec/Microsoft superpower contention and regime change combat. So what story is McAfee telling? Let's listen.

McAfee, like Symantec has chosen to position itself as a category 'leader', but with a twist. I quote from their corporate description of themselves. " *McAfee® is the **largest dedicated security company in the world** (my emphasis), and we proactively secure systems and networks from known and unknown threats. Home users, businesses, service providers, government agencies, and our partners all trust McAfee's **unmatched security expertise** (my emphasis again), and have confidence in our comprehensive, integrated, and proven solutions to effectively block attacks and prevent disruptions.*" The obvious implication here is that superpowers Symantec and Microsoft, both diversified companies with non-security lines of business, are less able to focus on solving actual problems in the market. And therefore, do not possess 'unmatched security expertise'.

Also...In distinction to Symantec's Security 2.0 positioning (which is designed to change the security market conversation and showcase the new, post-Veritas Symantec's overall expertise in protecting 'information, infrastructure and interactions'), McAfee positions itself as the proven *best of breed* provider focused on those problems John Thompson stated in his Vision 2006 speech are essentially under control. The problems folks face in the world of Security 1.0, i.e. viruses, spyware, hackers, etc.

And McAfee's CEO, like John Thompson, also delivers a message of 'leadership as innovation' which takes the form of touting first mover advantage in addressing various security challenges. Here's a quote from his annual report. " *We are dedicated to continuing McAfee's established record of innovation in 2006. We were the first to market with both host and network intrusion prevention, the **first to deliver consumer security as a service more than seven years ago,** (my emphasis) and the first to **integrate intrusion prevention with anti-virus** (my emphasis again). We are also the only company offering an integrated end-to-end mobile security solution.*"[38]

And while not actually coming right out and using the term 'monoculture', or implying that Microsoft's dominance in PC operating systems is in any way responsible for the multitude of evils presented in the White Paper cited above, McAfee has begun practicing conversational symbiosis. How? By leveraging Microsoft's high profile entry into PC security to get its own Best of Breed 'Proven Security' message to the market. Here's a telling headline from one of their press announcements[59], a headline presented in the context of Microsoft's ongoing high profile admissions of various new Windows vulnerabilities. McAfee uses it to make their messaging point and support their own brand promise.

> *VULNERABILITY ADVISORY: MCAFEE, INC. SOLUTIONS PROTECT AGAINST EIGHTEEN NEWLY DISCLOSED MICROSOFT WINDOWS VULNERABILITIES*
> *McAfee Intrusion Prevention and Security Risk Management Solutions Provide Protection to Identify and Block Potential New Attacks"*

The basic point of the press release---To openly declare that folks with PCs that have these vulnerabilities are already *safe if they have McAfee.*

So let's briefly summarize McAfee's storyline in the messaging mashup. Their positioning (largest *dedicated* security provider vs. Symantec and Microsoft) and brand promise (peace of mind from their proven security suite that any and all 'monoculture-related' bad things will be blocked) are that of a classical best of breed competitor (e.g. BEA Systems in middleware, Business Objects in business intelligence, Intuit in personal finance).

But here's the asymmetric marketing question. Is this 'best of breed' story rugged enough to defend them against their larger competitors?

Let me tackle this issue by assessing the effectiveness of the brand messaging of all 3 companies, prior to proceeding on to the 4th and final thread in the mashup, the emerging ISV, asymmetric marketer thread.

First Symantec. Symantec's incumbent leader positioning and new Security 2.0 brand promise, while compelling, are **not yet optimized to defend them against category regime change** in the age of the software superpowers. If I were advising their brand and PR agencies, I would not hesitate to let them know that they may be painting their client into a corner of classic cargo cult messaging missteps. Here are those missteps.

1. *Positioning yourself* (or allowing your agency to position you) *within a static snapshot of a category* is not the way to go in the

superpower sandstorm. *Positioning in the overall market conversation or messaging mashup is the way to go.* What do I mean by that?

Many brand and PR agencies in 2006 still continue to rely (lazily and inappropriately I might add) on analyst tools like the Gartner Magic Quadrant model, as their key source of input for messaging differentiation. For those folks who may have been vacationing on Mars, and are not familiar with the model, the Magic Quadrant is Gartner's proprietary tool to compare product functionality and vendor 'leadership' attributes within a given category at a given point in time.

John Thompson's well-articulated, fact-based assertion of leadership in the keynote speech I referenced above is straight out of the Magic Quadrant positioning playbook. In fact, Thompson mentions the Magic Quadrant in his Gartner interview I referenced earlier, even drawing a laugh from the audience when the interviewer challenges Symantec's claim of innovation leadership[60] relative to others. You guys put us the Magic Quadrant so we must be the best...is how I would paraphrase Thompson's spontaneous, and witty comeback.

But what the branding/PR agency advocates of the Magic Quadrant positioning playbook fail to incorporate in their microwavable 'stories' are all those *polarizing sound bite sandstorm issues.* Including continuous reputation conflict, monopoly market behaviors (and their spillover into values issues), as well as the 'everything on the table' stuff I referred to in my discussion of Google at the top of the chapter. Let me make clear that I don't blame Gartner for this. I place the blame on the shoulders of cargo cult branding and PR agencies that have *fallen into the habit of outsourcing their clients' positioning* (a core competency for asymmetric marketers) to an analyst firm. Because they think 'analyst validation' is the short cut to make the cargo planes land for their client.

If I were advising Symantec on how to participate in the messaging mashup, I'd recommend that they *assess every single hot button issue contained in the 'monoculture' thread* I referenced above. And systematically cherry-pick those specific issues that can be transformed into 'campaign-able' ideas. Ideas that will help them to defend themselves in the face of category regime change dynamics, and the no-fly-zone marketing of a competing superpower.

2. Regarding Symantec's new Security 2.0 brand promise, I'd tell them to start paying it off in spades or let it gracefully go away. Why? Because at this writing (4 months after Thompson's highly visible introduction of the idea at a customer conference), there are less than 1,840 references to "Symantec Security 2.0" on a Google search[61]. This means their brand and PR agency folks are not reinforcing the story enough for it to take on a life of it's own within the overall market conversation.

Instead, I recommend that they focus on a more 'intangible' brand promise (like their "Pure Confidence in a Connected World"), a promise that could be consistently paid off by *incorporating more of the kernel values in their operating culture into their messaging*.

For example, I'd leverage Symantec's decade-plus tribal experience around the question of vulnerability in all software platforms, and pay off the lessons learned by the Symantec tribe in their journey in PC security. I'd also recommend an aggressive campaign around the fact that no amount of 'integration' (Steve Ballmer's term) of security capability into the Microsoft (or any) platform is going to address the PC security challenge any time soon.

Something like this... *'We all know the connected world remains a dangerous world. We at Symantec have taken you this far. And we're the folks best prepared to take you the rest of the way'* ...That's how I'd recommend they begin *leveraging a culture of candor to pay off the intangible brand promise* of 'pure confidence'.

OK. On to Microsoft. As the leading software superpower, an asymmetric marketer that has had to face brand reputation conflict at every stage of its development, Microsoft messaging folks understand the points I just made relative to Symantec. When they enter a new category in force, they are smart enough not to position themselves relative to others as anything but the new entrant and underdog.

They *wisely do not position themselves as a leader relative to competitors, but as a partner in relation to their own installed base ecoregions*.

This is something asymmetric marketers with locked-in customer ecoregions can do. Position themselves in relation to their own customers. Seriously. If your cross-category ecozone already extends as far as the eye can see... Who else really matters but the inhabitants of that ecozone? The customers.

And in order to provide the messaging justification (within a polarizing sound bite sandstorm) for asymmetric marketing and category regime change, they *insist that their ecoregions and ISV partners 'demand innovation'*. Innovation that takes the form of the ongoing integration of new functionality into the Windows platform.

And around this positioning relative to one's own customers, Microsoft develops an increasingly sophisticated *'intangible' brand promise*. The *'Your Potential, Our Passion'* brand campaign is a representative example of the 'intangible' approach. A messaging approach which *flows naturally from seeing one's own operating culture as a source of competitive advantage*. It's all about paying off the Microsoft culture as a brand attribute. So is the new 'People Ready' messaging.

Let me also make clear that when I use the term 'intangible', I am specifically contrasting it to something like Oracle's *'Unbreakable'* brand promise. Which was *highly tangible and thus inevitably invited attack* by thousands of hackers and security gurus who set out to prove Oracle was not unbreakable.

So too is Google's use of the term 'evil', a seeming intangible. Which was actually *transformed into a negative tangible*, and picked up and run with on those protest placards carried by the Tibetan protesters (and countless bloggers around the planet).

I see an intangible brand promise of the 'Your Potential, Our Passion' type as the messaging equivalent of what Sun Tzu describes as *'formlessness'*. Shielding your actual market position from opponents. Defending your asymmetric marketing practices with the brand intangible of personal 'potential'. And the historic 'passion' of the Redmond tribe's operating culture.

So Microsoft has nailed those two elements. Asymmetric marketers should see these Microsoft messaging approaches as brand best practices carved in stone.

Position relative to your own customers.

Intangible brand promise that flows from your marketing culture.

Formlessness in defense of asymmetric marketing.

But there *is* a wild card of vulnerability in Microsoft's messaging. Especially as the company continues to enter new markets currently led by others. This vulnerability can be detected in various messaging components of the 'anti-monopoly on principle' thread I described above.

Just as Google's 'Don't Be Evil' was turned against them in the sound bite sandstorm, so too *Microsoft's 'integration' story is vulnerable,* as made clear in the arguments of the authors of the 'monoculture' white paper.

The only reason the monoculture story lacks resonance as an asymmetric brand messaging attack on Microsoft, is that it's proponents do not seek a competitive resolution in the marketplace. But in the halls of congress and the courts.

But that doesn't mean that *brass knuckles brand managers* will not *mine the elements of this particular monoculture story (and others) to either attack Microsoft's messaging, or practice conversational symbiosis with it.* How? By using it as one more compelling reason to tout their own 'complementary' offerings. Offerings that mitigate the risks inherent in the 'monoculture'.

On to McAfee. McAfee, like Symantec, is leaving way too much sandstorm messaging capital on the table by restricting itself to classical 'best of breed' positioning within the messaging mashup. As a billion dollar ISV with a powerful network of go-to-market partners, they have an unparalleled opportunity to capitalize on the contention between Symantec and Microsoft.

My recommended messaging would take the form of a 'McAfee has the moral high ground' story. A story told to every consumer and enterprise security customer who will listen. Something like this: *"While two market giants on power trips slug it out for your security dollars, you can count on us to protect you. We don't have an agenda of market dominance...Just the security products you demand. So stop looking to the leaders before it's too late."*

Maybe not these exact words, but you get the direction I'm going. The big point. When category regime change dynamics dominate a market conversation, capitalize on the contention between two superpowers to advance your own messaging agenda.

I'd also recommend that McAfee capitalize on a *values-focused message embracing 'anti-monopoly on principle' content, without all the government intervention baggage.*

Wow. You have no idea how really painful it was for me giving away all that free branding advice to billion dollar software companies. But what the hell, this is the last chapter.

And at the end of the day, the advice was for really for you, gentle reader. Advice designed to smash the monoculture of cargo cult messaging agencies.

OK on to our 4th and final thread in the mashup.

Thread Four: Emerging ISV Asymmetric Marketer Thread
Let's circle back to what I said about asymmetric marketers in Chapter One. That they do not run away from the simple (however counter-intuitive) conclusion that most of their future customers, whoever they may be, are *probably superpower customers today.*

For *startup and emerging category ISVs, asymmetric brand strategy is all about entering the messaging mashup with a story that, first and foremost, comes off as 'complementary' to the story told by the superpower(s) or other incumbent market leader.*

A story that picks up where the superpower messaging leaves off.

And because we are dealing with *composite conversations that fuse category issues and superpower contention issues,* you have lots of choices. You can articulate a complementary message with those superpowers actually competing in your category, or you can articulate a complementary message with superpowers adjacent to the category, or even nowhere near the category. And this is especially true when there are regime change dynamics driving the overall messaging mashup. For asymmetric marketers watching their precious marcom spend, practicing conversational symbiosis with the superpowers is where the brand action is.

So let's see how 4 different emerging ISVs have chosen to implement this idea within the PC security messaging mashup. (Note: By mentioning these folks I am not 'American Idol-izing' them, or even suggesting that they will win big someday. They may. Then again they may not. Too many factors to call an individual cage fight, unless I'm personally engaged in it. I'm simply making the point that they are representative examples of asymmetric brand messaging in the superpower sandstorm.)

1. ISV Practices Conversational Symbiosis with Superpower Symantec

Sana Security is a venture-funded ISV that has developed an alternative security model to the traditional security approaches used by Symantec, Microsoft and McAfee. Rather than developing software focused on preventing the spread of *known* malware by continuously updating the user with malware 'signatures', Sana has introduced what it calls Active Malware Defense Technology[62], i.e. behavioral protection that protects against *unknown or 'zero day' malware*. Sana's solution identifies malware by watching how a given software platform or application is supposed to behave, then enforcing that behavior and quarantining any suspicious activity before it can spread. From a product point of view, they are disruptive technology innovators.

But rather than message their disruptive technology innovation as something directly in opposition to superpower solutions, Sana has gone down the road of asymmetric brand messaging.

They have chosen to practice conversational symbiosis in the superpower sandstorm by *positioning their offering as complementary to Symantec.* Here's a sample of their messaging from a June 2006 press release titled, *" Sana Security Primary Response SafeConnect Complements Anti-Virus Solution and Delivers Comprehensive Malware Protection".*

"Sana Security, Inc., a security software company, today announced Primary Response SafeConnect for Norton AntiVirus to deliver broad threat protection against malware and unwanted programs. By pairing Sana's proactive anti-

malware technology with Norton AntiVirus, enterprise customers and end users receive complete protection against a scope of malicious threats, including unknown malware attacks, without requiring signatures and scanning."[63]

So what's the asymmetric brand messaging lesson here for ISVs? Simple. Even if your product strategy is based on disruptive technology innovation against incumbent market leaders, even if you do not embrace the asymmetric product model I suggested in this book, you can still practice asymmetric brand messaging. And position yourself as *complementary within the messaging mashup.*

Think of this as an example of messaging symbiosis of the type Google practices with Microsoft, i.e. positioning the Google Toolbar to attach to Microsoft's installed base of Internet Explorer customers. One thing for asymmetric marketers to keep in mind. These messaging doors don't stay open for ever, because the superpowers are intent on co-opting disruptive innovation to pre-empt emerging competitors. So walk through them while you can. The optimal outcome. The superpowers notice your symbiotic messaging, see your particular form of disruptive technology innovation as something they can co-opt, and buy you out at a premium.

2. ISV Practices Conversational Symbiosis with Microsoft

As part of its entry into security markets, Microsoft in late 2005 established the SecureIT Alliance, an organization now embracing scores of security ISVs with products and services that interoperate with, and complement, Microsoft offerings. The founding of this alliance provided smart startups with an opportunity to brand asymmetrically, and begin attaching their messaging to Microsoft's enterprise security initiatives in a symbiotic fashion.

Here's an example of asymmetric brand messaging from Centrify, a startup ISV focused on complementing Microsoft's server side offerings, and extending those offerings into the ecoregions of competing suppliers. I quote from a Centrify press release:

"Centrify Corporation, a leading provider of solutions that securely integrate non-Microsoft platforms with Microsoft® Active Directory® management services, today announced that it is a founding member of the new Microsoft SecureIT Alliance, a community of security providers who are working together to deliver more integrated security solutions for the Windows

Server Systems platform. In contribution to the alliance Centrify is focused on **helping define how non-Windows platforms can better integrate with** **Microsoft's security infrastructure** *(my emphasis)*[64].

After laying out this complementary, 3-dimensional product message, the Centrify folks take sides in the cage fight. They make the extremely smart move of openly validating Microsoft's security initiatives.

"Microsoft's leadership in establishing the SecureIT Alliance is a further demonstration of their **commitment to all levels of security for users and** **enterprises** *(my emphasis)," said Tom Kemp, CEO of Centrify Corporation. "Centrify is equally committed to ensuring that non-Microsoft platforms and applications benefit from the ongoing enhancements in identity management related to authentication, authorization and access control that Microsoft and fellow alliance members deliver."*[65]

No fence-sitting or brand equivocation here. Just pure asymmetric mutualism with both superpower platforms and messaging.

Centrify is an ISV that appears to instinctively understand that in this age of the software superpowers, the smart way to advance one's own brand messaging is through practicing conversational symbiosis.

3. ISV Practices Conversational Symbiosis with Google

With Google? How the hell did they get involved in this PC security messaging mashup? You didn't mention them in your 4-thread mashup framework.

Hey…Google came in through the back door of the cage. Through their Google Pack of PC utility software that runs on Windows.

Here's an example of how Lavasoft, a Swedish anti-spyware ISV, took advantage of their inclusion in the Google pack to practice conversational symbiosis with Google. And by association, with Symantec, Adobe and other superpowers also included in the pack.

Lavasoft Ad-Aware SE Personal Edition Included as Part of **Google Pack**
Award-winning Ad-Aware is bundled with Google's free software package

Lavasoft AB, the world leader in antispyware solutions has teamed with Google Inc. to include Ad-Aware SE Personal Edition in the Google Pack. Lavasoft is one of seven companies working with Google for the pack of free software utilities.

*"Lavasoft is excited to team with Google to include its award-winning and industry-leading antispyware solution in the Google Pack," said Merja Turpeinen, Marketing & PR Coordinator at Lavasoft AB. "We are **pleased to help Google deliver privacy protection to their users** (my emphasis).[65]"*

And then they raise the brand stakes by referring to themselves as the 'preferred antisypware solution.'

*Google Pack, launched on January 6, 2006 offers free, useful software to improve the user experience online and on the desktop. Google Pack is a combination of best-in-class software selected by Google users to effectively manage information, communicate better, and surf the web faster and safer. By Google's selection of Ad-Aware SE as a **preferred antispyware solution**, Lavasoft's role in the community of online users is invigorated.[66]*

'Invigorated'...there's a term you don't see used very often in American brand messaging. Kind of like borrowing brand equity from a Swedish massage. Uh, oh. I better watch myself.

But seriously, the lesson here is simple. Extend Superpower Thread 1 of the mashup from 'contending superpowers within a category' to contending cross-category superpowers in general. And then practice conversational symbiosis with your superpower 'host' of choice.

4. ISV Practices Conversational Symbiosis with AOL

Here's one final example in this thread. When you can't find a superpower with which to practice conversational symbiosis, find an incumbent market leader in *an adjacent category*. That's what ISV Kaspersky Lab has done with dialup ISP leader AOL.

How? By teaming with AOL on their free Active Virus Shield service, an alternative online PC health offering to Microsoft's Windows Live OneCare service. The AOL service is even co-branded as *'Powered by Kaspersky'*, a none-too-shabby asymmetric messaging coup[67].

And let's throw in the fact that Kaspersky's 'Powered by' branding approach is an extension of their asymmetric sales strategy focusing on OEM partners. Why go head to head with Symantec, Microsoft and McAfee, when you can embed your technology into the offerings of software and services providers in adjacent categories. And let the world see that little 'Powered by' branding button all over the place. It's the 'powered by Google' SaaS branding playbook applied to PC security.

OK. Let's close out this chapter by summing up 3 practical brand guidelines for participating in any messaging mashup.

Three Asymmetric Brand Messaging Guidelines (and a little bonus advice)

Guideline 1: Remember. This *4-thread conversation framework I've described above exists in all software markets in the age of the cross-category superpowers.*

Look for opportunities to practice conversational symbiosis in:
- the Superpower(s) thread
- the Anti-superpower 'monoculture' thread
- the 'Best of Breed' thread, and
- the Emerging ISV, complementary marketer thread

Try to *see this simple framework as your strategic messaging GPS in the superpower sandstorm.* It will save you lots of wasted time and dollars with those *'borrow your watch to tell you what time it is'* cargo cult branding and PR agencies that often need weeks to 'come up to speed on your category'. Before they produce job one.

I would suggest that it is your spiritual duty to help these kinds of agencies hit bottom and get into asymmetric marketing recovery. How? By gently informing them that you have read this book, and you've got your messaging strategy angle covered... *internally*.

And if they freak out when you tell them this, ask them to call me for a little bit of peer-to-peer intervention. They really are good people...In spite of all that metrosexual eyeware. They just need to regularly attend their Cargo Cult Marketers Anonymous meetings, and they will get better.

Guideline 2: *Position yourself within this 4-thread conversational framework, not in a category "magic quadrant".*

Why? Because then you can *begin leveraging the values issues and the 'everything on the table' reputation mini-crises* that will naturally emerge in the age of the superpowers.

Remember. There is no vendor in any 'magic quadrant' with the brand name 'monoculture'. But Mr. Monoculture has one of the loudest voices in the messaging mashup. This is where the messaging action is turning out to be in the age of the superpowers...an age in which category regime change, not best-of-breed tornado-chasing gorillas are the norm. An age in which brand conflict will inevitably place the issue of market monopoly (and all its values hot buttons) on the table.

Guideline 3: Strive to develop a more *'intangible' brand promise---One that begins incorporating the distinctive and unique elements of your own corporate culture* as a messaging differentiator.

'Your Potential, Our Passion'---that's intangible...Teflon and culture-driven. Sun Tzu called it strategic 'formlessness'.

'Oracle. Unbreakable'---that's very, very tangible and invites attack. Attack that only diverts your attention from the real world of cage-fighting competition. And forces you to do way too much messaging 'clarification'.

And here's a few asymmetric *brand messaging bonus rules* I like to live by.

Customer Name-Dropping Can Be a No-No: Don't reference any customer you are not prepared to lose. If your website lists all your marquee customers and lots of customer case studies, you are making it too easy for your asymmetric competitors. Hold back 90% of your customer names for *private* presentations. Make sure that the 10% of customers you do publicly list are customers you 'own' by virtue of some special relationship.

Create Your Own 'News': Despite what PR agencies tell you, you don't need any excuse to issue a press release. Remember---It's a persistent conversation, and you want your story and your voice in it as much as possible. In client engagements, I often sit in on agency review and decision-making processes for PR, brand and interactive agencies. It has been my experience that only the rare minority of agencies are not stuck in the cargo cult 90's. If they tell you that you can only issue a press release about some 'substantive' event, then tell them that substantive event will be your search for a new agency. Seriously, asymmetric PR doesn't look at 'core' for its messaging content. It looks at 'context' for its content. The context of the superpower sandstorm in which the next sound bite can provide you with an asymmetric brand messaging opportunity.

Search Marketing in the Sandstorm: Conversational symbiosis is all about capitalizing on market polarization. When in the course of writing this book I noticed that there were no competitive ads placed on Google next to the search term 'Microsoft monoculture', it became clear to me that the software industry has a long way to go before it recovers from cargo cult thinking. If the whole world is having a dotcomplexity-advantaged, search-optimized market conversation about the downside of natural monopoly, you want to inject yourself into that conversation. That's what search engine marketing is all about. Positioning your offering next to those sound bites in the conversation that have a persistent life of their own.

Word of Mouth Cuts Both Ways: Don't forget the lessons of the 2006 Google sound bite sandstorm. 'Don't be evil' morphed into 'Google don't be evil'. And when negative word-of-mouth jumps up, activate your tribal culture. Get one of your tribal chieftans (CEO, CMO, CTO) into the conversation with his or her own weblog, email interview, live webcast, etc. to start telling your side of the story 24/7.

Tie Money Spent to Money Received: Last but not least, don't do 'branding' in the abstract. Unless you are Microsoft, Oracle, eBay, Google or another superpower engaged in category regime change, and you need to spend money to shield yourself in the sound bite sandstorm. If you are an emerging or turnaround ISV, tie any and all brand messaging spend directly to your asymmetric sales strategy. Your trialware, your colonial channel recruitment, your OEM or powered-by selling. Isn't that why people invest in campaign management and EMM (enterprise marketing management) systems?

Hell...If it was up to me, every press release on every ISV website would contain a live link to click through to a landing page where you could download something... or sign up for a trial subscription to an on-demand app...or grab a white paper from your favorite tribal chieftan.

But hey, that's just me. As you know by now, I'm into marketing overkill. I'm into marketing candor. I'm into marketing sobriety. I'm into the rowdy culture of the garage. I'm into dominance... the Tao of Dominance.

And for those very reasons, I do pledge to you, gentle reader, to 'die hard'. Boldly co-opting the dotcomplexity machine gun of the cum-ba-ya 'Participation Age'. Being one of those 'only the paranoid survive', control-freak, asymmetric marketers who always seems to flunk their Electric Kool-Aid Marketing Test. Who has a weird asymmetric gene that keeps me from getting stoned on the fad-du-jour.

And I have a confession. I actually like the feeling of marketing brass knuckles on my hands. I thrive on market conflict. And values polarization. That's one reason why I've enormously enjoyed picking this public fight with an industry guru like Geoffrey Moore. But don't worry. I'm sure he'll handle it well. I'm sure, like a good Darwinian, he will adapt.

After all, Geoffrey Moore is the guy in the fight well-defended by a marketing monoculture.

A marketing monoculture fifteen years in the making.

I'm the romantic. The disruptive innovator in this game. The guy brawling with no rules.

The guy carrying asymmetric strategy across the marketing chasm.

Hoping to find a few, good marketing pragmatists. Pragmatists that want to succeed in the superpower sandstorm. And don't mind riding on the back of a marketing dinosaur to get there.

The bottom line. I can't help but love this age of the software superpowers. Why? Because I thrive on the challenge of helping the best and the brightest (*and the baddest*) win on this rugged market landscape of cross-category natural monopolies.

And with all due respect to Jacques Chirac and his new French search engine, I have a not very well disguised agenda that seeps through the cracks of this book.

I want the American software industry to remain second to none.

And I say that with no apology to the second place finisher, wherever they hang their hat. Whether Bangalore, Beijing, Berlin, Belfast or Buenos Aires.

And I'm convinced that if we in the U.S. get past our bubbleboy compulsion for the fad-du-jour, our penchant for cultural self-sabotage, our web-of-wealth entitlement, our recurring Electric Kool-Aid Marketing Tests...We *can* remain second to none. It won't be easy, but we have one thing, one small asymmetry in our favor.

To quote Sonny Barger, the founder of that world-recognized asymmetric brand, the Hell's Angels biker club,

"There is no reverse gear on a motorcycle".[68]

There is no reverse gear in asymmetric marketing.
There is no reverse gear in superpower market dynamics.
They groove in...*and then they move in.*
They are path dependent.
And if you have made it this far, you have been treated to a small glimpse of that path.
And in today's world, I'm glad that the longest, widest, most sunlit part of this path still runs through America.

But all that flag-waving, inappropriate marketing testosterone, and bloody brass knuckles aside, I am sad about one small thing.

When Bill Gates finally retires, from whom will I shoplift my ideas? Hey...There's always Larry Ellison. And who knows, maybe Eric Schmidt and those Russian rock stars down at the Googleplex have a few, new asymmetric moves up their sleeves.

Oh well. Time to go.

It's midnight in the global software industry, and the Seinfeld reruns are on.

It's that one about doing the opposite.

Obligatory Bonus Scenes

TEN PREDICTIONS FOR THE AGE OF ASYMMETRIC MARKETING

In an industry where everybody wants to be more like Hollywood (God help us), where software marketing is another form of 'Reality TV', you can't just finish your book and move on. Not enough 'value'. You have to throw in a 'bonus scene', or two, or three, to justify the twenty bucks. OK. I'm a player. Here's my obligatory bonus scenes.

It's a list of Ten Predictions that should prove to you my Asymmetric Marketing cage-fighter kung fu is strong. Strong enough to pierce through the sandstorm to see what is on the other side. Here goes. I'll shoplift the David Letterman model, and do them in reverse.

Prediction 10: The Cargo Cult Marketing Monoculture is Broken

While in the short term (next 5 years), 90% of the installed base of cargo cult marketing consultants and agencies will continue to hold on to any and every graphically correct marketing model they can find, their monoculture will eventually be broken. Why? The cultural, political, economic and values polarization that is inherent in today's global markets will catch up with them. I call this trend... *'partisan capitalism'*. Partisan capitalism will drive a 'sobering up' of the marketing profession, and not just in the tech industry. It will create a new generation of marketing 'realists', creative economic nationalists, and garage entrepreneurs capable of operating in the context of Post 9.11 global conflict. Marketing realists and economic nationalists who are forced to take sides. Marketing realists for whom the phrase World War Three is not an excuse to change the TV channel.

Prediction 9: Open Source Is Completely Co-opted by the Software Superpowers

It already has been to a large extent. But hopefully, its complete integration into the product portfolios of the software natural monopolies will lead to a more systematic focus by ISVs on *full spectrum marketing innovation as their key competitive differentiator*. And to symbiosis with the software superpowers. Not disruptive innovation against them.

Prediction 8: 'On-demand' Will Experience a Setback Around a Security Scandal

A high profile on-demand provider will experience a major security breach, in which valuable customer information will be compromised. This will temporarily cool down interest in on-demand approaches, and simultaneously stimulate renewed interest in traditional 'on-premises' ISV models. *ISVs with 'hybrid' approaches (on demand/on premises) will benefit.*

Prediction 7: Chinese "Dissidents" Will Win, & Punish Marketing Collaborators.

The downside of conforming to the Chinese government's dotcommunist policies will be apparent when the 'children' of Tienanmen Square eventually take power in their country. The shortsightedness of U.S. technology companies, including many of the software superpowers, will come back to bite them in their collective marketing booty. The new democratic leaders, many of whom will have had relatives and friends betrayed by the 'digital collaborators', will take their business elsewhere, including to a *new generation of Chinese, Taiwanese and Japanese startup companies*.

Prediction 6: Asymmetric Marketers Will Blossom in India

As price-based competition intensifies in the Indian software industry, a new generation of asymmetric marketers will emerge. They will *focus on delivering software and services to the Indian market*, and leverage that home marketing expertise elsewhere around the globe.

Prediction 5: M&A Activity Will Trend Toward "Merger of Equals" Advantage

As the superpower sandstorm intensifies, startups and emerging category players will increasingly turn to 'Merger of Equals' M&A activity to create an asymmetric advantage. It will become *common wisdom that the 'half life' of a software category in the superpower sandstorm is a fraction of what it was in the laissez-faire period of tech market development.* The faster that small companies combine and achieve self-sufficiency, the better position they will be in to practice superpower symbiosis. Boutique investment bankers will flourish along side this trend.

Prediction 4: VCs Will Align With Their Superpower of Choice

A minority of enlightened VCs will openly repudiate 'disruptive technology innovation' as a long-term investment strategy. They will align with specific superpower agendas, and *invest in 'colonized' startups* committed to practicing symbiosis with a superpower. They will make a fortune.

Prediction 3: Culture Management Systems Will Abound

More than one startup will integrate the discreet functions I have referred to in this book as a "Culture Management System". They will make it available as a single end-to-end offering that attaches to superpower platforms, and enterprise applications, as an internal "marketing OS". Don't forget to call me when you do. *I've got a little CMS 'dark-itecture' I held back.*

Prediction 2: The Next U.S. President Will Demand an Anti-terror "eFront"

In the after-bubble, the tech industry in the U.S. has not been fully engaged in doing its part to win the Global War on Terror. In the 2008 U.S. presidential campaign, this issue will come to the fore. One or more candidates will call for an 'eFront' along the lines of the Israeli tech industry, i.e a tech alliance to develop the next generation of e-technology to assist in the war. This issue of the "eFront" will also drive a backlash against 'outsourcing' of commercial software development, and a major revisiting of the prevailing 'core/context' ideation that justifies it. Don't say I didn't warn you Geoffrey.

Prediction 1: The Next Software Superpower Will Have Read This Book

The management team of an under-the-radar startup will successfully infiltrate a non-strategic market creation initiative of some incumbent market leader. They will co-opt the market momentum of this initiative to further their own agenda. Probably with an OEM or 'powered by' sales agreement. They will then practice full spectrum asymmetric marketing, and establish an early natural monopoly groove-in that they ride to cross-category superpower status. They will have used this book as their marketing GPS.

What do I want from their deal?

A thank you card would be nice.

GLOSSARY
OF
ASYMMETRIC MARKETING

Asymmetric Marketing: The winner-take-all marketing wisdom developed by the cross-category software superpowers over decades of market experience. A system of marketing that rejects disruptive technology innovation against the superpowers, in favor of the practice of effective symbiosis with incumbent market leaders. The application of asymmetric warfare thinking to software marketing across the full spectrum of the marketing challenge, including strategy, market development framework, products, sales approaches, customer lock-in, operating culture and brand messaging.

Bark-itecture: One of four aspects of asymmetric product shark-itecture. It refers to that aspect of an asymmetric offering that allows it to easily become "OEM-able" or 'powered-by'-able for inclusion in superpower and other incumbent leader offerings. The external 'bark' of the product tree may be another company's branding, user experience, etc., but the trunk of the tree is yours. This aspect of product strategy helps enable symbiotic cooptation of the market power of incumbent leaders.

Big Hat, No Cattle Syndrome: Grandiose marketing strategy (based on chasing the software fad-du-jour) coupled with anemic execution. A gap between strategy and execution in the superpower sandstorm based on cargo cult marketing addiction. Symptoms of Big Hat, No Cattle Syndrome include inability to identify a qualified sales prospect and leads falling through the organizational cracks.

Bubbleboy: A cargo cult marketer from the bubble period of history. A term shoplifted from the Seinfeld episode titled 'The Bubble Boy', loosely modeled on the experience of an individual raised in a germ-free, plastic bubble and protected from life's dangerous realities. Refers to marketers protected by, and dependent on, a cocoon of invested cash, and whose businesses never become self-sustaining due to their rejection of the best practices of the software superpowers, and their embrace of 'new rules for the new economy' in the context of the software fad-du-jour.

Cargo Cult Marketers: Marketers that are guided by delusional 'new rules' belief systems, and/or abstract market development models from the laissez-faire period of tech market development. Marketers that romanticize disruptive technology innovation (e.g. Geoffrey Moore's 'Chasm theory). Cargo cult marketing came to the fore in the bubble period during which 5000 'disruptive innovators' are estimated to have gone extinct. See 'cargo cult science'.

Cargo Cult Science: An expression coined by Nobel physicist Richard Feynman to describe those persons following the appearance of science, but not its substance. Term originates from Feynman's description of a tribe of tropical islanders who engaged in various imitative rituals designed to make cargo planes land. The rituals were unsuccessful.

Category Regime Change: The replacement of a category market share leader in an adjacent category by an asymmetric marketer possessing category-extensible market power. Example: Microsoft's defeat of WordPerfect and Lotus in desktop apps; Microsoft's defeat of Novell in network servers; Microsoft's defeat of Netscape in web browsers.

Cellularity: Underlying business biology of dotcomplexity-advantaged business. The natural end of a customer relationship. Customer churn as the normal state of affairs. Cells live, cells die, cells are created. Marketing apoptosis (programmed cell death).

Channel Colonization: The symbiotic relationship between a superpower and their loyal solutions partners. The state of the channel in the age of the software superpowers, resulting in the channel partner focus on superpower marketing agendas, and the abandoning of non-aligned vendors.

Chasm Theory: Developed by Geoffrey Moore in 1991 in his book 'Crossing the Chasm'. Systematically lays out a market development model for disruptive technology innovators based on a Technology Adoption Lifecycle (TALC) approach.

Cooptation: Creatively leveraging the market power of another through the practice of market symbiosis, in order to further one's own marketing agenda.

Culture Management System (CMS): Internal software platform designed to foster a sober, candid, self-organizing, ownership-driven asymmetric marketing organization. A mechanism to enable Marketing by Garage Values (MBGV). An asymmetric marketing tribal 'OS'. Can incorporate intranet, team weblog, conferencing, groupware, and Employee Incentive Management (EIM) capability.

Customer Barrier Management (CBM): The market-craft of locking in customers, and pre-emptively defeating parasitic competitors. The customer management strategy of asymmetric marketers. The conscious attempt by asymmetric marketers to make the law of path-dependent increasing returns operate in their favor, by implementing the best practices of the software superpowers.

Dark-itecture: One of four aspects of asymmetric product shark-itecture. The conscious incorporation of stealth into your product strategy. Dark-itecture is what you hold back in the form of undocumented features and APIs that can provide you with asymmetric advantage in follow-on markets.

Desertification: The over-cultivation of market landscapes. The driver of the superpower sandstorm. Results from both the IT 'do more with less' agenda, and the no-fly-zone market behaviors of the superpowers.

Digital Political Correctness: Refusal to dominate customers, often rationalized in the name of 'customer power', 'openness', and the Bubbleboy 2.0 'Participation Age'. Often used by big companies to attack the growing market power of smaller, asymmetric competitors. A form of intellectual elitism that attempts to invalidate the lessons of the rise of the software superpowers.

Disruptive Technology Innovation: Technology that obsoletes a prevailing paradigm. The primary market religion of Silicon Valley technical and financial elites.

Dotcomplexity Advantage: The embedding of one or more native web effects into the fabric of an asymmetric offering. Can take multiple forms, e.g. update-ness effect (never-ending product approach popularized by Windows update), self-organizing effect (eBay marketplace and platform), visibility effect (ability to see how discrete customers use your SaaS or on-demand application, and thereby optimize offering for all customers and/or sets of customer), network effect (Skype client download), and more. Complexity science applied to real-time, networked markets.

Ecoregion: A subset of an ecozone. Superpower market geography defined by a specific product-centric customer lock-in, e.g. the Oracle database ecoregion, the Adobe Acrobat Reader ecoregion, the eBay PayPal ecoregion. Often presents as a product/partner/customer cluster, e.g. the Microsoft .NET developer ecoregion. Focused Target of Asymmetric Opportunity (TAO) for marketers seeking to practice superpower symbiosis. (see ecozone)

Ecozone: A well-demarcated opportunity landscape defined by the market footprint of the superpower that dominates it. An installed base of cross-category locked-in superpower customers. Broad Target of Asymmetric Opportunity (TAO) for marketers seeking to practice superpower symbiosis.

Graphically Correct: Intentionally sarcastic expression used by this author to describe abstract, symmetrical market development models, e.g. 'chasm' theory.

ISV (Independent Software Vendor): Includes companies leveraging one or more software deployment models including conventional on-premises, web on-demand (also called SaaS-software as a service), appliance model, embedded, etc.

Inverse Selling: A selling model based on trialware. Use/sell vs. sell/ use. The prospect invests human bandwidth to use the product, and conventional 'selling' is only done on the basis of a successful trial evaluation. Helps eliminate Big Hat, No Cattle Syndrome by providing tangible evidence of 'qualified' lead.

Law of Increasing Returns: Developed by Brian Arthur. That which is ahead gets further ahead. Complexity science applied to economics. The basic law governing software economics in the age of the natural monopoly superpowers.

Market Power: Ability to influence the behavior of a market to conform to your marketing agenda, up to and including the ability to progressively displace incumbent market share leaders. The end result of practicing asymmetric marketing across the full spectrum of marketing activities, including products, selling approaches, and customer management.

Market Share: Percentage of a defined market category using your product. In and of itself, not necessarily a reflection of asymmetric market power.

Marketing by Garage Values (MBGV): The kernel values of a culture of asymmetric marketing. Sobriety, candor, self-organizing across silos, shared ownership of the revenue objective. 'Garage' refers to the legacy of pre-bubble high technology bootstrapped entrepreneurism, and is no way designed to infringe on the well-deserved brand equity and market reputation associated with Guy Kawasaki's *Garage Technology Ventures or Garage.com*.

Marketing Defense-in-Depth: A layered customer barrier management (CBM) approach incorporating barriers to customer exit, barriers to competitive entry, and barriers to product imitation. See Customer Barrier Management (CBM)

Messaging Mashup: Composite 24/7 market conversation in the age of the software superpowers that provides a working framework to develop ISV brand messaging strategy. Comprised of 4 conversational threads, including the superpower(s) thread, the anti-monopoly-on-principle or 'monoculture' thread, the 'best of breed' ISV or pragmatic anti-superpower thread, and the symbiotic, complementary, asymmetric ISV thread.

Narc-itecture: One of four aspects of asymmetric product shark-itecture. Means systematically designing in dotcomplexity advantage in two forms. 1-Update-ness that increases customer dependency, and 2-Continuous feedback , user profiling and actionable business intelligence. Narc-itecture in action is Windows Update, Symantec anti-virus signature updates, Yahoo's MyWeb personal page, Google's 'search history' capability, etc.

Natural Monopoly: Software vendor possessing a customer-sanctioned market lock-in. Distinguished from government-sanctioned monopoly, e.g. original AT&T. That natural state of software markets in the 21st century software industry.

N-glish: An Unorthodox Model Description Language used to describe self-organizing, dotcomplexity-advantaged business. E.G. N-formation (a many-to-many market), N-stitution (stable vendor-controlled market community, the 2nd stage of an N-formation), N-duplicatability (a high level of customer barrier management-in order to overcome or commoditize an N-duplicatable business it is necessary to equal or surpass the associated 'N' or network effect.)

No-fly-zone Imperative: The natural marketing behaviors of the cross-category software superpowers designed to pre-empt parasitic competitive encroachment on their market territory. Includes strategic control of installed base ecozones, containment of emerging market threats, colonization of partner networks, creation of new markets, and collusion and contention with each other. Based on the military metaphor, 'no fly zone'. The no-fly-zone imperative of the superpowers is the primary marketing 'GPS' (geo-positioning system) used by asymmetric marketers to detect Targets of Asymmetric Opportunity. It is the working alternative to the TALC in an age of natural monopolies.

Path Dependence: The initial market 'groove-in' that determines what product and which ISV will benefit from the law of increasing returns. Example: Microsoft's groove-in as the IBM PC operating system vendor defined the natural 'path' along which PC clone markets (Windows platform), adjacent markets (desktop Office Suite), and derivative markets (web browsers) developed.

Powered-by Deal: The SaaS (or on-demand) equivalent of an OEM agreement. It enables the 'powered by' provider to capitalize on the momentum of its customer.

Quark-itecture: One of four aspects of asymmetric product shark-itecture. The smallest aspect of your overall offering designed to be adopted by the greatest number of users in the shortest amount of time to begin driving and/or expanding a customer groove-in. E.G. Adobe Acrobat Reader, Skype client, free trial subscriptions to on-demand applications (Webex, Salesforce.com.).

Reverse Tornado: The 'death spiral' effect that regularly occurs when a market share leader deficient in market power faces category regime change from one or more cross-category software superpowers.

Sandstorm (aka **superpower sandstorm**): A metaphor to describe the marketing challenge facing ISVs in the age of the software superpowers. Characterized by reduced market and revenue visibility, positional confusion within eroding categories, board/investor heat and/or intervention into day-to-day management affairs , and broken marketing machinery. Exacerbated by both the desertification of IT and the no-fly-zone imperative of the superpowers.

Shark-itecture: Key element of product strategy implemented by asymmetric marketers to maximize customer dependency and pre-empt competitive encroachment. The product strategy of the software superpowers developed over the life of their offerings that allows them to 'eat' their competitors and carry out category regime change. Shark-itecture is how the superpowers anchor and defend their ecoregions, migrate their installed base of customers to their new products, and achieve multi-generational, cross-category product dominance. Comprised of 4 components, quark-itecture, bark-itecture, narc-itecture, dark-itecture. *See all.*

Software Superpowers: Natural monopoly, asymmetric marketers with cross-category *and* category-extensible market power. The superpowers dominate their installed base customers, i.e. their ecozones and ecoregions, dramatically outpace VCs in software R&D investment, co-opt disruptive innovation, and define the 21st century software market landscape. Microsoft, Oracle, IBM, Cisco, SAP, Symantec, Adobe, Yahoo, eBay, and Google.

Sound Bite Sandstorm: Polarizing, values-driven media coverage of software superpower market behaviors. E.G. Press frenzy around Google's business deal with Chinese government, Microsoft legal battles, pedophiles in Yahoo chat rooms, etc. A messaging opportunity for ISVs.

Superpower Symbiosis: The basic foundation of asymmetric marketing strategy, grounded in the natural sciences. Living together with the software superpowers. Can take multiple forms including mutualism (win/win), parasitism (win/lose), commensalism (win/neutral). Superpower symbiosis provides the conceptual framework for the development of marketing strategy, products, sales approaches, messaging, and more.

TAO (targets of asymmetric opportunity): The ecozones and ecoregions of the superpowers to which asymmetric marketers symbiotically attach their offerings. An approach to marketing strategy that shifts focus from 'end customer' markets to the locked-in ecoregions of the superpowers in order to capitalize on the momentum inherent in superpower (or incumbent leader) installed base dynamics. Microsoft's initial target of asymmetric opportunity was IBM. Google's initial target of asymmetric opportunity was Yahoo. Adobe's initial target of asymmetric opportunity was Apple.

Three-Dimensional value proposition: An ISV value proposition that benefits the end customer, the ISV, and the 'host' superpower or superpowers with which the ISV is practicing symbiosis. The value proposition of "Microsoft-the-startup" is a good example of a 3-D value prop. PC users received benefits, IBM received benefits, and Microsoft received benefits. An important aspect of both asymmetric products based on continuous technology innovation on top of superpower platforms, and asymmetric brand messaging that carries a 'complementary' storyline.

Tribal Chieftanship: The leadership style of asymmetric marketers. Hands on, lead by example, thought leadership-driven, individual value contributor/doer. Personal reputation equity-rich model which results in the 'street-cred' needed for rapid response to competitive threats and market opportunity.

Two-Dimensional value proposition: An ISV value proposition that benefits the end customer and the ISV. A characteristic of many dead bubble companies that abandoned pre-existing value chains in favor of go-it-alone disruptive technology innovation, e.g. WebVan, Napster, GovWorks.

Endnotes

Chapter One

[1] Richard Feynman, "Cargo Cult Science", <u>Caltech Commencement Address</u>. 1974
<http://www.physics.brocku.ca/etc/cargo_cult_science.html>

[2] Larry David, Larry Charles, "Seinfeld, The Bubble Boy". 1992
<http://www.seinfeldscripts.com/TheBubbleBoy.htm>

[3] Silicon Valley/San Jose Business Journal, "Dot-com 'casualties' near 5000". March 11, 2003
<http://sanjose.bizjournals.com/sanjose/stories/2003/03/10/daily19.html>

[4] Bill Mann, "Burning Fast: The Pain of Being Right". August 30, 2002. <u>The Motley Fool</u>
<http://www.fool.com/news/foth/2002/foth020830.htm>

[5] Kevin Kelly, "New Rules for the New Economy". 1998 Viking Penguin.
You can read it online at <http://www.kk.org/newrules/contents.php>

[6] Kevin Kelly "New Rules for the New Economy". Rule 6: *"Let Go at the Top". As innovation accelerates, abandoning the highly successful in order to escape from its eventual obsolescence (my emphasis) becomes the most difficult and yet most essential task."*
<http://www.kk.org/newrules/newrules-list.html>

[7] US District Court of Northern California, Class Action Complaint Against Ventro Corporation, a B2B Marketplace provider. *"By December 1999, defendants knew that Ventro's existing business model did not work and that the Company did not possess the technology to successfully compete in the B2B market (emphasis JEB).Defendants knew these problems would severely impair Ventro's future revenue growth. However,*

defendants wanted to raise money through debt offerings before the bottom fell out of Ventro's stock price. Thus, defendants continued to make positive but false statements about Ventro's business and future revenues. As a result, Ventro's stock traded as high as $243-1/2 per share during the Class Period."
<   http://securities.stanford.edu/1017/VNTR01/20010508_003c_011790.htm>

[8] Sneaky Kings, "Dot". 2002
<http://movies2.nytimes.com/gst/movies/movie.html?v_id=273162>

[9] Comments of Enron Corporation Regarding B2B Electronic Marketplaces
< http://ftc.gov/bc/b2b/comments/enron.htm>

[10] Online News Hour, PBS, "Enron After the Collapse"
"Shortly after Enron's sudden bankruptcy, the SEC questioned Andersen CEO Joseph Berardino about his firm's inaccurate audit statements and Enron's overstated profits. Berardino told the SEC that Enron's audited statements were misleading since Andersen accountants did not include Enron's money-losing partnerships, like Chewco, in the main financial statements."
<http://www.pbs.org/newshour/bb/business/enron/player6.html>

[11] Price Waterhouse Coopers, Thomson Venture Economics, National Venture Capital Association, The MoneyTree Survey News Release "VENTURE CAPITAL INVESTING STEADY AT $21.7 BILLION IN 2005 HOLDING ON TO 2004's GAIN". January 24, 2006
"Software investments slipped 10% in 2005 to **$4.7 billion** in 840 deals. However,
Software easily held its position as the largest single industry category with 22% of total
dollars and 29% of all deals." Internet-specific investing has grown slowly over the last three years with 2005 ending at **$2.9 billion** in 450 deals, up slightly from $2.8 billion in 2004. Companies classified as Internet-specific represented 13% of all venture dollars and 15% of all deals in 2005.

[12] Price Waterhouse Coopers, Thomson Venture Economics, National Venture Capital Association, The MoneyTree Survey News Release "VENTURE CAPITAL INVESTING STEADY AT $21.7 BILLION IN 2005 HOLDING ON TO 2004's GAIN". January 24, 2006

"Among the standard industry classifications, the Software industry attracted the most first-time activity with $1.2 billion (of $4.7 billion, JEB) going to 238 companies."

"The continuing shift toward Later stage investing over the past five years reflects venture capitalists ongoing support of existing portfolio companies via additional follow-on rounds. Given the lackluster IPO market, portfolio companies may be waiting longer to exit than in previous years."

[13] Microsoft Corporation, Microsoft Fourth Quarter FY 2006 Earnings Release. July 20, 2006
<http://www.microsoft.com/msft/earnings/FY06/earn_rel_q4_06.mspx#income>

[14] Jenni Lehman, Gartner Group,"Magic Quadrants and MarketScopes: How Gartner Evaluates Vendors Within a Market." 13 October 2005

[15] Geoffrey Moore, "Crossing the Chasm". Harper Collins. 1991

[16] Geoffrey Moore, "Inside the Tornado". Harper Collins. 1995

[17] Joseph E Bentzel, "Tossing the Chasm?". Marketing Magnified Newsletter, CMO Council. February, 2004
< http://www.cmocouncil.org/Marketing_Magnified/MM_newsletter_3.html#tossing>
"Instead of tossing the chasm and looking for the latest new rules for the new economy, smart marketers try to identify and develop non-conventional, unorthodox, asymmetric counter-measures for those specific market conditions that contribute to adoption interruption. Since asymmetric marketing is a roadmap for unconventional marketing warfare, its practitioners pay close attention to symptoms of on-the-ground "adoption erosion" that may alter the dynamics of a specific adoption lifecycle and force in-the-field adjustments to strategy and execution."

[18] Geoffrey Moore, "Resolving the "Nasty Bit" in Innovation Strategy". Always-On Network. June 27, 2004. Report from Moore's speech at the Silicon Valley 4.0 Conference.
< http://www.alwayson-network.com/comments.php?id=P4471_0_4_0_C>

[19] Wikipedia, Seattle Computer Products
< http://en.wikipedia.org/wiki/Seattle_Computer_Products>
" In 1980 Paterson wrote the QDOS operating system, later known as
86-DOS, over a four month period. Microsoft purchased a license for
the system in December 1980 for $25,000, which it in turn provided to
IBM as the first PC operating system, MS-DOS, which IBM adapted as
PC-DOS. Subsequently, in July 1981, Microsoft purchased full rights to
QDOS for an additional $50,000. However, Microsoft did not disclose
it was reselling the system to IBM. As a result, SCP sued Microsoft, and
settled for $1 million in 1986. SCP is no longer in business."

[20] Wikipedia, IBM PS/2
< http://en.wikipedia.org/wiki/IBM_PS/2>
" The Personal System/2 or PS/2 was IBM's second generation of
personal computers. The PS/2 line, released to the public in 1987, was
created by IBM in an attempt to recapture control of the PC market
by introducing an advanced proprietary architecture. Although IBM's
considerable market presence ensured the PS/2 would sell in relatively
large numbers, the PS/2 architecture ultimately failed in its bid to return
control of the PC market to IBM."

[21] Wikipedia, OS/2
< http://en.wikipedia.org/wiki/OS/2>
" The increasing popularity of Windows prompted Microsoft to shift
its development focus from cooperating on OS/2 with IBM to building
a franchise based on Windows."

[22] Wikipedia, Extreme Programming
< http://en.wikipedia.org/wiki/Extreme_programming>
" Extreme Programming applies incremental changes: for example, a
system might have small releases every three weeks. By making many
little steps the customer has more control over the development process
and the system that is being developed. The principle of embracing
change is about not working against changes but embracing them. For
instance, if at one of the iterative meetings it appears that the *customer's
requirements have changed dramatically (JEB emphasis)*, programmers are
to embrace this and plan the new requirements for the next iteration."

[23] Brian Utley, "25th Anniversary of the IBM PC". Technology Evangelist
Weblog. August 12, 2006
<   http://www.technologyevangelist.com/2006/08/25th_anniversary_
of.html>

" Every major functional organization had written off the possibility that the concept of the PC was viable or that it was in the best interest of IBM to pursue this class of product (my emphasis). Manufacturing said that the cost objectives could not be met. Marketing said that it could not be economically marketed. Corporate finance said that there was no money in this kind of a venture. Corporate technical staff said that such an effort was diversionary to the primary thrust of IBM Research and Development. So what happened? The IBM Chairman was Frank T. Cary. He had observed the dramatic growth of the Apple II acceptance and believed that the visible trend was a harbinger of what was to come. Given the denial of the Corporate and Functional Units Heads he felt compelled to make a very fundamental decision. He concluded that the only way to insure IBM was not left out in the cold was to create a Product Island that was isolated from all the non-believers. The Personal Computer Business Unit was formed reporting directly to the Chairman. Twelve months later the PC was born. The only IBM technology in the product was the keyboard."

[24] W. Brian Arthur, "Increasing Returns & Path Dependence in the Economy". University of Michigan Press, Ann Arbor, MI 1994

[25] W. Brian Arthur, "Increasing Returns and the New World of Business". Harvard Business Review, July-August 1996
<http://www.santafe.edu/-wbarthur/Papers/Pdf_files/HRB.doc>
"If a product or a company or a technology—one of many competing in a market—*gets ahead by chance or clever strategy (JEB emphasis)*, increasing returns can magnify this advantage, and the product or company or technology can go on to lock in the market."

[26] W.E. Pete Peterson, "Almost Perfect". Prima Publishing, 1994. (out of print)
Author's online edition available at <http://www.wordplace.com/ap/>
"By mid-1993 they (WordPerfect) claimed to have a 51% share of the Windows word processing market..."

[27] David M. Katz, "The taking of Lotus 1-2-3? Blame Microsoft". CFO. com, December 31, 2002
<http://www.cfo.com/article.cfm/3007634>
"Lotus 1-2-3 never recovered from the advent of Excel. Although the program still has a substantial number of users today, Hayward proclaims, "Lotus is clearly a legacy product." In fact, Excel so dominates the field

today that Gartner no longer bothers to collect usage numbers on Lotus 1-2-3."

[28] Wikipedia, Novell
<http://en.wikipedia.org/wiki/Novell>
"...by 1990, Novell had an almost monopolistic position in NOS for any business requiring a network."

[29] Sun Tzu, "The Art of War". Shambhala Publications. 1988, Thomas Cleary translation
Boston MA; Page 94: "For the impact of armed forces to be like stones thrown on eggs is a matter of emptiness and fullness".

[30] Wikipedia, Browser wars.
<http://en.wikipedia.org/wiki/Browser_wars>
" Netscape's business model was not to give away its browser but sell server software. Microsoft understood this and attacked Netscape's revenue sources, bundling Microsoft's Internet Information Server web server "free" with server versions of Windows, and offering Microsoft customers workalike clones of Netscape's proxy server, mail server, news server, and other software free or at steep discounts. This didn't have much effect at first, as much of Netscape's revenues came from customers using Sun Microsystems servers, but the gradual result was to make Windows NT more popular as a server for Internet and intranet while cutting off Netscape's income."

[31] Geoffrey Moore, "Darwin's Dictionary" 2006
<http://www.dealingwithdarwin.com/theBook/darwinDictionary.php #Technologyadoptionlifecycle>
"Tornado: A stage in the technology adoption life cycle during which pragmatist customers, spurred by the appearance of a killer app, enter the market in droves, driving demand to exceed supply, creating a frenzy of expansion and a meteoric rise in equity valuations."
" Killer app: An application with broad horizontal appeal that catapults a category into the tornado phase of the technology adoption life cycle."
" Disruptive innovation: An innovation type that initiates a growth market by creating a new category through one of two mechanisms: discontinuous technology or value-chain discontinuity."

[32] Geoffrey Moore, "Darwin's Dictionary" 2006
<http://www.dealingwithdarwin.com/theBook/darwinDictionary.php
#Technologyadoptionlifecycle>
" Gorilla: A market-share leader whose position is sustained by proprietary technology that has high switching costs, leading to both high GAP and long CAP, the marks of exceptional shareholder value."

[33] AllBusiness.com, " IDC Ranks BroadVision First In The E-commerce Software Market." Originally published in EDP Weekly's IT Monitor, July 10, 2000 issue
" According to the recent figures from IDC on e-commerce software applications revenue, BroadVision was the leader among 250 other vendors worldwide competing in the $1.8 billion e-commerce software applications market in 1999. Oracle, Open Market, Vignette, IBM and SAP completed in the top six. Ranked second in last year's report, BroadVision penetrated the top position this year with double the amount of license revenues, surpassing last year's leader Sun/Netscape. "We are thrilled to rank number one among the world's e-commerce application companies," says Dr. Pehong Chen, president and CEO of BroadVision Inc. "BroadVision's winning business strategies are credited to the record rate of sales of our BroadVision One-To-One Web- and wireless-based applications packages. Companies using BroadVision are realizing measurable benefits and competing effectively in the new era of e-relationships."

[34] Nadaq.com BVSN Financials
< http://www.nasdaq.com/asp/extendfund.asp?symbol=BVSN&selected=BVSN&page=full>

[35] Broadvision.com Company Information, Press Releases
" REDWOOD CITY, CA -- July 26, 2005 -- BroadVision, Inc. (Nasdaq: BVSN), a global provider of web self-service solutions, and Vector Capital, a San Francisco-based private equity firm, today announced that BroadVision has entered into a definitive agreement to be acquired by a newly-formed Vector portfolio company. Under the terms of the merger agreement, current BroadVision stockholders will receive $0.84 per share in cash and BroadVision will operate going forward as a privately-held, independent software vendor."
" In November 2005, we announced the termination of the merger agreement that was entered into with Vector Capital Corporation in July 2005."

[36] Wikipedia, Symbiosis
< http://en.wikipedia.org/wiki/Symbiosis>

[37] SAP.com
< http://www.sap.com/solutions/duet/index.epx>

[38] Scot Petersen, "For Sun, Microsoft Settlement is No Joke". eWeek
April 19, 2004
< http://www.eweek.com/article2/0,1759,1569460,00.asp>

[39] Scot Petersen, "For Sun, Microsoft Settlement is No Joke". eWeek
April 19, 2004
< http://www.eweek.com/article2/0,1759,1569460,00.asp>
" Sun officials probably feel they own Microsoft now because millions
of dollars will be flowing from Redmond for at least the next 10 years.
But what Sun does with that cash will determine whether Sun will again
be a force or a mere sideline player in the enterprise. The less publicized
but potentially bigger deal of April 2 was the promotion of Jonathan
Schwartz to president and chief operating officer of Sun, placing the
software wunderkind one step away from McNealy's post. Both men
agree software is what will drive growth for Sun. How much they focus
on the real threats to their company—IBM and other Linux vendors,
rather than Microsoft and Windows—remains to be seen."

[40] Wikipedia, Howard Dean
< http://en.wikipedia.org/wiki/Howard_Dean>

[41] Geoffrey Moore, "Darwin's Dictionary" 2006
<http://www.dealingwithdarwin.com/theBook/darwinDictionary.php
#Technologyadoptionlifecycle>
"Bowling alley - See Technology adoption life cycle.
A stage in the technology adoption life cycle during which technology
is being adopted for niche markets but not yet for broad horizontal
usage."
"Technology adoption life cycle
A model that describes how communities react to the introduction
of a discontinuous technology, consisting of a progression through
five adoption strategies: technology enthusiast, visionary, pragmatist,
conservative, and skeptic."

[42] Akamai Corporate Website
< http://www.akamai.com/en/html/services/application_performance_ solutions.html>

[43] Line56.com
< http://www.line56.com/articles/story_index.asp?StoryType=11>
You're going to have to click on the link for the poster and supply an email address to download it.

[44] Tom Kaneshige, "Barriers to B2B". Line56.com January 2001
<http://www.line56.com/articles/default.asp?ArticleID=1984>
"In addition to bringing you face to face with competitors, B2B undermines important strategic advantages. Matt Lekstutis, principal with A.T. Kearney, has seen any number of companies—especially those that have traditionally relied on proprietary relationships with suppliers, information availability, or IT connectivity to supply chains to attract sales—struggle with this issue. "With B2B, these competitive advantages are essentially going to become available to everyone, and at the same price," says Lekstutis. "Companies are asking themselves, 'Do I want to be actively engaged in the demise of my competitive advantages?' (JEB emphasis)"

[45] David Jablonski, "Extinction: past and present" Nature. Vol. 427. February 12, 2004
<http://66.102.7.104/search?q=cache:WLF83_jYjKEJ:pondside. uchicago.edu/ceb/Nature04.pdf+99%25+species+extinct&hl=en&gl=us &ct=clnk&cd=58>
"Extinction is a fundamental part of nature — more than 99% of all species that ever lived are now extinct."

[46] Wikipedia, Ecozones.
<http://en.wikipedia.org/wiki/Ecozone>

[47] Wikipedia, Ecoregions
<http://en.wikipedia.org/wiki/Ecoregion>

[48] Elise Ackerman, "Google expresses concerns over Microsoft's Internet Explorer". San Jose Mercury News. May. 01, 2006
<http://www.mercurynews.com/mld/mercurynews/news/14476260. htm>

"Google accused Microsoft of not playing fair in its quest for a bigger share of the $10 billion online advertising market on Monday and revealed that it has shared its concerns with antitrust regulators in the United States and Europe. Google's gripe: An upcoming release of Microsoft's Internet Explorer Web browser will contain a search box that in some cases defaults to the MSN search engine. As a result, Microsoft might be able to persuade more people to use its search technology and potentially win a larger share of the extremely lucrative market for Internet advertising. Someone who wants to use Google to find information on the Internet would be forced to choose the Mountain View-based company from a list of almost two dozen other search providers."

[49] CNN.com, "Microsoft hit by record EU fine." March 25, 2004
<http://www.cnn.com/2004/BUSINESS/03/24/microsoft.eu/>
"The complaint against Microsoft centered on the Microsoft Media Player, which plays music and video clips. It is a free add-on to Windows. Microsoft, based in Redmond, Washington, says this feature benefits consumers, but competitors like Real Network's player and Apple's Quicktime say it threatens their business and they want it unbundled. At stake is Microsoft's market share in the rapidly growing home entertainment market."

Chapter 2

[1] Fox Television, 24.
<http://www.fox.com/24/profiles/>

[2] Geoffrey Moore, "Darwin's Dictionary" 2006
<http://www.dealingwithdarwin.com/theBook/darwinDictionary.php
#Technologyadoptionlifecycle>
"Technology adoption life cycle: A model that describes how communities react to the introduction of a discontinuous technology, consisting of a progression through five adoption strategies: technology enthusiast, visionary, pragmatist, conservative, and skeptic."

[3] Wikipedia, Laissez-faire.
<http://en.wikipedia.org/wiki/Laissez-faire>
" The term laissez-faire is often used interchangeably with the term "free market.""

[4] Sarah Lacy, " Charting a New Course at Siebel". An Interview with Siebel Executive Bruce Cleveland. Business Week , March 30, 2005
<   http://www.businessweek.com/technology/content/mar2005/tc20 0503300353_tc121.htm>
"For the first eight years, the company largely had no strong competitors. Over the years, we saw tremendous growth rate. That growth rate was tied to the health of a growing economy. Once companies retrench and cut costs, they don't invest in sales and marketing. So, two big things jumped in front of our growth. The global economy took a nosedive, and this became an interesting market segment to Oracle and SAP. That really impacted our growth after 2001."

[5] Denis Pombriant, "Where Does Siebel Go from Here?". CRMBuyer. com, Part of the ECT News Network. May 4, 2005
<http://www.ecommercetimes.com/story/42790.html>

[6] Geoffrey Moore, "Darwin's Dictionary" 2006
<http://www.dealingwithdarwin.com/theBook/darwinDictionary.php #Technologyadoptionlifecycle>
"Main Street: The last stage of the technology adoption life cycle, coming at the end of the tornado, it signals a rise in the strategic importance of the conservative customer."

[7] Geoffrey Moore, "Darwin's Dictionary" 2006
<http://www.dealingwithdarwin.com/theBook/darwinDictionary.php #Technologyadoptionlifecycle>
"Gorilla - See Market share hierarchies
A market-share leader whose position is sustained by proprietary technology that has high switching costs, leading to both high GAP and long CAP, the marks of exceptional shareholder value."
"Market share hierarchies
A model for describing the pecking order in marketplace power among the market leader, a close challenger, and an also-ran. In proprietary-technology-enabled markets with high switching costs, the roles are gorilla, chimp, and monkey. In commoditized markets with low switching costs, the corresponding roles are king, prince, and serf."

[8] Salesforce.com Inc. FORM 10-Q, Quarterly report pursuant to Section 13 or 15(d) of the Securities Exchange Act of 1934 For the quarterly period ended July 31, 2006.
<http://secfilings.nasdaq.com/filingFrameset.asp?FileName=00011931

25%2D06%2D176211%2Etxt&FilePath=%5C2006%5C08%5C18%5C
&CoName=SALESFORCE+COM+INC&FormType=10%2DQ&Rcvd
Date=8%2F18%2F2006&pdf=>

" Marketing and Sales: Marketing and sales expenses were $59.8 million,
or 51 percent of total revenues, during the three months ended July
31, 2006, compared to $34.7 million, or 48 percent of total revenues,
during the same period a year ago, an increase of $25.1 million. The
increase in absolute dollars was primarily due to an increase of $17.2
million in employee-related costs, $4.4 million in stock-based expenses,
$0.9 million in marketing, advertising and event costs and a $2.1 million
increase in allocated overhead. Our marketing and sales headcount
increased by 54 percent since July 31, 2005 as we hired additional sales
personnel to focus on adding new customers and increasing penetration
within our existing customer base."

" Marketing and Sales: Marketing and sales expenses are our largest
cost and consist primarily of salaries and related expenses, including
stock-based expenses, for our sales and marketing staff, including
commissions, payments to partners, marketing programs and
allocated overhead. Marketing programs consist of advertising, events,
corporate communications and brand building and product marketing
activities."

[9] Connie Guglielmo, Bloomberg News, "Conway says he made
PeopleSoft 'too successful'". Contra Costa Times Sep. 24, 2005
<http://66.102.7.104/search?q=cache:yVzmix5AjDcJ:www.
contracostatimes.com/mld/cctimes/business/12731486.htm+craig+con
way+peoplesoft+fired+twist+in+the+wind&hl=en&gl=us&ct=clnk&cd=
7>
"Oracle formed a "twist in the wind" strategy to scare customers and
drive down PeopleSoft's sales and share price, Conway said. Conway
decided to use "strong words" to characterize the hostile bid, "words
that I knew would be carried by the press to every customer around the
world." "It was during this first 48 hours that you probably read quotes
from me referring to 'Genghis Khan' and 'a shotgun wedding.'"Conway
testified in October last year that he "may have" overreacted to Oracle's
bid. Conway in one instance described Ellison as "sociopathic" and said
he wouldn't sell PeopleSoft at any price. PeopleSoft fired Conway after
*the board learned about a deposition in which he admitted to lying to analysts
by telling them that Oracle's offer was no longer chasing away customers. In the
deposition, Conway said the statements were "promotional, not true, absolutely
not true." (JEB emphasis)*

[10] Rita K. Farrell, " Oracle Chief Testifies in Trial on Hostile Bid for PeopleSoft". New York Times, October 9, 2004
<http://www.nytimes.com/2004/10/09/technology/09soft.html?ei=508 8&en=1a1055a753e4de7e&ex=1255060800&partner=rssnyt&pagewante d=all&position=>
" But during cross-examination of Mr. Ellison, a PeopleSoft lawyer, Max Gitter, said Oracle's "twist in the wind" strategy of making a "stingy" bid of $16 as a placeholder - allowed Oracle executives and sales teams to urge potential PeopleSoft customers to hold off on purchases. That created the perception among analysts, investors, customers and employees that if Oracle acquired PeopleSoft, it would be shut down, Mr. Gitter said. Under questioning by his lawyer, Michael Carroll, Mr. Ellison insisted that he always intended to sell PeopleSoft programs on request but not actively market them. And he said that he did not intend to force PeopleSoft customers to migrate to Oracle products."

[11] Drew Robb, " SAP AG and Microsoft Corp.'s Duet: Glue for SAP And Office
Jointly developed software provides the link between two applications, right off the shelf." Computerworld. August 21, 2006
<http://www.computerworld.com/action/article.do?command=viewAr ticleBasic&taxonomyName=development&articleId=9002554&taxon omyId=11>
< "Customers wanted the ease and familiarity of their Office environment and yet wanted the ability to access and use the robust, secure business processes from the SAP back-end systems," says Moore. "As Web services and SOA became integrated features of both companies' product lines, the feasibility of providing contextual business information from SAP within Office 2003 increased, and the idea of Duet was born."

[12] The Economist (print edition), " The alliance against Google. What today's internet firms can learn from 19th-century history." Aug 10th 2006
<http://www.economist.com/business/displaystory.cfm?story_ id=7277064>
" In May, Yahoo! and eBay struck an alliance in which eBay will use technology from Yahoo! to place advertisements on its auction site. On the other side of the bargain, Yahoo! will use PayPal, eBay's online payment mechanism, for transactions from Yahoo!'s pages. (Google recently launched a rival payment system of its own.)"

[13] Microsoft.com
<   http://www.microsoft.com/athome/security/spyware/software/
default.mspx>

[14] Ed Scannell & Scott Bekker, " Ballmer Asks Partners to Bet on Microsoft in Security, Search, Unified Communications". Redmond Channel Partner Magazine, July 11, 2006.
< http://rcpmag.com/news/article.aspx?editorialsid=7595>
"Search and portal, unified communications and security" are the areas where partners will have to choose Microsoft or competitors, Ballmer said. "Those three businesses we want to build together." Calling his talk "The Winning Choice," Ballmer asked partners to support Microsoft's effort, place a bet with Microsoft and get trained on Microsoft technologies. Ballmer acknowledged it wouldn't be comfortable for partners to choose. Without naming competitors in security, such as Symantec or McAfee, or the other fields, Ballmer asked, "Will you choose to work with us or your traditional partners?"

[15] Gartner Group Press Release, "Gartner Says Worldwide Application Integration and Middleware Market Increased 7 Percent in 2005" 8 June 2006
< http://www.gartner.com/press_releases/asset_153343_11.html>
" In 2005, the top five vendors accounted for 69 percent of the total worldwide AIM market (see Table 1). IBM maintained a commanding lead in the market, with 37.2 percent market share in 2005."

[16] Wikipedia, LaserWriter
< http://en.wikipedia.org/wiki/LaserWriter>
"When it was introduced in late 1985, the LaserWriter was the first laser printer for the Macintosh world. With a printer resolution of 300 dpi and printing speed of 8ppm, the LaserWriter may have seemed like just another ordinary printer. *But at the heart of the Laserwriter's raster image processor lay the Adobe PostScript interpreter, a feature that would ultimately transform the landscape of computer desktop publishing (JEB emphasis).*
[17] McKinsey & Company/Sand Hill Group, Software 2006 CIO Insight Survey.
<http://www.sandhill.com/conferences/sw2006_materials/sw2006_
CIO_InsightSurvey.pdf>
"Enterprises with 1,000 or more employees seem to be decreasing investment in new initiatives in favor of software licenses, maintenance,and training for existing infrastructure."

[18] General Peter Schoomaker, "Special Operations Forces: The Way Ahead". Defense Issues: Volume 13 Number 10. February 1, 1998 <http://www.defenselink.mil/Speeches/Speech.aspx?SpeechID=651>

[19] US Army Space and Missile Defense Command (SMDC) Press Release, "Space and Missile Defense Command contributions and lessons from Operation Iraqi Freedom". October 14, 2003.
GlobalSecurity.org.
<   http://www.globalsecurity.org/space/library/report/2003/bernstein_mccullough.htm>
" In a flat, featureless desert environment prone to blinding sandstorms, the lack of distinguishing landmarks and sandstorm-related loss of visibility severely limited navigation and position determinations. Under these conditions, GPS navigation was indispensable and the GPS accuracy predictions provided by the ARSSTs to supported units were integrated into the ATO cycle to support precision fires and deep operations."

[20] Anne-Francoise Pele, " France Launches 'Quaero' Search Engine Project". EE Times. Apr 25, 2006 (republished in Information Week)
<   http://www.informationweek.com/story/showArticle.jhtml?articleID=186700938>
" In hopes of stimulating local technological, industrial, and economic development, President Jacques Chirac of France has announced a 2 billion euro (about $2.5 billion) plan to back a series of projects, including one on a Franco-German search engine intended to rival Google."

[21] Andy Reinhardt, Raphael Kahane, Gail Edmondson, " Not So Fast, Linux". Business Week November 8, 2004
<   http://www.businessweek.com/magazine/content/04_45/b3907083_mz054.htm>
"In Europe, software isn't just about bits and bytes anymore. It has become a matter of politics. In city governments from Paris to Vienna to Rome, civil servants and politicians are caught in a fight over competing visions of the future of computing. On one side is Microsoft, which is trying to hold on to its dominant position in PC and server software. On the other are factions backing the open-source model, which flouts convention by selling software cheaply -- or giving it away -- and sharing code. The contest playing out in city halls has turned Europe into a key battleground in the global software wars. It's no wonder open-source is fueling such passion. European governments chafe at Microsoft's

market power and want to encourage alternatives. "They don't like being beholden to a monopoly," says analyst Philip Carnelley of researcher Ovum in London. *At the same time, many policymakers see Linux as Europe's best chance to reclaim a role in an industry dominated by American giants. Two of the world's three largest Linux sellers started in Europe (JEB emphasis).* There's a cultural element, too. Europeans have an affinity for Linux because it was created by a Finn, Linus Torvalds. And the communitarian culture of the open-source movement strikes a chord with the political Left. "There's an attraction to a business model that is closer to utopian socialism," says François Bancilhon, chief executive of Paris-based Linux software maker Mandrakesoft (MDKFF), which sells and supports Linux software."

[22] Dennis Normile, "Is China the next R&D superpower?" Electronic Business. July 1, 2005
< http://www.reed-electronics.com/eb-mag/article/CA610433?pubdate=7%2F1%2F2005>
" When Chinese Premier Wen Jiabao visited India in April 2005, he suggested that if India contributed its expertise in software and China its strengths in hardware, they could form
a world-beating information and computer technology combination."

[23] President Bush's Technology Agenda, " Promoting Innovation and Competitiveness". April 26, 2004
< http://www.whitehouse.gov/infocus/technology/economic_policy200404/toc.html>

[24] United Nations, "International Year of Deserts and Desertification 2006". United Nations Website
< http://www.un.org/issues/gallery/iydd/iyddintro.htm>
" Fertile topsoil takes centuries to form, but it can be washed or blown away in a few seasons. Human activities such as over-cultivation, deforestation and poor irrigation practices combined with climate change are turning once fertile soils into barren patches of land. Arable land per person is shrinking throughout the world, threatening food security, particularly in poor rural areas, and triggering humanitarian and economic crises."

[25] Asian Development Bank, "Combating Desertification in Asia"
< http://www.adb.org/Environment/desertification.asp>
" One of the most troubling problems associated with desertification

and land degradation processes is the creation of dust and sandstorms. In the PRC and other countries of Northeast Asia, dust and sandstorms represent serious transboundary environmental concerns, and unfortunately they have become almost regular phenomena-sweeping across Mongolia and the northern part of the PRC, to the Korean Peninsula and Japan.

[26] Nicholas G. Carr, "IT Doesn't Matter". Harvard Business Review. May 2003
< http://www.nicholasgcarr.com/articles/matter.html>
"In this article, published in the May 2003 edition of the Harvard Business Review, I examine the evolution of information technology in business and show that it follows a pattern strikingly similar to that of earlier technologies like railroads and electric power. For a brief period, as they are being built into the infrastructure of commerce, these "infrastructural technologies," as I call them, open opportunities for forward-looking companies to gain strong competitive advantages. But as their availability increases and their cost decreases - as they become ubiquitous - they become commodity inputs. From a strategic standpoint, they become invisible; they no longer matter."

[27] Paul Deninger, "Terrorist Companies". Always-On Network. November 25, 2003
<http://www.alwayson-network.com/comments.php?id=P1740_0_4_0_C>
"In my opinion, the VC industry is one of the things that is holding back the recovery. This is my terrorist analogy. Part of the reason why this recovery has taken so long is because our industry was filled with terrorists. In our business, a terrorist is a company that has too much cash. *It's the public company that doesn't have a real business, but it's got a hundred million bucks in cash sitting on its balance sheet. Or it's a private company in a particular market segment with 50 million bucks in cash. These companies are making a fortune just to give some money away. In doing so, they screw up the market for everybody else. You cannot defend yourself against an irrational competitor. If your competitor doesn't have to make money, you can't defend yourself against it. So these guys are no different than terrorists (JEB emphasis).* You can't defend yourself against somebody who is willing to strap a bomb to their body and grab you when they pull the trigger. That's what happened in our industry. We had all these companies running around pissing away money when we were losing money. They were like terrorists with bombs strapped to their body. When they

pulled the ripcord everybody in the room got blown up. We have got to flush all those companies out of the system. There are still too many of them. Just because the VCs aren't giving these companies $50 million anymore (they're only giving them $20 million), and just because they're doing it at a $25 million pre-valuation as opposed to $200 million, doesn't mean the system sticks.

[28] Walker Stapleton, Brian Benjamin, ""General Oelstrom Addresses Students on Military Strategy. Highlights many connections between military planning and corporate strategy". Harbus Online (Harvard Business School News & Community) March 11, 2002 <http://www.harbus.org/media/storage/paper343/news/2002/03/11/News/General.Oelstrom.Addresses.Students.On.Military.Strategy-207411.shtml?norewrite20060828l837&sourcedomain   =www.harbus.org>
""General Oelstrom, a Three Star retired Air Force General, spoke of strategy in the context of a mission he directed to protect Shiite Muslims in marshes in Iraq. The result of the operation was the establishment of the often tested "no fly zone" for Iraqi aircraft. He outlined the importance of contingency planning surrounding the establishment of rules surrounding the no fly zone in Iraq. *How we came to define the no fly zone in terms of air superiority (my emphasis)*, the response of our allied forces to potential violations, and the involvement of the Saudis all required careful strategic planning prior to implementation," Oelstrom said."

[29] Washington Speakers Bureau, Tom Peters <http://www.washingtonspeakers.com/speakers/speaker.cfm?SpeakerID=474#>
Click on the link for 'Brawl With No Rules' under the Preview Videos Heading

[30] Wikipedia, United States vs. Microsoft <http://en.wikipedia.org/wiki/United_States_v._Microsoft>

[31] UNITED STATES OF AMERICA, Plaintiff, v. MICROSOFT CORPORATION, Defendant. Civil Action No. 94-1564 (SS) Competitive Impact Statement.
< http://www.usdoj.gov/atr/cases/f0000/0045.htm>
" The Complaint alleges that Microsoft has used its monopoly power to induce PC manufacturers to enter into anticompetitive, long-term

licenses under which they must pay Microsoft not only when they sell PCs containing Microsoft's operating systems, but also when they sell PCs containing non-Microsoft operating systems."

[32] Lisa Bowman, Mary Foley, " Microsoft vs. DOJ: It's all in the APIs". ZDNet News June 1, 2000.
< http://news.zdnet.com/2100-9595_22-502453.html>
"Microsoft has come under fire for not documenting some of the internal Windows APIs, a move that competitors claim gives the company's own software makers a huge advantage over external developers because they know about certain features in Windows that others don't."

[33] Graham Lea, "How MS played the incompatibility card against DR-DOS". The Register. November 5,1999
< http://www.theregister.co.uk/1999/11/05/how_ms_played_the_ incompatibility/>
"One of the claims by Caldera that Microsoft wanted dismissed concerned intentional incompatibilities between Windows and DR-DOS. David Cole and Phil Barrett exchanged emails on 30 September 1991: " "It's pretty clear we need to make sure Windows 3.1 only runs on top of MS DOS or an OEM version of it," and "The approach we will take is to detect dr 6 and refuse to load. The error message should be something like 'Invalid device driver interface.'"

[34] Microsoft Announces Principles to Guide Future Development of Windows. Twelve tenets to continue to apply after major parts of U.S. antitrust ruling expire. July 19, 2006.
< http://www.microsoft.com/presspass/press/2006/jul06/07-19PrinciplesPR.mspx>

[35] Jim Hu, " Yahoo to Trillian: Talk to the hand". CNET News.com. June 23, 2004
<   http://news.com/Yahoo+to+Trillian+Talk+to+the+hand/2100-1032_3-5245821.html>
" Yahoo on Wednesday began blocking Cerulean Studios' Trillian software from communicating with its instant messaging service in its latest step to fence its popular client from third-party integrators. Beginning at about 6 p.m. Wednesday, Yahoo changed its instant messaging language to prevent third-party services, such as Trillian, from accessing its service. Like previous statements, the company said the block is meant as a pre-emptive measure against spammers from

its Yahoo Messenger service. "Spammers are being aided by entities that are abusing our systems, where they effortlessly gain knowledge of pathways and back-alley access to send spam," Yahoo spokeswoman Mary Osako said. A Trillian spokesperson did not immediately return an e-mail seeking comment. Trillian software essentially folds in multiple IM clients under one interface. Although IM services from Yahoo, America Online and MSN cannot directly communicate, Trillian allows a user to chat with their buddies on all three systems under a common look and feel."

[36] Trusted Computing Group (member list)
< https://www.trustedcomputinggroup.org/about/members/>

[37] Trusted Computing Group Website (product search 'software')
<https://www.trustedcomputinggroup.org/kshowcase/view/catalog_search/simple_search/process?step%3Aint=1&referring_url=https%3A%2F%2Fwww.trustedcomputinggroup.org%2Fnews%2F&category_text=b534c65449767cdfccf73899ee9e9e3f774df9c8&keywords=&submit=Go>

[38] Microsoft Next-Generation Secure Computing Base - Technical FAQ. July 2003
<   http://www.microsoft.com/technet/archive/security/news/ngscb.mspx?mfr=true>
" Q: In what ways do TCG and the NGSCB architecture differ, and what do they have in common?
A: The *NGSCB architecture encompasses a much broader set of functionality than TCG (JEB emphasis)*, but both efforts are designed to enable a more secure and trustworthy computing platform. TCG has defined a set of functional specifications for a component known as the trusted platform module (TPM). The upcoming TPM version 1.2 is expected to work as the security support component (SSC) in NGSCB to provide certain cryptographic and data storage services. In addition, NGSCB involves the following enhancements to further secure the platform:
• CPU and memory controller changes to enable strong process isolation (each application has its own execution memory space)
• Changes to secure user input (keyboard and mouse) and output (display integrity and confidentiality) to enable a secure path to and from the user
• Authenticated booting of nexus"

[39] Microsoft Next-Generation Secure Computing Base - Technical FAQ. July 2003
< http://www.microsoft.com/technet/archive/security/news/ngscb. mspx?mfr=true>
"Q. What is the difference between NGSCB and DRM?
A: First, digital rights management refers to a category of software and/ or hardware systems that enforce policies that mediate access to digital content or services on machines in the control of entities other than the content publisher or service provider. Once the user of a machine accepts a set of policies, DRM systems are designed to enforce those policies even if the machine owner (or malicious software running on the user's machine) subsequently tries to subvert them.
NGSCB is not DRM. The NGSCB architecture encompasses significant enhancements to the overall PC ecosystem, adding a layer of security that does not exist today. Thus, DRM applications can be developed on systems that are built under the NGSCB architecture. The operating system and hardware changes introduced by NGSCB offer a way to isolate applications (to avoid snooping and modification by other software) and store secrets for them while ensuring that only software trusted by the person granting access to the content or service has access to the enabling secrets. A DRM system can take advantage of this environment to help ensure that content is obtained and used only in accordance with a mutually understood set of rules."

[40] Wikipedia, 2005 Sony CD copy protection scandal.
<http://en.wikipedia.org/wiki/2005_Sony_CD_copy_protection_ scandal>

[41] Mike Ricciuti, "PeopleSoft bid a sign of weakness for Oracle". CNET News.com. June 12, 2003
<http://news.com.com/2030-1012_3-1016001.html>
'George Koch remembers the moment he identified Oracle's chief enemy in the business applications market to Larry Ellison and other top brass at the company more than a decade ago.
To the astonishment of many colleagues, it wasn't one of the usual rivals: It was a company based in Germany that had no customers in the United States. "I said that there is one company we will need to face, that all of this will come down to, and that's SAP," said Koch, the former head of Oracle's business application division. *Thirteen years later, the company is still struggling to cut the German software maker's lead in the same market--a contest that should have been a slam dunk for Oracle, given*

its dominance in the database systems that form the foundation for business applications. The applications industry has become increasingly important as Oracle has lost market share in a slowing database business, a fact that was underscored in the company's $5 billion hostile takeover bid for PeopleSoft last week (JEB emphasis).

[42]Matthew Hicks, " Sun, Microsoft Promise End to Patent Feud". April 2, 2004
< http://www.eweek.com/article2/0,1895,1561360,00.asp>
" Ballmer and Sun Chairman and CEO Scott McNealy played up the two companies' plans to collaborate on making their server and client software more interoperable, initially focusing on Microsoft Windows but also to include e-mail and database software and identity management."

[43]2006 VARBusiness 500
<http://www.varbusiness.com/sections/main/2006vb500.jhtml;jsession id=XHFQQK41SEVAKQSNDLRSKHSCJUNN2JVN>

[44]Cristina McEachern, "VAR500 Research: Is Vendor Exclusivity Right For You? VARs view vendor loyalty through the lens of their business needs." VAR Business. April 17, 2006.
<http://www.varbusiness.com/article/showArticle.jhtml?articleId=1844 28948>
"Forty-nine percent said they prefer to lead with a particular vendor in any given technology category and sell exclusively that vendor's products, if possible."

[45]Cristina McEachern, "VAR500 Research: Is Vendor Exclusivity Right For You? VARs view vendor loyalty through the lens of their business needs." VAR Business. April 17, 2006.
<http://www.varbusiness.com/article/showArticle.jhtml?articleId=1844 28948>
" Take Henry Cheli, president of Herkimer, N.Y.-based Annese & Associates (No. 368 on the
VARBusiness 500). He uses Cisco Systems hardware exclusively for his IP-telephony business.
"We can do best-of-breed this way, and if a customer asks for a different product, we'll say we don't do it because we don't think it's a great solution." But to put together an end-to-end IP-telephony solution, customers usually need some things that Cisco can't provide, such

as application software. In that case, Cheli tries to go with Cisco-recommended vendors, or with ones he has worked with in the past. So, in a nutshell, he's Cisco-exclusive when he can be."

[46] Microsoft.com Press Release, " Microsoft SPOT Unveils Next Generation of Smart Watches, Expands Smart Product Suite With Weather Stations" Jan. 4, 2006
< http://www.microsoft.com/presspass/press/2006/jan06/01-04Expand sWeatherStationsPR .mspx>

Chapter 3

[1] Wikipedia, 'Die Hard'
<http://en.wikipedia.org/wiki/Die_Hard>
"When Die Hard was released, it was considered one of the best action films of its era. It is said to have reinvented the action genre and set the 90's with action/thriller movies such as Speed. Die Hard grossed $80,707,729 at the U.S. Box Office[1]. It was highly acclaimed by critics and spawned two sequels Die Hard 2: Die Harder (1990) and Die Hard with a Vengeance (1995). The fourth film in the series, titled Live Free or Die Hard is currently in production (as of 2006). A previous attempt at a fourth Die Hard eventually evolved into Tears of the Sun."

[2] Steven Metz, Douglas V. Johnson II, "ASYMMETRY AND U.S. MILITARY STRATEGY: DEFINITION, BACKGROUND, AND STRATEGIC CONCEPTS" Strategic Studies Institute. January 2001
< http://www.strategicstudiesinstitute.army.mil/pdffiles/PUB223.pdf>

[3] Sun Tzu, "The Art of War". Shambhala Publications. 1988, Thomas Cleary translation
Boston MA. Page 148
"According to the rule for military operations, there are nine kinds of ground."

[4] DOD Definition of 'Force Multiplier'
<http://www.dtic.mil/doctrine/jel/doddict/data/f/02166.html>

[5] GlobalSecurity.org, "What's new with smart weapons"
<http://www.globalsecurity.org/military/systems/munitions/intro-smart.htm>
"A Precision Guided Munitions [PGM] is a missile, bomb or artillery

shell equipped with a terminal guidance system. It contains electrical equipment that guides it in the last phase before impact."

[6] Microsoft.com, "Shared Source Initiative Overview"
< http://www.microsoft.com/resources/sharedsource/Initiative/Overview.mspx#EHC>
" *The software industry often is depicted as irreconcilably divided into mutually exclusive, rival camps of commercial and open-source providers. Market forces, however, are rendering this portrayal obsolete (JEB emphasis)*. Both models have proven beneficial to the software market, which has determined that they should coexist in healthy competition, and has even driven them to converge.
Traditionally, commercial software developers relied on licenses that protected ownership rights by limiting access to source code, while open-source developers employed licenses that restricted developer control in favor of universal access. However, the market now requires that each camp embraces each other's principles, driving adherents of both models toward neutral, hybrid ground.
For many open-source providers, this "move to the middle" is the adoption of certain commercial licensing and business strategies. These developers seek to emulate the success of companies that have attained stability by providing commercial enhancements or services for open-source platforms (JEB emphasis). They have also learned the lessons from other companies that abandoned early open-source efforts and from those organizations that proved unable to adapt to market demands and consequently met their demise.
For commercial software providers like Microsoft, this middle ground is represented by programs like the Shared Source Initiative, through which source code is made broadly accessible without forfeiture of intellectual property protections that have served as the linchpin of commercial software innovation for decades."

[7] Geoffrey Moore, "Darwin's Dictionary" 2006
<http://www.dealingwithdarwin.com/theBook/darwinDictionary.php#Technologyadoptionlifecycle>

[8] Nasdaq.com, Company Financials (superpower 2006 R&D in billions)
MSFT $6.584; IBM $5.84; CSCO $3.32; ORCL $1,87; SAP $1.28; SYMC $.94; GOOG $.6; YHOO $.56; EBAY $.48; ADBE $.36
<http://www.nasdaq.com/asp/ExtendFund.asp?mode=&kind=&symbo

l=ORCL&symbol=IBM&symbol=SYMC&symbol=CSCO&symbol=Y
HOO&symbol=GOOG&symbol=ADBE&symbol=EBAY&symbol=SA
P&symbol=MSFT&FormType=&mkttype=&pathname=&page=full&s
elected=ADBE>

[9] Wikipedia, Napster
<http://en.wikipedia.org/wiki/Napster>
"Napster's facilitation of illegal activity raised the ire of several major
recording companies, who almost immediately — in December 1999
— filed a lawsuit against the popular service.[6] [7] The service would
only get bigger as the trial, meant to shut down Napster, also gave it
a great deal of publicity. Soon millions of users, many of them college
students, flocked to it. After a failed appeal to the Ninth Circuit Court,
an injunction was issued on March 5, 2001 ordering Napster to prevent
the trading of copyrighted music on its network.[8] In July 2001, Napster
shut down its entire network in order to comply with the injunction.
On September 24, 2001, the case was partially settled. Napster agreed
to pay music creators and copyright owners a $26 million settlement for
past, unauthorized uses of music, as well as an advance against future
licensing royalties of $10 million. In order to pay those fees, Napster
attempted to convert their free service to a subscription system. A
prototype solution was tested in the spring of 2002: the Napster 3.0
Alpha, using audio fingerprinting technology licensed from Relatable.
Napster 3.0 was, according to many former Napster employees, ready
to deploy, but it had significant trouble obtaining licenses to distribute
major-label music. On May 17, 2002, Napster announced that its assets
would be acquired by German media firm Bertelsmann for $8 million.
Pursuant to terms of that agreement, on June 3 Napster filed for Chapter
11 protection under United States bankruptcy laws. On September 3,
2002, an American bankruptcy judge blocked the sale to Bertelsmann
and forced Napster to liquidate its assets according to Chapter 7 of the
U.S. bankruptcy laws.[9] Most of the Napster staff were laid off, and the
website changed to display "Napster was here".

[10] Wikipedia, Webvan
<http://en.wikipedia.org/wiki/Webvan>
"Webvan was founded in the heyday of the dot-com boom in the
late 1990s, and *its original investors encouraged it to build rapidly its own
infrastructure to deliver groceries in a number of markets. The idea of online
grocery shopping was sound, as established retailers have since proven with their
own Web sites. The mistake Webvan made was trying to build everything on*

their own (JEB emphasis), instead of partnering with existing supermarket chains, wholesalers, or a network of small chains or independent grocers. Some journalists and analysts blamed this serious error of judgment on the fact that none of Webvan's senior executives (or major investors) had any management experience in the supermarket industry, including its CEO George Shaheen who had resigned the top spot at Andersen Consulting, a management consulting firm, to join the venture."

[11] Amazon.com Target Online Storefront
<http://www.amazon.com/Target/b/104-0005817-4170353?ie=UTF8&node=1079726>
"Sales of products by third-party sellers on our websites continue to increase year-over-year, representing 29% and 28% of unit sales in Q2 2006 and Q2 2005, and 29% and 28% for the six months ended June 30, 2006 and 2005. Since revenues from these sales are recorded as a net amount, they generally result in lower revenues but higher gross margin per unit." Exerpted from Amazon.com 10Q, quarter ending June 30, 2006.

[12] Washington Technology, "GovWorks Tale Hits Big Screen". May 7, 2001
<http://www.washingtontechnology.com/news/16_3/datastream/16484-1.html>

[13] Santa Fe Institute, Stuart Kauffman
<http://www.santafe.edu/sfi/People/kauffman/>

[14] Stuart Kauffman, "At Home in the Universe. The Search for the Laws of Self-Organization and Complexity" 1995 Oxford University Press. p. 8

[15] Paul Wiefels, "The Chasm Companion". 2002 HarperCollins Publishers Inc. p 64-65

[16] Brian Arthur, "Interview (by Dominic Gates) in Pretext Magazine" 1998

[17] Clint Boulton, " Microsoft to Buy Groove Networks". March 10, 2005. InternetNews.com
< http://www.internetnews.com/bus-news/article.php/3488951>
"Groove launched in 2000, and has accrued $155 million in venture

capital involving Microsoft, Accel Partners, Intel Capital, and private investors."

[18] Wikipedia, "Beetlejuice".
< http://en.wikipedia.org/wiki/Beetlejuice>
"Beetlejuice is a film directed by Tim Burton, first released in the USA on March 30, 1988, and produced by The Geffen Film Company for Warner Bros. Pictures. It features two recently deceased ghosts, Adam Maitland (Alec Baldwin) and his wife, Barbara, (Geena Davis), who seek the help of an obnoxious bio-exorcist, Betelgeuse (Michael Keaton), to remove the Deetz family — metropolitan yuppies who recently moved from New York City and now occupy their old house."

[19] Sun Tzu, 'The Art of War'. "Shambhala Publications. 1988, Thomas Cleary translation
Boston MA; p. 98

[20] Jim Hu,"Yahoo sheds Inktomi for new search technology". CNET News.com June 26, 2000.
<http://news.com.com/2100-1023-242392.html>

[21] George Mannes, "Search Party Rocks as Yahoo! Buys Inktomi". The Street.com. December 23, 2002

[22] Danny Sullivan, "Yahoo to Buy Overture." July 15, 2003. SearchEngineWatch.com
<http://searchenginewatch.com/showPage.html?page=2234821>

[23] Microsoft.com, "Microsoft and RealNetworks Resolve Antitrust Case and Announce Digital Music and Games Partnership. New partnership brings Rhapsody subscription service and RealNetworks' games to millions of Microsoft's MSN users."
<http://www.microsoft.com/presspass/press/2005/oct05/10-11MSRealPR.mspx>
"The three agreements include an agreement to resolve all the companies' antitrust disputes worldwide; an agreement for a wide-ranging digital music collaboration between the parties, including promotional and marketing support of Real's leading digital music subscription service, Rhapsody®, on MSN properties; and an agreement to offer RealNetworks' digital games through MSN Games and Xbox Live Arcade for Xbox 360."

[24] PrintOnDemand.com, "Kinko's Recognized in BusinessWeek Web Smart 50". December 19, 2003
<http://www.printondemand.com/mt/archives/002048.html>

[25] Steven J. Vaughan-Nichols, "Sun Insists Red Hat Linux Is Proprietary But Red Hat and Experts Disagree". eWeek.com, May 26, 2004
<http://www.eweek.com/article2/0,1895,1601494,00.asp>

[26] Sun Tzu, 'The Art of War'. "Shambhala Publications. 1988, Thomas Cleary translation
Boston MA; p. 104
"Be extremely subtle, even to the point of formless-ness".

[27] Sun Tzu, 'The Art of War'. "Shambhala Publications. 1988, Thomas Cleary translation
Boston MA; p. 95

Chapter 4

[1] Wikipedia, Digital Equipment Corporation.
< http://en.wikipedia.org/wiki/Digital_Equipment_Corporation>
" At its peak in the late 1980s, Digital was the second-largest computer company in the world, with over 100,000 employees."

[2] Ken Jacobs, "Oracle Database Changed the World". Oracle Magazine, May/June 2003.
< http://www.cs.iupui.edu/~ateal/n311/history.htm>
" In March 1983, RSI (previous name of Oracle, JEB) released a new version of Oracle that was entirely rewritten in the then-new C programming language, increasing its portability beyond the range of operating systems that ran on the Digital Equipment Corporation PDP-11."

[3] Amey Stone, " SPECIAL REPORT--AFTER THE MELTDOWN, Crawling from the Dot-Com Wreckage". Business Week Online. December 19, 2000.
< http://www.businessweek.com/bwdaily/dnflash/dec2000/nf20001219_800.htm>
" For Web companies that hope to make the bulk of their profits from advertising, the near-term prospects are bleak, but there's light at the end of the tunnel. Content sites have suffered as struggling dot-coms

cut their ad budgets and mainstream advertisers largely remain on the sidelines, unconvinced that Web advertising works. Result: Ad rates on the Web are falling through the floor. Wit Soundview media analyst Jordan Rohan says some second-tier sites that used to charge $2.50 for each 1,000 page views generated by a banner ad, are now charging only 50 cents -- which is getting close to a site's actual marginal cost of running the ad. He believes the pricing environment will probably deteriorate more in the first quarter of next year as more inventory at Web sites goes unsold."

[4] Nasdaq.com, Google 10Q. For the period ending June 30, 2006.
<http://secfilings.nasdaq.com/filingFrameset.asp?FileName=00011931 25%2D06%2D167945%2Etxt&FilePath=%5C2006%5C08%5C09%5C &CoName=GOOGLE+INC%2E&FormType=10%2DQ&RcvdDate= 8%2F9%2F2006&pdf=>

[5] Answers.com, Tao.
< http://www.answers.com/topic/tao>

[6] Chapter 11, Lao Tzu, Tao Te Ching
< http://www.ling.su.se/staff/kicki/LaoZi.htm>

[7] Press Release, " RSA Security Joins with Microsoft to Bring Strong Authentication to Windows Environments". February 24, 2004.
< http://www.rsasecurity.com/press_release.asp?doc_id=3374&id=1034>
" The RSA SecurID for Microsoft Windows solution is designed to provide a simple, consistent user login experience, regardless of whether the user is working on- or offline, remotely or inside the walls of the enterprise. By combining something the user knows (i.e., a secret PIN) with something the user possesses (i.e., a unique RSA SecurID token that generates a random, one-time password every 60 seconds), Microsoft Windows enterprise customers will have an effective, easy way to secure user access to sensitive company information. The RSA SecurID for Microsoft Windows solution is designed to provide significantly greater security than static passwords – without requiring any additional hardware on the desktop."

[8] Remarks by Bill Gates, Chairman and Chief Software Architect, Microsoft Corporation
RSA Conference 2004. San Francisco, Calif. February 24, 2004
< http://www.microsoft.com/billgates/speeches/2004/02-24rsa.asp>

" A key partner in a lot of this has been RSA and the work they do to give people various smart card type options. And we recently announced a new development between us, which is a way you can use the RSA Secure ID that's a very simple little ID card and actually I've got one of them here -- (applause) -- clearly very popular with RSA employees -- (laughter) -- and everyone here."

[9] Susan Kuchinskas, "Microsoft Brings Smart Cards In-House". September 19, 2005. InternetNews.com.
< http://www.internetnews.com/bus-news/article.php/3549926>

[10] EMC Website, "EMC Announces Definitive Agreement to Acquire RSA Security, Further Advancing Information-Centric Security". June 29, 2006
< http://www.emc.com/news/emc_releases/showRelease.jsp?id=4487>
" Joe Tucci, EMC's Chairman, President and CEO, said, "Information security is a top priority among executives around the world, and it has become an inseparable attribute of information management. Businesses can't secure what they don't manage, and when it comes to securing information, that means simply two things – managing the data and managing access to the data. EMC is the leading provider of information management solutions. Bringing RSA into the fold provides EMC with industry-leading identity and access management technologies and best-in-class encryption and key management software to help EMC deliver information lifecycle management securely."

[11] SAP.com, " SAP Offers Safe Passage for Enterprises Running PeopleSoft, JD Edwards, Siebel, or Retek Solutions"
< http://www.sap.com/usa/solutions/safepassage/index.epx>
"You should concentrate on your business -- not worry about the effects of the Oracle acquisition on your PeopleSoft, JDE, Siebel, or Retek software. If your current provider is spending more time on its business than on your software, then turn to the company that has spent more than 30 years delivering flexible, open, and reliable solutions: SAP."

[12] Oracle.com, " 5 Questions You Should Ask SAP".
<   http://www.oracle.com/applications/five-questions-you-should-ask-sap.html?pageregion=ocom_hp_c_main_1_fiveQuestions_083006>

[13] BEA.com, " BEA AquaLogic™ Product Family. Service Infrastructure for managing SOAs in heterogeneous IT environments.

< http://www.bea.com/framework.jsp?CNT=index.htm&FP=/content/products/aqualogic/>
"Business agility depends on the free flow of information, services, and business processes across the organization. This flow may be stymied by the heterogeneous nature of the typical large enterprise's IT environment. Multiple platforms (such as IBM, BEA, Microsoft, SAP, and Oracle) and technologies (J2EE, .NET, legacy, etc.) require IT to hard-code the point-to-point connections, hampering information flow and slowing the delivery of new business services."

[14] Duet.com, "Developer Center".
< http://www.duet.com/DeveloperCenter/tabid/75/Default.aspx>

[15] Paul DeGroot, " Crashing the Channel Party". September 01, 2005. Redmond Channel Partner Online
< http://rcpmag.com/columns/article.aspx?editorialsid=1088>
" Now you'd think that the host at such a party would be careful to make sure the limelight rarely strayed from the main stage, to wit, what Microsoft was saying. *The striking thing about Microsoft's approach to the channel is that the company not only doesn't mind if partners use its events to talk to each other, it actually encourages it (JEB emphasis).* The RIO networking system for the conference lets you browse a conference Web site for other partners who have published their particulars. You can then arrange a time to sit down with them at the conference, even during a keynote. More important, the schmoozing goes on 24x7 with Partner Channel Builder, a Web site where Microsoft Partners can profile their solutions and services and browse for other Microsoft Partners who might make a good fit."

[16] Kevin Newcomb, " MSN Renews With Overture -- for Now". November 18, 2004. ClickZ News.
< http://www.clickz.com/showPage.html?page=3437891>
"Microsoft today extended its three-year-old agreement with Yahoo to provide Overture paid listings on MSN sites in the U.S., Canada, Europe, and Asia through June 2006. The previous agreement ran through June 2005. Microsoft has been working feverishly to increase its own exposure in the search space. It launched a beta of the new MSN Search service last week, which is expected to displace the Yahoo-owned technology currently powering its algorithmic search as soon as the end of this year. "Our timeline is driven by the quality of the service. When we feel the product has effectively incorporated the consumer

feedback we receive, we will release the final product. At this point, we are aiming to release the final service early next year," said an MSN spokesperson."

[17] Shamus McGillicuddy, " CIOS IN THE DARK OVER MAINTENANCE COST CREEP". SearchCIO.com. June 28, 2006. < http://searchcio.techtarget.com/originalContent/0,289142,sid19_gci1196469,00.html> "A Forrester survey, cited in a new research report by Murphy, revealed CIOs will spend only 20% of their 2006 IT budgets on new projects. Murphy said CIOs are spending the other 80% of their budgets to "keep everything else running."

[18] Barracuda Networks, Request Evaluation Unit. <https://www.barracudanetworks.com/ns/products/request_eval_unit.php>

[19] Paul Wiefels, "The Chasm Companion". 2002 HarperCollins Publishers Inc. p.51

[20] Hasbro.com, REAL AND INCREDIBLE FACTS ABOUT THE MONOPOLY® GAME < http://www.hasbro.com/monopoly/pl/page.funfacts/dn/default.cfm>

[21] National Association of Corporate Directors, Houston Branch. < http://www.nacdhouston.com/bios.html#vince> Note: This link points to the website version prior to his passing.

[22] Wikipedia, Videotex < http://en.wikipedia.org/wiki/Videotex> " Nearly all books and articles from videotex's heyday (the late 1970s and early 1980s) seem to reflect a common assumption that in any given videotex system, there would be a single company that would build and operate the network. Although this appears shortsighted in retrospect, it is important to realize that communications had been perceived as a natural monopoly for almost a century — indeed, in much of the world, telephone networks were then and still are explicitly operated as a government monopoly. The Internet as we know it today was still in its infancy in the 1970s, and was mainly operated on telephone lines owned by AT&T which were leased by ARPA. At the time, AT&T did not take seriously the threat posed by packet switching; it actually turned down the opportunity to take over ARPANET. Other computer networks

at the time were not really decentralized; for example, the private network Tymnet had central control computers called supervisors which controlled each other in an automatically determined hierarchy. It would take another decade of hard work to transform the Internet from an academic toy into the basis for a modern information utility."

[23] Troy G. Miller, Eric P. Gist, "Selling in Turbulent Times". 2003. Accenture
<http://www.accenture.com/Global/Research_and_Insights/By_Subject/Customer_Relationship_Mgmt/SellingInTurbulentTimes.htm>
Click on the link on this page to download the PDF of the report.

[24] Sun Tzu, 'The Art of War'. "Shambhala Publications. 1988, Thomas Cleary translation
Boston MA; p. 98

[25] Wikipedia, Hyman Roth.
< http://en.wikipedia.org/wiki/Hyman_Roth>

[26] John Furrier, PodTech Network, " Microsoft in Silicon Valley with Dan'l Lewin" Interview Transcript. July 16th, 2005
< http://www.podtech.net/?p=75>

[27] Ina Fried, " Microsoft readying Vista marketing blitz". March 7, 2006. CNet News.com.
< http://m.news.com/Microsoft+readying+Vista+marketing+blitz/2163-1012_3-6047217.html>

[28] Oracle.com Press Release, " Oracle Database 10g Release 2 Now Available on Microsoft Windows Platform. Oracle Showcases Microsoft Windows and .NET Platform Integration
at Microsoft Tech.Ed China". September 13, 2005.
< http://www.oracle.com/global/hk/corporate/press_050913.html>

[29] Brian Utley, "25th Anniversary of the IBM PC". Technology Evangelist Weblog. August 12, 2006
<   http://www.technologyevangelist.com/2006/08/25th_anniversary_of.html>
" *Every major functional organization had written off the possibility that the concept of the PC was viable or that it was in the best interest of IBM*

to pursue this class of product (my emphasis). Manufacturing said that the cost objectives could not be met. Marketing said that it could not be economically marketed. Corporate finance said that there was no money in this kind of a venture. Corporate technical staff said that such an effort was diversionary to the primary thrust of IBM Research and Development. So what happened? The IBM Chairman was Frank T. Cary. He had observed the dramatic growth of the Apple II acceptance and believed that the visible trend was a harbinger of what was to come. Given the denial of the Corporate and Functional Units Heads he felt compelled to make a very fundamental decision. He concluded that the only way to insure IBM was not left out in the cold was to create a Product Island that was isolated from all the non-believers. The Personal Computer Business Unit was formed reporting directly to the Chairman. Twelve months later the PC was born. The only IBM technology in the product was the keyboard."

[30] Geoffrey Moore, "Top 10 Innovation Myths." SandHill.com. February 6, 2006.
< http://www.sandhill.com/newsletter_archive/20060206.htm>

[31] John C. Dvorak, " The Microsoft malaise. Commentary: Eight signs that the software giant is dead in the water" May 3, 2006. MarketWatch from Dow Jones.
< http://www.marketwatch.com/News/Story/Story.
aspx?guid=%7B629B28CD-9E0E-48CA-8E8B-243AA6E2CB92%7D
&dist=lycos&siteid=lycos>

[32] Ed Yourdon, "Death March Projects Are Back". Yourdon.com. August 31st, 2006
< http://yourdon.com/personal/blog/2006/08/31/death-march-projects-are-back/>
"For whatever it's worth, technology-based solutions are at the bottom of my list of recommendations for surviving and succeeding with death march projects. At the top of my list is politics — e.g., *figuring out who the key stakeholders and decision-makers really are, figuring out why the death march project has been initiated in the first place, and who will be allowed to define "success."* (JEB emphasis) That's followed by negotiation and estimation techniques, followed by "peopleware" practices, followed by "processes" (e.g., agile processes, SEI-CMM/ISO-9000 processes, risk management processes, etc.). All of these are things we should

be doing for any software development project, but they are the key differentiators between success and failure in a death march project."

Chapter 5

[1] Steven J. Vaughan-Nichols, "Sun Insists Red Hat Linux Is Proprietary But Red Hat and Experts Disagree". eWeek.com, May 26, 2004
<http://www.eweek.com/article2/0,1895,1601494,00.asp>

[2] Wikipedia, "Let's get ready to rumble!"
< http://en.wikipedia.org/wiki/Let's_get_ready_to_rumble!>
" "Let's get ready to rumble!" is the trademarked catchphrase of American boxing announcer Michael Buffer."

[3] Wikipedia, Color Commentator
< http://en.wikipedia.org/wiki/Color_commentator>
" A color (or colour) commentator, sometimes known as a color analyst, is a member of the broadcasting team for a sporting event who assists the play-by-play announcer by filling in any time when play is not in progress. The color commentator provides expert analysis and background information, such as statistics, strategy and injury reports, on the teams and athletes, and occasionally light humor. Color commentators are usually people who used to play and/or coach the sport that they broadcast."

[4] Steven J. Vaughan-Nichols, "Sun Insists Red Hat Linux Is Proprietary But Red Hat and Experts Disagree". eWeek.com, May 26, 2004
<http://www.eweek.com/article2/0,1895,1601494,00.asp>

[5] Wikipedia, "Austin Powers in Goldmember".
< http://en.wikipedia.org/wiki/Austin_Powers:_Goldmember>
" The names of the Japanese twins, Fook Mi and Fook Yu, are not romanized correctly; the more correct spelling (using Hepburn romanization) would be "Fuku Mi" and "Fuku Yu" (sailor fuku also being the Japanese word for schoolgirls' uniform). However, a deleted scene indicates that the two girls are actually American, and that they made up these names without knowing Japanese."

[6] Webopedia.com, Fork
< http://www.webopedia.com/TERM/f/fork.html>

[7] Steven J. Vaughan-Nichols, "Sun Insists Red Hat Linux Is Proprietary But Red Hat and Experts Disagree". eWeek.com, May 26, 2004
<http://www.eweek.com/article2/0,1895,1601494,00.asp>

[8] Ibid.

[9] Wikipedia, Mother Teresa.
< http://en.wikipedia.org/wiki/Mother_Theresa>

[10] Steven J. Vaughan-Nichols, "Sun Insists Red Hat Linux Is Proprietary But Red Hat and Experts Disagree". eWeek.com, May 26, 2004
<http://www.eweek.com/article2/0,1895,1601494,00.asp>

[11] Seinfeld Quotes, "The Opposite".
< http://www.pkmeco.com/seinfeld/opposite.htm>

[12] Steven J. Vaughan-Nichols, "Sun Insists Red Hat Linux Is Proprietary But Red Hat and Experts Disagree". eWeek.com, May 26, 2004
<http://www.eweek.com/article2/0,1895,1601494,00.asp>

[13] Wikipedia, Orwellian.
< http://en.wikipedia.org/wiki/Orwellian>

[14] Scott McNealy, "A Letter from Scott McNealy". Sun Participation Age Event - United Nations. June 6, 2005
< http://www.sun.com/aboutsun/media/features/participate-un.html>

[15] Tom Wolfe, "The Electric Kool-Aid Acid Test". 1968. Farrar, Straus and Giroux
< http://www.tomwolfe.com/KoolAid.html>

" Tom Wolfe, a journalist already widely known for his exuberant portraiture of the American Bizarre, plunged into the psychedelic world of the Pranksters and emerged with The Electric Kool-Aid Acid Test, a now-classic portrait of the coterie which gave the hippie world of the 1960s much of its philosophy and vocabulary. He recounts their romp across America in the first psychedelic bus, their alliance with the Hell's Angels, their Be-elzebubbling takeover of a Unitarian Church convention, their conversion of the biggest anti-Vietnam rally of all time into a freak-out, their zany games of hide-and-seek from the law in two countries—all with a depth of exploration and a stylistic inventiveness which make The Electric Kool-Aid Acid Test one of the most memorable journalistic odysseys of our time."

[16] M.R. Rangaswami, "The Birth of Enterprise 2.0". September 1, 2006. Sand Hill Group.
< http://www.sandhill.com/opinion/editorial.php?id=98>
" Whether created by software vendors, internal IT departments, line-of-business units or service providers, the software of Enterprise 2.0 will be flexible, simple and lightweight. It will be created using an infinite combination of the latest - and possibly, some old-fashioned - ingredients, including the following:
- Technologies - Open source, SOA/Web services (AJAX, RSS, blogs, wikis, tagging, social networking, and so on) Web 2.0, legacy and proprietary - or some combination
- Development Models - Relying on in-house, outsourced or offshore resources - or any combination; pursuing a global development strategy; and/or pursuing co-creation with users, partners or both
- Delivery Methods -Downloading individually; paying for a license; and/or, using on-demand/SaaS or via a service provider

[17] Karl Marx, Friedrich Engels, "The Communist Manifesto."
<http://www.anu.edu.au/polsci/marx/classics/manifesto.html>
"A spectre is haunting Europe -- the spectre of communism. All the powers of old Europe have entered into a holy alliance to exorcise this spectre: Pope and Tsar, Metternich and Guizot, French Radicals and German police-spies."

[18] Wikipedia, Newspeak
< http://en.wikipedia.org/wiki/Newspeak>
"Newspeak is a fictional language in George Orwell's novel Nineteen Eighty-Four. In the novel, it is stated as being "the only language in the world whose vocabulary gets smaller every year." Orwell included an essay about it in the form of an Appendix (in the past tense)[1] after the end of the novel, in which the basic principles of the language are explained. Newspeak is closely based on English but has a greatly reduced and simplified vocabulary and grammar. This suited the totalitarian regime of the Party, whose aim was to make any alternative thinking ("thoughtcrime") or speech impossible by removing any words or possible constructs which describe the ideas of freedom, rebellion

and so on. The Newspeak term for the English language is Oldspeak. Oldspeak was intended to have been completely eclipsed by Newspeak before 2050. The genesis of Orwell's Newspeak can be seen in his earlier essay, "Politics and the English Language," where he laments the quality of the English of his day, citing examples of dying metaphors, pretentious diction or rhetoric, and meaningless words — all of which contribute to fuzzy ideas and a lack of logical thinking. Towards the end of this essay, having argued his case, Orwell muses: "I said earlier that the decadence of our language is probably curable. Those who deny this would argue, if they produced an argument at all, that language merely reflects existing social conditions, and that we cannot influence its development by any direct tinkering with words or constructions." Thus Newspeak is an attempt by Orwell to describe a deliberate intent to exploit this decadence with the aim of oppressing its speakers."

[19] Patricia Seybold, with Ronni Marshak, "The Customer Revolution. How to Thrive When Customers Are in Control". 2001. Crown Publishing Group.
<http://www2.darwinmag.com/connect/books/book.cfm?ID=202>

[20] Sun Tzu, "The Art of War". Shambhala Publications. 1988, Thomas Cleary translation
Boston MA. P. 62

[21] Connie Guglielmo, Bloomberg News, "Conway says he made PeopleSoft 'too successful'". Contra Costa Times Sep. 24, 2005
<http://66.102.7.104/search?q=cache:yVzmix5AjDcJ:www.contracostatimes.com/mld/cctimes/business/12731486.htm+craig+conway+peoplesoft+fired+twist+in+the+wind&hl=en&gl=us&ct=clnk&cd=7>

[22] U.S. Federal Trade Commision, "An Antitrust Primer".
< http://www.ftc.gov/bc/compguide/antitrst.htm>
"Section 2 of the Sherman Act makes it unlawful for a company to "monopolize, or attempt to monopolize," trade or commerce. As that law has been interpreted, it is not necessarily illegal for a company to have a monopoly or to try to achieve a monopoly position. The law is violated only if the company tries to maintain or acquire a monopoly position through unreasonable methods. For the courts, a key factor in determining what is unreasonable is whether the practice has a legitimate business justification."

[23] Sun Tzu, "The Art of War". Shambhala Publications. 1988, Thomas Cleary translation
Boston MA. P. 155

[24] Bill Gates, "The Internet Tidal Wave". Microsoft Internal Memo. May, 1995
< http://www.usdoj.gov/atr/cases/exhibits/20.pdf>

[25] Bill Gates, "Internet Software Services." Microsoft Internal Memo. October 2005.
< http://www.scripting.com/disruption/mail.html>

[26] Wikipedia, "Apoptosis".
<http://en.wikipedia.org/wiki/Apoptosis>
" Between 50 billion and 70 billion cells die each day due to apoptosis in the average human adult. In a year, this amounts to the proliferation and subsequent destruction of a mass of cells equal to an individual's body weight."

Chapter 6

[1] Bill Gates, "The Internet Tidal Wave". Microsoft Internal Memo. May, 1995
< http://www.usdoj.gov/atr/cases/exhibits/20.pdf>

[2] Wikipedia, Big Kahuna.
< http://en.wikipedia.org/wiki/Big_kahuna>
" "Big kahuna" is a common slang term for the person in charge of something. It comes from the Hawaiian word kahuna, meaning shaman or wizard."

3 Phil Wainewright "CSFB says 'traditional software is dead'". ZDNet Blogs
< http://blogs.zdnet.com/SAAS/?p=91>

[4] Wikipedia, Roger Ailes
< http://en.wikipedia.org/wiki/Roger_Ailes>

[5] Bill Gates, "The Internet Tidal Wave". Microsoft Internal Memo. May, 1995

< http://www.usdoj.gov/atr/cases/exhibits/20.pdf>

[6] Ibid.

[7] Ibid.

[8] Ibid.

[9] Ibid.

[10] Ibid.

[11] Ibid.

[12] Ibid.

[13] Ibid.

[14] Ibid.

[15] AlwaysOn-Network Poll, "Does your company have a Chief Marketing Officer "CMO" titled executive?". December 1, 2003.
<http://www.alwayson-network.com/polling/index.php>

[16] Judith Kautz, Small Business Notes. Tribute to William Hewlett upon his passing in 2001.
<http://www.smallbusinessnotes.com/history/hewlett.html>
"Hewlett-Packard Advertisement --"Rules of the Garage: Believe you can change the world. Work quickly, keep the tools unlocked, work whenever. Know when to work alone and when to work together. Share - tools, ideas. Trust your colleagues. No politics. No bureaucracy. (These are ridiculous in a garage.) The customer defines a job well done. Radical ideas are not bad ideas. Invent different ways of working. Make a contribution every day. If it doesn't contribute, it doesn't leave the garage. Believe that together we can do anything."

[17] Time Magazine, "Life in the Googleplex". Photo Essay. February 2006
< http://www.time.com/time/photoessays/2006/inside_google/>

[18] Wired News, "Al-Jazeera: No Help With Hackers". April 4, 2003
< http://www.wired.com/news/business/0,1367,58352,00.html>

[19] Larry Bossidy, Ram Charan, "Execution. The Discipline of Getting Things Done". Crown Business. 2002. p. 85

[20] Photo of the Crew of the Chow Hound
< http://www.91stbombgroup.com/chowhound.html>

[21] Captain Robert Crawford, "Wild Blue Yonder". U.S.A.F. Anthem. 1939
< http://www.scoutsongs.com/lyrics/offwego.html>
"Off we go into the wild blue yonder,
Climbing high into the sun;
Here they come zooming to meet our thunder,
At 'em boys, Give 'er the gun! (Give 'er the gun now!)
Down we dive, spouting our flame from under,
Off with one heckuva roar!
We live in fame or go down in flame.
Hey! Nothing'll stop the U.S. Air Force!"

[22] Wikipedia, Frank Quattrone
< http://en.wikipedia.org/wiki/Frank_Quattrone>

[23] Wikipedia, "Murder on the Orient Express".
< http://en.wikipedia.org/wiki/Murder_on_the_Orient_Express>
" This book was also noted for its surprise ending, where it is revealed that all of them did it - the suspects (including Pierre Michel) are the twelve executioners, taking justice into their own hands for a crime that the law did not punish. The only suspect not participating in the crime was Countess Andreyni, whose place was taken by her husband instead. Poirot provides two explanations, one bearing the truth and the other being farfetched theory incriminating no one on the train. Poirot agrees to let Dr. Constantine and M.Bouc decide which is correct. The story given to the police is that the murderer escaped the snowed-in train after committing the murder. The 12 are allowed to walk free and the truth is hidden from the police."

[24] Wikipedia, "Wag the Dog".
< http://en.wikipedia.org/wiki/Wag_the_Dog>

[25] Wikipedia, "Click Fraud".
<http://en.wikipedia.org/wiki/Click_fraud>

[26] Karl E. Weick, "Sense and Reliability: A Conversation with Celebrated Psychologist Karl E. Weick". Harvard Business Review. April 1, 2003

[27] Ibid.

[28] Intel.com, Andrew S. Grove.
<http://www.intel.com/pressroom/kits/bios/grove/paranoid.htm>
"I'm often credited with the motto, "Only the paranoid survive." I have no idea when I first said this, but the fact remains that, when it comes to business, I believe in the value of paranoia. Business success contains the seeds of its own destruction. The more successful you are, the more people want a chunk of your business and then another chunk and then another until there is nothing left. I believe that the prime responsibility of a manager is to guard constantly against other people's attacks and to inculcate this guardian attitude in the people under his or her management."

[29] Wikipedia, Stripes.
<http://en.wikipedia.org/wiki/Stripes_(film)>
"Winger (Bill Murray's character---JEB) manages to motivate his platoon, and begins to get them in shape for graduation. However, after a long night of studying, they oversleep and almost sleep through graduation. Without time to get dressed properly, they run to the parade grounds thoroughly out of uniform and give a highly unconventional, but nevertheless impressive, drill display led by Winger. When the General finds out that they had to complete their Basic Training before their injured Drill Sergeant could be replaced (and developed this routine on their own), he decides they are just the kind of "go-getters" he wants working on a special project in Italy."

[30] Alcoholics Anonymous, 'The Big Book Online'
< http://www.aa.org/bigbookonline/en_appendiceI.cfm>

[31] Sun Tzu, "The Art of War". Shambhala Publications. 1988, Thomas Cleary translation
Boston MA; Page 99

Chapter 7

[1] Google.com, "Investor Relations. Google Code of Conduct."
< http://investor.google.com/conduct.html>
" Our informal corporate motto is "Don't be evil." We Googlers generally
relate those words to the way we serve our users – as well we should.
But being "a different kind of company" means more than the products
we make and the business we're building; it means making sure that
our core values inform our conduct in all aspects of our lives as Google
employees."

[2] Ashwini Bhatia, " Exiled Tibetans Protest Google Censorship".
Associated Press. February 14, 2006.
< http://www.breitbart.com/news/2006/02/14/D8FOTFL85.html>
"Scores of angry Tibetans on Tuesday protested Google's launch of a
censored version of its search engine in China which adheres to that
country's government restrictions on free speech.
The protesters assembled in the central square of Dharmsala, the
northern Indian headquarters of the exiled Tibetan government,
carrying placards reading "Google, Don't be Evil," and "Gulag, Censoring
Search by Search.""

[3] Robin D. Rusch, "The Search Is Over: Google Wins in 2005". January
23, 2006. BrandChannel.com.
<http://www.brandchannel.com/start1.asp?fa_id=298>

[4] Wikipedia, Kryptonite.
<http://en.wikipedia.org/wiki/Kryptonite>
"Kryptonite is a fictional element from the Superman comic book series
(and subsequent related media). The element, usually shown as having
been created from the remains of Superman's native planet of Krypton,
generally has detrimental effects on Superman. The name "kryptonite"
covers a variety of forms of the element, but usually refers to the most
common "green" form.
Kryptonite was produced from the material of Krypton, when it was
destroyed in an explosion."

[5] Wikipedia, Bizarro
<http://en.wikipedia.org/wiki/Bizarro>
"Due somewhat in part to the Seinfeld episode "The Bizarro Jerry,"
Bizarro and the Bizarro world have become somewhat well-known in

popular culture and the term Bizarro is used as to describe anything that utilizes twisted logic or that is the opposite of something else."

[6] Joseph Kahn, "So Long, Dalai Lama: Google Adapts to China". New York Times. February 12, 2006
<http://www.nytimes.com/2006/02/12/weekinreview/12kahn.html?ex=1 297400400&en=5cd44b3b85bec8c1&ei=5090&partner=rssuserland&e mc=rss>
"Chinese Tibetans or other Buddhists who might be curious could try finding images of the spiritual leader on Google.cn, a new search engine that Google tailored for China and is now, two weeks after its unveiling, on full display to local Web users. Is he that guy with puffy cheeks wearing a Western suit? No, that's Liu Jianchao, China's foreign ministry spokesman, demanding that the Dalai Lama stop trying to split the motherland. What about that balding man leading a big delegation? No, that's Chen Yi, a late Chinese vice prime minister, offering grain to the Tibetan people. Only one of the 161 images produced by searching in Chinese for the Dalai Lama on Google.cn shows the 14th Dalai Lama, the spiritual leader of Tibet since 1940."

[7] Hon. Christopher H. Smith, New Jersey. Member U.S. House of Representatives. Contained in report titled "THE INTERNET IN CHINA: A TOOL FOR FREEDOM OR SUPPRESSION? WEDNESDAY, FEBRUARY 15, 2006 HOUSE OF REPRESENTATIVES, SUBCOMMITTEE ON AFRICA, GLOBAL HUMAN RIGHTS AND INTERNATIONAL OPERATIONS, SUBCOMMITTEE ON ASIA AND THE PACIFIC, COMMITTEE ON INTERNATIONAL RELATIONS, Washington, DC.
<http://wwwc.house.gov/international_relations/109/26075.pdf>
"Google.cn, China's search engine, is guaranteed to take you to the virtual land of deceit, disinformation, and the big lie. As such, the Chinese Government utilizes the technology of United
States IT companies combined with human censors, led by an estimated force of 30,000 cyber police, to control information in China. Web sites that provide the Chinese people with news about their country and the world, such as the BCC, much of CCN, as well as Voice of America and Radio Free Asia, are routinely blocked in China. In addition, when a user enters a forbidden word, such as "democracy" or "Chinese torture" or "Falun Gong," the search results are blocked, or you are redirected to a misleading site, and the user's computer can be frozen for unspecified periods of time."

"Similarly, Google censors what is euphemistically called "politically sensitive" terms like "democracy," "China human rights," and "China torture" on the new Chinese search site, Google.cn. Let us take a look at what that means in practice. A search for terms such as "Tiananmen Square" produces two very different results. The one from Google.cn shows a picture of a smiling company, but the results from Google.com show scores of photos depicting the mayhem and brutality of the 1989 Tiananmen Square massacre. Another example: Let us look at "China and torture." Google has said that some information is better than nothing, but in this case, the limited information displayed amounts to disinformation. A half truth is not the truth; it is a lie, and a lie is worse than nothing. It is hard not to draw the conclusion that Google has seriously compromised its "Don't Be Evil" policy. Indeed, it has become evil's accomplice, and hopefully that will change."

[8] Therese Hoffman, Ph.D., "The Chinese Cultural Revolution: Autobiographical Accounts of a National Trauma" Lourdes College, Sylvania, Ohio, USA
<www.ipsonet.org/congress/5/papers_pdf/th16.pdf>
"Big characters posters condemning the guilty, public denunciations, forcing victims to assume the jet plane style1, shaving half the teachers' heads in the yin-yang style, parading victims through the streets wearing tall dunce hats, and escalating violence turned Universities and middle schools into arenas of chaos (Wang, 1996; Tsou, 1986; Fairbanks, 1992; Huang, 1996)."

[9] Joseph Farah, "Google: Enemy of Freedom". January 27, 2006. WorldNetDaily.com
<http://www.worldnetdaily.com>

[10] Weekly Standard (online edition), "Googling "human rights" in China. Visit Despotipedia--the People's free encyclopedia!" February 6,2006, Volume 011, Issue 20
<http://www.weeklystandard.com/content/public/articles/000/000/006/646qdhjk.asp>

[11] Howard Mintz, "Feds after Google data. Records sought in U.S. quest to revive porn law." January 19, 2006. Mercury News.
<http://www.keepmedia.com/pubs/MercuryNews/2006/01/19/1161246?extID=10032&oliID=213>

[12] Press Release, "Authors Guild Sues Google, Citing "Massive Copyright Infringement"
September 20, 2005
<http://www.authorsguild.org/?article=86>

[13] WorldNetDaily, "Google dumps news sites that criticize radical Islam. Search giant axes another news page, calls terrorism discussion 'hate content'." May 23, 2006
<http://www.worldnetdaily.com>

[14] Michael Liedtke, "Click Fraud Concerns Hound Google". Associated Press. May 7, 2006
<http://www.usatoday.com/tech/news/2006-05-07-google-click-fraud_x.htm>

[15] Stephen Foley, "To google or not to google? It's a legal question. Search engine's sense of humour crashes as it fires off warning letters over use of name as a verb". August 13, 2006
<http://news.independent.co.uk/business/news/article1218805.ece>

[16] Associated Press, "India: Google Maps Too Graphic". October 16, 2005
<http://www.wired.com/news/technology/0,69230-0.html>

[17] Markus Dettmer, Marcel Rosenbach, "Fear of an American Internet". February 1, 2006. Spiegel Online International.
<http://service.spiegel.de/cache/international/spiegel/0,1518,398519,00.html>

[18] Jim Hopkins, "Google's givers go Democratic". February 14, 2005. USA Today.
<http://www.usatoday.com/money/industries/technology/2005-02-13-google-give-usat_x.htm>

[19] Ted Bridis, "Google compromised its principles in China, founder says". June 6,2006. Associated Press.
<http://www.usatoday.com/tech/news/2006-06-06-google-china_x.htm>

[20] Kate Phillips, "Google Joins the Lobbying Herd". March 28, 2006. New York Times.

<http://www.nytimes.com/2006/03/28/politics/28google.html?ex=13012
02000&en=8d58f2770d53f9db&ei=5088&partner=rssnyt&emc=rss>

[21] Stefanie Olsen, Elinor Mills, "Google pledges $900 million for MySpace honors". August 7, 2006. CNet News.com.
<http://news.com.com/Google+pledges+900+million+for+MySpace+ho
nors/2100-1032_3-6102952.html>

[22] Ed Leefeldt, "Yahoo shuts chat rooms promoting adult-child sex". October 13, 2005. Reuters.
<http://in.tech.yahoo.com/051012/137/60jb6.html>

[23] MSNBC Interactive, "EBay bans sale of endangered sawfish. Snouts fetched hundreds of dollars in U.S., U.K., Australia". January 24, 2006.
<http://www.msnbc.msn.com/id/11007937/>

[24] Alorie Gilbert, "Oracle to PeopleSoft: The pink slip's in the mail". January 14, 2005. CNet News.com.
<http://news.com.com/Oracle+to+PeopleSoft+The+pink+slips+in+the+
mail/2100-1014_3-5536612.html>

[25] Mike Ricciuti, "Oracle: Unbreakable no more?" July 28, 2005. CNet News.com.
<http://news.com.com/2061-10789_3-5808928.html>

[26] Steven J. Vaughan-Nichols, "Cisco Source Code Reportedly Stolen". May 18, 2004. eWeek.com.
<http://www.eweek.com/article2/0,1759,1593862,00.asp?kc=EWNKT0
209KTX1K0100440>

[27] JULIA ANGWIN and JOSEPH T. HALLINAN, "Newspaper Circulation Continues
Decline, Forcing Tough Decisions". May 2, 2005 . Wall Street Journal Online.
< http://online.wsj.com/public/article/SB111499919608621875-72vA7sU
kzSQ76dPiTXytqgOMS5A_20050601.html?mod=tff_main_tff_top>

[28] Associated Press, " Hollywood Sees Big Box Office Slump in 2005" December 15, 2005
< http://www.foxnews.com/story/0,2933,178864,00.html>

[29] The Project for Excellence in Journalism, "The State of the News Media 2006. An Annual Report on American Journalism".
<http://www.stateofthenewsmedia.org/2006/narrative_cabletv_audience.asp?cat=3&media=6>
" By either measurement, one thing is clear: Fox News channel was the ratings leader in 2005. Wherever one looks, more than half the cable news audience was watching Fox News. In the evenings, or prime time, an average of 1.59 million people watched Fox News in 2005, up from 1.47 million in 2004. That is more than double the 725,000 watching CNN, whose median prime time viewership dropped by 90,000, from 815,000 in 2004. MSNBC had a median prime time audience in 2005 of 335,000 viewers, slightly less than the 341,000 viewers a year earlier."

[30] CNN.com, " Fox anchor named Bush press secretary. Snow replaces McClellan as White House continues makeover." April 26, 2006.
< http://www.cnn.com/2006/POLITICS/04/26/snow/index.html>

[31] Jenn Shreve, "MySpace Faces a Perp Problem" Apr, 18, 2006. Wired News.
< http://www.wired.com/news/culture/0,70675-0.html>

[32] Joris Evers, "Microsoft shakes up security fray. Debut of company's OneCare product has started a new security software race where consumers are likely to be winners." June 7, 2006.
CNet News.com.
<   http://news.com.com/Microsoft+shakes+up+security+fray/2100-7350_3-6080718.html>

[33] Jeremy Kirk, "Antivirus software market jumped 13.6% in 2005. According to Gartner, industry"
<http://www.computerworld.com/action/article.do?command=viewArticleBasic&articleId=9001332>

[34] Symantec Corporation Annual 10K Report For the Fiscal Year Ended March 31, 2006
<http://secfilings.nasdaq.com/filingFrameset.asp?FileName=00008916
18%2D06%2D000254%2Etxt&FilePath=%5C2006%5C06%5C09%5C&CoName=SYMANTEC+CORP&FormType=10%2DK&RcvdDate=6%2F9%2F2006&pdf=>
" Sales in the Consumer Products business are trending more towards our electronic channels which are comprised of online stores, including

our Symantec store, and OEM and ISP relationships. During fiscal 2006, nearly 65% of revenue in the Consumer Products segment came from our electronic channels. We also made infrastructure improvements in order to capture more direct renewal business from customers originally reached through these channels. In fiscal 2006, we partnered with more than 150 ISPs and 50 OEMs around the world."

[35] Ibid.
"During fiscal 2006, we began offering multi-year consumer subscriptions in order to deliver new technology capability and functionality to our customers throughout the year, rather than only once a year."

[36] Symantec.com, News Release. "Symantec's New View: Security+ Availability = Information Integrity" CUPERTINO, Calif. Oct. 26, 2004
< http://www.symantec.com/press/2004/n041026a.html>
"Symantec Corp. (Nasdaq: SYMC), the global leader in information security, today unveiled a fundamentally new way for enterprise customers to view and manage the risks around protecting, securing, and using their most valuable asset, their information. Backed by partners and customers, the concept that Symantec calls "Information Integrity" addresses the need to keep businesses up, running and growing, even in the event of Internet threats or other disruptive events."

[37] Joris Evers, " Collision course for Symantec and Microsoft". May 23 2006. CNet News.com.
< http://www.zdnetasia.com/news/security/0,39044215,39361300,00.htm>

[38] Symantec Corporation. "Symantec Vision 2006 Online" John Thompson Keynote Speech. San Francisco, California May 8, 2006
< http://www.veritas.com/van/vision2006/index.jsp>

[39] Ibid.

[40] Ibid.

[41] Ibid.

[42] Ibid.

[43] Microsoft Corporation. " Remarks by Steve Ballmer, CEO, Microsoft Corporation
Worldwide Partner Conference" Boston, Massachusetts. July 11, 2006
<http://www.microsoft.com/presspass/exec/steve/2006/07-11WPC2006.mspx>

[44] Ibid.

[45] Ibid.

[46] Ibid.

[47] Daniel Geer,Charles P. Pfleeger, Bruce Schneier, John S. Quarterman, Perry Metzger, Rebecca Bace, Peter Gutmann, " CYBERINSECURITY: THE COST OF MONOPOLY. HOW THE DOMINANCE OF MICROSOFT'S PRODUCTS POSES A RISK TO SECURITY." September 24, 2003. Computer & Communications Industry Association.

[48] Ibid. page 5

[49] Ibid.

[50] Ibid. page 11

[51] Google Search, Microsoft monoculture. September 9, 2006.
< http://www.google.com/search?hl=en&lr=&q=microsoft+monocultur e>

[52] John Thompson Interview, " Video: Symantec's relevance in a Microsoft world" Gartner Symposium ITExpo. May 17, 2006.
< http://news.com.com/1606-2-6073553.html>

[53] Apple.com, "Why You'll Love a Mac". TV commercial.
<http://www.apple.com/getamac/>

[54] McAfee.com, "Chairman's Letter. McAfee 2005 Annual Report"

[55] Jeremy Kirk, "Antivirus software market jumped 13.6% in 2005. According to Gartner, industry"

<http://www.computerworld.com/action/article.do?command=viewAr
ticleBasic&articleId=9001332>

[56] McAfee.com, "Chairman's Letter. McAfee 2005 Annual Report"
" Last year, McAfee made an important transformation. We shifted
away from our previous direct sales model, so that today we conduct
nearly 100% of our business through channel partnerships."
[57] Ibid.
" Additionally, in 2005 we added over $145 million to deferred revenue,
which reached an all-time high of $746 million, providing increased
visibility into our future results."

[58] Ibid.

[59] McAfee.com, Press Release. July 11, 2006.
<http://www.mcafee.com/us/about/press/corporate/2006/20060711_
120000_d.html>

[60] John Thompson Interview, " Video: Symantec's relevance in a
Microsoft world" Gartner Symposium ITExpo. May 17, 2006.
< http://news.com.com/1606-2-6073553.html>

[61] Google Search, "Symantec Security 2.0" (September 9, 2006)
< http://www.google.com/search?hl=en&q=%22symantec+security+2.0
%22>

[62] Sana Security Website, "Active Malware Defense Technology".
< http://www.sanasecurity.com/products/technology/activeMDT.php>

[63] Sana Security Website, Press Releases.
< http://www.sanasecurity.com/press/pressreleases/062706.php>

[64] Centrify.com, Press Release. "Centrify Joins the SecureIT Alliance".
October 2005.
<http://www.centrify.com/news/release.asp?id=2005100601>

[65] LavaSoft.com, Press Release. " Lavasoft Ad-Aware SE Personal
Edition Included as Part of Google Pack . Award-winning Ad-Aware is
bundled with Google's free software package" January 10, 2006
<http://www.lavasoft.com>

[66] Ibid.

[67] AOL Active Virus Shield Web Page
<http://www.activevirusshield.com/antivirus/freeav/index.adp>

[68] Sonny Barger, "Freedom, Credos from the Road" Harper Collins, 2005. page 73